Silence: Entering the Cosmic Sea of Consciousness

SILENCE: ENTERING THE COSMIC SEA OF CONSCIOUSNESS

A WESTERN YOGI'S JOURNAL: 2000–2001

Yogacharya David R. Hickenbottom

Editor: Ruth M. Lamb, Ph.D

The Cross and The Lotus Publishing
Camano Island, Washington, USA

For permission requests, contact the publisher at:
http://www.crossandlotus.com/contact.html

ISBN: 978-1-957811-11-6 (softcover)
ISBN: 978-1-957811-12-3 (eBook)

All photos courtesy of Carla Hickenbottom Portfolio

Edited by Ruth Lamb

Book design by Jan Westendorp/Kato Design and Photo (katodesignandphoto.com)

Cover design by Rob Landers, Ruth Lamb, and Jan Westendorp

Published by
The Cross and The Lotus Publishing
Camano Island, Washington, USA
Website: www.crossandlotus.com

CONTENTS

FOREWORD   ix
INTRODUCTION   xxi

PART ONE
Chapter One: Prelude to a Year in Silence   3

Chapter Two: Entering-In: Silence at Cloud Mountain   19
    September: Stillness and Oppositional Forces   20
    October: Sadhaka Homecoming and Babaji's Blessing   45
    November: Tests and Dreams   95
    December: Deepening Faith   106
    January: A Guru's Strange Life   120
    February: Inward Mind: Tackling Adverse Forces   132
    March: All Experiences Come from God   143

Chapter Three: Life's Deeper Meaning   163
    April: Standing at a Crossroads   163
    May: My Cells Fly Apart: I Climb a Mountain   171
    June: The Masters Visit and Marriage   182
    July: Universal Consciousness   198
    August: Fire of Renunciation   217

Chapter Four: Summer Teachings   231
    Jnana-Wisdom   231
    Breaking the Binary Code of God   234
    Detachment: The Way to Freedom and Harmony   240
    O Ram, Thou Art the Infinite   243
    Master I   245
    Master II   248
    Vision Illumined   256
    O Infinite Divine   257
    Full-Time Awareness   258

Krishna   259
Freedom In Action: Prem-Ananda   261
Jesus: Blended Thoughts of the East   264
Introduction To Peace Pilgrim   266
The Guru's Glory is God's Glory   268
The Mystic Light Within   270
Affirmation for Meditation   272
Deepening Kriya   273
September: Journey of the Soul   277

Chapter Five: Re-entering the World   291

Chapter Six: Closure   301

PART TWO
**Chapter Seven: Notes To Sadhakas—How Dharma
    Works in Everyday Life**   307
Sadhaka's Homecoming   308
Introduction: Living a Spiritually Centered and
    Principled Life   310
Dharma: How It Works in Everyday Life   313
Babaji On Faith   317
Tithing   320
Four Lions and The Diamond Light   322
Blessings from the Guru   324
Of Will and Surrender   328
Balanced Sadhana   337
Awaken O Divine Mother   345
God: With and Without Form   345
Gardening with God   353
Brahmacharya   356
The Means of Brahmacharya   363
Dragons at the Door   374
The Razor's Edge   378

A Songbird's Verse 387

What is in a Word? 389

Unlimited Power 393

The World is a Reflection of Your Consciousness 397

Plateaus 402

Becoming Poor in Spirit 408

A World Stood on Its Head 415

The Washerman—Washerwoman 416

Sadhakas go to the Movies 416

Know a Gift's Value 417

Be an Instrument of Joy 418

Guru 419

Inner Renunciation 420

Kundalini 423

Karma and Kundalini 428

The String of Intuition 431

Meditation as Renunciation 435

Loyalty 438

The Universal Religion 442

You Are a Divine Instrument 447

Moral Courage 452

Compassion 454

Where East and West Meet 459

What is True Joy 463

The Twenty-Four Aspects of Creation 465

Creation Story 480

APPENDIX

Babaji-Inspired Clearing/Charging Exercises 489

REFERENCES 537

EDITOR'S ACKNOWLEDGMENTS 539

Yogacharya David at Cloud Mountain.

FOREWORD

The search for the sacred has been with humankind since the beginning of time as shared in the earliest transcriptions from ancient sculpture, cave art, and writing. Yogacharya David (1954–2019), a Western man born in Washington State, USA, dedicated his adult life to the search inward, constantly seeking to reawaken the highest order of sacred, spiritual-universal connection with the cosmic Divine. Here is a brief introduction to the man and the yogi, stated in his own words as much as possible.[1]

Throughout the ages, great masters have spoken of the sacred climb to access Divine-realization, to connect humanity with the highest truth of existence. Yogacharya David, even as a child, knew there was more than "surface life," or what could be experienced through the five senses. He sought answers through the church as well as through science and philosophy. Then he found a teacher who spoke a new language, one of such deep inner awareness that a whole world of freedom began unfolding.

David reflects:

> My life is a dedication to God. In fumbling steps and in the precision of movement, I steer my life toward that precious Goal. My Great Guru set the course, direction, and Goal. She beckons me still from her deeper life. God awakened me to that purpose when my own will would have taken me to self-destruction, or at best, to a mundane, senseless life. I pretend no greatness, nor even goodness, for there is none other good than my Heavenly Father. Truly, I can say wholeheartedly that it is by God and Guru's Grace that I have found my Self.

> I suppose it is natural to want all the world to share the sacred mystery that I feel, and it would be sheer arrogance to assume that no others do. But there is the

---

1   This Foreword, or a similar version, is designed to introduce the reader to David the man and David the Yogacharya and is placed in David's books in order to provide context.

songbird within that bursts into Divine verse and aches
to share that deepest Intimacy.

In 2007, David wrote an autobiographical sketch. He told the
story of a young man in search of something of vaster meaning
than he had so far discovered. Excerpts from this sketch place his
writings and teachings into context as he takes us with him on his
magnificent, challenging journey up the sacred mountain. The full
autobiography can be found on The Cross and The Lotus website
at: www.crossandlotus.com.

When David was nineteen years old, he had a tremendous
experience:

> I remember sitting under the stars on a warm summer
> night; it was around midnight. The stars were spread
> like a carpet of tiny lights above; my heart felt like it was
> physically breaking right down the middle. I felt a crush-
> ing weight pressing down on me and I was breaking
> under the strain. It was all too much for me and I made a
> spontaneous prayer in my agony, "Oh God, I don't know
> if you exist, but if you do, if I have never needed you
> before, I need you now. Help me!"
>
> Amazingly, with that prayer came an instant relief. I
> felt that a thousand pounds of weight came off me in that
> moment. The tremendous pain in my heart was soothed.
> I was aware that in a split second, the agony I had been
> feeling was gone. Immediately after this unseen help
> came to my aid, my mind began to reason, "Well, since
> I prayed to God, my mind imagined getting some help
> and I felt relief as a result." It was my mind, not anything
> else, that helped me. No, it was more than the mind. I
> had connected with something wonderful and powerful
> and definitely beyond me.

David had other search experiences, but here we focus on his
being invited to a talk by a wise "grandmother." David says:

> Well, this "grandmother" description did not appeal
> to me. But… eventually, I said yes. On a Wednesday

evening in March 1974, we all piled into a car and drove to a nice home in North Seattle... Mother Hamilton began to speak with such spiritual power that I felt as if my long hair was being blown straight back. She spoke of God, of Self-realization, Christ Consciousness, and renunciation. Many of the concepts were foreign to me, but I recognized that this was someone who spoke with authority and wisdom. After the talk, Mother gave each of us a hug. As I stood in line waiting, getting one person closer to Mother, my heart was beating so hard I could feel it thumping in my chest. After I hugged Mother, I remember little until I found myself sitting in the back seat of the car... Each time I came to hear Mother speak, I wondered if I would feel the same power of God, and each time it proved itself true... Before meeting Mother, I would be looking for the nearest exit if someone started speaking about God, but when Mother used the word, I knew there was a new and enlarged meaning.

David speaks of initiation into Kriya Yoga that spring. He shares, "I felt I had the means for making spiritual progress, something I could take with me everywhere. How I made contact with one of the greatest masters this world has ever seen is a great mystery to me. Every day, I thank the heavens for this greatest of gifts, a sense of gratitude that does not diminish with time, but only grows sweeter."

David's Guru, the Reverend Mother Yogacharya Mildred Hamilton (1904–1991) met Paramhansa Yogananda (1893–1952), whom she affectionately called "Master," in 1925. At that time, she had been seeking deeper meaning in her life and spiritual guidance towards a truth she intuited was available but hidden from her view. Her first meeting with Master was in Seattle, Washington, USA. David said: "At that meeting when Master looked at Mother, she experienced a shock that went through her entire being."

Over time, Mother Hamilton became a Center Leader, then a Reverend, and finally, in front of thousands, Mother Hamilton received the title Yogacharya from Yogananda. She was the only woman to receive this honor, and one of only seven in total in his worldwide organization.

Yogananda followed the great Kriya lineage from India that came through Jesus, Babaji, Lahiri Mahasaya, and then Sri Yukteswar, who was Yogananda's teacher. Yogananda created a large organization in America. His aim was to "bring all into the spiritual heights he enjoyed in God." As David says: "This is the work of a spiritual master. A true Master makes you feel as if God is very close, very intimate, and very knowable."

David finds his way to this great lineage of teachers. He says:

> When I came to Mother, I was definitely a diamond in the rough. Not even a diamond, but more a lump of coal hoping one day to shine with light like a brightly-lit diamond! An inner pain brought me to the path, most unwillingly. And this inner pain kept me on the path when I would have gladly wandered away, back into the world.

In his autobiography, David speaks of the testing of his resolve and the testing of his commitment by Mother Hamilton. In 1982, not only did she invite David to give talks to the devotees, but she also asked him to speak of his inner experiences. He tells us: "I had never spoken to anyone about my deepest inner experiences except to Mother, and now she was asking me to say aloud in front of others my most sacred experiences. Mother had always cautioned against talking to others about spiritual experiences." David realized the reasons not to talk and now the reasons to talk. "Not easy, this," he says. The testing was for a purpose.

Two years later, Mother Hamilton ordained David as a minister. He agreed, thinking, "I can serve. I can serve Mother, serve Truth, be a servant of God, and serve the God that is within all people—that I can do! I found a way to be a minister." David's growth continued as he developed his inner agreement to find the Divine path. He speaks of a time in the fall of 1976 when he experienced a sudden rising of the Kundalini and entered what is called a "Mystical Crucifixion" state. He found himself living in two worlds: one the familiar, physical reality and the other a profound and difficult spiritual reality that had physical effects. Working between the polar opposites of physical and spiritual, a transformation gradually took place that changed his very core nature.

With his inward journey progressing, David accepted an ever-growing ministerial role while Mother Hamilton's health challenges increased as she continued in her resolve to serve God to her last breath. Supporting Mother Hamilton came at the same time as full-time school, full-time work, and full-time sadhana. Over time, David attended academic institutions; he received a Bachelor of Psychology and a master's degree in Applied Behavioral Science. Starting in 1984, he worked full-time as a counselor, and by 1985, he was volunteering as a mediator. Later, he was a founding partner of an innovative conflict resolution service.

Meanwhile, Mother, in planning for the continuation of the Guru-disciple lineage, told David that she was going to make him Yogacharya (teacher or master of yoga) and that she would be passing her spiritual mantle on to him. David shares: this gift "came as a deep Mystery, with inner potency and meaning that continues to unveil itself to me through the passing years. Far from feeling I deserved such an accolade, I felt deeply humbled and prayed that I would acquit myself to whatever capacity God would give me." David also says, "I, to the best of my ability, put my shoulder to the wheel of this Great Work begun so long ago."

On January 31, 1991, Yogacharya Mother Mildred Hamilton entered Mahasamadhi, a yogi's conscious exit from the body. David knew that Mother Hamilton was now in her light body. At this time, David says his task was "to find her in her universal Presence beyond the physical realm." That, plus other life decisions, led David to what he calls the "dark night of the soul," starting in 1992. David relates:

> At this time, I took a leave from ministerial duties as I felt
> I was in no condition to help others. I was entering a dark
> night of the soul. Mother described this dark night as a

time when the aspirant has had almost continuous communion with God, then all sense of connection disappears. This was my case, and it was to last for two years.
Meanwhile, I was working full-time, going to school full-
time, working part-time in an internship, and experiencing a deep emptiness inside that had no solution but to
go on. Never did I doubt God or the path I was on; what
I keenly knew were my own errors, all the ways I lacked
the spiritual qualities I knew that I should have, and
most of all, how familiar God had been to me before, and
now with the curtain drawn, how helpless I felt, wanting
to get that inner Presence back. There was no joy for me,
and I struggled to just get through the day.

Time passed. One night I had a vision. I was walking
along a path in the desert. This desert was so beautiful,
green, and lush, with flowers like springtime. The path
I walked on was spongy feeling and the air smelled delicious. I felt God. Oh, it had been so long! Like parched
ground receiving fresh water, I soaked up the feeling of
God. As I looked behind me, from where I had come, the
land was charred black, the ground hard, cracked, and
broken from earthquakes, the air black with soot; I knew
the dark, ugly landscape I looked upon was a true representation of what I had been experiencing. When I saw it,
I let out a cry of anguish for all that I had been holding in
for so long! A prayer came: "Oh Lord of the Infinite, I have
missed you so much. Please never leave me again." For
the next six months, I gradually emerged from the darkened gloom into a new Light. I had completed my master's degree and went on to a work in my chosen field,
which was very satisfying.

One day, I received a call from some Kriyabans in
Canada who were asking me to help clarify their Kriya
practice, then an invitation to come and speak; there

were many thirsty souls awaiting my visit. For so long, I had felt I was the last one to help others; now the Light came to me at the same time as the expressed need of others. God's ways are perfect and mysterious!

This was in 1995 and yes, David answered the "call" to engage in his ministry in a new way. Canadians got to hear David's Kriya teachings, as did Americans, and later, people in India.

David worked as a counselor and mediator until 1998, when, through a powerful inner direction, he left his professional career to work as a full-time minister. While not knowing what would come next, he gave up a position he loved and turned this new phase of his life over to God's design.

Just at that moment, Peter Schultz offered to build a tiny apartment for David. He now had a home. Then in 1998, Phyllis Victory, a long-time devotee of Mother Hamilton, sponsored him on a pilgrimage to India. Of course, one very important destination was Anandashram, and Swami Satchidananda, who was now the God-man guardian of Anandashram. There, David found Swamiji to be "an indispensable help in my realization."

Returning to America, David led a busy life teaching, holding retreats, and meeting with devotees in many cities in both the USA and Canada. He says:

> On my return to America, I continued with a busy schedule of travel to work with various aspirants. Now, and after many years of fully scheduled days, I had time to simply go with the powerful stream up my spine into higher realms of consciousness. No longer was I daily crucified on the cross of vertically upward spiritual power meeting the horizontal daily demands of worldly activity. I was now free to sail into the mystical sea of consciousness without limit. One day, out of my mouth came the idea that I should spend a year in silence and solitude; again, it was an unsolicited idea that came unbidden from some unknown depth. Never before had

I considered such an idea. I don't think I had spent even a day in silence, except when there were no others about. Hence, from September 9th, 2000, to September 9th, 2001, I was in silence and seclusion.

During this time of silence, I became established in an inner state of stillness that has never left me. And then, another life surprise: toward the end of my year of solitude, an inner direction came to me. The inner direction was for me to marry Carla, a devoted aspirant who had given sincere service for the last several years to the Work. I realized that this was an important decision, one I did not take lightly as it affected many people, even the Work itself.

In his 2000–2001 journal, David speaks of the levels of reflection and inner and outer affirmation he sought to determine whether this was indeed the right direction for his life. On December 15, 2001, Reverend Larry Koler married David and Carla in a marriage ceremony that came from Mother Hamilton and was based on a ceremony Master created.

In early 2002, David and Carla left on a pilgrimage to India. David and Carla made pilgrimages to India in 2002, 2005, 2007, and 2013. Between these pilgrimages, and ongoing into 2018, David and Carla traveled to different Centers. David says:

Through this Master lineage, He has freely given the very highest means for making the journey of realization. God and the masters have decreed this Work out of love and compassion for those who desire nothing less than the highest realization. Far too often, we are unmindful of the underlying Reality that gives real peace, joy, and wisdom for all, no matter a person's circumstance. Jesus and Babaji are the headwaters of this Work, Lahiri Mahasaya, Sri Yukteswar, Master, and Mother bless it, and it will shine in this world as long as there are sincere seekers who desire spiritual transformation.

David closes the autobiography he wrote in 2007 with the words: "This spiritual evolution is the greatest hope for a strained world that is too often filled with conflict, intolerance, and separation. Only through individuals gaining realization of their spiritual Reality will this world come to know its full glory in the Light of the Infinite Divine."

From 1998 until his Mahasamadhi in 2019, David, and after their marriage, with the assistance of Carla, led a busy life hosting services in their home or in those of other sadhakas, traveling to Centers in both the USA and Canada, as well as making several pilgrimages to India. He shared his teachings in the form of retreats, poems, prayers, reflections, and discourses. David gave over one thousand talks to devotees. David described his inner journey more intimately through his journals. He conducted services for marriages, memorials, baptisms, and house blessings. In the latter part of his life, he felt called to pilgrimage to nature's cathedrals in beautiful wilderness settings and to spend time in the desert, always seeking the great Stillness.[2]

David knew that there was more to life than narrow materialism and superficial personality satisfactions. He sought answers; he found a teacher and teachings that nurtured an evolutionary process to realization, neverendingly bringing him surprises and taking him to new heights. David shares, as few can, the intimate internal processes required when we break free from a bound, programmed reality and truly claim our divine nature. His teachings interweave, from start to finish, a process that spirals upward to great height and promise, then descends into the valleys to gather up the lost pieces of shame, blame, and shadow, then carries these wounds lovingly up to the transformative heights. It is the climb of a sacred mountain, and, as it is with mountains, there are steep inclines, easy paths, valleys, and rivers to ford; there is false peak after false

---

2   *My Spiritual India* has David sharing his experiences during his 1998–99 pilgrimage to India and *Climbing the Sacred Mountain: Poems and Prayers of a Western Yogi*, features David's spiritual climb from 1978–2019.

peak until the grand summit is reached. This is the sacred mountain, unique for us all. Yogacharya David's teachings reach deep into our hearts and bring a higher dimensional perspective to each of us—a perspective that can take us into our own cosmic sea of consciousness, to our own potential for self-realization—our climb!

Editor's Note: David's words are important, the essence, the meaning, and the power, so I have changed very few words in his writings. Spelling is corrected and grammar has been adjusted as required. David's life's work comes in many forms, such as journals and a large number of writings in hard copy, other material from several computers, and there are tape recordings of talks that are currently being transcribed. Many writings are undated, some dated. Where individuals are mentioned with praise, their names are included in the texts; when personal inner work is described, names are replaced with an X or Y to honor privacy. All photo images have been gifted with legal permission granted. David's writings serve as magnificent reminders of the great consciousness, power, and wisdom within the human spirit. A series of books from Yogacharya David's teachings and journals is available at www.crossandlotus.com.

It is a privilege to bring Yogacharya David's teachings forward to unify people of all faiths, people who seek a deeper relationship with the sacred, with the wisdom of our multidimensional self, and with the brilliant intelligence of Nature when She is honored as an important co-creative aspect of the Cosmic whole.

I apologize for any errors, omissions, or missed documents, and request Guru's and reader's forgiveness.

May we all put our shoulders to the wheel of this great Work— the upliftment and spiritual evolution of the individual soul, and of this beautifully-created world.

Cloud Mountain Hermitage Retreat.

Yogacharya David prior to Silent Retreat.

INTRODUCTION

No soul can fathom all of that which we call God. But like crystal sugar, the soul may drop into the sea of consciousness, dissolve, and become one with the all-embracing love and Light of the Infinite. Yogacharya David. March 2001

I stand on the brink of going into a year of silence. By an inner command, this has come about. As I have contemplated this time, it has been shown to me how we, as human beings, avoid entering into the cosmic sea of consciousness that is God. Our true nature being the vast Spirit of Consciousness, one would think that all would be rushing to enter into that pure joy of Oneness. Yogacharya David. September 2000

Silence—a whole year—something that Yogacharya David had never considered. Actually, not even silence for one day! Yet, in the summer of 2000, David felt a potent inner prompting directing him to enter a year of silence. And, as with all great endeavors that come from an inner well-spring centered in Divine Source, Grace responded. A few months later, on September 9th, David entered a hermitage retreat cabin at Cloud Mountain Retreat Center, Washington State.

It was as if Mother Hamilton was endowing David with an even deeper meaning to her words:

Think of the wonder and the beauty of God—His power, His love, His peace, His infinite compassion and mercy, and then go deeper. Go deeper still, until you come into the silence of your soul, until you are face-to-face with the ocean of infinity—and then dive in. Go beyond all duality and feel yourself merge with that One who is All in everything. Go into the stillness of your soul and realize your oneness with Him.

Carla Gold, a devotee and friend of David at that time, later to become David's beloved wife, stated:

> When David told me he was thinking of going into a silent retreat for a year, it seemed the natural course of things. I thought this undertaking was an important and essential time in his sadhana, the natural next step in his quest (as Mother Hamilton would say) "to go over the top," immersing in complete Oneness with God.
>
> I knew that he was the Teacher/Guru who was helping and guiding me to my own complete God-realization. It didn't feel like he was leaving us (his devotees) behind, but that he would be taking us with him! The higher he soared, and reached his own goal, the higher the rest of us would go in our own attainment. I was in complete favor and told him I would support him in whatever capacity he needed.
>
> As Jesus said: "And I, if I am lifted up from the earth, will draw all peoples to Myself." (John 12:32)

We join David as he writes his summer 2000 journals before he enters his year of silence, and we follow through many journals as the full year continues to closure in September 2001. In these journals, David writes of his adjustment to silence, his daring to enter the deep subconscious sea that arises when outer activity is removed, and of his glorious times of peace, calm, and bliss as the superconscious realms also open. These momentous times are countered with obstructive forces, adverse situations, and even body pain. David finds the inner sacred power to overcome these apparent "obstacles" as they arise. David was ready for the initiation into the cosmic sea of consciousness that holds a vast potential for the human condition and connects to the super or cosmic spiritual realms available for all who seek with courage and wisdom.

As well as journaling, David wrote Dear Friends letters for the quarterly *The Cross and The Lotus Journal*; he wrote letters to the sadhakas, and he wrote a monthly greeting letter to the silent retreat sadhakas who joined him one Saturday a month on the mountain—this greeting was read aloud by a devotee. Many of these letters are included in the text. He also developed a whole series of teachings included in Part Two of this book.

Part One

Chapter One: Prelude to a Year in Silence—features David's words as he offers a brief introduction to the adesh/spiritual command that he ought to enter a year of silence in retreat. Here we also include poems written that summer.

Chapter Two: Entering and Sustaining Silence and Chapter Three: Life's Deeper Meaning—bring us to David's entry to Cloud Mountain and his retreat hermitage—where he enters and sustains a territory of silence. These chapters include all of David's year of silence journal writings and his four Dear Friends letters he had published in the quarterly *The Cross and The Lotus Journal*, plus his Dear Friends letters he had typed and sent out to sadhakas as well as the silent satsang greeting communications. These latter communications were handwritten, and the copies we were able to recover are included here.

The sections have been separated into months accompanied by a theme that seems to stand out as crucial to David's evolving soul journey toward Universal Oneness. Where David has provided dates, they have been included at the start of his sharing.

Chapter Four: Summer Teachings: 2001—brings us to the eleventh month of David's silent retreat. As summer progresses, David stops writing his personalized journal entries and documents a series of reflections as he prepares to re-enter the world. Most of these are not dated but were all in the same August journal.

Chapter Five: Re-entering the World—ends the silent Cloud Mountain journey as the auspicious day, September 9th, arrives. Retreatants had spent the night on Cloud Mountain at the retreat Center and are ready to hear David speak, chant, and dedicate the Babaji Grotto. Writings from this time are included as well as a selection of David's later reflections on his silent time at Cloud Mountain.

Chapter Six: Closure—brings an end to the more personal sharing portion of David's year in silence. Included are some selections of his later reflections on this special year that brought the cosmic sea of consciousness so much closer to his lived experience. And, amazingly, prepared him for another adventure, becoming a Householder Yogi.

Part Two

Chapter Seven: *Notes to Sadhakas*—includes a series of teachings David wrote, mainly between October 2000 and February 2001. Here, we find a fine synthesis of topics that support sadhana and bring many aspects of the human condition forward. An extended version of *Notes to Sadhakas* is available as a smaller booklet. In some cases, David wrote several versions of these teachings, some on computers, others in hard copy. In all cases, the latest version, or most complete version, was selected.

Appendix: Babaji-Inspired Clearing/Charging Exercises is a series on clearing and charging the subtle nadi nerves or pranic energy. These exercises, David says, were inspired by Babaji in the spring of 2001. David explains: "According to yogis, there are seventy-two thousand nadis, subtle astral nerves, in the human body. Each of these nerves is a carrier for a subtle intelligent energy called prana. Prana is responsible for our life in the physical, subtle, and astral bodies. It is the intelligent force of prana that makes us healthy. As well, it gives us the ability to move, breathe, and in all ways function."

Sadhakas were invited to a three-day retreat in April of 2001. David, still in silence, had others read from his notes. Information from that retreat has been compiled by David and is included in the Appendix.

Let us now turn to the voice of Yogacharya David.

PART ONE

CHAPTER ONE
PRELUDE TO A YEAR IN SILENCE

Dear Friends,[3]

I am writing to you all. My most humble apologies if I have not contacted you before this. My one excuse has been the demands on my time, which in no way reflect the love and caring in my heart. I have made a very big decision in my life. As of Saturday, September 9th, 2000, I am entering into a year of silence. An inner prompting has made me do this, and I have felt it to be the right thing to do. Cloud Mountain Retreat Center has opened its doors to me, and I will be staying in a cabin there. It has been built for this kind of retreat. They will provide me with food and check in on me if necessary. They have a wonderful staff, which currently includes my nephew, Chad. So, all is arranged for this year of time. I will not be taking my computer with me. Carla Gold will be monitoring my email for some time. If you wish to send me a message that way, she will get it to me. If you wish to write me, I will keep my P.O. Box. I would love to hear from you.

The purpose of this silent time is not known to me. I do not know if it is time to deepen my search for realization. I have also been reflecting on the decline in values, most directly here in the West, and the lack of desire by so many to seek and express the Light of Self-realization. So, this time seems connected with both of these issues. It should prove to be an interesting time for me, and I hope for you.

Carla Gold has also agreed to be the contact person for the Center Leaders, and we have a new tape of the month that Elaine Cone is coordinating. If you have questions of this nature or any

---

3   This Dear Friends letter is from September, placed here to provide context for the journal entries and the year of silence.

other, you may contact Carla. Know that you are in my heart, often in my thoughts, and in Spirit, we are forever connected. I once read that Good-Bye meant "God be with you." So Good-Bye and may blessings shower upon you without end.

Sadhana[4]

A sadhaka is one who practices sadhana. Sadhana is any spiritual practice taught by one's guru that puts the mind on God in order to purify the mind of desire nature and attachments. Desire nature and attachments are the stock and trade of the ego. Ego is the idea of separation from God and the identification with the body. Separation from God is a product of the human mind.

Therefore, it is the idea of separation that must be surrendered and crucified. Once this idea is eliminated through the crucifixion of the ego, the resurrection of the true Self-nature arises. This Self is the Christ, Krishna, or Buddha nature. With the resurrection of the Christ nature complete, then all sense of separation is ended.

The universal nature of Light, Consciousness, and Bliss is beheld to be everywhere, continuously, naturally. This realization is called Sahaja Samadhi, meaning natural or complete realization. All experience is then seen as a continuous manifestation of the Supreme Spirit of God. It is one, without a second. The sadhana, which is of the ego nature, disappears along with the idea of separation. Sadhana is no longer practiced, as the mind is totally purified of the idea of separation. There is literally no one left to do sadhana. This state of consciousness is rarely known today, but is attainable by all sadhakas everywhere, until complete realization—more sadhana!

---

4   Chapter One writings are from David's materials and are included to present a context for his time in silence.

Why Sadhana?

Why is sadhana necessary? From the beginning, God, Paramatman (the Supreme Self), gave his offspring, atmans (souls), free will. With free will, His atmans assumed masks of ignorance. Like Halloween characters, the masked children frightened and delighted one another. The masks became so familiar, the atmans began to think of themselves as the character of the mask they wore. Oh, what an enthralling play! And, the play has gone on and on as long as the atman children have wished. Sometimes, children here and there will tire of the game. Usually, it is at a time the other children are picking on them or they are frightened. But then the scene changes and once again they are enthralled with the play. So, the fickle-minded players return.

Finally, some of the players really desire to give the play up. Tired of the alternations between the pleasure and pain of the play, they focus their mind continuously on giving up the mask and the play. Others in the play want them to continue, so they seek to engage them over and over, trying to entice them back again. After some false starts, these others set about in earnest to give up the play. They ignore all the outer distractions, but new doubts assail them. "Who am I without the mask?" they ask. "Perhaps I wear one of those horrible masks beneath this one; what if I leave the play and I'm lonely? Perhaps I am no one without the mask." Thus, the doubts come again and again. For those who overcome the doubts, the moment of Truth finally comes. Even as they donned the mask in some unremembered past, now they doff it. Low and behold, what do they find? They are who they have always been deep down behind the mask. The atman. Not only that, but they now remember that they are also the Paramatman, the Supreme Self.

Adoration

Heavenly Father, Divine Mother
I lay the blossoms of my devotion
On the altar of my love for Thee
My listening mind waits in silence
While my soul softly opens in prayer to receive Thy light.
Gradually, I am aware of Thy presence
Enfolding me in Thy arms of everlasting bliss.
Suddenly I realize
I am not my body
I am not my mind
I am not my soul
Thou hast absorbed these in thy flame of eternal light.
I am forever one with Thee.

—YOGACHARYA MOTHER HAMILTON

Within the next couple of weeks, I'll be entering into a period of silence. The reason for this is not fully explained to me. I was speaking to my mother this morning. She said, "Well, you must feel very strongly about this." She's struggling to get her mind around this concept.

I think whenever any of us are confronted with some discipline, with some sadhana, it stirs something inside of us. Of course, we oftentimes try to project ourselves into that sadhana ourselves and see whether it's something that we could do—would be willing to do. We read about these great spiritual masters, and sometimes it's as if we're looking at a distant mountain, one that is very high, a powerful presence, one that stirs something deep inside of us. And yet at the same time, it seems distant, it seems unattainable, unreachable.

Whenever any one of us takes on some spiritual discipline, it helps to purify not only that one but the others who are around that one. That's true for every one of us. When you take time for deepened prayer and meditation, when you make the effort to purify your life and your consciousness, as you dig deeper beyond the everyday circumstances of your life and go into that higher realm of Divine Consciousness, then it creates a certain power within you, a certain ability to uplift not only your own consciousness but all consciousness.

Jesus once said, "And I, if I be lifted up from the earth, will draw all men unto me." (John 12:32) Now no one, I think, would deny that Jesus was lifted up, but when we look at all of humankind since that time, it doesn't appear that the second part may be true: has he lifted up all of humankind with him? In one sense, you can say not all humankind has entered into heavenly consciousness, but has that Divine Consciousness within Jesus had a powerful impact on this world? Did it help to uplift the consciousness of those who were around him, near him, following with him into the light? And has that continued to spread out over this world? And I think, you can say that he has had a very powerful effect.

But the inward meaning is something different. When the Christ Consciousness within you is lifted up, in other words, when you place it front and center of your own consciousness, and you draw all of your life-force up through the spine and into the Christ center—the ajna within your own body, within your own being—then all the humankind within you, all the human tendencies are lifted up in that action and drawn into heavenly consciousness. As you do that repeatedly, consistently, persistently, the mind is gradually purified. Eventually, you feel yourself more and more to be one with that Universal Divine Life that resides within you. Less and less do you feel identified with this body vehicle and with your tendencies that keep you glued to this world. More and more do you experience your freedom, your joy, your absolute consciousness, and, Sat Chit Ananda.

Unless this evidence is coming into our life, unless we are experiencing greater joy, greater light, greater purity, then we need to continue our sadhana. We need to intensify our sadhana, our prayer, our meditation, to ask God to intensify our own desire to know Him, to be embraced by Him, to be purified by Him, to be uplifted by Him, to attain to His consciousness.

It should be quite interesting. I've never done anything like this before. It's been interesting to watch myself. I haven't entertained any fear about it that I've noticed. It's like: "Well, God's just taking me on an adventure, and I'll just let Him lead me by the hand." He's the one who gave me the injunction. I trust that He'll give me everything needed to make this successful. But, of course, if you want to send prayers, I would never refuse those... I would like it very much if you all continue to meet and support each other, love each other, be an example for each other, be what a spiritual family should be.

I know that God's blessings and the masters' blessings are with you. And any time you focus here, at the heart, or here, at the ajna, that inner communion is there, that there is no separation, and that we might not ever be separate in any real way when that kind of communion is there. I've counted it as my greatest privilege in this lifetime to be with Mother and to serve her in whatever capacity.

Awaken the Light of the World

Not all can take this time in silence as I am doing, either due to circumstances or temperament. So, I do this for all. But be with me daily. For a minute, five minutes, an hour. Be in that silence. And from that silence, see the Light of the world, that Light which lighteth every man and woman, and awaken Itself in the world. Let that Light shake off sleep's angel's dust and awaken to a mighty roar! See that Light shining in your hands, your feet, your whole body, mind, and the altar of your heart. Then see sparks of that fiery wave jump to others, and from them to others still, awakening in them their own sleeping Light. Like a conflagration, that Light spreads over the world, awakening joy, peace, right thoughts and activity. The darkness of past ignorance seems as a dream. All the world arises to be a City of Light upon the hill. Every individual's antenna of heart and mind is attuned to that frequency of Light and harmony. "Arise, Awake!" is the thunderous call. "Forsake sleep and know your Divinity as never before."

Join with me. Bring the power of God within you and know this world is in for a change. Be on the crest of that wave of change and ride it in joy! Hari Om Tat Sat.

Two Thieves Steal Inward Sight

Two thieves steal from us inward sight
Closing our eyes to earthly pleasures and woes,
Yet focusing the attention on the One
We move inward the spinal Way.

Breathing slows
Mind stills
Heart rests
Hush, calm is here.

Lightning flashes in darkness,
Stream of Aum floods silence,
Constrained mind expands,
Blissful joy rises within.

Now inner revelation unfolds
Unspeakable truth makes itself known,
Transformation makes me new
At last, I know my Self true.

Truth comes in such hidden Ways,
The world continues its preoccupations,
One here and there hears the call,
The world thus-wise becomes enlightened![5]

---

5   All poems in Chapter One were in David's summer 2000 journals.

The Flower Glories in the Sun

The flower glories in the sun.
It proclaims:
"Is there any greater than I?"
And it listens intently to the echo.

The flower, today is, tomorrow is not.
It cares not for the branch that produces it.
It knows not the trunk that fed it.
It imagines not the roots that made life possible.

It sees the sun
But wants only praise from it.
Receives the breeze as a kiss
Only to increase the blossom's vanity.

O small insignificant flower,
You cannot appreciate the thousand other blooms around you,
But more than that
You deny yourself the joy of gratitude!

Birds Herald a New Day

The chirps of birds herald a new day,
Streaks of dawn pierce the dark,
Heaviness of night yields
Blessed Day begins!

Inner awakenings stir deep,
Signs of change come gradual,
Yearning outdistances knowing
Dawn comes too slowly!

I stumble in pre-dawn hours,
But see my faults more clearly.
Hope alternates with despair,
Far too gradually does the sun come!

Sight now awakens
Stronger my steps grow,
I help one here and there
Those whose eyes are darkened still.

A new day dawns
The world awakens
And shakes off the dreamer's trance
Songs of praise resonate from high towers.

The sun is for all,
Fear abandons itself to gratitude,
Loneliness becomes omnipresence
And life knows joy anew!

What Presence Moves Within?

What presence moves within?
Little do I know or realize
What wonders will come
In creeping Lightning streaks.

"Behold, I stand at the door and knock"
But who opens,
Who will open,
To inner Light and Beauty?

I, I open
Not to go out!
But to let Him in
I receive Him.

And in that communion
Of heart, of soul, of Spirit
A spiritual feast ensues,
Filled with love, wisdom, joy!

O what promise is there
To you and to me
But... who opens,
Who will open?

The feast is spread
And, who will receive
The universal One
Who knocks at our door?

O Lord, My Prayer

O Lord, Thou hast given me intelligence, reason, and feeling.
Please, O Lord, guide Thou my intelligence, reason, and feeling.
Thou hast also given power of will, movement, creativity, and energy.
Please O Lord, guide me in the use of will, movement, creativity, and energy.
O Lord, finally Thou hast given me things material: money, home, family and friends, and all possessions.

O Lord, make me a good steward of things material and a worthy member of the human race.
Thank You, Lord, for hearing my prayer, for I know You know my thoughts even before I do.
I pray this prayer to impress it into my own mind.
I pray not to change You; I pray to change my self!

One day God showed me how, in the same way, fear can sweep across a crowd and move humans to panic, that Light can sweep across this whole world and change the minds and hearts of all.

In that sweep of Light, hearts will soften, one towards the other. The Light of Supreme Intelligence will suddenly make dark and unseemly behavior look disagreeable. Humankind will look upon the past cruelties, unnatural passions, addictions, and oppressions as an inexplicable dream upon awakening to a bright new dawn. May the Light of that dawn speedily make its way to Now!

O Lord, change not my circumstances; change me!

When I was young, I used to pray, "Lord, give me friends and good grades," expecting them to come without effort on my part. I now see the folly of this. Today I might pray, "Lord, inspire me to study and learn well, and let me be a friend to all that I might earn their loyalty and friendship in return."

They said: "Show me a miracle!" and their eyes were blind. Closeness to God manifests as gratitude and awe at the stupendous miracles of the ordinary. I just used a rubber band and marveled at its ability to stretch and return to its original shape. I send an email and am astounded to be connected to anywhere in the world in an instant. To see planes the size of a palace suspended in the air. And these are the least. Recently, we had a birth. To think this baby started from two cells that became one. Think on that miracle that is also the pattern for all that is. Then that one became the many cells that make up the whole. Finally, the many cells come to realize they are really one. O the miracle of life. The heart bursts in love and appreciation for all that is. Yes, gratitude, wonder, and awe happen at the feet of the Infinite. What greater gift than this? What greater miracle?

Perfection Shining

The child smiles, warms the hearts of all,
Reflects the smile of God;
The student who ardently learns something new,
Understands something of God's intelligence;
The mother who suckles a newborn babe
Gives the life of God through her love;
The father who protects and serves his family
Watches with the care of God;
The teacher who awakens new light in another
Does the work of God;
The mystic who becomes pure Spirit,
Shines God's Light for all;
When all humanity lives in harmony with
The all-pervasive One
Fulfilling their highest nature,
Then we shall see perfection shining all about.

All in One

Enter gently
The inner Temple,

With pure intent
Upon the One,

Focus attention inwardly
Upon the single eye,

Stable is the mind
Drawing one step closer,

Moving deeper now
The Whole attention inward,

Absorbed, absorbed
In inner space absorbed,

The Light draws one further
Guiding the way,

The Sound
Calls one to holiness,

Becoming absorbed even deeper
Into the inner stillness,

Being is vast
Being is small,

Being rests
And creates,

Being is at rest
And revelations flow,

Being is without movement
And creation bursts,

Being is without compare
And is seen as the reflection that is All,

God is Being
And I am that,

I am the I Am
Of all selves,

And all are part of the whole
And each makes up the whole,

The seed becomes the tree
And the tree becomes the seed,

And all is One
All is One,

The dreamer awakens
And knows all is One,

And One is Peace
And One is Joy,

One is Self-aware
And One knows that It knows.

The intellect cannot reveal God. Using the intellect to study the scriptures and remaining satisfied with that alone is similar to the topographer. When the topographers make their maps, they draw lines on a flat piece of paper, describing the hills and valleys. They pace the number of feet for the gain or loss of altitude. But by drawing the lines, they do not scale the mountain, survey deep valleys, or courageously cross raging rivers. No, the topographers never take the journey by drawing their lines, and never know the glory of the adventure.

Now, the intellect can draw lines of thought. It can create rules and laws and fantasize about what the reality might be. But it does not, and can not, know. No one has seen God! Not with the human mind can it be done. But, like the topographers who leave their lines and paper and follow the map to reality, so too can the intellect leave its own limitations behind and enter the reality of Divine Mind. This can be, then, the only real use of the mind and topographer.

Yogacharya David lights Hermitage altar candle.

CHAPTER TWO
ENTERING-IN: SILENCE AT CLOUD MOUNTAIN

Enter In

To enter a family
Is to explore the Light and shadow
Of what it is to be human.

To enter the halls of Learning
Is to know the possibilities and limits
Of the mind.

To enter marriage
Is to learn the meaning of commitment
And to become softer of heart.

To enter parenthood
Is to experience sacrifice
And love unbounded.

To enter spiritual portages
Is to find who we truly are
And become one with the All-embracing One.

To enter old age
Is to see clearly the cycles of life
And learn the eternal youth of the heart.

To enter death
Is to leave this little human cage
And face the eternal youth of the heart.

To enter death
Is to leave this little human cage
And face what we have created.

To enter into stillness
Is to become the great I AM of Spirit
And realize we have always been that.

September: Stillness and Oppositional Forces

September 9, 2000

Today is the beginning of my year-long silent retreat. One-and-a-half months ago, I was given the inner command to start this venture. I asked for confirmation and a week later I was inwardly told, "You must do this." So, I began preparations for this day. Cloud Mountain Retreat graciously opened its doors for me, then I met with beloved ones from California to Prince Rupert, British Columbia. Then, the rush to get packed with the help of many friends, and here I am.

As I have checked in with my thoughts and feelings during my preparations, I entertained no doubts, no fear.

Today when I stood in front of Diamond Hall, for the first time I felt an oppressiveness in the silence. A doubt. Some fear was in me. The oppositional force fired a volley. My mind turned toward the One, my guide and comforter. I know It is here. The fear has stayed with me, and so too the Comforter. Who am I to contemplate a year of silence, a year of solitude? I am nothing, but the inner Light makes me know, "I am not the doer." I am following what I have been told to do.

Recently, I have been reading Sholem Asch's, *Moses*. What trials beset that great man and the people he led. My troubling fears look small in contrast.

O Lord, You have made me come here. By Your direction, I know this is the right place for me. You are my sole guide and comforter. The masters stand about me and I know I am not alone. You are my strength and shield.

I have said goodbye to many dear ones in this past little while. Feelings of loss, death, and grief have flooded many because of this change. Some part of me feels the sting of causing distress for others. Again, the temptation at seeing myself as the Doer.

Infinite Merciful One, I know You are the Supreme Self, the one who acts through all, so those who feel sorrow will be comforted. Those who keenly feel loss shall turn to You and know Your Presence. I release them into Your Keeping!

September 10, 2000

Today I have been feeling the sense of loss. I miss being in close physical connection with those I love. I know it is the idea of separation, rather than any reality on the outer plane. I release all ideas of separation into the Light. I focused on the group having Service this morning and felt myself there! A wonderful confirmation that in Spirit there is no separation by time nor space.

Any time I focus on the kutastha chaitanya (ajna point) I feel myself to be one with whom I am focusing my mind. In my heart, I know we are one. Where can there be separation when one has such knowledge? It is indeed the oppositional force once again trying to get entry. No fear, no loss, only softness of heart, only love of God, and through that love, a love of all.

O Blessed One, bless me always with the sure knowledge that we are One, and in that knowledge, Oneness with All in All. Be it so!

O Divine Mother

In purity You have called me to Yourself

But also in lurid outer forms

You come to tempt me away.

You are the sacred Power within

And You secretly yearn to rise

To awaken divine experience Itself

Through subtle channels that flow.

But age-old patterns divert

That steady-minded approach

And seek to divert that power to lesser gods

In vain pursuit of happiness.

Awaken in me O Divine Mother

Pure love for Thy Divine Form alone,

Burn those puny gods in sacred flame

And free me now and always, in Thee alone!

September 12, 2000

Reactions to entering silence have varied from, "I can't think of anything else to do in the world, how fortunate am I," to "Are you crazy?
Why are you doing this?" Fortunately, the latter are only fleeting.

Just For Today

Just for today
I will trust in you,
Just for today
I feel you close and present,
Just for today
I remain in the moment, unafraid.
Om Sri Ram Jai Ram Jai Jai Ram

What are realized masters like? They are like one who has vast wealth and power but has been born into this situation, so feels no need to show off or prove anything to anyone. In fact, their greatest joy comes in knowing they may be able to help another. It could be someone who owns a company that does well and prospers. Still, this person could oftentimes be in great joy just playing with a grandchild. At that time, completely forgetting vast wealth and power.

Spiritual masters too have vast wealth and power of a spiritual kind. They too, like the wealthy, vary in their display of it. Some show their attainment to all, like great showmen or women, but with non-attachment. Others live like ordinary people, wishing to be treated as anyone else. Both have their reasons, their purpose. Some like to have a small number of people know them and to work closely with that group. Others are known by millions. Perhaps you even know one, but you would never know if they did not want you to.

These masters have nothing to prove. They, in that sense, do not need us or anything. However, if we should ever have their boon, we would be the most fortunate on the earth.

September 12, continued:

I sat under the full moon light. It is always entrancing to me. The brightness revealed details of leaves and branches as I gazed over the hilly meadow. Noises came as some wild animal ambled noisily through the bush. A fear emanated from the stomach region. Ancient mental reflexes imagined a bear, some vicious marmot, something dangerous. A desire came over me to move into the safety of my cabin. I thought, it is good to expose these primal reactions. Do I put my trust in my walking stick or a wooden structure for my protection, or do I put myself in the hands of the all-protective Divine Mother? I chose the latter. I asked Divine Mother to come into that region of my stomach that felt fear and to give it courage. I asked Her to replace fear-laden thoughts with remembrance of Her. Calm came to me.

> O Divine Mother, teach me to
> Rely only upon You for my life,
> Safety, sustenance, and supply.
> You watch over me more carefully
> Than an audacious mother.
> Hari Om Tat Sat

September 20, 2000[6]

My life is a dedication to God. In fumbling steps and in the precision of movement, I steer my life toward that precious Goal. My Great Guru set the course, direction, and Goal. She beckons me still from her deeper life. God awakened me to that purpose when my own will would have taken me to self-destruction, or at best, to a mundane, senseless life. I pretend no greatness nor even goodness, for there is none other good than my Heavenly Father. Truly, I can say wholeheartedly that it is by God and Guru's Grace that I have found my Self.

I suppose it is natural to want all the world to share the sacred mystery that I feel, and it would be sheer arrogance to assume that

---

6   This beautiful writing came to David in September. As spring 2001 arrived, the songbird gave voice and David added to this song.

no others do. But there is the songbird within that bursts into Divine verse and aches to share that deepest Intimacy, yet finds that longing all the more painful as its song disappears into the void. The pain is nothing but God's constant yearning for His children to forsake their gloom-drenched dream of creation long enough to join once again in Divine Union.

Songs of Angels are not just beautiful voices, but the thrill of vibration that resounds throughout all space and is caught and finds resonance in the receptive soul.

THE CROSS AND THE LOTUS JOURNAL —SEPTEMBER 2000[7]

Dear Friends,

I stand on the brink of going into a year of silence. By an inner command, this has come about. As I have contemplated this time, it has been shown to me how we, as human beings, avoid entering into the cosmic sea of consciousness that is God. Our true nature, being the vast Spirit of Consciousness, one would think that all would be rushing to enter into that pure joy of Oneness. But as we look around, we see that it isn't so! The question comes, "Why do we not bend every effort to know this cosmic consciousness?" It is our freedom, our fulfillment, the purity of our Being, and yet, not only are we not diving into It, but we also devise every possible delay to avoid It! The answer has come to me in two parts.

One of the reasons for our dallying comes in the fear that we will have to face all that we have done in our journey while consciously separate from God. Consciously or unconsciously, we fear who we might really be. The horror of seeing what we have done against ourselves and others seems too overwhelming. We have had pounded into the brain since youth that we are bad; we fall short

---

7   The Journal was sent out just as David was entering Cloud Mountain.

of who we should be; we are sinners; we have the Id of Freud that is basically objectionable. In that way, we have learned not to look within, or at least not too closely.

The other reason is of the opposite extreme. Who and what we are is vast and powerful beyond our knowing, without boundaries, without limitation. Spirit threatens to overwhelm us with Its immense reach. "Who are we to know of this?" comes the question. Thus, poised between the two extremes, we settle for the known, no matter how dull to our eagle-soaring hearts. "Better to stay with what is known, than get in over our heads with the unknown," says the earth-bound soul. And so, we stay relatively the same. At best, we rearrange chairs on the soon-to-sink Titanic.

We seek to avoid the inevitable. We will all die; that is, leave this body and all its possessions. We will take that adventure without any preparation, hoping against hope that all will come out all right. But, Lahiri Mahasaya used to say, "Always remember that you belong to no one, and no one belongs to you. Reflect that some day you will suddenly have to leave everything in this world—so make acquaintanceship with God now." The great Master continued, "Prepare yourself for the coming astral journey of death by daily riding in the balloon of God-perception now."

To meditate deeply on the nature that is God is the way to prepare yourselves for the coming journey we call death. It gives us joy in the present. Imagine, if you will, breathing your last breath. The most natural thing to do in body consciousness is to reach for the next breath. Our future is then sealed for another lifetime in the physical body. Let us change the scenario and imagine you have been, each day, releasing your breath and expanding it into breathless cosmic consciousness. So, instead of reaching for the next breath, you release that last breath and let your consciousness rise into the vast Spiritual Consciousness that you have long realized yourself to be. In that precious moment, you feel yourself to be one with all that is. Freedom, bliss, and ever-new joy are yours as you free yourself from the restless tides of breath. A profound knowing comes to you that this is your real nature and human existence seems a dream.

To solve the mystery that is death even while living brings us such peace, which, perhaps ironically, allows us to live more fully while here in material existence. The key to this puzzle lies within us, always available to our all-knowing eye of intuition. But we busy ourselves with things of this world to such a degree that we obscure the Truth that would free us of our worst fears and ignorance. What is required is the courage to face ourselves, our past actions, and to face the wall of eternity. By becoming trusting in our Divine heritage, by taking a step at a time, we find we do not have to chase after what we seek.

Rather, if we become still, quiet, open-handed, then the answers we seek come to us. In the same way that we do not consciously digest our food, make our hearts to beat, and all the other functions that go on quite automatically in our bodies. We do not have to know all the functions required to make us ripe fruit to be Self-realized. What is required is that we become clear in our intention to know God, that all-embracing Consciousness that has created all that is. Unseen forces are then set into motion that make all possible. What is required is that we stay awake, ready! When that inner knowing says, "Do this, do that," we respond with pliancy. Then we make straight the path, the way to the Infinite. We feel as though every step of the way is guided by the Supreme Intelligence.

This thought guides me as I enter into this time of silence. I do not know all that will occur in this coming year. It is enough to take care of the things of the day. But one thing I do know, this guiding Presence will be with me and make everything that is to occur to be for the higher good of all. If you wish to join me in a day of silence once a month, once a week, once in a while, then we may commune with each other in that silence. And, during that time, pray for the world to be filled with Spiritual Light, even as I will be doing. You will be in my prayers every day, and in my heart always.

Namaste, (I bow to the Light within you) David

What Lies behind us and what lies before us are tiny matters compared to what lies within us.

—OLIVER WENDELL HOLMES (1841–1935)

September 21, 2000
Freddie

Freddie made his appearance the day before I started my silence. I asked him to go, but he did not. Freddie, by species, is... a fly. The day I started silence, I found him sitting on my chair. All others of his kindred kind, small flying machine types, I have ushered to the outdoors with a jar and lid. But Freddie? Well, for one thing, he was too quick. It was obvious he did not want to go. So, he stays.

After seeing him perched where I meditate, I began to wonder. I have spoken twice since taking silence, both on the first day. Once when I was reading something out loud that I had written, and the other was finding myself talking to Freddie. When later I sat to meditate, I saw Freddie on the desk. I patted my knee and mentally told him to come if he wanted to. In moments he was sitting on my lap. Well, what to do? I adopted Freddie!

Once, when I was meditating and the pulsation was very strong in my medulla and the top of my head, sure enough, I found Freddie glued to one or the other of these spots. He oftentimes comes and sits on my hands when I am in meditation posture. One thing I have cautioned Freddie about is being restless. He usually calms down, a real feat for one of a gadfly nature. If he cannot, a rarity, then he flies off.

One very interesting aspect to Freddie is that when he flies, he makes little or no sound. I find fly noises unbeautiful, so I appreciate this characteristic. One exception to this is when I lit some incense very near where I was meditating, Freddie made a lot of noise buzzing near my head. He was very unhappy, I take it, about the haze smoke being so close to me, making it uncomfortable for him to sit with me.

Yesterday, I told Freddie I really thought flies belong outside. I wondered whether he wouldn't be better off there. I opened the door while I swept the steps. I encouraged Freddie, mentally, to try it out here and if he didn't like it, he could go back into the house. Sure enough, Freddie came out the door. I had a thought to shut the door, flies can be a bit of a pest you know, but I remembered my promise; he could come back if he wanted to. Well, he flew around the porch a couple of times, then went right back in through the front door. All right then, he stays!

Since I started writing about Freddie, he has been busy sitting on my writing hand that is in constant motion, or on the pad of writing paper, or on my other hand. I mentally told him I was writing about him, and he seemed interested.

It seems when I have more isolated sadhana times, as when I was in the ashram, the animal kingdom responds. When on Sunday, Bob, Chad, and Carla accompanied me circumambulating the retreat center with Ram Nam, as I do every day, a black snake with three gold stripes came onto the trail as we walked along. When we walked by, it slithered under a rock. I felt a pang that we had not saluted it properly. When we had come full circle and returned to the same spot, the same snake came out on the trail as we approached. In unison, we sang Sri Ram and it listened. After some time, I decided to salute it with a pronam and continue on our walk. The snake then returned to its home under the rock.

Besides the fly and the snake, there were elk under the full moon light, a deer at dusk by Babaji's cave site, and a bluebird that sang next to my cabin—darshans of Ram in animal form. So, with great gratitude to these and more to come, Freddie and I are signing off for now.

September 22, 2000
Freddie Addendum

Since yesterday afternoon, I have not seen Freddie. Having glanced around a couple of times for him, I found him absent still. The thought came that he went outside after I had written the letter about him. The thought came, "Maybe he was insulted when I pictured him as a pest." Gone now for over twelve hours, I mentally called for Freddie, apologizing for calling him a pest. Within a moment, Freddie was again in sight, though at a distance. I tapped my lap and invited him to come. With a little coaxing, he came. But now he keeps more of a distance. He is now on my meditation chair whereas before he was "riding" my hand as I wrote. Frankly, this works better for me. Just now a bee came loudly against the screen. Freddie, on a nearby window, took off in the opposite direction. I mentally told Freddie it was all right; the bee is outside. Freddie is now sitting on my meditation chair. Such strange thoughts and occurrences. I know, critics will have no shortage of ammunition as I willingly hand them more!

Note: Father: Sat: Eternal Self
Son: Chid: Ever-aware Witness
Holy Ghost: Ananda: Comforter: Ever-new Bliss

Flowers of My Dreams

The flowers of my dreams
Are blooming on my altar for Thee,
For Thou hast seen my piteous cries
And bent Yourself to lift me up.

Who can say how sweet Your sweetness is?
Who can tell of Your glorious mantle white?
Who can serve as they ought to serve
The Light of unspeakable Beauty You are?

Fathomless is the love I feel for You, my Lord,

Breathless is my adoration at Your Feet.
Why? Because touching You I feel Your Nature
Breathing in, I taste Your nectar Presence.

And, in touching You, tasting You,
My Soul melts into Your Being
And naturally so, for Your lover,
I feel myself spreading over Your
Fathomless breathless nature.

A Nature so vast, no bird could wing,
A Beauty so rapturous, no artist could paint,
A Compassionate Empathy, no saint could ever tell,
A Love indescribable, no earthly love could approximate.

I die—I die in my Soul into Your Being!
And as I do, You are writing these very words with Your own hand.
Your love breaks this tiny human heart
Into a million prisms of Light that continue
To sing Your Name evermore.

Cloud Mountain Blossoms.

September 26, 2000

What a curious and marvelous world I live in. This morning's medi-tation after breakfast was a wonderful way to start the anniversary day of Lahiri Mahasaya's Mahasamadhi. It was two years ago today that I sat on the samadhi site of Lahiri Baba's in Haridwar. The beginning of *My Spiritual India* journey that started with my prayer to Babaji. Today was even more marvelous.

In my two weeks of being here at Cloud Mountain, I have not been indrawn as my nature has been prone to. That is, a feeling of being compelled to go within and be absorbed in communion with that inner Presence. I have wondered about this and have a few observations. It seems that there has been a period of time in build-ing a vibration here in the way one would build a house. First, the brush and waste must be cleared away. There were some psychic vibrations here that tried to intrude on my consciousness. Streams of images and conversations that suddenly came in. Those needed to be cleared.

Then the foundation needed to be set. Laying spiritual vibrations that began to fill this place. It started with the home-temple dedica-tion and has continued. Then for the landscaping. I have felt inner direction to circumambulate the property here every day, start-ing with the thrice rotation of Misty Meadows, silently chanting Sri Ram; once around the property at a slow gait with uninterrupted chanting, and then arriving back at Misty Meadows with another three revolutions and prayers for the establishment of Dharma in the world.

Now it seems the construction for the superstructure is ready. Yesterday, an ecstasy came over me and composed itself in a poem, "Flowers of my Dreams." For one hour afterwards, I felt positively and powerfully indrawn. It is interesting to note the oppositional forces at work during these past couple of weeks.

When circumambulating the property, people and situations would come to mind and I felt that I was walking into the power of negativity they held. By holding fast to the Name and affirming the

Almighty Light and Power of that Name they would eventually dissipate and leave. Then, only to have another negative power come in its wake. At different times in the following two weeks, powerful negative thoughts, feelings, or impressions would hit me. Many revolved around fear. Again, they were dispelled, fairly easily so far, with the power of Remembrance.

One of those oppositional forces came in the form of myself as powerless in meditation. As I said, the indrawing power that has been so strong in my life has been largely absent. Focused attention in meditation has been more scattered, more of a struggle. When some frustration built in me about his, I affirmed it was God Himself who meditated in me and it was with His power that I go below the surface of my thoughts or stay wading in shallow waters!

Well, this morning a powerful inner magnet drew me in. I had kept my appointments with God every day, starting at 4:00 a.m., and I am on a program through the day. I know it is with His power that results come. As I meditated this morning, that indrawing power did come. Inwardly, I perceived Babaji. A dialogue began that I will not relate in detail but resulted in my questions being answered by him. He said, "Come to me," in relation to my meditation dilemma. "Inwardly?" I asked.

"Yes," was his reply.

An inner Light, sometimes with a variation of the five-pointed star, but mostly as a pearl-colored luminescence, continued to draw me in. After some struggle to get the mind stable, I heard Dave moving lumber around in constructing the deck. I looked at the clock which read around 8:30 a.m. A brief process dictated I continue. The outer noise disappeared. The inner struggle continued with Babaji's inner voice as close to me as could be. Patiently, he led my strident thoughts back to "Come to me." Giving up on a formal meditation posture, as Babaji said, "Sit comfortably," I gave myself "easy pose." That is what allowed the body to sit comfortably.

Gradually, the mind became steadier but not in a constant way yet; it was still jumping. I thought once or twice, "Maybe I should take a break." The first time, Babaji indicated it would be better for me to continue. The second time, he indicated it would be better to continue, but it was okay to have a break. I told him I would come right back after the break. Would he still be there? "Yes," was the response. I had come to the point where, with Babaji's help, I knew that part of my struggle was seeing myself as the Doer. I had so much gratitude for his help and felt like such a poor student that I inwardly lay my head at his feet before taking the break. With that gesture, my mind became steady and I bathed in the Light of Consciousness. I remained in that way for some time.

At last, I felt it was now time to take a break. I outwardly bowed down at the feet of my wonderful Master, Babaji. When I opened my eyes, it was past 11:30 a.m. I went outside for some air and a stretch. Just then, I heard Dave walking up the path to work on the deck! What immaculate timing. The Infinite Mercy does all for this youngest of sadhakas, so beautifully that my heart overflows with gratitude.

O Infinite Babaji

Your Grace knows no bounds
You teach your most inept devotee
With such patience and love.

How can I say the gratitude I feel?
How can I show You my love?
How can I serve You with greater devotion?
Will you show me as the days of my life unfold?
Inwardly, I see you smile and nod affirmatively.

Babaji Statue.

September 27, 2000, Lahiri Mahasaya
Mahasamadhi Day

Dear Friends,

It was two years ago, September 27, 1998, that I sat on the banks of the Ganges. It was at Hardiwar, gateway to God, that I prayed:

O Babaji, in the form of Mother Ganges,
Please lead me to see Spiritual India.

It was the intense desire behind the prayer that brought quick results. Within the hour, our guide, Neelu, took us to the Samadhi (place of mortal remains) of Lahiri Mahasaya. What words can describe the blessings of finding a meditation group there celebrating the Mahasamadhi anniversary of the great Master in our lineage? The date and the existence of the group were unknown to me before that moment.

This Yogoda Satsang Group welcomed us with open arms. I listened, enthralled, at the story that Sri Tyagi told of his meeting with Babaji earlier that same year. The profound great Masters, Babaji and Lahiri Mahasaya, together as always, in coordinating a spiritual feast for their spiritual son. O blessings, I have received too many to count!

Now, two years later, I find myself on a new spiritual adventure, this one of a very different sort. I find myself again, and continually, in need of these most lovely Masters' blessings. I am now settled in this idyllic setting at Cloud Mountain Retreat Center for a year of silent retreat. As I settle up affairs for things to run smoothly in my absence, I feel a silence beginning to envelop me. Not an outward journey, as with India, but rather one dedicated to the inner reaches of Spirit.

My friends, I invite you to journey with me into that silence. We are led by the great Ones who started this work. We may glide over inner universes only to come into the lap of our Most beloved. Come, let us journey together through the inner space, the truly last frontier, and become ensconced in the Light that is the father of us all. Let us be as spiritual sojourners on a mighty crusade, a crusade to overcome ego's delusion.

Nigh, nigh comes the hour. Let not your lamps be without oil. In deep meditation, fill your reservoir with the oil of life-force, and in sacred Kriya, raise it to be a light upon the hill. O come, come with me as we follow the Light of lights, into the bridegroom's chamber and commune in union with Him! Let the joy of that union spread out and out until, like a conflagration of Light, It burns everywhere bright.

Let the names Babaji, Jesus, Lahiri Mahasaya, Sri Yukteswarji, Master, Mother, and all bearers of Light be emblazoned upon the heavens. And let there be a new Light, a new day, a splendid awakening upon this earth! May all worship according to the Light already shining in their soul.

So, my friends, in the spirit of Lahiri Mahasaya and the great ones, let us be bold partakers in the spiritual manna constantly pouring upon us. And, let us manifest dharma, our highest Light, now and always. And together, humankind can enjoy the blessings that arise from a life well-lived.

Om Namaste, David

Lahiri Mahasaya.

September 27, 2000

Arise, Awake!

Arise, Awake!
It may seem early
But who knows?
I may be Late!

Arise, Awake!
Crows a bird aloft
At heaven's sounding horn,
Leading us ever home to Pearl's gate.

And, rising, rising, rising,
Past paltry shimmering gold,
Finds erstwhile joys of old
Growing stale and putrefying.

Look neither left nor right
On thy morning ride,
But straight for the sun
Lest ye not wake before fall of night.

Onward, onward!
Cried the prophets since old,
But who cares to listen?
"Is it not tiresome to always go forward?"

But delay is quicksand!
And tempting as it might seem,
Turns wingéd flight to feet of lead
And sweet-scented dreams to thick mired land.

So, Arise, Awake!
Be it ever so with you
That you may know the One
And in Bliss forever stay!

I sent off, what is, for me, a very stark note to a devotee. My nature has been to be all kindness and love. This note insisted that when the devotee comes to perform some service, it must be without attachment. This devotee has provided a lot of service, but with some attachment. I checked in with the inner Self before I sent it and it gave the green light.

Since that time, I have felt mental and emotional anguish over the probable effect of the note. I have checked in with what feels to be Babaji's voice. He concurred that it had to be sent. Not only that, but it was for my good, as it helped break an attachment I too had formed. It has taken a toll on me. I feel that it is good, yet there are reverberations in me regarding this.

I am yet to be the detached pruner. That gardener who can precisely cut out the unwanted branches. Perhaps I will always feel the pain of the snips; if so, that is how God made me. In the meantime, I work to let go of my attachment and do what must be done.

I am sorry I cannot reproduce all the conversations between Divine Consciousness as Babaji and myself. I am slowly becoming convinced that is who I am in communion with. It was for the purpose of deepening my own Divine Communion. His responses come almost more quickly than my questions. He has me asking questions and he gives a short reply. He says by my formulating the questions, rather than him offering information, my attunement deepens. The thoughts and expressions he uses are akin to my own thought patterns, as he is using my mind as the receiver of his thoughts.

This has made me skeptical of the sources of this communication. "Is it simply my own mind?" It comes back very quickly that it is He indeed. Minutes ago, I was asking about Mother and why she did not feel close to him, Babaji.

"It was not necessary," was the reply. "She was focused on Master and Jesus."

"Was she connected with Meher Baba?"

Babaji: "Yes."

David: "Why did she not meet him in the physical body?"

Babaji: "It was not required."

David: "Can she hear me now?"

Babaji: "Yes, she is always very close to you."

At this point, I was washing some dishes. My heart convulsed and tears came.

Unable to stay standing, I had to sit and my whole body shook with—well, sadness over the aloneness of these last years, relief and joy at the confirmation of what I have known. So much came in those tears. Tears I've been longing to shed for some time now.

Many questions are being answered; some are not, being left for later times. I would like to share it all, but I cannot. What I do want to convey is the profound awe I have in regard to this. The questioning mind is still there, "Is this real?" But deep inside, I know that it is. A part of me feels that if I touch it too much, it will disperse into powder and be gone. Babaji assures me this year is to deepen our contact so there is clear communication between us, and he will help me with this part of my sadhana. Apparently, this is part of my karma. You know the analogy of being grateful for being the water boy, well this is it. Great gratitude and love overwhelm me. And to be in communion with all the gurus.

Yogacharya David walking and chanting.

One thing I've wondered is if Babaji had anything to do with Papa's initiation. He said he had "something to do with it," leaving it vague. I asked why Master didn't recognize Ramana Maharshi. He said because they did not have a strong connection. And is that why he felt so strongly about Bhramananda? When I asked for clarity, he said his answers were limited to my mind. I said that is what makes me suspicious about this. Babaji said, "Yes, they had a strong prior connection."

I asked about difficult relations and periods of my life I have not felt good about. He said they were part of my karma. I ran through a list, and he said yes to all, that they needed to happen. I asked about Kriyananda, and he said I was nothing like him. I asked if his problem stemmed from mental arrogance. He said that was part of it. He did not elaborate other than indicating the sexual problem ran very deep.

I asked about Freddie the fly, if he sent him. He said, "No." My karma had brought him. I have had such a nice connection with Freddie.

Well, that is a bit of a run down. I asked if I could write about this.

Babaji: "Don't you write about everything?"

I said: "Well it helps me to get it."

Babaji: "Yes, well, it's alright."

Babaji, I want to say, since I am writing this, that this is a dream come true. Thank you, from my whole heart and soul, thank you and all the lovely Masters who are working to make this world a better place for all.

Oh Yes, I don't know if I mentioned it, but earlier I had asked Babaji if we had a prior connection. He said yes but did not elaborate. As I have felt strongly also that Lahiri Baba and I have that connection, he said just now, "Yes, of course." He wants me to trust what I know more. He hesitates when I ask him things I already know. But you know after going it alone, that is, without verification of what I am getting other than I know that I know, it feels good to get confirmation. I promise I will not slacken up on inner attunement.

Om Namaste Babaji and sweet Mother and Masters, Om Shanti to one and all.

P.S. I asked about Carla, as she is so intimately involved in the work.

Babaji: "Yes, she is one of us." That too confirmed what I already knew. Blessings to her.

Chad Hickenbottom meditating.

September 28, Next morning, 5:00 a.m.

I inwardly ask Mother for confirmation. My mind not being calm, I reach out for a voice. A female voice answers. I question, "Is it Mother's?" I know it is not. The idea of psychic mischief-makers comes to mind. Inwardly, I call Babaji. He says, "Yes," my mind is not calm given that I had opened myself to a psychic influence. This throws my mind into doubt. The voice of Babaji instructs me to be calm. Yes, this is the right thing. Give the whole question over to God. In fact, earlier this inner dialogue had said it was Divine Consciousness coming in the form of Babaji. As I think about it now, the whole question is: "Is this coming from the superconscious realm or the negative psychic realm?"

When I first arrived here, I was getting interference from the psychic realm. If it is coming from Divine Consciousness, then it will be a constant knowing, not attached to "name or fame." I do not need to "reach out" to it, rather it is with me always, which is what the inner dialogue had said earlier. I can see now that putting the moniker "Babaji" to the one I am dialoguing with made my mind "outward," focused outside of my Self. In fact, it, this inner voice, supported this by its reluctance to respond when my mind was getting too outward focused. At those times, it did not answer at all, or more slowly.

This inner voice has been pointing me inward, asking the mind to be calm. As I reason this through, I feel a greater calm come over me—I think the emotions I felt when this inner voice confirmed that Mother and the Masters were with me, and Mother was always very close to me, made the mind get attached to an outer realm.

In fact, for perfect masters, there is no difference between themselves and God, for God expresses Himself flowing through their stainless consciousness. To become calm, to "Be still and know that I AM God" as the sign on my door reads. For some reason in this place, the hermitage, I seem to be more open to the psychic. The last (and first) teacher was a Tibetan Lama from the West Indies. Both the West Indies and Tibetan Buddhism have traditions of psychic phenomena. I asked the inner voice and it confirmed what I thought.

The thought came to me quickly: first, a question, "How to clear negative psychic phenomenon?" The answer, both mine and "His," was to keep my mind in higher consciousness—God.

I return to the same teachings, the ones Mother gave and that have kept me safe: "Keep your mind on God." I feel her smile. The reason she did not answer earlier, last night, is that my mental mirror was agitated and could not perfectly reflect her consciousness.

In all of this, the answer is to keep a perfectly calm mind. Babaji smiles with approval. In fact, since coming here, it has been clear that the work I was doing for God was talking to this mind and nervous system. In order for me to get established in this next state of consciousness, I needed a less agitating environment. The thought came, maybe I always will. Then I thought of Mother living in the city. I thought, no that is a limiting idea to think I would always need a remote, removed, environment. It is true for now. Well for now the thing is to bring this mind to a steady calm through Kriya meditation and focus on the Mind of God.

One thing I was reminded of the last couple of days is Papa's injunction not only to chant God's name but to remember His attributes. It seems as though, here at Cloud Mountain, teachers of the past have certain requirements of their students in silence: no eye contact, no personal connection, this being intrusive to the silent one. This has not been my mood so far. I have smiled and been open to all. And Jean has responded easily to this. David and Laura have the other pattern more ingrained, but David, who I see much more of, has shifted, and now makes eye contact and smiles. At least how I am feeling now fits better and relates to thinking of God's attributes. There are so many. God is joy, purity, love, peace, service-full, fun, an actor of supreme quality (adding to the fun), as tender as a mother, thoughtful and considerate, etc., ad infinitum.

Well, these qualities just don't fit well with no eye contact and no personality. I know the teachers here are trying to draw the mind inward and they try to do a lot in a short amount of time. But my time here is longer. The movement to be inward is more attuned to being naturally drawn in. I am long accustomed to having an inward life in combination with an outward life. The one does not disturb the other. But, this time away from my other life is necessary. Perhaps I will not be wanting any outer contact at some point. I did not want to go to lunch yesterday (Jean had invited me) because I did not want the outer stimulation, and I think they try to be careful around me, which is work for them. They need to be able to relax and enjoy their lunch, too!

Namaste, Peace, and Blessings.

Yogacharya David meditating.

October: Sadhaka Homecoming and Babaji's Blessing

October 3, 2000
Dreams

After the first day of my fast, I had a nice dream of X: Not much happened. I was in his apartment with some of his friends. He was wanting something from me but had not done anything on his own, so I was denying him. His friends were telling him they had told him so. The air was light and overall positive.

Then I had a much stranger dream. I was a strange fellow, a bit like the character of Forrest Gump. I took to speed walking and was walking all over the country. In fact, along the surf of the ocean, I was walking on the water. Then I found myself with some migrant workers who were being questioned about their citizenship by border police. I realized then that I had no I.D., no wallet, no money, or anything. The police were pretty rough and one, in particular, took us to a back room. He started twisting the arm of a man. The sense of this policeman was not good. He enjoyed inflicting pain for no seemingly good reason. I saw that we were all in trouble and in for a bad time of it. I went to the policeman and told him to stop. He turned his attention to me and started backing me up. His breath was hot and moist, and he had a definite sexual sadism sense to him. As he was backing me up, he was doing something that caused me pain. I told him that it was painful what he was doing. He replied that I probably liked that and I would like a lot more as he continued to press up close to me with that hot, steamy breath. Then I awoke.

As a result, a strange mixture of emotions has hung on to me for the last hour. The first thing I felt is a yearning compassion for all who may be in difficult situations such as this, with possible outcomes of torture, sadism, and death. The other is a deep feeling of disturbance regarding this border policeman.

The meaning of the dream came to me spontaneously while circumambulating the Center. Being out walking, was the soul doing sadhana, and then collecting souls who also wanted to return to their homeland? Sadhaka's Homecoming was written this morning, after I wrote about the dream. The migrants were souls I had come to lead home. They were no longer part of this world, thus their migrant status. The sadistic border policeman is the oppositional force. The fact I had no I.D. is that I have no ego attachment to this world. He turned his attention from the migrants to me, bringing about my role in helping them in their trouble. My dual feeling of yearning compassion and discomfort with his power and ugliness are both real.

Well, the game is afoot!

O Sadhaka

Let us journey home together
For each is born and dies alone,
But we have glad privilege to walk
Hand in hand while here.

And once knowing our joy
And finding it a boundless fount,
Each drinking deep their fill and more!
We find even more joy in sharing it with all.

So be glad, Sadhaka,
The journey may be long and difficult
But, it is in the right direction!
And we will yet live to see thy gentle homecoming.

The Seed that Yields Fruits

O Sadhaka
Long does the Master wish to share,
Share the wealth of Its heart and soul
The super abundant share of Its Spirit.
It longs for you to receive
To receive all It has to give
But a full pitcher cannot receive
Only when it is empty may it be receptive.

O Sadhaka
Open your heart and mind
Rid it of the contents of the world,
And like an opening bud become
The glorious warmth of morning Light.
Open yourselves to quiet yearning
Experientially awaiting the glance of inner Light,

Patiently be that expectancy
For it is not given to the over-anxious.

O Sadhaka
The opening is yours,
The Day is ripe for harvest
Of seed that yields such glorious fruits.

Reverend Larry Koler and Cate Koler, with
Reverend Peter Schultz in the background.

October 5, 2000

Last night after I walked in place and stretched, I stood out on the deck. I saw a star twinkle, and as usual, I thought of Babaji. Since Babaji has been coming to my inner mind, I have felt more drawn to, and more conflicted about, him. Early in this time of him coming to me, I asked Mother about this phenomenon. She said, "Keep your mind on God." Well, I have struggled with God with form, and God without form. At one point, Babaji said he was all-pervasive consciousness coming to me in the form of Babaji. Yes, it was Babaji speaking to me, but he was primarily the omniscient consciousness. I have felt my attachment and my struggle there.

Last night, as I felt myself yearning again for his physical darshan, I asked him plainly, "Is it best to surrender your form to the kutastha?"

"Yes," was the instant reply.

"All right, it's done!" And I surrendered all of it to the Light of the kutastha. And thank goodness, for now I see it was not a thing of peace. It was disturbing me, as I knew. But I needed to let it go. And of what was I letting go? It felt to me to be an ancient desire for the form of God.

A couple of times, hints of that attack have seemed to emerge and I immediately throw them too onto the flame of kutastha. Om Swaha!

October 5, continued:

O Divine Mother, Kundalini
Lift me past all human limitations
And reveal unlimited Divine Potential,
Raise me to Thy mystic Light!

As Yogiraj Baba would say so often, "The body is nothing but a nest of troubles." Only to the degree that it is made a living Temple of the Infinite does it find redemption.

David: "Om Babaji, have I done anything at all to pay for the air that I breathe?"

Babaji: "Yes, some."

Then the work I had done with other souls came to mind.

David: "Om Babaji, has the work I've done with others been alright?"

Babaji: "Yes, it has changed their lives."

Oh, the blessing of one of his words has the value of a thousand-thousand words of ordinary speech. Om Babaji.

October 5, continued:

Four nights ago, X had a dark shadow around him. When I inwardly examined him, he had two major astral entities on his back. They seek life-energy and attach themselves to the body. They are not human, but oftentimes have rather hideous reptilian or insect-like forms. They are parasitic and drain life-energy. I removed these two forms and a couple of minor ones. This is something I have to do for many people. I have not heard of this hideous issue, but discovered these form-energies on my own some time ago. Well, I did hear of someone on the radio who was talking in this vein once.

Anyway, with the fast, I have had some difficult days (today is the fourth day of a twelve-day fast). Inwardly, this morning, Babaji asked if I would like some of these astral creatures taken off me. I said yes and became aware of two of them attached to my back. On my left side, he removed a very large one that went from the nape of my neck to the bottom of my spine. The one on my right side was almost as big. When it came off, it bit Babaji. I asked if that caused pain and he said yes, although I suspect pain for him seems more like a dream. Upon removal, I felt immediate relief from the pain and difficulty I have been having on this fast. And, my vision got very clear, something I have been having trouble with for a while now. I asked if this creature was the cause of my blurry vision. Babaji said, "Yes." Then he peeled off a layer from my back that looked like a filmy plastic. It may have been a creature also, I don't know. Then he applied another type of layer that he said would make it difficult for them to attach to. He agreed that he would remove any future ones. My sense with the ones he removed was that they were connected with the oppositional force regarding this work I do.

P.S. While circumambulating today, as usual, interesting thoughts were occurring. I was remembering my Typhoid Fever at Anandashram and how it all seemed to strengthen me. All works for good. All works for God.

Your Will

Your Will
O Lord You know every part of me,
O Lord there is no nook or cranny unknown to You,
O Lord take this raw material and build a fit Temple for you.
O Lord make this mind glow with Your arduous Worship.

You are the protector to the humble,
You are strength to the faithful,
You are Bliss to the Yogi,

You are the All in All to the surrendered.

It is You Who has created this child in
Your Image and likeness,
It is You Who has spun this Divine Lila of separation,
It is You Who art the Savior to the wayward,
It is You Who must make the impossible possible.

I do not come as a beggar, someone unknown to You,
I do not seek for something that is not my rightful due,
I do not seek crumbs of paltry answered prayers,
I do not come for anything less than your very Self.

I know this cannot be bartered for as merchants do,
I know this does not come without paying full measure,
I know this does not come with study alone,
I know this does not come by being good alone.

I know the price for Your very self,
I do know it is love for You alone,
I do know it is surrender of all my self,
I do know that this is what is required.

I give to You my works,
I give to You my thoughts,
I give to You my love,
I give to You my all in all.

You will give me perfect love for You,
You will give me perfect service to You,
You will create a perfect temple Within,
You will give to me Your very Self!

My Challenge to You!

All my life, I was a secret yogi. Here and there, I would share some of my inner life. And when Providence had me bring someone to Mother, they stayed. But then God and Guru commanded me to go public. It was then I was told to make that which was secret open to all. To many, this might seem like a fine thing to do. To me, it was an act of submission. It was done for one reason. To give sadhakas the message that they might be able to attain something in this life. If such a poor sadhaka as myself could have some experiences and gain some realization, then anyone with a genuine hankering could do that and more.

Never think I have been perfect on this path. I do not say that with any pride. It is a source of deep regret for me. But, I have had a genuine and long-lasting sincere desire for God. Why? It can only be said that it is the Grace of God and Guru. I have the resolve that no matter how many times I fall, I will get back up. And I only tell you what I have realized or experienced myself. Otherwise, I will say this is what so and so has said.

Do not think that complete liberation is a joke. Sometimes people have some experiences and think, "I am realized!" That makes a joke of realization. There are those rare souls who Awaken with a touch. That is because they have attained that state previously. But they are rare.

Be in this for the long haul. But, you can know God now! You may know His Presence, His Bliss, His transforming Touch. If you do not know this, then make it your first business to realize it. Once that Transformation has begun, make it your first business to attune yourself to that Presence. Go where it tells you to go. Do what it tells you to do. As you do this, you will gradually Be as It is. This should be your first and primary goal in life. All other goals are sub-categories. If you want true fulfillment in your life, this is the way. And, you would not be reading these words if your soul was not calling you to your real Self, the great I Am.

This is the way I live my life. I do not propose anything I have not done myself. I am not here to cater to your fancies of what a spiritual life should be. I stand as a challenge saying to you, "Arise, Awake!" Follow with me as long as I am focused on the magnificent Light. And know for yourself the Truth of all truths, the unspeakable Truth of your Being.

October 8, 2000—Silent Satsang

Dear Satsang Friends: Greetings, David has asked me to read this to you.

Welcome to Silent Satsang at Cloud Mountain. Entering into silence means more than not speaking, it means entering into a spirit that is peaceful with deep movements of Spirit. As you enter the grounds, become still, not only the lips, but also, the heart. Feel the change and notice the peg on the outer entrance, hang your ego and worldly concerns there. Slow the mind, and breathe even, steady rhythms. Be open and aware of what the Infinite has to freely give to you today. The past is swept away; the future is but a dream; the present is pregnant with possibility. Empty the mind and let it open as a flower opens to receive the sun.

Hints to Silence: No whispering—that is not silence; become silent when you drive onto the property; bring a small writing tablet and pen for unavoidable questions; bring potluck food to the cabin;

proceed directly to Mist Haven on arrival; bring a water bottle; you may arrive at 9:00 a.m.; the program starts at 10:00 a.m.; bring layered, comfortable warm clothing; bring a meditation blanket or folding chair, whatever you need for prolonged meditation; at the top of the hour, we will have chanting and that is the time to take small breaks if necessary; do not come or go during the meditation hour; there will be time for a light lunch between 12:00 and 1:00; at 2:55, we will circumambulate the property with silent Ram Nam, then return to Mist Haven and repeat a prayer for world enlightenment; for those who wish to stay, meditation will continue at the Hermitage until 5:00 p.m.; then, time to go—carry peace and deep movement of Spirit home with you.

It has been a month now since entering Cloud Mountain. So far, it has been very interesting. Sadhana is thick in the air! As you might imagine, it takes some adjustment. Imagine, if you will, no radio, no television, no one to talk to, no movies, no news. Now everyone says, "I would love having time like that." But who does it? Not many. Because, for one, our lifestyle does not allow for it. But even more, it is not easy to adjust to. We are used to our stimulation and may feel we would go crazy without it! Well, I have not gone crazy yet, not any more than I have been in the past, at least.

I adopted a fly named Freddie. He is unusual in that he is a devotee fly. There may be more explanation later. And, Babaji has made his Presence known in new and more personal ways, also more of that may be coming later. Swami Vishwananda made a visit. The love was palpable in the air as this wonderful sage allowed me his darshan. We are blessed to have such a wonderful representative from India. My deepest thanks to Larry Koler and others who made this possible.

You will be receiving *Notes to Sadhakas* in the near future. These are some thoughts I have put down on paper while being here that relate to making this spiritual journey. My prayer is that you receive inspiration and some guidance through them during my physical absence.

During this last period of time, we celebrated Lahiri Mahasaya's birth and Mahasamadhi. A funny story comes to mind. Lahiri Mahasaya was walking home from the bathing ghat at the Ganges. As he walked by, someone noticed he had cut his leg and it was bleeding quite badly. They mentioned it to him. As he was absorbed in God, he had not noticed it. He tied a cloth around the leg and proceeded home. When he arrived, his wife said, "What happened to your leg?" He said, "I must have cut it. Why?" She said, while laughing at the sight, "You are bleeding all over. You tied the cloth to the wrong leg!" Well, he was so absorbed in God that he had not noticed which leg was cut.

So, let our minds be absorbed in the Infinite in order to gain peace and spiritual prosperity. And, to all Canadians, let your gratitude be plentiful in your Thanksgiving celebrations to the One who makes all life and happiness possible.

In Deepest Divine Joy, David

 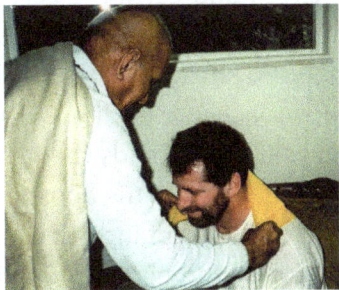

Yogacharya David with Swami Vishwananda.

October 8, 2000

Last night, I had a very interesting experience with Babaji. I looked at the stars from the deck. Since I have made my promise to not look for a material manifestation of Babaji, but an inward one, I shifted from looking for Babaji to descend from one of the lights in the sky to focusing on the inward star. When I did so, I asked, "Babaji, will you reveal your universal form, at the kutastha?"

Lightning quick, as always, there was a reply, "Yes!" Immediately, a magnetic force went into action at the third eye point and the medulla. It felt like a cork that is tightly placed in a bottle being pulled out of the ajna. After some time, I transferred indoors, and the force continued. Then into the next night, with some breaks, this force has continued to exert pressure at the ajna. When I asked Babaji what I could do, he said, "Look" at the ajna. Also, the celestial sound of the OM current is very strong.

Om Babaji, Jai Babaji!

October 9, 2000

On this day of Yom Kippur, this day of atonement, at-one-ment, Jesus has confirmed for me the rightness of my path. I felt a wrenching in my heart at this confirmation. It seems the veils between heaven and earth are very thin these days. The Presence of great masters is within my reach so easily, my mind races to keep up.

"Who am I, Lord?" comes the cry of my mind. Not yet does perfection reach into my life. Burning tears want to be released, but some invisible gate holds them. Ah, heaven and earth are certainly intermixed. I read of the apostle Paul's life as described by Sholem Asch, and the acceptance of Gentiles into the Faith. What a profound story for the ages, so graphically brought to life. Indeed, heaven reaches down and plucks us from the mundane and shows us how all the world is brimming with the beautiful.

Our Heavenly Father, Hallowed be Thy Name, Forever and Forever, Amen. Grace is the only word. I ask Jesus, "Will I know you perfectly?"

The answer: "My Father's mansion has many rooms. We continue to explore His infinite Kingdom." How confirming and thrilling. Then I ask, "Will You be with me always?" He says, "Babaji is helping you now, but I am with you always." My heart is touched to the core.

Om Sri Ram Jai Ram Jai Jai Ram

October 10, 2000

The story of Lahiri Mahasaya is so instructive. Soon after meeting Babaji, he asks Babaji to come for a "trifle"—that is, to satisfy some curiosity seekers. Somehow inside, if I seek out Babaji's Presence for a trifling, just a casual curiosity, I instantly feel its wrongness. My mind is then attuned to its proper direction. All of the answers I get come lightning-quick, in minimalist language but full meaning.

Hari Om Tat Sat

O Lord

I do not like Your game of hide and seek
Come now into Thy child's lonely heart.
Make Yourself known
And the sun to shine upon this one,
Be no miser of Spirit
But gracious evermore.
O Lord, I do not like this game
Come to me now!

October 12, 2000

I have been using the clearing exercises on my throat. An old symptom has re-emerged, like a stone in my throat. This is the place of illumined Buddhi. I suspect this "stone" is not mine, but I have a sense of whose it is. They are not doing well in their sadhana now. The obstruction is strong and uncomfortable. The game is afoot!

There has been a lot of anger and discord in the air; it swirls around. All individuals play a part in working out this larger karma.

Each tested to their capacity. The foundations have been laid, the stage set, who will rise and who falls is just the thing. Who slumbers, who awakes! Each master rightly acknowledges the truth of what I wrote. This is the spiritual path that comes in seemingly unspiritual ways.

Babaji continues to work on the ajna with a vice grip. To what end? To his end! In this, I am content to be in his sadhana.

Om Sri Ram Jai Ram Jai Jai Ram

Infinite Plays as Finite

The Infinite finds expression in the finite,
Water in the ocean is cast liquid
Then sun turns it to gas invisible
Becoming ethereal cloud vapors.

The Infinite plays as the finite
Coming to the next expression of water,
Clouds condense to rain or snowfall
Descending, descending, and descending.

The Infinite is frozen-finite,
The snow and rain may form sculptures
Once hardened as ice and snow on earthly plane,
Until quickening transmutes them to liquid again.

The Infinite builds movement as the finite,
Snow and rain descend to Mother earth
Gradually gather as streams, creeks, and rivers
Moving, moving, moving, into greater movement.

The Infinite finds diversity in the finite
The waters of different places blend and meld,
They complete and rush ever on
Seaward to their unknown destination.

The Infinite finds fulfillment in the finite
After a long, long journey of various forms,
Rivers of liquid rivers meet and dissolve
Into liquid ocean, vast and receptive.

Infinite and finite are not different,
Can the ocean and various forms of its manifestation
Be said to be disconnected? Can snowflake be without ocean?
Even though snowflake appears of a different nature?

October 13, 2000

Is not the snowflake a frozen piece of ocean? And can the ocean remain itself the ocean other than through the return of its children in tumbling, raucous majestic rivers?

It is the infinite that has become the finite. Does not God find expression in so many forms? Is it not me, and you, and all that is, and could God still be God, if all did not return to Him?

October 15, 2000

Receiving gifts of food and clothes and other items, as well as cards from devotees, I feel like the richest person on earth!

9:30 p.m. I have just finished *The Apostle* by Sholem Asch. From the time the slave of Tigellinus, Ofonious was seen crawling around the arena as he was being mauled by bloodhounds guarding the infant, to the end of the book when St. Paul saw the white wings of the angel, I have been convulsed by heart-wrenching tears. Tears of compassion, tears of joy run side by side. My mind reels at knowing why. Why for the heart and soul, compassion, love, and admiration for these enduring souls of the first order. Their courage is unassailable. Not that they did not have doubts, fears. Courage is not the lack of these ones. Rather, courage in the presence of fear and doubt, and continuing forward.

Sholem Asch has written two masterpieces in *The Nazarene* and *The Apostle*. With stunning clarity and breathtaking scope, he has made mythic figures take on flesh, bone, and blood and made the people and places come alive with an intuitive perception unmatched by any. My great gratitude for his most wonderful gift.

October 16, 2000, 4:00 a.m.

In *The Apostle*, Sholem Asch shows, in remarkable relief, the evolution of Paul. Beginning with a passionate young man studying with the most renowned Pharisee of the day, Paul exudes a tendency toward extremism. His rabbi warns him of the danger of embracing ideas that leave out Rabbi Hillel's core teaching to love thy neighbor as thyself.

Paul ignores such hints and in his zeal for the Torah, begins to persecute the fledgling Christian movement. The stunning conversion for Paul, Saul at that time, reveals an intense young man, full of shame and desirous to find his way into the "fold" of his Master's flock. Acceptance is not easy, but he has his supporters. Part of his revelation was to preach that the majority of believers at this time were Jews. The notion that a Messiah was Jewish, and the idea of God sending a redeemer, was not part of the lexicon of the Roman world at that time.

One of the great barriers to Gentiles converting in the early church was the ritual of circumcision. Adult males would be required to go through this procedure. As you might guess, in a world before anesthetics, this was more than getting some water sprinkled on the head and saying, "I do!" Not only that, but the converted Gentiles were expected to live by the Pharisee's laws of purity. Learning what those were, and abiding by them, could be a daunting task. It also set individuals apart from their old society.

The early Pharisees found no disagreement with the early Christians as long as they followed Mosaic Law and the complex laws of purity imposed upon being a Jew at the time. In fact, some Pharisees either dallied with the idea that Jesus was the Messiah they had been waiting for or took a wait-and-see attitude. The early church expected Jesus to come out of the Clouds of Heaven at any moment, literally any day.

Paul was intent on bringing the "good news" to the Gentiles and spreading it to the ends of the world. To do so, he started telling Gentiles they did not need to get circumcised nor follow the strict Pharisee codes. There was a hierarchy in the early church. Peter initiated those who were to be filled with the Holy Spirit and then could give communion to others. Paul was not one of those. When they tried to reel him in, the fiery Paul continued in his zeal. He was anxious to be a part of the fold, but on his own terms, according to his own understanding. He continued to drop more and more of the Jewish strictures, which created a break with the Pharisees and all those who maintained Moses' commandments.

Sholem Asch provides a beautiful description of the polarization created by Paul, and the schism between himself and the hierarchy of the new movement as Paul became more extreme. On one side are the early believers who see themselves as Jewish, only they believe the Messiah will return in a dramatic fashion any day. They mostly would like to see all in Judaism come to believe as they do. On the other hand, there is Paul who sees it as his role to be the apostle to the Gentiles and to remove all barriers.

To do this, Paul goes to the extreme, a huge extreme. For all early believers in Jerusalem, he says that all you have to do is to have faith in Jesus Christ. To the early church, this is beyond belief. Their anger at Paul, and their refusal of his message, is absolute. They have no means to stop him from saying what he is spreading to the hinterlands, but they are absolutely opposed to it.

Not only that, but Paul is equating Jesus with God. Again, this does not resemble their understanding at all. Their version is that the Messiah is sent by God to bring righteousness to the world and to vanquish the enemies of Israel.

Paul remains apart from the Jewish synagogue and his own brothers in the early faith. The word "Christians" started out as derision by other Jews. "Oh, look, there go those Christians, those anointed ones," would be the first. Paul liked the appellation and wore it with pride. The name eventually stuck, and they became known as the Christians, the anointed ones.

Sholem Asch shows that when Peter and Paul eventually make amends, Paul "corrects" his earlier extremism. A combination of acceptance and the reality of living the life of Gentiles lead to his realization that works are needed as well as faith. The Ten Commandments and basic laws become more emphasized in his later writings, along with the need to live by example. Not that Paul lived his life without observing the strict code of the Pharisees himself. Projecting his great desire for bringing Gentiles into the fold, he de-emphasized the need for following the basic laws. It was not his intention that they not do so. But he was such an ardent believer in his own faith, he presupposed all others proclaiming the faith would be as understanding of the need for purity as he was.

The great learning for him, as for many of us, is that human nature does not change with ease. Even with ardent faith, ego clings tight to its dark passions. An unremitting vigilance is needed along with guidelines for behavior. Until the mind has been purified to attune itself to Christ Consciousness and can draw constantly from those pure waters, and not mixing, in part or in whole, with the fetid waters of past tendencies, these guidelines of behavior are required.

Of course, the ego resists the bit and harness of abiding by any code other than its own. But, without obligation to anything higher than its own code, ego will continue upon its aimless walk to fulfill its own desires in life. If we be among those who follow the way of righteousness, of dharma, then we must be willing to put ourselves under the yoke of a higher law. Yoga means union, union with God. It also means yoke, the yoke of self-discipline, self-mastery.

Without accompanying works, faith is dead. To build an inner church of the Infinite, we must apply the principles we are taught. In applying those principles, we set a foundation built on rock and not the shifting sands of daily opinions.

The other side of that coin, of course, is when the laws and commandments become an end in themselves and not a means to an end. Always it should be held out that the goal is God-communion. This gives sweetness to an otherwise bitter cup. Front and center for the devotee is that the Kingdom of Heaven is here, now. The Clouds of Heaven are at the point between the eyebrows. The return of Christ Consciousness is within. Jesus said, "But I tell you a truth, there be some standing here, which shall not taste of death, till they see the Kingdom of God." (Matthew 16:28) Did he lie? No. His own followers were not able to grasp his meaning then. Most still do not know.

This is the good news. Let it be heard by all. To follow the way means to pick up your cross, the body, and do what Jesus did. He surrendered himself to the Supreme Being, God the Father, even unto death. If not death of the body, then death of the ego.

The great avatar was calling to humanity then; he continues to call to us today. The call has always been there, but there have been so few takers. "Therefore, he said unto them, the harvest truly is great, but the laborers few." (Luke 10:2) He was not referring to the conversions; he was speaking of the harvest of peace and joy that comes with the coming of the Kingdom, but the laborers, sincere aspirants, are few. Let us set our sights on us being among those chosen ones.

And what of the price, the sublimation of the ego self to the Eternal Self? Sholem Asch continues on to paint a compelling image of those stalwart individuals who literally gave their lives for not denying their adherence to their faith. Tortured, denied, horribly victimized, and killed, they held onto their faith. How? By uniting their minds with the Christ mind. "Remember the word that I said unto you, the servant is not greater than his lord, if they have persecuted me, they will also persecute you; if they have kept my saying, they will keep yours also." (John 15:20) They held onto their knowledge that each pain inflicted was uniting them to their ideal, their Christ. For some, that meant enduring the worst tortures. For others, it meant experiencing bliss and visions of bliss in the most excruciating circumstance.

Whose heart would not break confronted with such bestial behavior to others? Where is God's compassion if not in the softened hearts of devotees everywhere for even one person's suffering? One of the final scenes in *The Apostles* is that of Peter. His dilemma is whether to escape, or to go with his brethren to crucifixion. He has a vision of a man riding his horse into Rome. Slowly, it dawns on him it is his Master. Peter asks him where he goes. His Master says he is going to Rome to be crucified. He sees the nail wounds in the Master's hands. The vision is gone.

Peter returns to be crucified as his sentence has decreed. In each person who suffers, the heart of God is torn asunder. His saint's heart breaks at the suffering of humankind. They call us to live better. To remember to love thy neighbor as thyself. If one does, it affects thousands; if more do, who knows, it may be a contagion that sweeps the world. We have been called. Who will listen?

October 22, 2000

Well, this has been quite a day. Opposing force was working over-time, especially this afternoon. Started with some temptation thoughts. Then had terrific pain when my body was eliminating, a rare event. Then felt light as a feather afterwards on a walk, as if something had passed. Beautiful weather out and went for a walk to Black Daug Lake. It is the first time I have been off the property in a month. Felt very good until I came walking back down the gentle grade. My legs felt as if they had cement in them and I was walk-ing as if I had Multiple Sclerosis or some similar difficulty. All the life-energy left my legs, accompanied by terrific pain.

When I returned, it was time for my circumambulation of Cloud Mountain. I did the round chanting Ram Nam all the way as usual. I barely had control of my legs all the way down to the entrance. Coming back up was slightly better, otherwise, I don't know if I could have negotiated the grade. Once back on the deck, my legs almost gave way. In terrible pain, I made it indoors.

I had some chips and melted cheese for something to eat before Chad came. I usually don't eat then, and I have never made nachos here before. I felt it was a way to deal with the pain. I asked Babaji if this was paying the price for someone who was coming. He said I knew it already.

Meditation time with Chad went well. Toward the end, though, I thought of Larry, Cate, and Peter all out of town and thought of our small group. Why didn't more people come? This oppositional thought, for I consider it exactly that, hit me very hard. Occasionally, it happens that way. What am I doing wrong? I could be, should be, a better example, etc. I asked Babaji what I should be doing? He said to continue my sadhana. It then occurred to me that I would rather help guide a few souls to their complete realization than be involved in large groups of people that require organizations, etc. This seemed to answer my own dilemma, which is I don't have one!

By the time Chad came, my mood had lightened some, but I had a heavy heart still. Remarkably, my legs were working again with no pain. Then I opened a letter from Carla that Chad had brought with him. She described an incident of smelling Mother's perfume that had lifted her mood. Well, the gift brought tears and kept giving because it cleared my mood completely. I saw what a struggle I had been in all day. Thanks to God and Gurus, this little one seems to be clear of the struggle for the moment.

Jai Mother, Jai Babaji, Jai Gurus, Jai Ram

October 23, 2000

Each morning I awaken by 4:00 a.m. Oftentimes, I am awakened through the night, sometimes each hour. Some people have fear or anger about waking up through the night, or not being able to go to sleep. I feel as if it is God Himself who awakens me for the purpose of sadhana. Chanting God's name, thinking of His attributes, or puzzling on some problem He has given me to resolve. Waking and dreaming states seem to be the same. Both are for loving and serving God. It seems in my dreams I am in service to God all night. I am helping others as God gives me the power to do. Sometimes, I am teaching through words, but most often, helping through action— usually the dream has some oppositional force directed at me or the other person, or both. It is a matter of escaping the clutches of this force or suddenly removing it somehow. Each night, a new scenario presents itself. Oftentimes, when I awaken hourly, the dream continues from one hour to the next. I stay awake, but it seems only that my attention shifts from the interior dream world to the exterior dream world. Both have a reality and unreality to them. From the interior dream world, I often call on God and Gurus for their help as I feel that all overcoming is due to their power and intelligence. And, indeed, for both the interior and exterior dream worlds, they are my sole and sufficient means for all overcoming.

Overcoming is the ability of the mind to rise above the snare of sensory world attachments and float free in spiritual awareness. God is freedom, bliss, and a knowing oneness with the All Consciousness. Therefore, God is the antidote to cares, worries, and ignorance. To come to the feet of God means to surrender all human concerns of our human life to the Infinite and become the servant of the Divine. Freed from our burden of concerns, we focus the mind on God alone. We do as He directs from moment to moment. We then find our life is perfectly coordinated with truth, love, and justice. We find that we rise above the pettiness of daily human concerns and become envoys of peace and joy. These are some signs we may take as signs of progress in our sadhana.

When I awaken at 4:00 a.m., I chant for some time, do the Clearing-Charging Exercises I have been inspired with, then descend to the main floor to wash my face, scrape my tongue, and have some hot lemon water. I read or write a little, perhaps do some more chanting. My mind is awake and ready and at some point, it seems right to enter Kriya meditation.

Between 7:00 and 8:00 a.m., I have breakfast, usually a buckwheat pancake. This is how I start my day.

Om Namaste

Let Your Will Reign Supreme

Let Your Will Reign Supreme
It is Your Will that acts through this form,
You bring whom You will
You take whom You will away,
Of what concern is that to me?

All forms are Your forms
All happiness according to Thy Will,
I have but to reside in You within,
Reside as Witness to what You do.

I cannot concern myself for what may happen
For all happens at Thy instance,
Take all that I have called me and mine
And swallow those into Your Self.

A One without a second,
O ecstatic Love You bring to me,
Oneness of boundless Joy,
You fill this cup that is Yours with measureless Bliss.

Gone are past sorrows,
Evaporated future fears,
Only You, only Now exists,
Forever make me one with Thy own.

And in oneness who writes this,
As if there are two?
It is You, You in this form,
Also plays as if there is a lover and beloved,
Lover and beloved are one and interchangeable.

You make me write on, Beloved
Without scope or desire
Other than to express You,
To feel You flow through these veins, muscles, and thoughts.

This body that You have created
That You sustain
That You make to dance to Your tune
That You raise to enlightenment.

O Blessed of one Spirit
Let us all reside in Oneness;
Let us also play as two in One
And know total Joy in the play of
Many and as the One.

For my Beloved, You are none other,
None other but the One
Who plays the many,
But is always the One.

October 24, 2000
Forgiveness Exercise

If helpful, have a friend read this to you, or record it speaking slowly and play it back.

1. In your mind's eye, see the person you have yet to forgive. If it helps to make it more real, you can set a chair in front of you and mentally see that individual sitting in the chair.

2. Feel where the cords of energy connect between you and the other person. Once you have a clear sense of that connection:

3. Ask yourself, "Am I willing, am I ready to let this go (these cords of connection)?" Wait for an internal response. If the answer is yes, continue to step 4; if no:

   a. Ask yourself: "At what cost do I hold onto this?" For example, feelings of being stuck, heaviness in the body, pain, chronic anger, etc. Get in touch with the total cost of holding this lack of forgiveness, lack of letting go. Mentally place it on an old-fashioned balance scale. Put the cost on one side and the hoped-for benefit on the other. The hoped-for benefits can be, "I want to punish them," or "I never want to play the fool again, etc." Placing that hoped for benefit on one side and the cost to you on the other, see what happens to that balance scale. The scale usually becomes very lopsided, with the cost far weightier than any benefit that we might actually realize from holding it.

b. Ask for whatever support you think may help you in letting go. You might think to see Jesus, Mother, or one of the masters standing with you. You may find that seeing yourself standing next to the seashore or in a mountain meadow strengthening and calming. Whatever or whomever comes to mind, you may ask for them, or it, to come to you and support you in letting this go.

4. Once you have asked, "Am I ready and willing to let this go?" and, the answer comes back, "Yes," then mentally take out a sword or a large pair of scissors and cut that cord, or cords.

5. As you cut those cords, see your own energy coming back to yourself. Feel that energy coming back into your body and notice the effect it has on you.

6. See the negative, dark energy returning to the one you have been visualizing. As it goes back, notice the effect on them. If they disappear or change into a totally positive form, good. If they shrink but do not disappear, look for the other cords of connection and go back to step 3. (Do not become impatient. You may be letting go of years or lifetimes of backlog.)

7. When all the cords of connection are severed and the "other" image has disappeared or transformed, then see a column of Light sweeping from above and behind you, sweeping any residue of the darkness or negativity from you. Then see a column of Light coming from above and behind the other image,

or where the other image had been, and see the Light sweep away any residue of darkness or negativity from them.

Epilogue: You are done for now. Forgiveness may be complete, or it may be a step toward forgiveness. Future situations may trigger held-on-to feelings that are, as of yet, hidden in the unconsciousness. In that case, with patience and persistence, move through this exercise again until this area is completely cleansed of all holding.

May you know the blessings of forgiveness in your own life, and may those blessings spread to all whom you touch.

O Mighty Supreme Spirit
I pray that all souls may
Manifest Thy Light and Purity.
O Omnipotent force
You have created all;
Awaken Thy children
So that all may live in harmony
With Thy perfect will of peace and joy.

Cloud Mountain Light in Trees.

The Arena of Life

It is the Almighty Itself that has set the stage for this vast arena we call life. Prakriti sounds her horn of Aum and various actors spring into action. From one static whole moves minions of activity. All carry out their own part in the great pageantry. Row after row of atman lights don gay costumes that stretch limited conception. Wave after wave parades from the witness bleachers of eternity. Actors of different parts play in earnest their roles. Pleasure, pain, the high and the low, all have their place for the grand display. New soldiers of action stand ready for their time in the arena. Act I, Act II, and so on roll the scenes. When actors tire of their roles and wish to proceed home, they give one final act of sadhana. With glorious aplomb, the singular atman light rejoins omniscient Light for a joyous homecoming. Perhaps another scene will call its name and it cannot resist a curtain call!

October 25, 2000
The Flame of God

In my hermitage cabin, I have a gas burner. Each morning, I light it to make my hot lemon water. I strike my lighter, which produces a flame. When the gas switch is turned, a flame pops up on the burner and quickly multiplies as tiny flames from all the holes on the burner. Likewise, God exists separate from all creation. He manifests as Light, then through the magic of Maya, He assumes innumerable forms filled with light. Take away the structure of the burner and one would see one flame, one source that creates what appears to be the many little flames. Take away Maya and what is revealed is the fuel of Aum—the Light of Being that takes on the appearance of many.

Light of the Guru

Guru is the One Indivisible Light of God. Through God's grace and mercy, that Light assumes the form of a human being. Its purpose?

To bring devotees into the Light of God's own Being. Such is the tender mercy God has for all of His erring children who wander in the dark. One who knows their guru understands this. One who desires a guru but does not yet know one yearns for this. One who has no idea of the guru will be baffled by this. Such are the various states of sadhakas.

October 28, 2000
Scaling the Heights for Guru Darshan

Guru is the pure snow of white peaks above us. Guru shows Its grace by taking form as living waters in streams, rivulets, and mighty rivers. Some taste the waters, finding it good; they journey to the origin from where the waters run. Others try to dam up the river and say they are in charge of it, and all must come to them to drink. Such are religious institutions and factions. Others try to bottle the water and develop a brand name that others will buy. Such are the sectarian organizations and over-the-counter salesmen of God. Others say the water trickling through the dams and into the bottles is just ordinary tap water. Guru smiles at the play downstream and weeps for those who are thirsty and denied water. So, rivers and streamlets, one after another, are formed to quench the thirst of all.

Dam builders and bottlers rush in profuse anxiety, decrying other sources or try to quickly contain them. But Guru really loves the intrepid who scale the heights and enjoy the view from the peaks. Then, sometimes, one here and there says they will become a new stream for the guru. Guru is happy for He wants all to drink of the fresh living spring water and not the limpid dammed or bottled variety. And, perhaps another will so feel inspired by that taste to scale the heights for Guru's darshan.

Guru is not a person, place, or thing. Guru is Spirit. Guru is God. Guru is perfection. Human instruments of Guru grace this earth. They bring wisdom, teachings, and compassion to seekers every where. Guru is universal. Guru cannot belong to anyone alone, although He feels as though there is only lover and beloved in all the world. That is because Guru is love itself.

October 29, 2000
Divine Love

Why do great spiritual masters emphasize Love as the path and goal of realization? Once having tasted Divine Love, all such discussion ends. The superior merits of Divine Love are not to be found in romance novels or even the glorious descriptions of poets. Music may be a stepping stone, but no expression of Divine Love can be Love itself. Blunted materialists and absorbed intellectuals alike are quickened when touched by this all-absorbing State of Being. Tiny candles and even powerful search lights are left useless when the sun arises, so do all expressions of humanity become dull and limpid compared to the charm of Divine Love. Jnanis leave their dry intellect; those in service stop in rapt awe; those worshipping images lose sight of the images; and all Raja Yogis lose their breath in silent communion. All of nature stops, absorbed in the All-absorbing Nature of Divine Love that is more than a feeling of emotion, more than a thought or relationship, more than words or ideas can express. Inexpressible, Divine, Pure, and rapturous It is.

The reason saints sing Its glories is due to It surpassing all other glories. It is truth to say that God and Love are One. Unless you have drunk deep of Its virtue, you cannot say you know it. But realized masters have, and continue, to drink deep of It. Yet, the more they drink, the more they have the capacity to drink deeper. It is endless. And they are calling. These masters are calling to you, me, all: "Come, drink with me!" In fact, I have drunk to the point that I, myself, I became that Love Itself. I look and see nothing but That. So, drink me if you will! For the more that is drunk, the more plentiful the supply. Let us all drink to satisfy and continue drinking so others may drink of us for we are That, and That is ourselves.

This is the calling of the Great Ones. Come, let us drink Divine Love!

October 29, 2000
Dear Friends,

Silent greetings from Cloud Mountain. With the beautiful pageantry of gold, orange, yellow, red, and rust coming from all the fall leaves, it reminds me that the world is in constant change. Fall is always an enchanting time of year and makes me feel close to nature. Deer and chatty birds during the day, elk and owls at night, keep me company with nature's activity. I have been blessed with the beautiful surroundings of nature here at my hermitage cabin.

But outward surroundings play only a small part in my time here. My outward silence has led to unfolding inner events that are anything but quiet. Before coming here, many of my days were spent in absorption in the Divine. Although, the month or so directly before coming here saw me in much activity of travel and preparation. Upon arriving, I did not return to the inner absorption. Rather, the mind was more active and dealing with interior events.

Psychic phenomena, crowded in with conversations, images, and events, were very strong when I arrived. One by one, I put those to rest as the environment here was attuned to the higher Spiritual vibrations. The desire came to me one day to have the physical darshan of Babaji, and for Chad to have the same. This led to an inner interchange with Babaji, revealing that it was his will that brought me here, and it was for the sake of his teaching me inwardly and helping me to do this work at this time. Previously, I had had some experiences with Babaji, the supreme Param-Para Guru of our lineage. Since that day, there has been an open inner dialogue that has revealed yogic techniques and learning on a deeper level through inner renunciation and a focused mind.

Due to these inner teachings, and some writings that have been flowing from this pen, I have had a very active life inside! In addition, inner corridors of thought have connected me to distant people and situations, many times with great intensity. My dreams at night, daydreams, and my waking hours have continuity to the point that they all seem to be of the same experience.

One of the things I have been taught is how the Superconscious Mind can work through these channels of consciousness to effect changes in distant places and people. I have known of this before, but have never had an interest in such things as they draw the mind down to lower levels. But, my mind seems to be doing this spontaneously as part of the work that I am to do here. It has an interesting aspect to it, but I don't personally feel either drawn to it or repulsed by it, as it does not seem to interfere with my conscious communion with the Divine. So, it can come or go, as it wants, which it seems to do anyway.

Chad is doing well. He comes for meditation each night after he works very physically all day. He is a wonderful soul, and it is very nice to have him here. He has been the experiment for some new Raja Yoga techniques that will be taught in the Spring Retreat. He's not grown horns on his head yet, so I think it is going to be all right!

There is a Freddie the fly update. Freddie's a devotee fly. Unusual, it is true. He would sit himself on my meditation cushion whenever I was not there. When I meditated, he would sit on my leg or my hands. Sometimes he would get on my medulla, or crown of my head, but I asked him to stop, and he did. Any time he was not around, I could mentally call for him and he would come within a minute like a dog. One day, I thought that this hermitage cabin was no place for a fly; he should be enjoying the out-of-doors. I mentally told Freddie if he went outside, and didn't like it, he could come back in. He followed me out, flew around me a few times, and flew back in the door. Well, what could I do? I adopted him!

The story takes a darker turn here. To the day, one month after I moved in, I was using the facilities. I saw something dark in the water, but thought it was some thread or something. After answering the call, I flushed. It was at this time I saw it was Freddie! Treading water for all he was worth. Well, I must say he went to his watery grave valiantly. I wished him a higher birth next time, and even found myself missing the little guy after a while. I have never adopted a fly before, much less a devotee fly. I feel blessed.

I have established a fairly comfortable routine. My day usually starts at 4 a.m. and ends at 10:00 or 11:00 p.m. Each day, I walk around the property chanting Ram Nam for world peace and harmony. During this circumambulation, I experience a new theme every day. Some situation from the world surfaces and plays itself out in my mind. All through it, I chant the name of God, wishing it all peace and resolution. I feel the resistance caused by this situation both in my body and in the environment around me. This makes each day an adventure and by the time I finish my rounds, it feels I have really been through something. Before I start my round, I pray for purification of all minds, hearts, and bodies everywhere. When I end, I pray for the purity of the earth's atmosphere, dwelling places, and the earth itself.

This may sound a little grandiose to some, that this could effect any change in the world, but this is what I feel inwardly directed to do. There is a story of a squirrel that had her babies washed out to sea by a storm. She asked for the sea to give back her babies. Nothing doing. She then vowed that she would empty the sea of its water until she got her babies back. Using the brush of her tail, she took trip after trip, removing whatever water her tail would carry. One day, an angel saw the squirrel doing this strange action and asked her what the purpose was. The squirrel explained herself to the angel. The angel smiled at this and told the squirrel what she was doing would not make a dent in the amount of water in the sea. The squirrel said she didn't care, even if she had to be reincarnated countless times to accomplish her task, she would never give up. The squirrel continued this activity non-stop until her tail was worn to almost nothing. The angel revisited the squirrel and saw the condition of her tail. The angel, who was none other than God Himself, supplicated the sea, "Can you not see her efforts? She will not give up! Please return her babies." At this, the sea relented, and the mother squirrel saw all of her babies swimming ashore, as if they had never been gone. She was in so much joy that God had answered her unwavering prayer.

So never let us think that to do as we feel inwardly directed to do will not yield results. In spite of world opinion and outward results, let us persevere and never let go of the good fight. Verily, it is God Himself who moves through us in compassion when virtue guides and sustains us. Be It ever so. Om Sri Ram Jai Ram Jai Jai Ram

October 2000
The Bhakti of God

To experience Bhakti for God means to experience an overwhelming desire to be one with God. This desire is so strong that it takes over the entire being of the sadhaka. Imagine the love of a mother for her child, a love of an athlete for excellence of performance, a love of a miser for money, and a love of a new-found romance. Wrap those all into one love: bhakti is like that. When a saint was asked what was required to gain God, he took the sadhaka waist-deep into the river. He put the passive head of the sadhaka under water. Some little time went by. The sadhaka thought, "This is a strange thing the Master is doing. What is the lesson?" Then the sadhaka started to run short of air. He tried to rise up, but the strong hold the saint had on his neck would not allow it. Very soon, the sadhaka was getting desperate. He tried to push up. Nothing doing! He panicked with arms and legs flailing to get air. All he could think of was the need to get to the surface and get air. His lungs seemed about to explode, and he started losing consciousness when the saint lifted him to the surface. He clung to the Master, gasping for air. Finally, when he had recovered, his Master looked straight into his eyes. In a deep, resonant voice, he said, "When your desire for God is as intense as your desire for air was moments ago—then you shall have Him." The lesson sank deep into the sadhaka's mind.

This is the love of the sadhaka for God. But what of God's love for His sadhaka? Once, I sat with Mother in her later years. She said, "You know, sometimes I feel lonely." This hit me on a personal level as I too sometimes felt lonely, lonely for God, His Presence, compassion, intimacy, and love. It did not dawn on me at the time to ask her if she felt lonely for God, or if she was feeling God's loneliness for us. It may sound strange that God should feel lonely for us. And that God, who is whole and complete in Himself, would feel lonely, may not make sense. But from the standpoint that God divided Himself from Himself and became separate from Himself, it makes sense.

I have experienced God's loneliness for His complement in all of separate existence. The yearning desire for wholeness expressed by God is inexpressible. It is a huge and vast sea of ache, yearning, and desire for wholeness. With a constant flood of love and deepened desire, God surges in His need for reunification. But His need goes unheeded by a creation absorbed in play. Consumed by their play of the senses, humanity is unheedful of the call. Only when reversals of fortune occur do those souls of the world cry out for the comfort of union. The Divine Heart responds with Its all. But as soon as the crisis passes, and the scene changes, the soul is once again drawn into its preoccupations. Again, the Divine Heart is left without complement or comfort of union. Long does It wait. Long does It yearn. It yearns for the day when the soul will lift its head above the water of sensation and breathe the sweet Air of Spirit that longs to envelop, play with, and love Its very own.

Yogacharya David meditating.

Sholem Asch's *Prophet* is another beautifully written book. He has a curious mixture of themes. At one point, he expounds on the Universal Nature of God as the sole creator and actor in the world: that everything happens by the will of the creator, even an insect's ability to breathe. He, of course, is exactly right. Then he turns to the theme of Israel's suffering.

The time of the book's writing is the early 1950s—at least, it was first published in 1955. The horrors of Nazi Germany and its wholesale slaughter of people whose only "crime," so to speak, was that they were born Jewish. The prophet, in the book, is made to look to the depths of the river of tears and blood of all Jewish suffering. He reasons about what Isaiah had said, that the sins of the father visit the son. What could God be thinking of, to make so many go through so much, the holocaust, the pogroms down through the ages, etc.

Asch's solution is that Israel itself is taking on the world's sins as God's chosen people. This is part of the covenant, and even as Jesus laid down his life for many to be awakened to God's law and grace, so does Israel.

The flaw with this reasoning, and what the prophet struggles so much for in his understanding, is the people of Israel are not conscious, willing participants in this idea. Rather, they are willingly or unwillingly drawn to the slaughter for all other nations. Ultimately, it comes to this: if you can accept this duty, there is comfort in your acceptance. It is when one recants their duty that it becomes unbearable.

This line of reasoning is scattered with gems of truth, but the diamond has a flaw: that is, free will. Jesus came with a destiny; that is true. That destiny was to be a redemptive factor to the world. I say *a* redemptive factor and not *the* redemptive factor, because he, himself, said that he had not come to call the righteous, for they were not in need of the physician, but he had come to help those who had wandered from Truth. The apex of all the scriptures is in the Garden of Gethsemane. Jesus struggles with his duty, his destiny, and finally surrenders, "And he went a little further, and fell on his face, and prayed, saying, O my Father, if it be possible, let this cup pass from me: nevertheless, not as I will, but as thou wilt." (Matthew 26:39)

Without this conscious, willing surrender, the scriptures are without merit. For God, being the omnipotent Force of creation, to contrive for any and all to be unconscious, unwilling participants in a slaughter—it must be an act of surrender to the Infinite Will that makes something a holy, noble act.

What the prophet does not see in his vision is the complex weave of cause-and-effect, the Law of Karma whose law must be fulfilled. Stretching through time and lifetimes, a soul's story unfolds in a complex and fascinating storyline that affects not only an individual but groups of individuals as well. The Jews of one generation are not necessarily the Jews of the next. And it is not one suffering mass of souls forever stuck in a pattern, but an ever-changing pattern of persecutors, persecuted, redeemers willing to self-sacrifice, and those who willingly perform the sacrificial rites. On goes the story with souls moving in and out of this living fabric of life.

But, the message of God is not that your destiny of nobility is thrust upon you. Nobility comes from an act, or acts, of courage and surrender. It cannot be any other way. And while in the grief of the holocaust, when one is left reeling for some sense to it all, one must rise to a greater vision, a wider vision.

At the end of the book, the prophet sees all of creation coming back to the light from which it is issued. And indeed, this just may be the case. For if God be the sole creator of all, where else could it go? Would God throw a part of Himself away? It just doesn't stand the test of any reason, human or divine. If we accept the bitter herbs the world feeds us with acceptance, then it does add the sweetness of comfort to the taste. This is not to say we blithely accept injustice; far from it; for this, we need be warriors! But, to accept the bitters of soul medicine as God's will for our redemption makes it a sublime act of surrender.

A Bhakti's Meditation

Meditation is really an inner absorption in the Divine. Many people are interested in meditation, but few attain that blessed state. All meditation has a common theme: that is, the sadhaka starts out with concentration. Usually, the point of concentration is on a mantra, a particular sound, or words. Higher teachings come through the place of attention when the attention is put on the anahata, heart center, or the ajna, the point between the eyebrows. The reason for this is: where the focus of the mind goes, there also flows the life-force of the body.

The flow of this life-force, prana, enlivens wherever it flows and increases awareness of that area. Both the anahata and ajna are focal points for spiritual awakening, along with the sahasrara, the crown of the head. By repeated attention to these areas, they begin to awaken. People usually focus on the five senses, sex, survival, and power of will: i.e., gaining name, fame, and wealth. These constitute the realm of ego. The first awakening of a transcendent nature is love. That love is usually focused on a sweetheart, children, or friends, but it can also be nature or perhaps a locality or a country. This love is usually a mixture of ego and some transcendent nature. Ego is based on self-interest: i.e., "If I love you, you will love me back." Transcendent love is, "I love you for your own sake and because it is my nature to love, not for what I get in return."

Divine love is the fullest expression of transcendent love. It is purified of ego considerations and the ledger book of quid and pro quo. Love becomes the very nature of the sadhaka, being a fulfillment unto itself. This is why the heart center is the first center in the upward ascension considered worthy of awakening spiritual growth.

The next center mentioned is the ajna, the point between the eyebrows. This area is universally acclaimed as the doorway to higher consciousness. It is here that one may enter into states of consciousness that transcend the sense of "I,"—that is, the idea of separation, and can then enter into the grand union of Spirit. "The light of the body is the eye: if therefore thine eye be single, thy whole body shall be full of light," said Jesus. (Matthew 6:22) In addition, "The light of the body is the eye: therefore, when thine eye is single, thy whole body also is full of light, but when thine eye is evil, thy body also is full of darkness." (Luke 11:34) This eye is the ajna, the astral eye of omniscience. This center is considered to be the most important center of transcendence and leads automatically to the sahasrara when entered.

The mantra used should be under the guidance of a guru. The guru has the consciousness to awaken the sadhaka's higher centers. Like inert metal that is exposed to a strong magnet, the inmost metal itself becomes magnetized, and so does the sadhaka become inwardly charged through the spiritual magnetism of the guru. This magnetism increases the positive draw to spiritual consciousness and helps to open these inner centers. In concert with the sadhana performed by the sadhaka, this inner draw works a secret alchemy that gradually purifies the mind of vasanas, desire nature, and latent downward tendencies. This sadhana is twofold. The first is to turn away from attachment to things of the world, vairagya, or inner renunciation. The second, to reorient the mind to higher consciousness, to make the mind inward or bhakti.

Meditation is one of the means to do this. By focusing on the ajna and refusing the pull to things of the senses, either in the body or in the imaginal body, we are practicing sadhana. But this practice is not easy to come by. Habit nature of body consciousness tends to be strong—after all, that is the place where we have lived most of our lives. And, the focus on the material world may have yielded some nice results. The other side of that is just pure fear of releasing the known world of the senses, even if it has mostly produced misery for us. These two lions, one desire nature, the other fear, stand at the door of inner consciousness. We may be mindful that these two lions are not a weakness of the sadhaka alone, but are universal to all seekers. Overcoming these opposing forces is the very stuff of which sadhana is composed.

As we know, there are four paths of Yoga: Yoga of action, Yoga of love, Yoga of discernment, and Yoga of life-force control. Each personality will naturally feel more drawn to Karma Yoga, Bhakti Yoga, Jnana Yoga, or Raja Yoga. And it may be that there will be a combination of all four. I like to think of our path as the Fourfold Path.

That is, it uses elements from all four disciplines. And, even if your nature is oriented to Karma Yoga, selfless service, nevertheless, you can greatly benefit from Karma Yoga by Kriya Yoga meditation. Mother Teresa, a great Karma Yogini, spent early morning hours and evening hours in deep prayer and meditation. This time spent was essential to keep her focus truly on serving the Christ each day.

I was speaking to a social worker one day. She said rather off-handedly, "Oh yes, I used to do the Mother Teresa thing, then I burned out." Well, I doubted she really did the Mother Teresa "thing." Those hours Mother Teresa spent in God-communication with her focus on seeing the Christ in each one she met made her service very pure and was the source of seemingly boundless energy. That deep communion with God served as an inoculation against burn-out. Whatever our main calling, we must cultivate that inner communion in order to keep balance, perspective, and clear focus. That communion comes through deepened prayer and meditation.

Learning to still the mind takes persistence and patience. We may make it a priority to first enter into prayer. When you go to visit a good friend, you start the visit with talking about important things in your life. You can cultivate friendship with God in the same way. You can talk over the day, important, trivial, and fun matters of your life. This cultivates an inner intimacy. If there are questions about your life, you may even spend time without talking. You may rest, do some hard work, or just sit quietly together. With God, too, you can spend time in silent contemplation. This moves us to a greater sense of intimacy. Do not feel that kind of intimacy should come "just like that." Most of us are not used to that much intimacy.

Imagine, if you will, cultivating intimacy with God as a gradual unfoldment, as the petals of a flower opening and surrendering themselves to the sun, rather than a picture of storming the castle gates to take possession of the city. It is not for God's sake that we go to this place, but our own. We can willingly surrender ourselves if we feel the absolute good inherent in what we are surrendering ourselves to. But if fear, guilt, and suspicion are in the mind, then surrender will seem like a battle. It does not need to be that way between us and that inmost Friendship. Here we can gently, calmly, go inwards in a way that suits us. Move around the edges, test the feeling nature here and there. Sit in the Presence at a little distance, then try moving a little closer. We may have innate fear and distrust; that is all right, just test the waters a little at a time.

When we are ready, and only when we are ready, we can ask God to come into us. We can open ourselves to exploring the ways this Spirit comes to us. Calmly observing, it may be different than we imagined. The differences can be noted. It may be enough intimacy for the moment, and we can enjoy exactly what it is. God is not going anywhere, He is right there, very willing to be with us exactly as we would like Him to be. Intimacy does not usually come in big, fantastic displays, but in gradual unfoldment. Learn to discern the subtle flavors of Spirit. Keep the focus right there. It is right under your breath, a sensation close to you, even a slight thrill throughout your body cells, a feeling of peace and gentleness. Cultivate this fine and delicious aroma. This is God come to you as a rare and gentle Spirit. This may be different than how you usually think of meditation. This is the heart and soul of a Bhakti. God as friend, lover, intimate.

The Bhakti thinks of God's qualities, especially as an intimate. "O Lord, you are the Friend of all friends; you come with everything to give. You lack only one thing, that one thing I may give or withhold; that is my friendship, my love. O Lord, you are the beauteous feeling within, the glow of colors in nature. You are my all in all." In this way, Bhaktis talk to God. And as they say these things, the Bhaktis start to feel even more intimacy with the Beloved. A rapturous feeling can grow, an opening of the heart in a love song of Spirit that then subsides in a gentle manner into a caress. Rapt in this intimate world of lover and Beloved, that soul opens gradually to the love spreading out to all creation. The whole universe feels to be one's body, all throbbing in wonderous waves of joyful love. Free of body-limiting thoughts. Consciousness "centered everywhere, circumference nowhere." It knows Its Omniscient home once again. This universal embrace into omnipresent Love and Joy is the ultimate sacramental bond where lines of lover and beloved dissolve into the oneness of Love.

This rapture then descends again and lover and Beloved once again start their dance. Ever at one, ever apart do they dance and play, ever in the rapture of love. It is difficult to convey to one whose heart has not awakened to at least a hint of this dance. Perhaps a glimpse comes when one's heart and spirit are touched by some music, picture, or film. But earthly hearts are fickle: there today, gone tomorrow. God's heart is ever-ready; ours are unsteady, unrefined, inconstant. To make the attention steady, bringing all moods, thoughts, and awareness into that Divine Aura brings ultimate union. It makes no difference what the mood may be. One may be a lover, in anger, fearful, lonely; it makes no difference. The key is that one does not shrink from the Beloved through fear, shame, or, worst of all, indifference.

Only with a steady, meditative mind can that kind of devotion be brought to its fullness. This intense love affair is exemplified by Krishna, Christ, Ramakrishna, Saint Francis, Paramhansa Yogananda, and Mother Hamilton. In some, the love was transcendent only, never focused on a deity or image; such is the case with Krishna and Christ. In others, a deity or personality was the focal point, as with Saint Francis on Christ, and Mother Hamilton on Paramhansa Yogananda.

The devotee/lover of God with form must ultimately transcend that form. But the form plays a distinctive and important role in the devotee's life. That form becomes the focal point for the mind. A focal point like this is necessary for most. Even as children focus their attention on their mother most of all, so devotees find a focus for their object of love. This objectification needs to be understood in its right context. If it is seen as a doorway through which the devotee enters into universal consciousness, then it is rightly understood. If it leads to separation and sectarianism: such as, "My object of devotion is the only way, or the superior way, and your way, your religion, is inferior or wrong." Then it changes worship from sattvic, sweet devotion, to tamasic, or darkness. It can also lead to, "My religion is the only right way, and I am going to snub out all other ways." This is a rajasic tendency for domination. Neither the tamasic nor rajasic reflect true spirituality.

What is essential in any devotee is the true Spirit that comes with an open heart guided by wisdom. This may be recognized in a Christian, Hindu, Buddhist, Muslim, Jew, or in any of the countless theologies of the world. Within any religion, we may find those that are alive in an inner Spirit and Light. And Jesus said, "Not everyone that saith unto me, Lord, Lord, shall enter into the kingdom of heaven; but he that doeth the will of my Father which is in heaven." (Matthew 7:21) You may see such ones sitting here and there in congregations around the world. Their faces glow with Light; their hearts open, they are alive to an inner Light that cannot be denied and cannot be missed by one attuned to the Light. They reflect the qualities of Light: i.e., purity, softness of heart, standing by principle, inwardly directed. And, oftentimes, they are not the ones up in front, or on a board of directors. They may be, but they may just as easily be sitting in the back, or walking in the woods, or tending to someone who needs their care.

You see, this is the thing that defies circumscription by rule and law yet carries its own rule and law by its own virtue. Now ego can get a hold of that teaching and run rampant in a life of license. But devotees would not be doing the will of the Father in that case. To awaken inwardly to that Light, that Love, that devotion, is the meditation of the Bhakti. And, once fully awakened, it is a light unto itself. It guides, directs, accompanies, and comforts the devotee through thick and thin. Why? Because devotees have put God first, have meditated on love's ecstasy, and given themselves, heart, mind, and soul, to their Infinite Beloved. And it is a law: as ye give, so shall ye receive. When you give all, without expectation, you receive all unreservedly.

So, my blessed friends, learn the secrets of this open heart, be guided by the clarity of inner Light. Learn to meditate on love's ecstasy, and you will step into a world that is beyond the scope of human imagination. For it is a Divinely inspired world of Spirit that may be vouchsafed only to those who give their all. If you are luke-warm: "Oh I will meditate some; if I realize God sometime in the future, that's alright," then pray ardently that God makes you one of those awakened ones whose light will so shine, that it will be a beacon for all those thirsting to find the Light. Better to be clear: awaken to your Bhakti spirit even now, and know the inner glory of that Love and Bliss divine.

Breath and Function[8]

The function of breath is twofold: to clear the system and to charge the system. On a physical plane, this clearing is to take waste discharged from the blood to the lungs out of the body system. Charging then is to bring in the needed nutrients from the air into the lungs, to be absorbed in the blood.

Prana, subtle life-energy, also operates in this bifurcated method. Throughout the body system runs a subtle system of pathways that allows prana to cleanse and charge the subtle body in a similar way to how blood feeds and then carries waste away from the cells. This subtle system of nadis—astral nerves—may not be observable with a microscope, but can be intuited. This system affects our energy level, creativity, and moods. Why does someone with depression feel they have no energy? They eat the same food, drink the same liquids, breathe the same air, yet the body feels more like an inert mass than living tissue.

The reason, of course, is due to a suppression of pranic life-en-ergy. Without this essential element, life is literally not possible. Anyone who has been in close proximity to a dead body recognizes intuitively that "something" is missing. It is more than the body not

---

8   See Appendix for full description.

moving, talking, etc., but the absence of life-energy and soul are unmistakable.

This essential life-force that keeps us alive, and when properly functioning in good physical and emotional health, is also under the influence of the personal will. Easy proof of this can be demonstrated if you follow along with a little visualization with me. Imagine a time in your life when you felt very down, as if nothing was turning out the way you wanted. It does not have to be *the* time, so don't search too hard, just whatever comes to mind. Once you have this pictured in your mind, move into that picture, really feel how you felt at the time. Now, notice what you feel in your body right now—low energy, heaviness, etc.? Don't worry, I won't leave you there! Now, imagine a time in your life when something quite wonderful happened and you felt buoyant, alive, "walking on air." Once pictured, move into that scene and feel what that felt like at the time. Now notice how your body feels. Do you see how we can change the life-energy in our body, clearing away blockages that inhibit the flow?

These Clearing-Charging exercises are designed to do just that, clear away blockages in the flow of prana life-force and charge the system with life-giving, creative energy. What was revealed to me was the connection with the movement of the stomach-diaphragm and the function of the Clearing-cleansing breath and the Charging breath. Some simple examples will show you what I mean. Imagine you are going to lift an end of a couch. Slow down this picture and notice what happens to the stomach as you bend over to lift. Do you notice how the stomach is drawn up? Another example: imagine you are going to jump into a cold-water lake. Again, notice what happens to the stomach, drawn up again. This is to retain and charge the body system to prepare for some exertion or stress.

In contrast, imagine you are going to relax, lie down on the couch. You may feel some warm sunshine on you, a lazy morning or afternoon, maybe reading a favorite book. Now, notice how your stomach is operating in concert with your breath? You will notice that, in a relaxed state, the stomach moves out when the breath comes in. This clears and cleanses the subtle nadis. And, we have devised various methods in life to accomplish this balance in our lives. For instance, we create stress and strain on the body for exercise, creating breathing rhythms designed, usually unconsciously, to either charge and/or clear the pranic nerves. Or we may drink alcohol, overeat, or use other negative influences designed to effect changes in the physical and astral, pranic, bodies.

We may be more conscious of creating balance without outside stimulation. Not only that, but most of us have locked within the physical body and the pranic body memories of past traumas that affect our physical and emotional health today. This system of Pranic Life-Force Clearing/Charging Exercises will work to help resolve blockages created by these past experiences.

Just like the blood system needs to operate as it should, one should get fresh air and eat food compatible with one's system. So should one tend to the pranic system with fresh air and the food of good thoughts. Once the pranic passageways are clear, then regular use of the Clearing/Charging Exercises will act as maintenance.

Pranic health will clear the way for deeper, more sustained meditation as well. Much of the difficulty in concentration for meditation is due to blocked passages and imbalances in the pranic nadis. With the Clearing and Charging Exercises, these blockages can be eliminated, creating balance in the system. The attention can then be more easily focused on the higher centers. This offers even more potential than physical-emotional health. With a steady, balanced system to support the meditator, the withdrawal of life-force up the spinal stairway becomes an accomplished fact when the lower body system is cleansed and balanced. This Clearing/Charging Exercise promises the Raja Yogi or Yogini ultimate union in Sat-Consciousness.

Two Come to Visit

God has arranged for two visitors at my hermitage retreat. Like twin pros and cons, they have simultaneously brought their points of view. On one side, Sholem Asch's book, *What I Believe*, proclaims Judaism, and its offshoot Christianity, as the only true fount of faith in the world. On the other side enters Joseph Campbell through a series of taped lectures, *Transformations of Myth Through Time*. Campbell puts forward that there is nothing drearier in mythic lore than the idea of sin and the fall of humankind described in Genesis. And, that Genesis and the story of Moses are nothing more than the retelling of Hammurabic law and Babylonian myths. These earlier myths had no taint of the fall, but like those of India, projected voluntary incarnation and the joy of creation.

These two visitors are a bit like having an angel on each shoulder, whispering, or loudly proclaiming, their opposite views. I am of the mind that both have a glint of the diamond, but neither views the full effect. Judaism believers are not the "naysayers," when viewed in mystic light, that Campbell believes them to be. The mythologist has lucid insights aplenty for the ancient cultures, but has grudging apprehension of ancient Judaism. Overlooking many flaws of the cultures, Campbell speaks almost wistfully and poetically of burial sites and how woman's heroism wins eternal life for the couple. But, he seems to take a boxer's stance when it comes to problematic aspects of Judaism. Throughout his teachings, Joseph Campbell points us to the door of mystery, but does not guide us into it, nor does he give us the keys for entry.

For his part, Sholem Asch overlooks much of world history and of the spiritual understanding of other cultures and their religions. His writings convey other religions as cardboard caricatures of depravity. He does give a grudging nod to the Greeks for a sublime human philosophy, but considers them lacking in a true faith that would lead them to divinity. And, he totally ignores the religions of the East. Like a provincial youth, he projects his known village against the other villages he has heard tales of but has not visited himself. His descriptions lack a certain depth, a realness. I do not believe that God can be portrayed as the wholesaler of faith with only one authorized distributor to whom all others must come for their supply.

Both Campbell and Asch are eloquent speakers of their hearts' perspectives. But neither sway this listener to the rightness of their view. Discernment of Truth cannot be won by passionate argument only. A full view of Truth must have two elements to it. One: it must lift one above the mind to Soul Knowledge, and two: it must have a universal outlook. Campbell tends toward universality but lacks elevating one past the mind. Asch lacks universality, but soars, at times, to realms spiritual. However, he does not maintain height but comes crashing down into narrow tribalism and sectarian views. Both offer marvelous contributions, and I am glad for their visits. Neither make me a follower to any ultimate aim but both give firm stair steps to wider, if limited, vistas. I bow to the brilliant sparks of light emitted by both but will not rest myself in either.

The Reverend Mother Yogacharya Mildred Hamilton

The Reverend Mother Yogacharya Mildred Hamilton was a direct disciple of Paramhansa Yogananda, whom she affectionately referred to as "Master." Mother met Master in the year of 1925. Her love and devotion to Master were unequaled as her one and only Guru. Master healed Mother of several serious illnesses, as well as her children. Master made Mother a minister in 1949, to add to her duties as Center Leader of Seattle. He also gave her direct permission to initiate others into Kriya Yoga, and later gave her the unique distinction as the only woman Yogacharya in his worldwide organization, and one of only seven Yogacharyas in total.

Mother once said she was the product of two fully realized Masters. After Yogananda's passing, Mother received inner direction to go to India. There, in an ashram in the South of India, Swami Ramdas, affectionately known as Papa, put Mother through the Mystical Crucifixion. Through these terrific experiences, the New

Testament scripture's inner meanings were revealed to Mother. Hidden beneath the outward story of Jesus was the story of what everyone goes through in their ascent from the human to the Divine. This is Mother's unique contribution to the fund of world knowledge. Mother's love and service to God and Guru were complete, and she was a blessing to all who knew her. She was born on Christmas Day, December 25th, 1904, and achieved Mahasamadhi on January 31st, 1991.

Swami Ramdas
(Papa).

Yogacharya
Mother Hamilton.

Paramhansa
Yogananda.

October 28, 2000

Well, the interesting times have continued. I have been "clearing house" from devotees, former devotees of Mother's, to President Clinton. This strong current continues through inner corridors of consciousness. Vigorous censure runs through me to various ones. X received a pruning, then Y, and today President Clinton received a lecture from none other than me! Well, it came through the inner voice of this body, but the scene and words are not of my doing, at least not in a conscious way. It feels to me the power of God the Father coming through, as it never has come through me in the past.

In the past, my nature has been more of the Divine Mother: loving, compassionate, ever long-suffering. But this new temperament is forceful, direct, and does not hesitate to take any quarter.

And they seem to come of their own. The scenario unfolds and it becomes quite an undertaking to correct others.

Today my knees and legs are in great pain. The thought/memory came to me that Mother broke both of her knees when going to the Fiji Islands. That is how my knees feel, and the joints in my legs, from ankles to hips, are very sore. I do not know the meaning, but it seems very connected to coming here and working for God for the greater good of the world.

An insight came around X. He came with the desire to be the leader of the group. I had that position at some time past and he thought he was the better man for it. Well, he had his opportunity and found out it was not as it appeared. I pray he will rejoin the flock one day and make his peace with Mother and God. I certainly cannot do this work alone. He is a gifted soul. We shall see. All is God's doing, of this I know.

When it comes to this body, I don't seem to have any fear. I know that whatever suffering God may have in mind for it will be accompanied by corresponding Grace. Would He abandon one who is so utterly dependent upon Him alone? He would not be my God if that were true.

Om Sri Ram Jai Ram Jai Jai Ram

November: Tests and Dreams

November 2, 2000

Our true nature is spontaneous Joy, Ananda, and Love; Chit, rooted in the sure knowledge of the Eternal Self, or at least, that is how Ram reassures me. We may at times feel the knocks of the world; that is natural. This should not overshadow our free nature. Reject anything less than this as delusion and always attune yourself to the Divine Vibration, Aum, ever residing within and guiding you to your one Father-God.

To do sadhana, one must feel an inner Presence and direction. Guru comes to give us a lift in this direction. If one strains too hard for sadhana without the inner sweetness of God's Presence, it is vanity and produces imbalance, fanaticism, poor health, etc. If one knows of the path and makes no effort, that too will produce negative consequences. If the inner Life or Presence is missing or weak, then one should pray daily for God to awaken sincere desire for Him within us. Self-directed sadhana: i.e., from the ego, is like standing in the dark with a torch. But when the sun of inner Presence rises, one dispenses with the torch as it is no longer necessary. When God inspires you to pray for that awakening, that too is God awakening Himself within you.

November 10, 2000

This morning I awoke to a conversation. Question: "What is the meaning of the virgin birth?" Answer: "When the mind becomes still, it is like an empty womb: still, but full of possibility. Then Divine Consciousness may project into the stillness like a streak of lightning, illuminating the consciousness. This enacts the inner virgin birth."

My inner teacher went further. "When groups of souls come together and co-create a state of stillness, then as a group they may give birth to a collective Christ Consciousness. There is the saying, 'Be still and know that I am God.' To be still means to bring the mind to that inner state of stillness. This happens as a result of prayer and meditation. These prepare the mind for stillness, but Grace is the activating force for it. Once that state of stillness is achieved, to know God means the realization of God. That realization can only come in that stillness."

My mind went to the esoteric teachings of Sri Yukteswar in *The Holy Science*. I thought of Ananda as being the womb of silence with its holy vibration of Aumen. The Chit comes as a lightning strike. If the attention is directed "outward," it gives birth to the universe.

But if the mind is withdrawn with the desire for realization, Sat is revealed, and birth of God-realization occurs.

Associated thoughts of the physiology of the virgin birth came to me. The pituitary and pineal glands are connected to the Ida and Pingala nerves of the astral spine. The secretions of these two glands come together to form the Christ seed. It makes its way through the nervous system down behind the stomach. At this point, through God-tuned meditation, the mind is held in stillness, the star of the East is seen, and wise men of the three gunas surrender themselves to the inner King of Consciousness. Christ Consciousness is born into the being of humankind. The beauty of it all struck me in this feeling of silence.

I share here some snippets of how God teaches me. What is more difficult to share is the feeling and pure insight that come with this inner revelation. I pray as you read this that God grant you the feeling of stillness and the clarity of revelation that He has made me experience.

November 10, 2000 (Postal)

Dearest Swamiji,

In just a few days from the time of writing this letter, you will celebrate your birthday. I want to wish you the happiest birthday and fulfillment of your prayer that you be absorbed into Papa-Mataji, in Consciousness, of course. I have heard from Marge that your health is very good and that she and her grandson Travis had a good visit there at the ashram. I am very glad to hear all this news.

I am in receipt of your letter of October 13, 2000. Thank you so much for your blessings for my Sadhana here. As you know, I consider you to be my second Mother, next to my beloved Guru. Anytime I think of you and your darshan room, I feel that I am there, sitting at your feet. Love and gratitude swell in my heart for the many blessings I receive from your sacred form. And those blessed ones who help you in your work, Swami Muktananda, Swami Shuddhananda, Anantraman, Sri Ram Bhat, Kamalakar, please convey my sincere regards. How they shine in my mind as the personification of seva. Also, if the list is not too long, my regards to: Thankamma, Rama, Lakshmi Maha Devi, Ram, Babu, Kumar, Vinay, Shyam, Ramdas, Krishna, and all friends there. My only thought in mentioning some is that I will leave out others who should be mentioned, but that is the way of the world, I suppose.

I am doing well, and enjoyed Swami Vishwananda's visit here very much. I understand he had a very good visit to see devotees here in America. Special mention should be made of Larry Koler, his support for Swamiji's visit, and his taking long stretches of time from a very busy schedule to escort Swamiji to all the various places they visited.

Here at Cloud Mountain, I have established a routine of sadhana which includes daily circumambulating of the property, silently chanting Ram Nam. My hermitage cabin is in a beautiful setting, all the leaves have turned brilliant gold, orange, red, and yellow colors. The first thick frost is on the ground this morning, but the sun is shining brilliantly through for an early morning mist. Deer and singing birds in the day, and elk and owls at night, keep me company in my secluded retreat. I am going on two months of being here and sadhana has been intense and good. As Papa often said, realization of God is no joke. I pray that with God's blessings and the blessings of His saints, this poor Sadhaka may see some Grace from God to have pure aspiration for Him alone. Otherwise, I do what little I can to keep my mind on Him always, and surrender all results to His ever-loving Hands. My one desire is to realize Him completely, until there is no me and Him, but One. Will that day come? Ram's will be done.

With all Love and Gratitude. David

Yogacharya David and Swami Satchidananda.

Yogacharya David, Jerry Hickenbottom,
and others on a silent forest walk.

November 11, 2000—Silent Satsang

Dear Satsang Friends: Greetings, David asked me to read this to you.

I am very glad to see you all on this beautiful fall morning. All is going well. Every day seems too short for all I would like to do. Many writings have flowed from this pen, and I have some *Notes to Sadhakas* this morning. These are some short essays about being on the path. More will follow each month as they are completed. I would like to thank Carla for preparing these, and Larry and Cate for looking them over before their release. I hope you find them helpful.

We had a wonderful visit with Barbara Anderson, Ananda Mata. I think her life story is very interesting, instructive, and ultimately for the upliftment of the traditional Christian world.

Some points of business. Due to the size of the hermitage cabin, I thought it best not to have potlucks. But, due to God's sweet will, it is a beautiful day, and if you wish to bring a chair and sit on the deck there, you are more than welcome. I have about four chairs for outside.

We will begin each hour with Ram Nam, walking around the room. If you wish to stay meditating, of course you can do that. During the 3:00 hour, I will walk around the property silently chanting Ram Nam. It is a slow walk. Over some places, there are rough trails. You may join me, leave at that time, or stay meditating until my return.

There is a bathroom in my cabin. Be very careful to read the sign on the toilet and do as the sign states. Also, there are bathrooms at the bottom of the steep gravel path.

I am glad to have you come and look forward to our silent time together.

Namaste. David

P.S. If you would like more silent time, you may come down to the hermitage cabin after the meditation until 5:00 p.m.

November 20, 2000 (Email)

Dearest Swami Satchidananda,

Silent Greetings from Cloud Mountain. I am writing to wish you the very happiest of birthdays. May you be well and Papa-Mataji's blessings be very abundant. The day of your birth was, indeed, a fortunate day for the world.

I count as one of my greatest blessings to have had your darshan and the many kindnesses you bestowed upon me, and continue to bestow upon me. All of us here are richly blessed by you, and everyone sends their loving greetings and best wishes for a wonderful birthday celebration. I know you do not crave such special occasions, but indulge all the rest of us who enjoy showing you our love and appreciation for all seva you have done for your Gurus and all of us through the years.

Papa-Mataji's blessings be upon you always. David

November 21, 2000 (Email response from Swamiji)

We have duly received your loving email message. Thank you very much for your kind greetings on the occasion of my birthday and we are indeed deeply grateful to you for your kind words.

Things are going on well here. We had over 500 devotees from different parts of the country take part in the joint meeting of Anandashram Satsang Samiti members, from the 11th to the 13th. We also had some spiritual discourses, Bhajans, and the usual 36-hour continuous chanting of Ram Nam in the Homa Mandir. Altogether, we had a blissful time.

We note that you have mailed a letter to us. We eagerly look forward to seeing the same. Trust you are keeping good health and busy with your usual activities.

We pray for Beloved Papa and Mataji's blessings on you and all friends there for eternal happiness in His constant remembrance and service.

Satchidananda

November 20, 2000

Every night when lying down, I have been taking God to task: O God, You made me lukewarm in my sadhana. You make me as You wish, a creation of Your own Being. And You give me attraction for creature comforts. I take particular pleasure in eating some foods. When I lie down, I like the comfort of a bed. Why do You make me focus on the body at all? I have nothing in this world I feel attached to, yet this waking death of a body holds some attraction. It is You Who has made this atman. It is You who must make the desire, for You burn strong! I think of what I have left, my profession, thoughts of earning money, having a home, etc., and I am not sorry for it at all. So, if I care not for things of the world, then why do You make me lukewarm in sadhana! O Papa, you say it is all Grace. Mataji proclaims you are the same as the Omniscient Presence. Then You must Grace me with absolute desire for You alone. Nothing less will do! It is You. You have put this thought, this prayer, into my mind. It must be answered by You alone. Will that day ever come? Surely it must come.

November 20, continued:

I read Mataji's admonitions to those visiting the ashram. Her words are like nectar to me. "Arise, Awake!" is the essence of her command. Like teenage children, we awaken, then drift back to sleep, awaken again for a short time and return to sleep. The teenager has a love affair with the mattress. So, we too have a love affair with the body and the world. This body is in a process of decay once it has matured. Why do we ignore the inevitable death? We see life only stretching on and on. But it is not so. "Arise, Awake! To the Real Substance!" encourage all the saints. "Nothing doing." We roll over and go back to sleep and dream of living in a tiny, decaying world, hanging onto it as if it were our all. "Arise, Awake!" goes the call. Slumbering snores are the response.

November 21, 2000

Oppositional forces have been knocking at the door. Are they mine? Are they the world's? I cannot tell the difference anymore.

I had a dream. I was out in a medium-size fishing boat with a few others. The downrigger was set for deep fishing. I had seen a fish caught and brought into the boat. It struggled on the deck and finally, someone clubbed it dead. I asked God, "O Lord, why did you bring me to such a place? What have I to do with this?" I was given charge of the downrigger, now set deep. I asked if it could be a hook that was a set-and-release type that would not cause damage and that we might release the fish once caught. This was not received well. Then there was a hit on the line. What emerged from the water was not just a fish. It had the shape of a fish, but was many times larger than the fishing boat! Rising perhaps three or four stories above the water level, it approached the boat. I told the others to get into the cabin. Three options crossed my mind. With spiritual power, I would stop the fish from swallowing us all. I would offer myself as its meal and perhaps it would be satisfied with that and leave the boat and others alone, or third, it would swallow us all and that would be the end of that.

I stood on the aft of the boat, feet together and arms stretched up, my body taking the shape of a "Y." The fish came near and stopped. Through mental transference, it said: "You summoned me." I recognized this as the voice of a Being with a great Nature. The idea of all the oppositional forces arrayed against me came to mind. I said, "Can you help clear these oppositional forces? I cannot perceive the clear springs of God-Consciousness." The fish indicated it would help. It bit the cable line of the downrigger in two easily, and submerged.

I felt a deep vibration made by the fish from its home in the sea. It reminded me of the vibration that I felt at Babaji's Cave. In fact, I came to understand the fish had been none other than Babaji. I felt the vibration loosen the things that were bound around me. Babaji asked if I was surprised that a Being such as himself would be under water. I knew he referred to the Bible interpretation when I said the underwater subconscious mind was the repository for tamasic energy. I answered that the subconscious may be the repository for tamasic energy, but like life, it was of mixed nature. The superconscious could also be reflected in the subconscious. He said no more. I took this as agreement. The dream was done.

November 29, 2000

Last evening, a clear knowledge came to me that Larry would have disciples of his own. I thought that I should authorize him to give Kriya at some future point, not long after I come out of seclusion, I would think. Also, there are other potentials for this I have no doubt. The Kriya lineage is meant to grow from this branch. I feel a thrill at this portent, not of human excitement, but of a firmly-rooted idea of the Divine.

Two dreams: Lorraine and I were walking about a neighborhood. The love felt on both sides was tremendous. I think she may have been pregnant. I was so happy for her and felt a fulfillment at the unqualified love between us, not as man-woman, but soul to soul. At the end, someone drove up, a bit familiar, then I recognized him. He was in a large, older model Cadillac type of car. He had been looking for me. I think it may have been Rich, Carla's friend.

The other dream: Phyllis was coming and we were to meet her. She came in at an airport. She was very joyful. There were a number of us there to meet her. She greeted several as I waited, a little in the back. She saw me and the meeting was wonderful, although she gave me a hug with one arm and hugged someone else with the other, then was swept toward others. I stood and waited. She came back and introduced me to a woman who was quite thrilled to meet the "Yogacharya."

Actually, there was a third dream; this one was about the three-story house in West Seattle that I had been thinking of renting or buying. I had a dream (within my dream) of an older couple who had owned the house. The man told me there were several buried parcels that may be worth a lot of money now. I was not sure, as they were stocks and perhaps bonds and some other valuables. Others had looked for this wealth, but not found it. He indicated if I looked for it, I should be careful as others knew of the rumor that the treasure was buried in that house, and they may make trouble for me if they came to know of its reality. There was excitement and some anxiety as I found some parcels hidden in foundation bricks. He had wanted me to use the money for "God's Work." He had no family or children, although distant relatives may try to make a claim on it. When I awoke, I thought, "O Lord, make me free of women and gold!" Create in me pure desire for you alone. Let me yearn for thy riches as my wealth. Let me yearn for union with You as my marriage.

November 29, continued:

Entering into my third month of silence, I find some increased desire nature for outside stimulation. I imagine this is a sense of isolation. Like all my tests, these are passing phases, from a few moments to some minutes or more. Or, a gradual unrest coming on me, till I realize something is happening and needs tending to. This desire for outside stimulation is for the ordinary things of life in America: getting in the car and going to the store, visiting with friends, making plans to do something or go somewhere.

Here, there is nothing to plan, other than meals. Today, I am on the sixth day of a fast and so even that is not current. As I realize this desire for outside stimulation, my attention is drawn more inward. My inner world is the place to put this desire for stimulation. Bring the attention inward, look to resolve desire nature completely in Oneness Consciousness. How the mind continues to run after sense-consciousness. My daily prayer has been, "Lord, instill in me the desire for You alone. You who have made me, made me with desire nature. Now that desire nature is mixed. Some for the body, some for You. Make me so that all my desire is to realize You, serve You, love You. Make Yourself my All in All. You are All-powerful, and You can do this now. Make it so."

Charmie Gilcrease and Michele Rogan: a silent walk in the rain.

December: Deepening Faith

December 4, 2000
Tests

Tests: today, God told me a letter I wrote and sent out two days ago responded wrongly to what someone wrote. I had misinterpreted what was said. I asked God why He, who is the One acting in this form, gave me that information now and not when I wrote the letter! The answer: a test. It is a test to me about detachment, seeing fame and shame as the same. It is also a test for the recipient of the letter, of sincerity, of desire for Truth, and attraction to God in this form. Even actions that appear wrong are right when one is surrendered to God. No fear or pride accompanies one who is surrendered. When God is the sole (soul) companion, then only oneness exists.

Yesterday, a feeling of total serenity surrounded me like a blanket. Absolute faith brings one to absolute serenity. It is the security of the child playing near the ideal mother and father. No harm can befall it. Surrounded by love and assurance, the child plays without care or worry. Ah! Such a state cannot be truly described, only experienced.

The magnetized state of the ajna continues. Since Babaji's promise of absolute Union, it has been there off and on. For the last several days, it has been almost continuous. It is a sensation lower than normal, at the top part of the nose rather than the point between the eyebrows or a little above. Ram's will be done!

December 5, 2000

I experience a "heavy spot" on the origin of my nose, like someone pushing their finger on that spot. Sometimes it is like a very firm pressing, sometimes more intense than that. It moved, last night, to the bridge of my nose. Now it is at the beginning of my left eyebrow. It intensifies when I am in deeper meditation, but will continue even when, as now, I am writing, or during other activities. I believe, although I have felt such pressures in the past, that this started when Babaji agreed to give me the consciousness I have yearned for, pure God Consciousness. I have asked for its meaning, but nothing is clear about it at this point. As always, God is at work.

Deepening lessons on faith: all anxiety, all self-consciousness, all fear and anger are a result of lack of faith. When we reside in the secure lap of faith, we know all things happen by Divine Will; therefore, for our good. When we know, through and through, that all is occurring for this purpose, a deep faith abides in us that is unshak-able. This knowing faith is the rock of Peter. Once we gain knowl-edge that the Christ is in our midst, then we rest, assured. Peace, fulfillment, and deep realization are then integral parts of our being. Neither storm, destruction, nor outer success threatens it.

Om Nama Papa

December 6, 2000

When washing our clothes, we may find an old beloved garment marked with holes, even stains that do not come out. Close inspec-tion reveals the fabric feels and smells clean, even delightful—even so with God's saints. Having used their bodies in service to him and for His realization, the fabric of the body may have many signs of wear. Close inspection will show only purity and pure vibrations. Other garments may look perfect on the outside, but when we draw closer, they smell rancid and do not feel right. The ego is a terrific showman. It can don the outer garb and some affectation of a saint, but the tree is known by its fruits and the ego-saint's faults will eventually come to be known.

If you feel bored or without direction, don't just act out of rest-lessness. Rather, go inside and pray to God. Tell Him you know each moment is precious and for some reason, you are having this rest-lessness. Ask Him what His will is for you. Listen, when you get a direction and you feel good about it, follow that, even if it doesn't make total sense to you in the moment. As long as the feeling of God's Presence is with you and you feel the purity in your being, you are all right.

December 6, continued:

When we are sincere on the path, then we should be thankful for any knocks the ego gets. It is by those experiences, taken with grati-tude, that we lose attachment to what others think. When the storm passes, mostly the storm of restlessness inside when some fault is exposed, we find we are still breathing, still able to think and carry on. Really, we can have joy and see the humor in such things. It is as if the whole cosmos, at times, conspires to make us look foolish. Ninety-nine percent of the time, we do all right. That one percent is shown to the whole world!

A sadhaka should be able to analyze any situation that may have occurred. We then own up to our part in it, whatever that might be, big or small. Then we are free to go forward without looking over our shoulder for what may come if we are discovered. To live simple and free of ego is best. Little children naturally do not know shame. Through time, they have to learn it. If we feel right with God in our hearts, then all right. If there is a problem in the heart, we must do everything we can to change that and make it right. If we do our best to mend broken fences but others refuse our efforts, then let it go, knowing you did your best after the fact.

Never forget, life is just a play. Do not lose perspective. It doesn't mean we don't have compassion for others. Even an actor can bring tears to our eyes. But always know this life is for learning and the joy of participation. So, live free in your thoughts. Attune yourself to the all-joyful Presence of God and know you are made in His likeness and image.

Om Sri Ram Jai Ram Jai Jai Ram

> They looked ahead to the time when they too would be living beneath the broken slates of New England's burying ground. And they asked themselves one question: 'If their acts would be worthy of generations yet unborn?'

—DAVID HACKET-FISHER, REVOLUTIONARY WAR HISTORIAN (1935–)

Christmas 2000
Dear Friends,

It is so wonderful to be able to share this time of year together. It is clear, from the historical story as it is told, that Jesus was not born this time of year, yet it has deep symbolic significance. The winter solstice is the darkest time of the year. It is said that when the world is in the greatest darkness and cries out for a savior, that God Himself incarnates into the world to re-establish Dharma. This incarnation of God, an Avatar, comes to lead all humanity back to Himself and to destroy all evil tendencies. As humans, we are the microcosm reflection of the macrocosm world in which we live. The savior in us is also born when we have tired of living in the darkness. Then God, in all of His purity, is born within us in order to destroy ignorance and to establish His kingdom of Light within. To celebrate the birth of Christ, that perfect Light of God, at this time of the year re-enacts the pattern set for all humankind.

One way of thinking of Christmas is to consider a festival of lights. Homes are decorated with colorful displays of lights; trees and symbols of humankind are glowing with lit ornaments. Gaily wrapped gifts bring a promise of new things to come. When seen for its many symbols, and what it represents within, it is inspiring to find such celebrations. For me, the most precious experiences I have of the season are in communing with God and spending time with our spiritual family. It is here that the deepened meaning of the season comes alive. By attuning hearts and minds to the universal Christ and celebrating this birth into humankind, we may soar to the realm of angels that resound in the spiritual vibration that radiates peace and goodwill toward the entire world. What a wonderful, powerful vibration that emanates from the highest reaches of God and floods all the world. Like a radio receiver, we must attune ourselves to the proper frequency in order to feel that vibration. We not only are then a receiver, but also become a transmitter of those most holy vibrations of peace, love, and joy. The Light of the world thus becomes magnified, and the Festival of Lights becomes a spiritual celebration of kindred souls.

It is also the time of year that our most beloved Guru comes to mind. An incarnation of the Divine Mother, she too came as a savior of humankind. Like many of God's perfect incarnations, their lives do not take on the true significance until viewed from the distance of time. I think we will see a flowering of her teachings that will help to change the world and universalize the minds of aspirants everywhere. Of course, she had great love for her family, both her spiritual and her little human family. One of her great joys was to prepare a special meal for her family. Later, that became the preparation of a spiritual feast for her spiritual family. I know she takes great joy when you open yourselves to loving your own family and expanding that love out toward the family of humankind. We cannot say that we love God and not our neighbor. For our neighbor is truly God in that human form, perhaps asleep, perhaps awake, but never absent. Mother's very nature was love. So, when we love, we enter into her and commune with her in more intimate terms. May your celebrations be joyful; may you find the Christ Spirit ever residing within you, and may God and the Masters bless you richly with inner gifts of Spirit that you may share with all.

Peace, Bliss, Amen

THE CROSS AND THE LOTUS JOURNAL
—DECEMBER 2000

Dear Friends,

Silent sacred greetings. During this time of year, much of the world recognizes the birth of Jesus. When one enters the inner way of God-realization, one sees universal teaching in the sayings of Jesus and his life story. From time immemorial, spiritual masters have used stories, some fact, some fiction, to point the minds of aspirants towards ultimate Truth. The masters have always known absolute Truth could only be the product of direct, transcendent perception.

Thus, the essence, the kernel of Truth, is not in the outer husk of the story, but in realizing the ultimate Truth at its core. By entering into the story, itself, we follow the Way as it has been laid out for us. When the story is told by a realized master, the story itself becomes a way of salvation. That is, by following in the footstep principles of the story, we will be led to the realized state from which its author is speaking. This is the great marvel and mystery of a really good story. In the story of Jesus, we have a story for the ages.

I invite you all to take time during this busy season and read the story of the birth of Jesus. Then go into the quietness of your own being, asking God to show you that inner core of Truth, something to take with you that will help guide your daily life. Do not be discouraged if, at the first diving or two, you do not get any pearls of wisdom. Keep going deeper into silence until a glistening of Light lets you know you are near your goal. It may come as a sudden insight, or a remembrance of something you have always known, but now know more deeply, more profoundly.

If gift-giving is part of your celebration, then soak the gifts in love. When you give, give mostly with your heart. Then the gift you receive in the giving is the love that permeates the gift itself. Nothing more is needed. This is also a wonderful time of year to give to a stranger. Make an extra effort to know how God would like to give through you to another. Again, with love, as it were, flowing like liquid to the recipient. It makes life quite fun and alive if we spend our days looking for opportunities to give, without thought of return. It may be the gift of a smile, some small encouragement, or a secret gift of some money to someone in need; it can take the shape of countless forms, but all in the spirit of life giving to life. The life exemplified by Jesus was such a life, and we see that in the lives of all the great masters.

Christmas is also the birth date of our beloved Guru, Mother Hamilton. Her life was an example of one who picked up her cross, her body, to follow the Christ. In her own Master, Paramhansa Yogananda, she found that Christ Light blazing so brilliantly. And through the Christ-like experiences she went through, she realized the inner truths contained in the scriptures. Through her life, we have a modern living example of one who 'went all the way' in the realization of God. We honor her most when we emulate her example in her love of God and Gurus, and her surrender to God's will.

It is in that spirit of Divine love that I send this greeting to all of you. Although I may not be able to be with you physically during this season, nevertheless I am with you in Spirit. My one desire, my one gift I wish for all of you to receive is the gift of the Presence of the Infinite One. When you open your heart, mind, and soul in sincerity and humility, you become a Holy Grail for the wine of Spirit to fill to overflowing. May you always be filled to overflowing with the Grace of that Spirit.

Merry Christmas and Happy Birthday, Mother.

In Divine Love, David

Spring Retreat (Announcement)

April 6–9th, 2001

Everyone is invited to the Spring Silent Three-Day Retreat at Cloud Mountain Retreat Center. A Raja Yoga Technique for clearing the subtle astral nerves and charging them as well will be taught for the first time. New and experienced meditators will benefit by practicing this Clearing/Charging Technique that will clear the three bodies of distractions and prepare sadhakas for deeper meditation. It will also help to clear past mental, emotional, and physical traumas, again helping sadhakas in their spiritual quest. The cost will be $150 USD for the three days for food and lodging. Please contact Carla Gold for more information.

Loving Care

At Cloud Mountain, months ago (early in my retreat), I was reading the last chapter of *The Perfect Master*[9] about Meher Baba. The book concluded with a statement to the effect, by Baba, that meditation does no good. The method to know God is to repeatedly read Baba's story of creation, given at the end of the book. This method, he said, would take one to God. Well, I started the story, got bored with it, and then I gave full vent to the anger that had begun with his statements that story reading was the method and meditation practices did no good. For a couple of months, I did not pick up the book, and for a month after I set it down, I did not want to look at his picture. This was the first "interference" or falling out I had had with Baba ever since I came to know him through his picture that transmitted its purifying Light several years before. I knew this anger, this resistance, I was feeling reflected some inner working by Baba.

After some months, I felt a relaxing of the tension between us. Later, I picked up where I left off with the book, *The Perfect Master*. I started the story over and found it good. I was devoid of the previous intense reaction. I somehow felt back to being okay with Baba, with some wariness of his methods prescribed, but feeling better about him. When Larry notified me of Don Stevens coming to Seattle to give classes on the book *God Speaks*, I felt an immediate prompting to attend.

The first night, it was clear to me that Don was using the same method as Baba: to meditate and think about the story. He went on to explain that every word of the story was impregnated with the energy of an atomic bomb. The key, as I understood it from Don, is to read the story until it "sings in your veins." Through this attention to the words—in this case, it was the book, *God Speaks*—one will receive intuitive insights that unleashed some of the spiritual power of the words. With the obvious care of a trained scientist (Don's background is that of a scientist, a chemist, I believe), he

---

9   Now only found as *The God-Man* by C. B. Purdom.

noted, sometimes a voice in the back of the head (although he says he is not generally a "voice man") reminds him of something he has known, or some sudden insight comes to him from or about the words.

After the first night's class, there was a general acknowledgment by those of our spiritual family who attended that they liked the feeling in the room very much. I too enjoyed Don, but was still wondering why I was prompted to come. The feeling was nice; it is always a privilege to get the darshan of one with some realization, and clearly, Don is one in this category. But I knew, in my prompting to go, that there was something very personal to happen to me, and I knew on the first night, it had not happened. However, others were having very strong reactions: anger, feeling it was time poorly spent, and other criticisms.

The first night spurred a desire to read more of *God Speaks*. Two questions began to form themselves in me. One, the main one, had to do with a question I have been having around the purification of the mind in the causal sixth center and moving into the seventh center. The question was not yet fully formed. The second question concerned Baba speaking the word that would change the world. "What is the nature of that word, and did he speak it?" In asking the second question, I wanted to see what Don's response would be, looking for his level of understanding. I was not sure I would ask either question directly to Don, but I could feel both questions forming themselves.

On the night of the second class, Don went into some detail about a story Baba told, in *God Speaks*, of a boy throwing a rock into a pond. This action, a whim of the boy, started a wave. This story was used to illustrate that the beginning of creation was begun by a whim, which started a force: energy in motion. Using Einstein's equation that says energy is equal to matter, Don said that matter is the natural outcome of the energy. The wave also created some other characteristics: it had high and low, front and back; this was the introduction of duality. Having personally heard Carl Jung, Don used an analogy in which Jung said that the creation of conscious-ness could be thought of as two pieces of material that electricity could pass between. This passing of electricity can occur because there is tension between the two poles. Similarly, the tension in duality creates conscious awareness.

As "drop souls," we each have some original tension, a knot, from the very beginning. We decided on what that knot would be from the very beginning, before creation came forth from the unconscious God. Since we were part of that unconscious God, we decided what that original samskara, that knot or twist, would be from the very beginning. Due to loneliness, on a soul level, we took on other samskaras in the hope of avoiding that loneliness. Since these samskaras do not really remove loneliness, they turn into irritants.

As a result, we take on additional layers to protect ourselves from these samskaric irritants. This results in increasing complexities in our nature. What was important in all of that, Don said, was that he more clearly realized he was fully responsible for his own life.

In the midst of Don's storytelling, he described how, over many years, a new understanding of the nuances of the story has come to him through intuition. Through questions and guiding the discus-sion, Don designed the class to prompt others to share their intui-tive insights regarding the story as well. Using the telling of the story, his own intuition as illustrations for others, and guiding the discus-sion, I was being given a view of how Baba's method for realization was being used by one of his close, direct disciples. It suddenly became clear to me: Baba had brought me here to show me first-hand his method for awakening intuition through the story. With this realization, I felt wonderful gratitude that Baba had arranged with such careful detail for me to get firsthand experience of this. Months before, he had disturbed me by touting this method above all others; now, he was showing it to me firsthand. How lovely!

Also, the second question about whether Baba had spoken the word and what the nature of that word was also answered by way of inference. The Mandali, Baba's chosen disciples, teach that the coming of the Avatar has not yet occurred. The "second coming" apparently will occur in seven hundred years. By inference, I take it they would say the word was not spoken, and will not be spoken until the second coming. Now, Don continued on to say, he thought possibly the word *had* been spoken, but the Mandali would not agree with him on this point. As I say, the primary teaching seems to be that the word has not been spoken. My second question was to test to what extent Don and those who follow Baba have "concretized" the message. My sense, as far as the Mandali and general consensus of the followers is concerned, the message is taken on a literal plane; Don was indicating a deeper understanding.

The thing I feel that brought me here was the Love and care that Baba is taking in showing me his ways and methods. I know there is more that will be shown to me about the use of the story for sadhana. Baba, directly or indirectly, influences the work I am doing for God and Gurus; Mother has clearly put Baba in our lives, and he has taken a keen interest in us. The love and goodness of it come through again and again. The wisdom of his methods is still unfolding for me, but I do feel the power in "the story" told by a master. After all, have not the stories of Jesus initiated, sustained, lifted, purified, and enlightened devotees for thousands of years? Yes, there can be no doubt: there is great power of transformation in a story.

As an aside comment, Don reiterated a truth said by other masters and sufficiently answered my first question: the guru raises one from the sixth to the seventh center. I willingly, gladly, put myself in Mother's care for this eventuality.

God has been showing me consciousness beyond time. This whole notion that God "created," and before this, God was unconscious, I see not in reference to time but rather a focus on a particular aspect. Like a large painting, whole and complete, and when studying it you focus on the details. To do that, you become voluntarily unconscious of the rest of the painting—that is, a point in time—then move to another detail—the next moment in time, etc. Baba—as a certain point in the picture—says, "I Am That I Am." He speaks to consciousness that is focused on another aspect of the painting. And he says, "You are also the I AM—the one observing the painting—but you are so focused on that one image, you have forgotten you are really the one looking at the image. As long as you think of yourself as the image in the painting, you are not identified with the I AM—you are not me. But when you do realize you are the one looking at the painting, you are the I AM. Then you will know you and I are the same."

December 22, 2000
The Blissful Body

Creation, we know, is of three sorts of bodies. The causal, the first cause through thought, ideas; the astral, the energetic body that has form and sensory perception; the physical, made up of matter, providing a vehicle to interact with the physical cosmos.

If you think of the creation of a computer, it has chips, circuits, a screen, typing keys, etc. These are equitable to the physical body. Then there is the electricity that makes its way through the physical mechanisms of the hardware, without which nothing would work. This power of electricity may be thought of as the astral body. Then there is the software, encoded information, the ideas that make the hardware and the power of electricity have meaning. Beyond these three is the operator of the computer, for the meaning of having a computer is lost if not for the operator. The operator may be thought of as the soul.

These three bodies as analogous to a computer and its operator have limitations. For unlike the operator of the computer, the soul is in touch with realms beyond the three aspects of a computer and its operator. The soul has direct access to Ananda, the blissful body. Bliss is unlike any sensation derived through the physical, astral, or causal bodies.

Ananda, you might say, is the body of God. That is, it contains and manifests all creation, in potential and in its perceived reality. Bliss is the true Nature of creation. Bliss is akin to what we call feeling. Feelings of happiness, joy, love, the thrill of subtle appreciation. It cannot truly be said what bliss is, it cannot be defined or qualified. It is the true pleasure through the body. The pleasure of smelling, touching, tasting, seeing, and hearing are the five mechanisms by which this body senses the world.

Ananda transcends all such sensations. It also is beyond the artist's thrill of creation, the intellectual's joy of deep thought. Bliss uplifts and purifies the soul. It is ever new, giving added subtle power and meaning with each new expression. Ananda is intoxicating, ennobling, and enlightening beyond total comprehension. Yet one may be on the most intimate terms in appreciation of Bliss Nature. Perhaps to say it most simply: Bliss is simply BLISS.

Lotus Flower-Soul-Force.

January: A Guru's Strange Life

January 13, 2001—Silent Satsang

Dear Satsang Friends: Greetings, David has asked me to read this to you.[10]

Mother's Mahasamadhi Graveside Service

We gather here today to honor the life of one who has touched us all. To honor Mother's life best is not to just wax eloquent about the past. God, great spiritual masters, everyone, all of life is, was, and will be, thoughts in the mind. But the word "is" connotates the present, and eternity.

The life that "is" Mother resides with us as we honor the life she lived. Her teachings, her example, her ever-living, knowable Spirit are present. We pray that we may be conscious of her Spirit, and that we might rise up to meet her in heavenly consciousness as we honor her.

Mother

I do not think of funerals and memorials as a time of grief, so much, as a time of honoring. It is ten years now since Mother left her body, what for great yogis like Mother is called Mahasamadhi. Maha means great or large. Samadhi is union with God. During a yogi's life, such as Mother's, union with God has become a constant feature. At the time of leaving the body, however, that soul willfully releases its hold on the idea of body consciousness and dissolves into the great spiritual sea of divine consciousness that is God. This glorious

10   This was read by Reverend Peter Schultz at the January Graveside Service.

moment, as the wave of consciousness explosively unites with the sea of universal consciousness, is what is known as Mahasamadhi. Such a blessed event is this, that all who are present at such a time consider it a sacred privilege. Far from thinking of this as a time of sadness, which may exist, it is a time of great joy!

I will not speak here of the details of Mother's life; that can be for another time and place. But I will mention one thing. The thing that inspired Mother, drove her, and took her to heights beyond knowing, that one thing, of course, was God. Mother's life was a romance, in the greatest sense of the word. A romance as strong as any husband and wife, as any mother and child, as any hero ever had for a noble cause. It is an internal, Divine Romance. And when Mother got bit by that romance bug, she got bit bad! Not just a little bite that comes and goes, not just a medium bite that lasts for a time but gradually fades, but a bite that would withstand fierce storms of difficulty, desert wanderings of lonely years, humiliations of misunderstanding, and even deaths on the cross rising to resurrection in the heavens. This one thing of a Divine Romance is finer than any golden, bejeweled crown that any king or queen has ever worn.

There is one thing that is so closely linked with Mother's Divine Romance with her Lord, that it scarce can be separated. That was, and is, and will be, Mother's everlasting desire that we also be consumed with that kind of desire, and ultimate union, that she had with her Beloved. Her great desire is for us to be bit, and bit hard. So that our love and devotion are strong. So strong that it will withstand the storms, the deserts, humiliations, and even deaths that surely come with such a life. Not for vain or egoistic reasons does she ever have that desire. One reason alone drives her in this quest for our souls. She wishes that we will join her in her resurrection in God-Consciousness. That we will know what she knows. We will feel what she feels. We will become what she is: gloriously free in God. Bound no more by a self-imposed separation. Ever-free, ever-one with her Infinite beloved. Her love for God and for us is inextricably joined together.

The greatest way to honor Mother is to emulate her, to follow her in her Divine Romance. Not like a parrot emulates, but as a devoted, mentally attuned disciple. To ask for, pray for, allow for that bite to enter into our heart and soul that will carry us to the Infinite Beloved. It is with great joy that I am privileged to join here with you all to honor the greatest soul I have known, that I have heard of. That is how I feel about Mother, my beloved Guru.

January 14, 2001
The Guru's Strange Life

Yesterday, we had Silent Satsang here at Cloud Mountain. As to context, I have been reading *The Perfect Master*, by C. D. Purdom. An "unadorned" account of Meher Baba's life up to 1936. It gives daily accounts and places of movement of the inexplicable Master caught in the maze of seemingly irrational behavior. I feel myself in the midst of a spiritual whirlwind. Larry had often commented on the strange behavior of this Master, but I had yet to be caught in it until picking up this narrative. My inner consciousness has reflected not the calm eye of the storm, but the whirling, twirling bits blown by the random gusts of activity of this Master.

And what is it that differentiates the mad-man, the eccentric egoist, and the God-man? The mad-man has no center, only activity without real or lasting purpose. The egoist acts for the sake of self alone, for greed, power, lust, excitement, whatever desire the self of ego entails. And what of the God-man? The God-man acts in total surrender to the God-Self. This Self has a defined purpose: the upliftment and spiritual healing of all with whom God brings them into contact. The God-man has no ego, having surrendered selfhood into Self-hood. No longer the self defined by the body and its relationship to the world, the God-man exists as a Spiritual entity, an expression of vast universal Self-hood.

And how does one differentiate between the mad-man, the ego-driven-man, and the God-man? There is a saying: "It takes one to know one." In Meher Baba's case, he had three of the great, known saints of that day confirm his spiritual status. But God-men and women are not easy to read. It all comes down to this, "The sheep know the shepherd's voice." There is something beyond reason and words that awakens the sleeping God within. The waking can be uncomfortable, painful even. Nevertheless, it is the awakening.

The other saying of Jesus that applies is this: "A tree shall be known by its fruit." (Matthew 12:33) The result of following such a one will bring the followers to their own realization of their own oneness with God. However, this has its difficulties as well. Many Christians today say they are followers of the man from Galilee. With two thousand years of tradition and vast institutions erected in his honor, one feels the sustainability of the man and the movement. Imagine an event today. Some man or woman declaring themselves to be an anointed one, a Christ. You are one of a dozen followers of such a one. No millennium of history, no art and edifices built in their honor. Not only that, but many of their actions defy logical explanation! Others criticize; you are thought by some to belong to a cult, perhaps a dangerous cult. Now, you were asked to sacrifice all to follow this leader: how many current-day Christians would be eager to respond to such a call, I wonder?

These are the questions that come to one in reading Meher Baba's life—in fact, in following the lives of many of the great masters. It is a matter of inner faith that gives one the resolve to answer such a call. Although one can prop up such a response with logic, logic alone will not be the rock upon which such a spiritual life will be built. The God-given intuitive knowledge that Peter had, "You are the Messiah, the son of God," brings the aspirant to the clear realization of their spiritual destiny. But even this is not enough. For that faith will be tested, storms of hell will shake that faith and attempt to bring it all to naught. Only the humble, only those that persevere, will know the resurrection of their Christ-Selves from the ashes of their egoistic embers. That one may then rise, resurrect in three days or in three bodies, to become fully manifest Christhood. In that journey, they may assume some burdens for those who follow.

Like a Scoutmaster who removes the pack from a child while out on a long hike so that child can make it to the end of the trail, so the realized-being alleviates the load for the devotee-disciple.

Yesterday, during our silent Satsang, some loads were transferred to this body and consciousness. Surrendered to what God wants for this expression of Himself, this self takes whatever is given.

In vision, I went outside the hall, vomiting up unbelievable amounts of material. Someone got some buckets and I filled two, two-gallon buckets full.

It was a disturbing sight of blood, small bones, and physical remains. Both buckets had the manifestation of two abortions. This, of course, was distressing and revolting to all who saw it.

Another thing I took on manifested as a dream this morning. It was the forcible rape by two women of another woman. All the feelings, the physical manifestations, are experienced in the three bodies as these visions and dreams manifest.

What has long been held onto by the individual is transferred to this body. All the results of that experience are then gone through, knowing all the thoughts, all the trauma, every sensation, all of it comes through. The difference is that because this consciousness is united to the Divine, the results of those experiences are gradually (sometimes fairly quickly, sometimes more slowly, depending on the karmic complexity) worked through this body and mind. If this consciousness were not united with the Divine, then it would remain a troubled history in their conscious mind, or stored, perhaps even unknowingly, in their subconscious mind. Therefore, it is not a work sought out by the ego, only adding to its own current burden of gaining its own freedom.

This earlier experience has definitely confirmed for me that abortions carry a very high price for the one who chooses such an action. This world is a difficult training ground; there is no doubt about that. Like a Marine boot camp, perhaps the best thing that can be said for it is that you got through it!

January 14, continued:

This morning, I was looking at pictures of Mother for the calendar—getting ready for Mother's Mahasamadhi. In thinking about possible pictures, memories of Mother being very particular about what pictures were to be reproduced for wider distribution came to mind.

Only being able to guess at much of the criteria Mother used in making these judgments, I have done my best to reproduce only those pictures that I thought she would definitely approve of. Looking at the December picture, Mother holding angels on either side of her shoulders, I wondered what Mother would have thought of reproducing that picture for the calendar. Then I thought to myself, "Mother, a devotee's perspective is different from the Guru's. We find charm, captivation, and beguilement in some ways about you that you may not find about yourself. Therefore, as disciples, we may choose differently." Without flippancy or being disrespectful, we may present those sides of Mother that endear her to our hearts, minds, and souls.

January 15, 2001, 9:15 p.m.
Meditation is Both a Noun and a Verb

- Meditation is both a noun and a verb. It is an action, a rite, a process, and it is also a State of Being.
- Meditation as a technique is ultimately simple to learn. To become one who is in meditation is the most difficult of tasks.
- Meditation begins with concentration. Concentration on a single word, phrase, or image of Divinity. For the verb meditation points to God. The noun meditation *is* God.
- Meditation as a technique may be taught. Meditation as a State of Being defies teaching or description.
- Meditation is a practice—actually, a way of life. Practice and Being ultimately meet. Meditator and meditation become fused.

- Is discussion helpful to meditation? Perhaps not. It may help point the way and confirm the complexity of what is an apparently simple procedure for the meditator.

January 21, 2001
Dear Friends,

It has been a busy month here in silence. I spent some extra time in Seattle at the beginning of the month, in order to help get things prepared for Mother's Tenth Mahasamadhi Anniversary. I am very pleased with the special projects we have in the works. Many of these things will be available to you, whether you can be here in person or not.

We have been busy putting together a book celebrating the life of Mother. It will be a collection of writings from all of you! I have reviewed some of the writings and I think you will agree: they are touching, interesting, and a wonderful tribute to a great God-woman. We will have a suggested donation for these books, but if you cannot afford the donation price at this time, please do not let that stop you from picking one up or ordering one from us.

We will also be opening our long-awaited website for The Cross and The Lotus Publishing. This site will include items we have published as well as the Anandashram books we carry; many of the writings and pictures can be downloaded, if you wish; the site will also have some interesting aspects, such as a calendar of events for the month. I hope you will visit the site later this week when we 'open the doors.'

On Mother's Mahasamadhi day, we have available the second release of Barbara's *Songs to the Infinite*. The CD will have a new cover with a beautiful picture of Barbara sitting behind her harmonium. The words of the songs are included in a booklet. I think you will be very pleased with this new edition. We are also issuing, in commemoration of Mother's Tenth Anniversary, a calendar for the year 2001, with a different picture and quote from Mother for each month.

Well, that gives you a sense of what we have been working on and the many busy hands, minds, and talents that have been working on the projects. My thanks go out to those who have made time in their busy schedules for participating. I am sure that they, like myself, experience a special grace, a feeling of closeness to God, Mother, and the Masters when involved in any such project. As a result of these many activities, I have not been able to respond to your letters from the month of December. Please accept my sincere apologies for this, and know that I will answer your letters as soon as I possibly can.

My time here has been going well. Despite my involvement with these outer activities, my silence has grown deeper. There is something that seems contradictory about 'talking' about silence. I feel the changes happening in me: the communion with Spirit grows deeper, stronger, on even more solid ground. One of the things Mother used to say about realization was, "You know, and you know that you know." With each deepening of that inner knowingness in me, my awareness becomes broader—a more total absorption of my being—and more penetrating. In some ways, I can use the same words for describing what I know, but the realization has sunk more deeply into my soul than ever before.

One of the hallmarks of God-consciousness is the fact that it is ever-new. Mother would say that God-realization is not the end of growth or the end of discovery. Really, through realizing your oneness with God, you are more prepared than ever for plumbing the depths of Eternity. Can you conceptualize what that is? It is difficult because the nature of the human mind is to put parameters around everything. That is why you have to go beyond the human mind and connect with the unlimited Nature of the Divine Mind. So, in gaining Self-realization, the revelations continue and exploration broadens: the main difference is that in Self-realization you have your absolute conscious oneness and complete harmony with the All and All in All.

From that oneness, you are directed, guided, protected, and comforted throughout all of your activities. You no longer wander, ignorant of that inner wisdom, making decisions with the imperfect human reasoning, you become a conscious witness of the beauty, intelligence, and grace of the Divine Mind. If you could but know that the same creative intelligence that created this vast universe and all that resides in it is right here, within you. Then who would bother to tinker with the paltry pickings of limited human reasoning alone, not when you can know that Omniscience, feel it, and become one with it? But most do not know, and what is worse is that most do not even bother to know. But if you take what has been taught to you by the great spiritual masters, and get to work in gaining that realization, then you may know. And in that knowing, you will realize the truth that has been taught for all time: Ye are the temple of the living God.

May you be inspired to reach daily for this realization until you come into the conscious knowledge of that Truth.

In God, Christ, Gurus, David

January 23, 2001

Lessons: The projects for Mother's Mahasamadhi anniversary have not all gone smoothly.

My lessons from this include:

- Clarity on who the leader of the project is. This was done initially, but leaders did not always lead.
- Ensure Roles and Responsibilities are clear: this too was done in general. My idea that overall responsibility is given, and specifics are worked out by those individuals—this has been part of the problem. Those individuals did not "take-up" many of the details.

-SO-

My desire continues to not micro-manage projects given to others.

-SO-

An alternative is to set intermediate dates to check in on progress, timelines, etc. One problem has been that I have been in silent seclusion—leaves it interesting as to how to do these intermediate check-ins, but I now have the computer and internet.
Another issue: setting reasonable timelines with the calendar in particular. I felt the timelines for printing inadequate. I suggested this—but left it in the hands of those doing it.

-SO-

When setting timelines—be willing to challenge those in charge of the work as to reasonable timelines.
One of the familiar themes for me is around personal authority. I have noticed in these projects that not only have I been removed by my circumstances, but I am slow to challenge those I put, and they agree, into leads of projects.

-SO-

- I choose to be clearer about what my expectations are with project leaders.
- I will challenge timelines, etc. when I perceive too little time has been allowed for a project.
- I will create intermediate goals and check in with project leaders at scheduled times.
- I will makeup a written timeline, have one for myself and the project leader—or the project leader can do this and give it to me.

Summary:
- Clarity of roles
- Clarity of responsibilities
- Establish reasonable timelines
- Schedule intermittent check-ins
- Have a written schedule

Suppose you are to do some construction. You are remodeling a room. You remove the drywall and find the timbers beneath have rotted. Now, one has two choices. You may quickly put new drywall up over the rotted timbers, plaster it, sand it, and paint it. It looks beautiful, much time and effort have been saved. Only problem is, of course, that underneath, the foundation is weak, and will get weaker with time. Cracks in the surface start to show and it will not hold up.

On the other hand, to tear off the outer covering of the wall, expose every rotted place, tear out the rot, replace it with solid timber, reinforce joints, etc., takes time, effort, and expense. One may regret ever having started the project at all. Exposing one area may only reveal other problems not even guessed at before. On and on the project goes, until all problems are exposed and resolved.

Even so with the sadhaka. One may dress the part of a holy person, assume a rank in a spiritual organization, be thought well of by all, yet underneath resides rotting desire nature and attachment— or the sadhaka can ruthlessly expose every inner fault to the examination of discernment, and cast the rotting carcass into the fire, to be totally consumed. To continue this work until all that is not good is gone, then to use high-quality materials in building.

To the untrained observer, the walls done in these two manners may look the same from the outside. Even an expert can be fooled for a little while. But soon, the problems emerge. When the faulty construction is explained away by the contractor, some may believe the confabulated explanations offered. But the wise will see the difference quickly. Later, when the outer wall crumbles, then the inner faults will be well known.

Contrast this to the proper constructing that stands the stress and wear of time. Then will the true merit of a finely constructed life bear its real fruit. O Sadhakas, always construct to the highest quality.

Does God Have a Form? Is He Formless?

A person has a body. An individual is also spirit. Which is the greater? One would say that spirit determines character traits that uplift and ennoble, so spirit is greater; in this one speaks the truth.

But, let us reason further. If not for the body, that spirit could do none of the works by which others could recognize this greatness. He or she would perform no acts of art, literature, or music for the benefit of others. There would be no acts of courage, self-sacrifice, or loyalty. With no chance of falling, there is no gaining of merit by rising. Without the body, the spirit goes unexpressed.

Therefore, to say the spirit of the individual is greater than the body is true; it cannot be denied. But, a body is a necessary instrument for the spirit in this world. Like a hand in a glove, the spirit fills and animates the body.

Humanity, made in the design that reflects God, reveals God, reveals God's nature to have the form of creation as His body and formless Spirit. He is, in fact, the All and All in All.

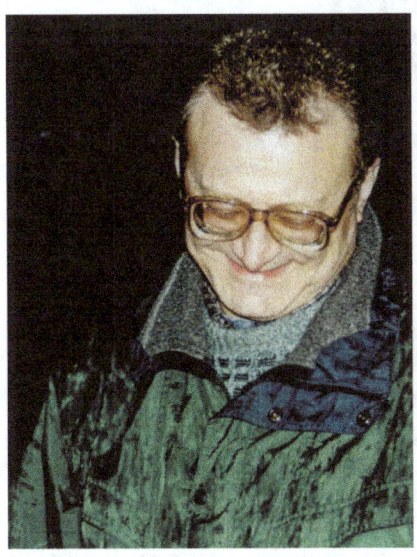

Jerry Trofimchuk reflecting.

Reverend Peter Schultz in Stillness.

Yogacharya David and Carla (Gold) Hickenbottom in Silent Communication.

February: Inward Mind: Tackling Adverse Forces

February 6, 2001

To those of definite beliefs who believe their mode of worship is sanctified and those of differing sects or religions are not, I have a question for you. Whether you be Jewish, Christian, Muslim, Hindu, Buddhist, or any sect or "ism" that believes yours is the only true way:

When a mother or father of a different religion prays for their sick child, do they pray to a different God than the God you would pray to for your own sick child?

To Papa's Sri Ram
Victory to the Christ
Praise Him Amen
Victory to the Christ
Praise Him Amen

Rely on the Light. It is your All and All in All. When you learn to rely on the Light, you gain peace; it is the supplier of all your needs. Be less dependent on things of the world and more Self-reliant on the Light of your being.

February 6, continued:

Larry chose an ascension transcription for the Spring Journal. It feels to me as if this is confirmation from Mother on my current state. She spoke specifically of the ten subtle qualities of the mind and their purification. She even told of Master relating how one great soul can have a fall in that ascension; one might even have two falls and God's Grace would lift one up if one was sincerely repentant. It seemed she was speaking directly to my situation. She reiterated that she could not live our lives for us, but we must live with the consequences of our actions. I pray for God's Grace that He purify this vessel so it may become a proper receptacle of His Divine Grace.

I had two dreams: met Win and Kathy at a wedding at Lincoln Park. They were both surprised and eager to see me. Both were emotional, especially Kathy.

I had a waking dream, or I was awake in a dream; it's hard to distinguish anymore. I received a legal notice from Self-Realization Fellowship (SRF) asking me to desist from using Master's picture, etc. I went to their headquarters and business offices. I was insistent (openly, verbally, flamboyantly so), that I meet a "real" person and decision-maker. I did not succeed. I was offered to see X at her home on her sick bed. I went back to, "What have I to do with her?" I seemed to be testing them, desiring to awaken those there who are caught up in their magic dream. At times, I seemed to be in the spirit of Shirdi Sai Babaji. At one point, I said, "Fie on this organization!" Are they so lost? I pray not.

Yesterday, I put it again to Babaji why I am unable to do Kriya. He showed me. The flow up my spine is like a large, strong current. When I go to do Kriya, it is designed to magnetize the spine and begin the flow of this current. A simile may be that of a siphon. A siphon is used to start the flow of a fluid. Once the fluid has begun to flow, a siphon action would only interfere with the flow in full motion. I will continue to verify this instruction.

February 10, 2001—Silent Satsang

Dear Satsang Friends: Greetings, David has asked me to read this to you.

This last month was a full month, with preparations and the celebration for Mother's Mahasamadhi Anniversary. Celebration may sound like a strange word to some for the passing of such a beloved one. Consider that death of the body is like taking off a well-used, but heavy, old overcoat. Envision the freedom experienced upon leaving that old heavy coat behind, then that day may be marked as a wonderful day indeed. However, the real celebration aspect of the anniversary is in honoring and having gratitude for all that Mother did for us during her life. For, without Mother, and the selfless lives of our spiritual lineage, none of us would be sitting here today, and our lives would be much the poorer if not for them.

All has gone well here for me here at Cloud Mountain. God continues to pour His grace on this child of His. He seems intent on finishing the task He started so many years ago. Certainly, if He had better raw material, His job would be easier. When I think of Mother, Master, and Papa, and their clear focus on God alone, it is a wonder that God has made any headway with this one at all! Perhaps He was feeling bored on the day He selected me for sadhana and thought to Himself He would like a really good challenge. Whatever the case, He has taken me to the point to where He has and is making strong efforts at moving forward.

This has been the most fascinating journey. I remember so many years ago, over twenty-five of them now, when He started the kundalini activity within my own body. I went through times of singing and dancing, moving in very specific ways that were all geared to align the very atomic structure of body cells, as a magnet aligns metal filings. And all for one purpose: to prepare the body, mind, and soul for upliftment into cosmic consciousness. I was constantly being taken from one experience to the next; each movement purified the physical body, and then the astral body; finally, God brought me to the causal body. In the causal body resides the ten subtle qualities of the mind, those memory storehouses of all human experience and tendency, and they have to be purified from stem to stern. It is an exacting task, for every thought has a charge of life-energy behind it, and all thought tendencies of the mind are revealed and have to be transcended. One lesson taught in this: we are responsible for every thought that is sent across the threshold of the mind. For every thought is a creation. It is a profound and humbling reality. It is in this deep inner work that God has been working through this body and mind for the past while.

One point has been driven home: the whole journey is within. When Babaji first came into my conscious awareness here at Cloud Mountain, I was still attached to outer events. Deep in my mind, I wanted the kind of miracles that occurred in the *Autobiography of a Yogi*. I think this is natural, but it is now a distraction. When I would look up to the stars, I would think of Babaji coming down as one of those stars and manifesting physically, in a sattvic thought, for it was rooted in a devotional mood, but this was the wrong focus for my mind; I must have an inward mind. This was a hard pattern to break. For so many years, any time I saw brilliant stars at night, I made this association with Babaji. Now, when I see those stars, I think of the star at the center of my forehead. And Babaji, as quick as a thought, so quick it sometimes startles me, is nearer than any mortal could be. I tell of these experiences in hopes that you may be saved from making this same mistake, so that you may be guided perfectly in all ways.

I am glad that you made the effort to come here today. Satsang, association with Sat, the true Self, is the most noble purpose for which to gather. Remember when you come together for times of meditation, times of listening to Mother's tapes, don't jump up afterwards and start talking about anything and everything. This is a sacred time, and should be treated as such. It is easy to trample on fragile things, without thought or care for the damage done. Being in uplifted consciousness should be treated as the most precious, fragile experience we can have. It should not be trampled upon, not only in ourselves, but in others as well. When we come together, each of us is a custodian for creating a holy environment. With a gust of vibration here, a loud comment there, those subtle vibrations quickly retire before such audacity.

It is common when a spiritual vibration is built up that we will want to project it out, for we are not used to holding so much life-energy within us. So, after meditations, there is often-time loud talk and laughter, and a focus on anything other than God. We are disgorging the precious vital energy we have built during the meditation time; like a thief who runs off with the precious jewels only to sell them cheap at the pawnshop. So let us not be like the foolish thief, cheating ourselves as well as others who have come to worship. Expand your ability to be an instrument for the powerful vibrations of God, and do not waste them on the trivial. That is why I ask you to leave quietly. Learn to hold that tremendous conscious energy and lift it up the spine so it may carry you to supernal realms. Don't be an unwitting agent for the devil, of lower vibration. Today, let us invite the Masters to be present with us. Let us strive to attune ourselves to their vibration. Inward attunement with the Guru brings us into heavenly realms and protects us from lower vibrational forces. Let us upwardly reach for higher experience, and inwardly petition the great Ones to bring us to their inner realms of heavenly consciousness.

Hari Om, Tat, Sat, David

Yogacharya David offering silent birthday blessing.

Reverend Jill Hough and Honor (Wells) Baldigara in Delight.

February 15, 2001

This morning, I unwittingly opened an attachment that sent a virus to all on my mailing list. This produced an angry state of mind in me. I thoroughly took God to task for using me in this way. The anger continued for most of the morning. Finally, through some frustrations, I was able to send out a notice to all, warning them of the dangerous email. The production of this rajasic state made a most powerful impression on my mind. Why does God make a fist of one hand in order to hit the open palm of the other? This remains a great mystery, an enigma. However, even in tense circumstances, it must be recognized that all happens by Divine Fiat.

Truly, there cannot be two wills in the universe, since the sole Creator is singular. Painful circumstances are a stern reminder not to be attached to this passing show. Health and unhealth, comfort and discomfort, pain and pleasure are all passing phases that have no true bearing on Who and What we truly are. Only by clear and decisive renunciation of attachment to these passing phases can we re-identify with our true nature. Once we know that we are spiritual beings, we can have constant comfort in our human drama.

Jesus assured all that they need not have fear; he would send the Holy Spirit, the Comforter. Once established in the Holy Spirit, the world will seem as a dream. Different states of mind may visit us for a while, but they quickly disappear, leaving not a trace. This promise has been the teachings of all great spiritual masters. We may rely on it and set our sights clearly on the goal. Wherever we are, whatever we are doing, this immortal truth may be awakened within us and guide us to our freedom. Om Sri Ram Jai Ram Jai Jai Ram

February 16, 2001

One of the roles I have to play is helping others by taking what they carry in themselves into my own body. Recently, I was helping to work out the difficulties of another, and as if in confirmation, I received reports of how much calmer and more centered that same person was.

Today, I have been receiving the anger of a devotee into this body. The connection is felt in the solar plexus and shakes the whole body when these vibrations come. Recognizing that we are one, I accept these violent knocks as if they are my own. It has disrupted my digestion and created stress in different parts of the body. Every day, there are various effects from different ones that come to me. Due to my identification with the Self, I am able to work through these various negative vibrations. The Infinite, in all of Its kindness, has willed these transferences to occur. Infinitely kind, because it is a help to those struggling to make progress on the path to their realization; infinitely kind, because it gives me an opportunity to serve. No barriers of distance keep this progress at bay. I only ask that God graces me with constant remembrance of Him, ever holding both hands to His sacred Feet.

February 16, continued:

This evening, there are some rajasic shadows from this morning's events. On recognizing them, they began to dissipate. Then the word "specter" came to mind. A sudden recognition that an entity had come in with the violent knocks of anger that this body had taken on. At the time of that energy/specter leaving, a steady calm ensued. When I reflected on the one whose energy I took, it has been known to me that he has had difficulties with entities along with his mental problems. It is something to be in service to in this way. Carla was the recipient of some of this spillover. In some strange way, I feel these events are somehow connected with the internet virus. It is as if the unleashing of the virus is connected with these entities. By being a part of the spreading of the virus, I became connected (as part of the Divine Plan), with the mischief unleashed. When I sent out the follow-up emails, I felt cleansed of something foul. The one whose energy came my way reacted violently when I sent the virus out, saying, "Why did you send that killer virus to me?" It was 24 hours after my computer sent out the virus that the angry vibration, and this entity, came. This may seem to be a madman's rantings, but the sequence is all very clear to me.

I have burned incense and asked Carla to burn some as well. May God and the Masters surround and protect us and no harm come to us as our minds are fixed on Him.

Om Sri Ram Jai Ram Jai Jai Ram

P.S. Unlike other entities I have worked with, sending them to the Light, this entity I banished from its earthly influence. It had no interest in the Light. I intuitively knew that, so I sent it out of this realm into the dark astral regions. There it may work out its evil karma without molesting those here. Ram's inscrutable play. Om Sri Ram Jai Ram Jai Jai Ram

February 21, 2001

For over these past many weeks, the back of my head has had a very interesting sensation. On my left side, just above the medulla, it feels as if a fairly large area, perhaps two inches in diameter, has been opened. Through this area, a sound/vibration pours into my brain. It has a very definite sound, the high pitch of (unknown). Not being trained in sound, and the fact the sounds are not generated from an earthly source, I find it difficult to say exactly what it sounds like. It is either what is described as the flute, a very high-pitched flute, or a bell. I imagine those tests done to measure hearing may have a pitch such as this—well, perhaps. It is steady and remains for long periods of time. It has been ringing for the entire time I have been writing. I "know" it is doing a work in me, but I cannot say at this point what that work is.

Also today, I have been in a terrific struggle. The psychic realm has been filled with the Self-Realization Fellowship. It started with a conscious dream this morning. I had received legal papers to desist from using Master's name and his picture. I went to Los Angeles to find someone to speak to who had authority and <u>was</u> a real person. I only encountered lawyers and MBA types. I was offered to be taken to see X at her private home in her sick bed. I declined. "What have I to do with her?" I feel she is set in her ways and attitudes. (Or, not this exactly. It is more that I am clear she is not the one I am to deal with.)

I spent the day in an inner struggle with them. I felt Master several times acting in disguise through me. I am willing to go through whatever he wants in order to fulfill his will. Sometimes, I find myself wishing I was smarter, stronger, clearer, better, more charismatic. But the clear advantage to my many faults is that I know I may not rely on my own merits, but on God alone. My attitude all day has been one of simplicity; whatever cleverness there has been has come through me rather than from me. I am pleased for that.

O Lord
You see to it
That this situation
Fulfills the highest good
For all concerned.
Hari Om Tat Sat

February 25, 2001

The knocks (February 16) have continued, hitting the solar plexus and shaking the whole body. Inwardly, I told God if I needed protection, He must do it. No more noticeable effects of anger-entities as before. I can feel the hit on the body—I am reverberating throughout. There are after-shocks, but it seems all right for now.

Carla drove down to bring fasting supplies and celebrate my birthday. She, Chad, and I drove up to Mt. St. Helens and visited the Cold Creek Ridge facility that has focused on the recovery since the May 17, 1980, eruption. We saw a film that showed the whole side of the mountain slide down and then the gases and ash fumed up in a roiling mass 12 miles high. For months before, via their instruments, they observed the active area building up, inches and feet at a time. This pressure finally found weak areas in the side of the mountain that caused it to give way.

It made me think of the internal processes of breaking human consciousness apart so that Divine Consciousness can erupt. The pounding from internal workings shows small signs of changes. If the internal workings are active enough, it eventually breaks away large pieces of human consciousness, causing huge landslides to occur. This mighty process changes the inner, and sometimes the outer, landscapes of the individual, and, many times, extends out even further. It may be that a spiritual master's life will affect very few people in their lives. It can be they will change a world. The light that resides in these, those of little or massive change, is the same. Why some are but a whisper, and why some, like the fallout of Mt. St. Helen's, encircle the earth is a great mystery. But we may be assured, the light is exactly the same for both.

February 27, 2001

It's been an interesting day. Started last night when I returned to the cabin. Larry had taken Chad and me out for my birthday. I had been feeling fine. Almost upon entering the cabin, my whole insides started shaking. They vibrated for some time, producing some nausea. I am not sure how long this continued, an hour or so, then it started to settle. The knocks to the solar plexus have also continued. It feels to be some major assault from the psychic realm. Thoughts of the website come to me. Could it be in reaction to that?

Tonight, I received a letter from X, an ex-member of SRF. She was told by Brother Y that reading Master's original words was being disloyal to Master. It is difficult to believe, but also, I believe it. Can this body withstand this assault? The pressure and pain are terrific. When I check in with Babaji, he is right there. I prayed to Master, saw myself hanging on to the hem of his robe. He was wearing tiger skin shoes; I could only see below his knees. Everything in me tells me I am on the right track with all of this. May the Masters help me through.

Om Sri Ram Jai Ram Jai Jai Ram

February 28, 2001

The inner shaking and knocks on the solar plexus continue. I hang on to Master's hem. I cling to his left leg as he is seated. I feel the fabric of his robe. I see the dark ochre color, and I see his tiger skin shoes.

Thoughts of Brother Y come. His words echo around. I know what will happen to them (the groups splintered off from SRF), but I will not tell. I am sure that the Brother has only loving thoughts about the fate of us! I am so glad He knows my destiny. Surely, I must arrive at God's feet, as I have nowhere else to go.

Other thoughts: the organization, SRF, is the same as Master. Brother Y said, "Loyalty to SRF is the same as loyalty to Master. If you doubt SRF, you are doubting the Guru. It is a question of attunement." Yes, I would say it is a question of attunement, and attainment. The implications of his statements are vast. For his assertions to be true means that everyone who acts on behalf of SRF would have the same attainment as Master, for how else could they have such perfect attunement without corresponding purity of mind that leads to attainment? That, to me, is the clear implication. Otherwise, you could doubt actions of any or all of those who speak, edit, or write on behalf of the organization. Does having faith mean never to have differences of opinion? Does that mean the entire organization moves, speaks, and acts as one mind, one purpose, one thought? I think one would have to become very simple indeed in order to conceive of such a thing.

An entire organization standing in as Guru. An interesting and untried notion. We shall see. For myself, I am glad for what I have in God and Guru.

March: All Experiences Come from God

March 6, 2001

Later on in the day of my last entry, February 28, we had the worst earthquake in a half-century. Its epicenter was nearby. I went to stand in the doorway as the whole cabin shook very hard. Only one jar broke, with books thrown off the bookshelves and various items knocked off their surfaces. There was some serious damage done from Olympia to Seattle. But remarkably few injuries. The one death I heard reported was due to a heart attack. There were many comments on how lucky we were.

After the quake, the shaking inside calmed down. The aftereffects continued for three or four days. I felt I had been pretty beaten up, did not have much physical energy, no ease of movement. I find now that difficulties of the body, and, for that matter, the emotions and mind, do not overwhelm me. I stay constant in God, seeing all experiences as coming from Him. My humble gratitude goes up as wordless prayer that God has seen fit to send His Grace to one such as me. My deepening prayer is that He forever makes me His own. As I feel emotions well up in that wordless prayer, it reminds me that until the time of the quake, I was having Bhakti tears on the outside of my eyes every day. Since that time, I have not. Today is the first day of feeling back to my "normal" self.

I pray that God break the last container of separation, no matter how thick or thin the veil. Whatever He deems necessary for me to go through, I will do. I had a false inner voice this morning. For a couple of minutes, I listened and responded. Then I realized it was not a true voice of God.

> O Lord, You, lead me,
> Let no inferior force near me,
> You alone are my guide,
> See to it, O Lord
> That I be guided aright!

A heavy, pressing feeling on the bridge of my nose is quite constant. I have some anxiety that God will let me languish in mediocrity.

> O Lord, it is by Your Grace
> That I may be lifted up,
> How is it if You delay?
> Will You not come now!
> And release Your son from this prison?

THE CROSS AND THE LOTUS JOURNAL
—MARCH 2001

Dear Friends,

I am very pleased we were able to come together to celebrate the anniversary of Mother's Mahasamadhi at the end of January. It called forth service from many people to have all the preparations, publications, and website in readiness for the event. Even in my silence, I had the opportunity to be involved in these projects. To be of service is one of the greatest joys this life has to offer.

I have come to think of this path to God we follow as embracing and utilizing all four major systems of Yoga. The four aspects are: Karma Yoga, that of selfless service; Bhakti Yoga, love and devotion for God; Jnana Yoga, use of discriminative intelligence; and Raja Yoga, the path of meditation and life-force control. Deeper under-standing of Karma Yoga in particular gives us the means to trans-form our daily lives into a continuous state of prayer and joy.

Anyone who breathes, eats, sleeps, and moves in the body is involved in the field of action. Karma means action, and Yoga means to be yoked with, or in union with, the Infinite all-pervading Consciousness of God. Initially, Karma Yoga involves dedicating all actions to God. When we work for our families, in a profession, for a noble cause, or in service for a spiritual work, we train the mind to see the work as a Divine mission that fulfills our real purpose for being here, even in the most mundane activities. Through this ded-ication, our lives become charged with a higher purpose and we experience joy in the activity. Since everyone is involved in some activity, all are called to this life of dedicated service and have access to this joy in action.

One of the hallmarks of this dedicated life is letting go of the results of our actions. Of course, we begin with some end in mind when we start an activity. But, an over-mindfulness of the end product robs of us our concentration and the joy inherent in doing the activity itself. An accountant-devotee was telling me of the mound of papers she faced every day piled on her desk. Looking at that mound produced a tamasic depression and a loss of energy and enthusiasm for her work. Through letting go of the idea of the mound and focusing on the one piece of paper she had at the center of her desk, she discovered a joy and freedom by doing the identical task, but with a shift of focus. Poor training of the mind makes us overwhelmed with details and the sheer abundance of tasks in our life. A disciplined focus makes us properly prioritize our tasks, and then take one thing at a time. This letting go of the end result, and staying focused on what is at hand, moves us from a hectic, rajasic energy, to a calm, centered sattvic mode of service.

Through this inner calm, we awaken to the play of the Divine energy moving through us. We feel this life-energy flowing throughout our body; it is, in reality, moving through our subtle astral body. Awareness of this flow brings a tingling, flowing, energizing life-energy throughout our being. We feel that we are being carried along with this life-energy, versus having to push hard to get through the very air and gravity of this material world. This life-energy brings with it a joyful awareness that makes us feel in tune with our true nature; we then act in accordance with others, not out of a self-centered agenda, but in dedicated selfless service.

This life-energy will not only flow in our direction, but it also directs us. As I sat on the deck this morning, the idea for writing this article came to mind, as it has been generating itself in me for several days now. This movement within built up and became an inner imperative, go in and write now! Through surrender to the inner direction, this flow of intelligence comes with increasing force and awareness. Humans, endowed with free will, may ignore this inner prompting, but experience has proven that willful disobedience comes at a great price. **True happiness and bliss come about through the sensitive attunement and surrender to this inner guidance.** It is a direct link to the Superconscious Mind that has perfect attunement with the Supreme Divine Consciousness.

Through total surrender of individual will to this inner Divine Will, the body, mind, and soul become instruments of God. With humble obedience to this inner direction, this fusion with the Divine Mind makes one a silent witness. Eventually, Divine Consciousness and human consciousness meld into a singular whole. The Divine may then play the human instrument as a master musician would play a grand piano. Even as a grand piano may have extra keys for higher notes, so does the human instrument have extra keys of consciousness in the sublime heights of Sacred Union. Selfless service is the means for achieving this great Union with God.

When we work in this attitude of service, life becomes joyful and blissful, and we naturally fulfill the will of the Divine. In that state of complete freedom, we transcend even the sattvic quality and use all aspects of consciousness in service, but none bind the soul. Therefore, one may express joy, disappointment, humor, anger, or sadness in a natural fashion. But unlike the past, when identification with these states produced a mood that drew one into a bound state of mind, it now blows through as a breeze, leaving no residue of latent feeling-states of mind. While in action, the Karma Yogi moves, acts, speaks in the world as any other, but inwardly remains ever-free! We need not be called to any "great work," as the world measures it, to be doing Karma Yoga; we can be right where we are, doing exactly what we are doing, fulfilling this Divine mission of selfless service.

May you know the joy and freedom that comes with this exalted calling today, and every day, as you go about fulfilling your mission as a Karma Yogi. David

Announcing: Babaji-Inspired Clearing/Charging Exercises

Which of us has not sat for our practice of meditation and not felt restless, distracted, wanting to do "anything other than this," tired (all of a sudden)—in short: resistant? We may have the will power to move through such obstructions; we may develop a pattern of avoidance, cut our meditation short, or we may find other less-than-helpful ways of dealing with the resistance. The problem, in case you were wondering, is not unique to you! Our spiritual path requires constant vigilance, tenacity, strength, and surrender. And, fortunately for those on the Kriya path, there are methods for moving us along at a faster pace.

Yogis, as do those practicing any discipline, benefit from finding better ways to reach their goal. Through the intelligent application of meditation techniques, we can accelerate and better use our time and energy for calming and stilling the mind. A new process for helping to clear the physical, energetic, and mental bodies is being presented. This process of breath work will help clear the subtle nerves of the astral body (the nadis) and recharge the whole system.

In a three-day silent retreat, you will learn how to cleanse the body of disturbances that lead to physical, emotional, and mental unrest and imbalances. These imbalances, left untreated, may also result in illnesses in any of the three bodies. In doing these safe, simple but powerful techniques, you will learn the step-by-step methods for clearing disturbances and powerfully charging the system with pranic life-force.

In addition to these techniques, there will be group chanting, meditation, simple yoga stretching, and for initiates, Kriya Yoga. This retreat is not restricted to initiates, and all are most welcome.

March 7, 2001
Dear Friends,

Today is the anniversary of Paramhansa Yogananda's Mahasamadhi, March 7, 1952. I think it is hard for most of us to comprehend what Master achieved in his lifetime.

Imagine coming to the United States in the 1920s, a country that was very strongly Christian with little tolerance for someone else's Christian sect, much less another religion altogether. Master brought the liberating message of Yoga. As he traveled from city to city, crowds turned out in such vast numbers that thousands would come. Some arrived hours early, and many others were turned away due to the lack of space. He was a sensation. These were free lectures, followed up by smaller classes for those wanting to know more. Despite the strongly Christian orientation, there were many souls who hungered for something more.

When I traveled to India, one of the things that struck me was the close relationship between men in particular and families in general. Men often gathered in groups, in a familiar intimacy that is uncommon to see here in America. I pictured Master coming to Boston, with cold winters, and cool citizens who had a suspicious reserve. Then I pictured Master living in a small apartment, working with some devotees who led busy lives. Despite what Master had in God, I am sure he felt lonely at times and wondered what he would achieve. But with the strength of God and the Masters, he persevered through the cold winters and his love thawed the cool reserve of interested future yogis.

After living in Boston for a few years and traveling about the country, Master yearned to settle down and work with earnest students/disciples. When he saw the hotel on Mount Washington that had faded a bit from its earlier glory, he recognized it as the site of his earlier visions, one of three sites from which he was to build a worldwide movement. Through determination and God-tuned will, he was able to purchase the property, thanks to someone being inspired to give him money at the last moment. Thus, he found a home base from which to operate and train devotees on the path.

Thousands had come to the free lectures, but Master was disappointed in the number of students who were really willing to get down to work on doing sadhana. With patience and perseverance, he continued to teach, love, and sometimes scold those who followed the path of Yoga.

Imagine, if you will, Master trying to make ends meet during the long worldwide Depression of the 1930s. Master had heard of a wealthy man interested in Yoga, and when he met James Lynn in the 1930s, they made an immediate connection. James Lynn, later to become Rajasi Janakananda, helped Master survive financially, and Master helped James Lynn become reborn again in his Soul.

Through Master's amazing autobiography, expressing his heart and soul as well as that of the many-thousand-year-old tradition of Yoga, he has changed the Western world. Certainly, Master could not have accomplished all that he did without the support of the Masters of our lineage. He was made for the task in many ways. He loved to travel; he loved people, but most of all, he loved God. Without doubt, his having been here, for devotees and for all, enriches the world.

I have often marveled at the obituaries in the newspapers. In a few sentences or paragraphs, an entire life is summarized. It includes family members and sometimes the work someone did, accomplishments, and perhaps some clubs of which they had been a part. Sixty, eighty, or more years summarized just like that. Life is precious; the human soul is priceless, yet so hard to quantify or describe. On this day of remembrance, I hope these few words will bring to mind a feeling of gratitude and communion with this great soul in God. Mukunda Lal Ghosh became Swami Yogananda, became Paramhansa Yogananda. He has affected our lives in immeasurable ways. In my mind's eye, I spontaneously bow to his feet in love and gratitude for who he was, what he did, who he is, and what he does. Masters such as Paramhansa Yogananda are ever-present when we call upon them with love.

May you be blessed today with his remembrance and the sweetness of his Presence.

In God, Christ, and Gurus, David

Paramhansa Yogananda.

March 10, 2001—Silent Satsang

Dear Satsang Friends: Greetings, David has asked me to read this to you.

I want to welcome you here today. There are some devotees not here today, and later I will ask for prayers for some of them. It has been another interesting month and I will tell you some of what happened. As you all know, we recently had the worst earthquake in over half a century in the Seattle area. I know Larry shared with many, an email I had sent to him Wednesday morning before the earthquake. So, I thought I would share a bit more of the story with you all.

On Monday evening, Larry came down to celebrate my birthday and had taken Chad and me out to dinner. When I returned to the cabin, I experienced a violent inner shaking. It was not the physical body shaking, but the subtle astral body. I was very glad to be back in the cabin because I was incapacitated for quite a while after-wards. The next morning, I felt a little worn out, but okay beyond that. Throughout Tuesday, I had several more episodes like the first one. They are very difficult to describe to you, but it felt like my whole nervous system was being violently shaken back and forth, and of course, there was nothing to do about it. It was so hard on my nervous system that I asked God if my body could withstand all this or whether He was going to have me leave my body at this time. He indicated to me that the body would survive.

Wednesday morning, I had two more episodes and was feeling very fatigued by this latest strange adventure. I have many such strange adventures; once in a while, Ram prompts me to share one with you. Around eleven in the morning, the cabin started to shake, and it did not take me long to recognize that this was an earthquake. The ground and cabin were shaking much like my insides had been for the last couple of days and it was all very interesting. We are close here, at Cloud Mountain, to the epicenter, so I think we got a pretty good hit. Some bottles fell and one broke; books were thrown from the bookcase as I stood in the door frame of the front door. I learned later that for the size of the quake, it was remarkable that there was as little property damage and harm done to people as there was; we can thank God for that.

After the earthquake, I didn't have any more shaking episodes, although I was laid pretty low until this last Monday. It just goes to show that when you travel with God, it is a real adventure, and you never know where it is going to take you. You never know exactly how things are going to turn out. What you can be assured of is whatever happens in following the ways of God, it will be for the highest good of all.

The other thing I would like to share with you is something from last night, Friday evening. For Sri Yukteswar's Mahasamadhi anniversary, Chad and I listened to Ben Kingsley's audiotape of "The Resurrection of Sri Yukteswar" from the *Autobiography of a Yogi*. In this chapter, Master describes his Master coming to him in physical form three months after leaving his body. During this visit, Sri Yukteswar described the astral and causal worlds in some detail. I want to tell you it is all true. What Sri Yukteswar says, what Mother says, what Yogananda and Papa say, is all true. This creation and its Creator are incredibly vast, beautiful, powerful, and filled with intelligence beyond description, and it is knowable to the soul through inner perception.

We do not have to build it; we need no machinery or high-powered computers to access it, and in fact, none of those things will get us anywhere. This path we are on is really quite remarkable. We may see some things in life that are awe-inspiring: a large or beautiful building, towering mountains, the blast-off of a spaceship, even astronomical photography that shows the stars and constellations. And yet as wonderful as these things are, they reveal but a tiny piece of all that is, and all that we can realize ourselves to be.

I know that I am trying to describe the indescribable, but when truth reveals itself to you and shows you something more than what you have known before, there is something in the soul that would like all to know the joy of that discovery. I want you to know that we are on the right track, and that the age of discovery is now. Who we are, what we know, the experiences we may have are vast and without limit—and they are ours to have by making the effort of going inside the laboratory of our own Being. Well, I have tried my best to convey to you what I can of the power, the mystery, and the loveliness of it all, but it all seems so inadequate when expressed in language. Perhaps there is something in this that will inspire you to plunge ahead in your own exploration.

This day marks the completion of six months here at Cloud Mountain. I want to thank everyone for the wonderful support you have given to this work and to me. Truly, no work can be carried on by a single person. God has given us each other to love one another, even as He loves us, to help each other, and to encourage one another on our path back to Him. My heart expands with love when I think of all those God has given me so that we may journey together back to our Infinite Beloved. This is our time on the stage of life. How many lifetimes have we lived, only to ask ourselves at the end: "Why didn't I make more effort to know God?" Well, here we are, not at the end, but in the midst of the action; the place is here, the time is now. We can know God, and God is bigger, grander, and more wonderful than we could ever imagine. So let us journey forward together on our pathway to the Infinite.

Om Namaste, I bow to the Infinite in you.

Plus: let us keep in our prayers Swami Satchidananda who is having some heart problems, and for other devotees—Chad, please lead us in healing Oms.

March 20, 2001
Dear David and Laura,[11]

This month marks the completion of six months of my year-long silent retreat. I thought I would give you a note of how things are going.

The cabin and setting have been a perfect "yogi's cave" for me to practice this year of silence. All the arrangements around food and necessities have gone very smoothly. Jean has been most accommodating in finding the right foods for me and even helpful in finding some experimental items, such as cereal with Kamut, quinoa, and spelt. The deck has been a nice addition, especially for sunny days; the various birds and deer have made for nice company.

My work here has also gone on quite smoothly. Before coming, I was not sure what it would all look like, although I knew what it would sound like—silence. I have been writing *Notes to Sadhakas*, which reflect some of my thoughts about being on the path. We also had a large anniversary at the end of January for my Guru's Mahasamadhi that required much planning and coordination. It was at this time I brought my computer here and started to use the Internet as well on a more regular basis. I want to thank you for the access to the 'net, as I know it has made the work of those elsewhere better and more efficient, having access to me in this way. There are additional writings and work, as well.

The inner work has gone very nicely. It is intense, often straining, but always rewarding and I know I'm on the right track. We all bring different perspectives to the path and follow various disciplines, but Truth is one. Whenever one makes progress toward their goal,

---

11   David and Laura Branscomb, the owners of Cloud Mountain Retreat Center.

all benefit. To whatever degree I have been able to do that, I want to thank you for helping to provide a supportive environment for me. I know that others have expressed that they have received benefit from my time here, so there is a ripple effect that goes beyond us. It is rare here in the West to have such places dedicated to the fulfillment of Dharma. My prayer is that we all become living examples of the best of what that word means.

I look forward to the upcoming retreat. There will be a Raja Yoga technique that has been inspired during my time here. I have instructed a few sadhakas in this technique and all have received excellent benefits from its practice. Our path brings elements of all four Yoga disciplines to it, so it will have perhaps a few novel aspects from the more typical teachings presented here. We will have time for chanting and some simple hatha yoga stretching as well as the instruction on the pranayam technique and practice time. We will also use, with your permission, the fire pit near the canteen on Saturday night.

What will the remaining time here bring? Well, it is a mystery to me. But I trust that it will continue to fulfill the purpose for which I was brought here. My current plans for September are to be moving out in the second half of the month. I don't have a date at this point, but one of my thoughts is that you will have it available for the first of October; with some time (a couple of weeks?) to finish the outside siding or whatever may be needed. My thinking right now is that we will not be using the retreat time in September. The organizing of this retreat has shown it would be a challenge to do two such retreats so close to each other. I hope this does not prove to be a difficulty for you.

I trust that all is well with you and that you have not had problems connected with my stay here. If there are issues that have not been addressed, then please let me know, as it will give us an opportunity to create peaceful solutions. I feel badly that my use of the phone line in the evening proved an inconvenience for staff, and trust that my use of it, typically at 11 a.m. is working out satisfactorily. It just so happens that today is the Spring Equinox, and, according to Sri Yukteswar, an opportune time for meditation. May you know the blessings of Peace and unbounded Love in all you do.

With all love and blessings, David

Yogacharya David and George Baldigara.

March 21, 2001

Devotees have different needs. It is like the various needs of plants. Some plants need a lot of water, and little sun. Some do well with a lot of sun and a lot of water to boot. Give a plant too much water, the roots rot, and the plant dies. Give a plant too much sun and it dries out and dies. The guru gives water in the form of affection and outward caring. The sun is the guru's teachings. Both are necessary to each devotee, but in varying amounts. Some devotees do not believe they get all the water or sun they would like. But God knows our real needs and sees to them. The guru's water and sun may also be given through underground springs and light filtered through the branches of trees; that is, in hidden ways. Each is given according to their need. God orchestrates each instrument perfectly so that all may play in harmony. If children are given too many sweets, and they may relish the sweets, in no time they get cavities, their teeth rot and fall out.

We should take it on faith that we get exactly what is needed, for God loves us more than the doting mother loves her child.

The guru is here to do a great work. Transforming the devil-nature in man to the Son of God secretly residing within is no mean task. Devotees must make a one-hundred-percent effort to live the teachings. They must keep their mind on the goal. However, often the goal slips from their grip and they lose their way. Their inner compass should bring them back to north. North is the direction; up the spine to the highest regions of enlightened mind. The devotee should always feel that even if they cannot keep their grip on God, that God has a firm grip on the devotee. God is ushering us into His Kingdom and there is no doubt about it! Make that note a constant in your symphony of devotion.

Om Sri Ram Jai Ram Jai Jai Ram

Yogacharya David and Christine Baldigara.

Charmie Gilcrease on Hermitage Deck.

March 23, 2001
Dear Friends,

I was touched by the recent plea by Swami Satchidananda for assistance to the earthquake survivors in India. I will quote some of his request:

> Mother Nature's recent, furious Thandav in Gujarat in the form of an earthquake has caused most severe damage in and around Ahmedabad, Bhuj, and other places, resulting in the loss of thousands of lives, thus rendering many orphans and homeless. The number of persons who sustained major and minor injuries is also enormous. Though the exact details of the loss of property are not available, it is estimated to cross several hundred crores.

This is the time for all of us to rise to the occasion by extending our hand of help to the distressed and needy, to offset at least a considerable portion of the damage to life and property. No individual, or Government, or other voluntary agencies can singly handle this crisis. There is urgent need for everyone to be involved in this humanitarian work, whether through personal service or offerings in kind, or by rendering prayer to the all-merciful Almighty Lord of the universe for the speedy restoration to normal life.

I thought to send seventy-five dollars for this help. The ashram has a Satsang Samiti, a Center in the area that can get the funds directly to those in need without administrative filters to go through. I have absolutely no doubt that the money will be well spent. Then I thought perhaps others would also like to help. If you feel so inspired to render some financial help to those truly in need, you may send the money, cash or check, to Carla Gold, designated for this purpose. You may make me the payee for the check or money order; of course, you may send however much you feel directed. We will include all names of donors and send one sum to the Mother Krishnabai Trust. Whether or not you contribute financially, please keep in mind the all-important prayers for the speedy restoration to normal life in this area. As we have recently under-gone a large earthquake and suffered such little loss of life and limb, it is even more pertinent to the people in this area to render some aid in gratitude for our being spared a worse catastrophe.

I will plan to send the total sum collected by April 8. You may also bring the amount with you to the retreat. April 8 is the day of Passover and Papa Ramdas's Jayanthi (birthday), a doubly mean-ingful day.

Thank you for your due consideration and prayers.

David

Reverend Larry Koler, Cate Koler, and Jerry Trofimchuck.

March 23, 2001

I was ruminating just now: spiritually I am with Papa in bhakti, with Master in Raja, and with Mother in how she blended them. Also, like Mother, politically I like Ronald Reagan. I have found, over time, that I have become even more like her. Some say this is because I do whatever Mother does. I don't believe that is true. With diet, for instance, Mother thought most people do better eating some meat and fish. My own experimentations and research prove just that.

Morally, I think Mother took the right stand on the issues. With abortion, I started out on the choice side, now it's right to life. She voiced some thoughts I do not know about. She did not like Japanese culture; she thought Shivananda was the opposing force. I know that Mother would love individual Japanese people, but something about their culture she did not like. So, on some things I may differ, but so many other things are similar. I may be the most surprised at this, of all. I was reading Papa; he said Russia and America are the same. I don't believe that for a moment. In that, I am like Mother, and probably Master, who thought Korea was a holy war. Well, just random thoughts, but very interesting.

Most every day, I have tears of God. Tears of joy, tears of yearning, tears for the sorrows of the world. No soul can fathom all of that which we call God. But like crystal sugar, the soul may drop into the sea of consciousness, dissolve, and become one with the all-embracing love and Light of the Infinite. How timely, how loving God is. I speak to God, "O Lord, why do You delay, your Jivas cry out for You, yet You delay? Should You not rush to Your beloved ones and lift them in Your arms when they cry out so for You? Please, delay no longer, lift them into Your Presence. And look to their needs; they have a body and families. Will You not take some cares off their shoulders by seeing to their needs and comforts?" These things I say to God, and tears form on the outer edges of my eyes.

O Bhaktas, when God comes to you, be like the grateful lover that cannot believe that one so perfect or beautiful should love them. Be tender and soft-hearted, God, sensitive to each touch and caress; attentive to every word spoken, and let the delight of that Presence be our first, middle, and last, and you will know that unending Presence. Into that ocean of the Presence, you will willingly, gladly, surrender yourself in Holy Joy, Peace, Bliss, Consciousness.

Hari Om Tat Sat

Chapter Three
Life's Deeper Meaning

April: Standing at a Crossroads

Satsang Silent Retreat April 6–9, 2001
(Message sent out in February)

An Invitation to All!

The retreat begins on Friday evening and goes until mid-day Monday. "Silence is Golden," so the saying goes, and it is in silence that we will all come together. There will be a chance to talk and greet everyone on Friday evening until the orientation, and there will be time to say goodbye on Monday. In between time will be Golden Silence. During these retreat days, we will have time for meditation, silent walks, and classes on some new yoga methods.

The classes will have verbal presentations by teachers. The teachings will encompass a Raja Yoga technique that has been inspired while I have been here at Cloud Mountain. I have used the techniques myself, and taught them to some others with wonderful results. These techniques involve the breath and focused attention on the nadis, the subtle astral nerves that run throughout the body. The nadis carry the source of what makes life possible in all creation, prana, or life-energy.

By removing blockages in these nadi-channels, the life-force will be freed to flow naturally along its normal routes. Physical, emotional, and mental dis-ease creates blockages that affect our health and well-being. When we sit to meditate, these blockages create restlessness, fatigue, and other barriers to concentration. You will find that these simple techniques can make for profound changes in your physical, mental, and spiritual balance.

You will also have time for yourself: time for reflection, meditation, and writing; whatever helps to take you deeper into the silence. I think some may feel a little trepidation at spending this length of time in silence and meditation. You will not be asked to spend 24 hours of the day in sitting posture! You will have freedom of movement and time for walking in nature, etc. Wear comfortable clothing and you may bring seats for meditation, blankets, stools, chairs, whatever will make you comfortable. This will be an informative and relaxing time, and it may stretch you in some new ways, but that will be for the good.

If you would like to do some preparation beforehand, you may begin by creating three lists. The three categories are physical, emotional, and mental. These lists will be statements of those things you want to let go of in each one of these categories. The contents of these lists are for your eyes only, so you may feel free to be as thorough and open as you would like. Also, bring three plain envelopes, each one marked with a name of one of the categories. You will also have some time to work on these Friday night and Saturday, but it is good to spend some time beforehand formulating your thoughts for what you will be letting go of.

Carla Gold is helping to coordinate the retreat on our end. She will be giving you details about how to register and what you will need and what to expect. The cost for the three days at Cloud Mountain is $150 USD. This pays for your sleeping quarters (most of them are shared) and your meals. I think $50 a day is very reasonable. There is also a time to tip the staff generously at the end of the three days. There are a few single rooms. I would like to leave them for those who have special needs. For instance, I know there are those who have breathing machines at night that might disturb others. If the single rooms are not all needed by those in need, then you may indicate your preference for a single room; those will be determined by the first to request them. You will also be assigned some chores to do during the retreat for upkeep. I am asking that you plan to stay for the entire time of the retreat. I look forward to our time together, and in creating an atmosphere that will be informative, rejuvenating, healing, and uplifting.

In blessings of God and the Masters, David

April 6, 2001—Silent Satsang Retreat[12]

Dear Satsang Friends: David asked me to read this to you.

Entering into Silence

My dear friends, thank you for joining me on this weekend retreat. It is one of the dear privileges of life to be able to step out of everyday activity and direct the mind and all the life-energies toward the One, the source of all life.

Entering into silence is a way to withdraw the life-energy that is constantly being channeled out through the senses. One of the things noticed by being silent is how much energy goes into speech. But not just the act of speech; it is the thought (hopefully) that goes into speech, listening (hopefully) to what others say, and anticipating what you will say in response. All of this draws the mind and the energy outward. To refrain from speech and redirect that energy inwardly is a powerful thing to do.

Such powerful events can sometimes bring up anxiety. As with all sadhana, there is a sense, many times, that it is outside your conscious awareness, that coming into union with God brings with it mortal danger. The mortal danger of course is to the ego, which believes, rightfully so, that it will die. This feeling that going deeper into God is dangerous explains why you have so much resistance. When you are told that going to God fulfills all your desires, is unending Bliss, is the fount of Wisdom, what in the world would

---

12   See Appendix for the outline of the retreat schedule and to review the educational outline of the Babaji-inspired Clearing/Charging Exercises.

seem more important than that?! Yet, that is how you act when you allow distractions and excuses to keep you from entering into deeper states of communion with the Infinite.

Even when you are keeping your mind on God and serving Him in all you do, the energy of the body can have rajasic qualities. Living in a high level of activity, rubbing shoulders with others in constant anxiety, being in environments that bombard you with sights and sounds, can result in the energy body being activated with restless rajasic energy that floods the senses.

There is the story Swami Satchidananda told of the woman who came to see a great yogi. She approached the yogi with respect, bowed at his feet, and waited for him to respond. She waited quite a long time, but nothing doing, the yogi remained with an inward focus. At last, the lady devotee decided to leave. As she was doing so, the yogi stirred, and she turned back to him. After some time, the yogi was again focused on the world, and they began to talk. The lady devotee was a bit miffed that the yogi seemed to take his sweet time in acknowledging her presence, and said so! The yogi calmly explained that he had been sweeping. "What!" She exclaimed, "I did not see you sweeping, I only saw you sitting here staring at your navel." The yogi patiently went on to say that he had been out traveling the day before and picked up many things from the world that he was sweeping out of his mind! The lady was so full of rajasic energy she could not fully comprehend what the yogi was saying, but she was satisfied with this explanation and went on to ask her questions.

You may find that you will need time for sweeping as well! The echoes of worldly consciousness may haunt you: memories of yesterdays, anticipation of tomorrows, and your energy body revved up for action will follow you into your time in silence.

When I entered Cloud Mountain, I knew that there would be a period of adjustment. I had been traveling continuously beforehand, meeting with so many devotees and preparing to move; my thought and energy bodies were adjusted to the flow of activity.

There would certainly be a time of sweeping the energy and thought impressions of activity so that I might enter into deeper states of silence. Knowing these echoes would take their time, but would eventually settle down, gave a perspective that helped me to know there would be a time of transition.

Silence is not only about not speaking; it also means becoming inwardly quiet. When the echoes of activity begin to die down, the mind continues to spin its web of ideas. Silence is ultimately entering into a completely still state of mind. When the mind is still, all eternity reveals Itself to the Soul. When the body is so rapt in attention that nary a breath ensues, nor an eyelid blinks, and the power of the Name lifts the Soul into supernal realms, then one has entered into the deeper silence of God. Not an empty silence, but a silence filled with the power of all creation. This is not just poetic license, but a genuine experience that moves the Soul to both its depths and its heights of Being.

I am joyful to be with you for a time when this is our complete focus. Do not be discouraged if this exalted state does not come in a moment. Also, do not think it is so far away that you cannot attain it. Feel as if you are on a journey and your destination lies just beyond the next curve, yet if it is not there, you have the courage and tenacity to go to whatever lengths it takes, however many curves must be negotiated, until you come to your ultimate Self.

May God and the Masters be present with us as we seek that ultimate Union they so ardently desire for us.

Om Shanti, Shanti, Shanti. (The vibration of Peace, Peace, Peace) David

Deeper Meaning

Teachings from Paramhansa Yogananda[13]

"Sir, what should I do to find God?" a student asked. The Master said: "During every little period of leisure, plunge your mind into the infinite thought of Him. Talk to Him intimately; He is the nearest of the near, the dearest of the dear. Love Him as a miser loves money, as an ardent man loves his sweetheart, as a drowning person loves breath. When you yearn for God with intensity, He will come to you."

"I wish I had faith, Master," a man said. Parmhansaji replied: "Faith has to be cultivated, or rather, uncovered within us. It is there but has to be brought out. If you watch your life, you will see the innumerable ways in which God works through it; your faith will thus be strengthened. Few people look for His hidden hand. Most men consider the course of events as natural and inevitable. They little know what radical changes are possible through prayer."

Truth is never afraid of questions.

Try to realize you are a divine traveler. You are here for only a little while, then depart for a dissimilar and fascinating (astral) world. Do not limit your thought to one brief life and one small earth. Remember the vastness of the Spirit that dwells within you.

From the depths of silence, the geyser of God's bliss shoots up unfailingly and flows over man's being.

"In the absence of inward joy, men turn to evil," the Master said. "Meditation on the God of Bliss permeates us with goodness."

God is Eternal Bliss... His being is love, wisdom, and joy. He is both impersonal and personal, and manifests Himself in whatever way He pleases. He appears before His saints in the form each of them holds dear: a Christian sees Christ, a Hindu beholds Krishna or the Divine Mother, and so on. Devotees whose worship takes an

---

13   Paramhansa Yogananda. (1994). *Sayings of Paramhansa Yogananda*. Los Angeles, California: Self-Realization Fellowship (pp. 1–19). We could not locate the reference for the quote David used in this section, so we replaced it with this selection from Paramhansa Yogananda.

impersonal turn become conscious of the Lord as an infinite Light or as the wonderous sound of Aum, the primal Word, the Holy Ghost. The highest experience man can have is to feel that Bliss in which every other aspect of Divinity-love, wisdom, immortality—is fully contained. But how can I convey to you in words the nature of God? He is ineffable, indescribable. Only in deep meditation shall you know His unique essence.

April 12, 2001

My life is a dedication to God. In fumbling steps and in the precision of movement, I steer my life toward that precious Goal. My Great Guru set the course, direction, and Goal. She beckons me still from her deeper life. God awakened me to that purpose when my own will would have taken me to self-destruction, or at best, to a mundane, senseless life. I pretend no greatness, nor even goodness, for there is none other good than my Heavenly Father. Truly, I can say wholeheartedly that it is by God and Guru's Grace that I have found my Self.

I suppose it is natural to want all the world to share the sacred mystery that I feel, and it would be sheer arrogance to assume that no others do. But there is the songbird within that bursts into Divine verse and aches to share that deepest Intimacy, yet finds that longing all the more painful as its song disappears into the void. The pain is nothing but God's constant yearning for His children to forsake their gloom-drenched dream of creation long enough to join once again in Divine Union.

Songs of Angels are not just beautiful voices, but the thrill of vibration that resounds throughout all space and is caught and finds resonance in the receptive soul. Like strings and reeds of various instruments, the receptive places in the soul begin to quiver, but unlike the instruments, the soul feels the thrill of that glorious vibration. Thrill after thrill moves the soul, then settles into a quiet pool of peace. A whispered breeze of joy gently plays on the surface and then an inspiration of thought rises like a great whale out of the depths, revealing a portion of its massive body, then sinks down below the surface again. All Nature, all existence, is seen to thrill in the ecstasy as a single Life in various motions. The heart heaves under the fruit of the gifts it bears. The little mind is stilled, and the great Mind encompasses all of its own. No boundaries are there, circumference melts into infinitude. Peace, gentle, powerful, intimate, and expansive without limit exists simultaneously in total harmony. Divine Song moves in the ether in constant waves, but ears and eyes are dulled by muddied coverings of earthly pre-occupations, and those reeds and strings of the soul are dampened by material desire.

Oh, children of the Infinite, awaken to your vast mansion within! Let your soul sing in mystic vibration the thrilling tunes of your Soul's song. Dying to the vain preoccupation of separateness is to resurrect into your vast, dimensionless Self.

No birth, nor death, nor body am I,

I AM HE! I AM HE!

Blessed Spirit, I AM HE!

I AM HE! I AM HE!

Blessed Spirit, I AM HE!

Let this be our anthem, our affirmation, and our realization. Let us die in our surrender to the Infinite Creator, our Heavenly Father, and resurrect in our perfect oneness with God alone.

April 25, 2001
Crossroads

I stand at a crossroads. The question has come to me: am I to be married? The question has remained with neither a yes nor a no. Yes, means to partnership in this work for God. Whether married or not, it seems to me the balance of a partner is what I do best with. Is this of the highest truth or is this a temptation on the way up? I am told the stars and planets support the union. But stars and planets, while foretelling our pattern in life, do not include the moving sea of grace. Cannot God's Grace lift us beyond the push-and-pull of stellar systems? Yes, the answer rings clear and without doubt. What is God's wish for me? I stand on the crossroads; the logic of it does not find the answer, finding both roads logical. Obviously, I am feeling a pull in the direction of marriage, or the question would not exist at all. What is God's will? What will fulfill the highest good of all? What will help the work of the Masters best? For this answer, I will consult one who is the greatest expert I know in following God and Guru's will, Swami Satchidananda.

May: My Cells Fly Apart: I Climb a Mountain

May 5, 2001, 2 a.m.

Some great work is in process. For the last two days, tremendous movements of God's force are coming through this body. Awoke at 1:30 a.m., moon shining through the (body) window (interesting slip of the pen). Two days to a full moon. Much of the flow of energy over the last two days has been focused on the 5th and 6th chakras of the spine. Pain and tension have been terrific. The Clearing Breath has been a God-send. Thank you, Babaji. This morning, however, the vibration was coming from the 1st chakra. Like the whole ground shaking from some large and heavy machinery moving. Sometimes, I wonder how much this body can withstand? As past experience has proven, quite a bit. And what does it matter if the cells of this body fly apart as they sometimes feel they must? All is He! And, if that fulfills God and Guru's purpose, then so be it! It is my greatest privilege to give my life to them and for them.

Om Sri Ram Jai Ram

Michele Rogan on an early Spring walk.

Jonni Anderson.

Charmie Gilcrease with Jerry Trofimchuk,
Reverend Peter Schultz, and Yogacharya David.

May 12, 2001—Silent Satsang

Dear Satsang Friends: Greetings, David has asked me to read this to you.

Good Morning, everyone. We are meeting here once more in silence with the full attention on God. Last month, it was with great joy that I was able to bring to you the Clearing/Charging Exercises. I know, hearing from many, you have had wonderful experiences, and that is very gratifying. With continual application, I look forward to sharing with you all more ways of using these breathing exercises, and if in your practice you find new applications that you think others will find helpful, please feel free to write to me about them.

As we enter into what I think of as your real entry into spring, blooming azaleas and rhododendrons, it reminds me of the cycles of life and how, after every period of darkness, comes the promise of spring: new growth, flowering, and then the fulfillment of sweet fruit. So, in our spiritual journey, if during those times of darkness, we always know that spring will come, then we can always take comfort in that thought and persevere until that time comes.

And oh, the beauty of that spiritual fruit; how lovely, no words can describe, though poets and saints have tried to give wings to those words that will lift them to heaven. But words are of an earthbound nature and will never reach to those heavenly heights. We need not despair, though, for the heart and soul have no such restrictions; they are made of heavenly stuff. Like a booster rocket, the words of poets and realized ones may give lift to what is inside each of us. And where the words drop off and fall earthwards, our heart and soul may leave earth's gravity and enter into the boundless heavens.

I am glad to see each one here, those who made the effort to come. Realizing God is like that, there are many who say, "Oh I want to realize God more than anything." And then you see how many make the sincere effort to do so and the ranks begin to thin pretty quickly. Krishna tells us that out of many thousands, only a few, here and there, really seek Him out. And out of those who rise, and rise high, very few attain to Him in all His purity and perfection.

This is not because the way is barred, but due to human indifference. How easy it is to get sidetracked with worldly concerns and entertainments, but how much is given to our reach for God? This is not to say we are not to lead a life of balance, but really how much do we give to God each day? Without God, we would not be able to take a single breath, or have the power of thought or action. Yet, so many give God short shrift in their lives.

The strange thing about this is that attaining God will give us perfect Joy, Peace, and the inner direction for the attainment of all things perfect. As the song goes: "When will I ever learn, to live in God, when will I ever learn?" So that is why we are here: to learn to live in God. In the Temple of Silence, we learn that our roots are in God, inescapable. Once having our minds so purified in that Silence, we never again forget our roots, and the knowledge that the place we draw our life from, is in God. Then we are ever free, ever free.

Thank you for coming so we might seek out that source of life together. We will follow the same format as before. I think it would be nice to have lunch down on the deck of the hermitage cabin. For those who would like to stay, you may come down to the cabin from three till five.

Om Sri Ram Jai Ram Jai Jai Ram, David

May 13, 2001
Premanand

It came to me that if I were to ever choose a name, it would be Premanand, Bliss through Love. This thought led to a very unusual communication within me. I found myself communing with some other souls. They were sending thoughts to me and receiving mine as well. This all started when I was thinking Premanand. I don't know how much I can reconstruct it now, but I will try, as the communication was so swift and came in words and pictures, as well as feelings. The other beings I was communicating with I shall refer to as AC; it will get clear as to why. My thought was: Love is the way to bliss.

A.C.: Yes, love is the greatest thing.

David: Yes. (The feeling of great love between us, love heading into bliss; I was clear there were several of these souls.)

David: Who are YOU? (I felt they were from another planet when I asked this.)

A.C.: We are from a great distance.

David: Can you tell me?

A.C.: What you call Alpha Centauri.

David: How have we connected?

A.C.: We are communicating in love—that is how we are connected.

David: How did you know of me?

A.C.: Your teacher (Mother) told us.

David: You know of her?

A.C.: Yes—she has come and taught us here. (My sense was that this was recent and may be ongoing.)

David: She is all love.

A.C.: Yes.

David: Light.

A.C.: Yes.

David: Wisdom.

A.C.: Yes.

David: Will.

A.C.: Yes!

David: Ahhh… (Mentally bowing at Mother's feet. Then we all rose into ineffable love and bliss.)

David: And she told you about me?

A.C.: Yes—you have that love.

David: Yes—Premanand. (I repeated that word and it vibrated out with such power and uplifting force, over and over again.)

David: Are all on your planet such as you? (Attuned and filled with love and bliss.)

Pause

A.C.: Not all—but in general, we are attuned to this. (Some sadness, it seemed, about the ones who were not—but more like they were struggling to get there rather than any kind of preoccupation with war and strife as we have.)

David: How wonderful to have a planet attuned to Premanand (and the vibration of that name resonated deeply between us).

David: Why is your planet so advanced? Have you always been this way?

A.C.: Due to our position and realized ones (Masters—this was a picture and felt sense rather than words, so like most of this—the wording is my best attempt at description—although some came in definite mental words) guiding us.

David: Yes—where would we be without great ones leading us?

A.C.: Yes. (And the resonance of truth reverberated out and out.)

David: And the position of your planet? So, Sri Yukteswar was right—the position of a planet influences the evolution of that planet?

Pause

A.C.: Yes, position makes a difference.

David: Pause on my end to let this sink in. The image of the Centaur came to me (they knew it), complete with bow and arrow.

David: The image we have of your system is war-like?

A.C.: Yes—that is imagination from your civilization—though there was a time when we had war. (The feeling of the violence from this planet overcame me and the lack of real love by so many.)

David: Yes—it is lonely here at times; there are those who love, love a great deal—but it is not constant or pervasive.

A.C.: Yes, we can imagine—you may commune with us at any time.

David: How do I know this is not just in my mind?

A.C.: Feel the power of love. (The vibration was ringing in every cell of my body and I felt my mind extending over vast space, in communion with them.)

David: But it may be just my mind.

A.C.: What if it is—but we are real. (With these simple unequivocal words, the love rang out.)

David: I have such great love—I know—but I sometimes fall short of perfect purity.

A.C.: That will pass—your nature is love.

David: What do I need to do for my complete realization?

A.C.: Love, Premanand.

David: That is all I want.

A.C.: Yes.

(I could feel my awareness drawing back.)

David: Will I commune with you again?

A.C.: Whenever you focus on the heart—we will be there. (And as I focused on the heart, I felt the strength of that connection.)

Om Sri Ram Jai Ram Jai Jai Ram

May 13, 2001, continued:

A little while later, I listened to my Sunday tape of Mother speaking. Before I turned it on, I asked Mother to confirm this experience if it was true. During her talk, she spoke of being able to communicate with beings from other planets without having to leave her chair, no need for a spaceship. She had experiences that she could scarcely believe happened to her; in fact (at the time of her speaking in 1969), she still had a hard time believing all that had happened to her, but she knew it was true and it was what God had given to her. I could well understand her dilemma. Then I received this email with a quote from Papa that seemed to me another confirmation:

> There is no more potent power in the life of a human being than love which ennobles, enlightens, and sanctifies life. The heart imbued with this love feels for the suffering of humanity. It is this Love that freely forgives and returns good for evil, because it is born of the Divine Spirit and dwells within you. It is the expression of Truth— the Light that radiates from your purified, illumined soul.

Such a love is the ideal to be aspired for. The person in whom it has revealed itself is really holy. He is the channel of God's power and glory.

—SWAMI RAMDAS

Om Sri Ram Jai Ram Jai Jai Ram

May 28, 2001

God is not religion. Religions are so many approaches to scaling the mountain of God. Most often, the religion sets up a station at some distance, but within sight of the mountain, and says, "Worship God from here, safe within our compound."

But the realized ones have scaled the mountainsides. From viewpoints along the way, poems, music, and scriptures, they describe vistas that move and inspire the soul. Some souls climb so far and no more. Some climb to some height and descend to set up some temple of worship to say this is purer than the other temple-religions already established.

Some souls are too busy climbing to the top and simply disappear into the blue sky-clad ceiling above the mountain. A few souls climb to the top, and through inspiration guide others to scale those peaks. They inspire others to transcend the many false peaks, to continue on to their emancipation at the summit of the All in All.

What is required to scale the mountain that is God? The first requirement is sincerity, without it nothing can be done of real value. The next thing needed is an all-consuming desire for the peak; nothing less will do. The third necessity is a way-shower, one who has been there and makes the journey possible for the aspirant. Finally, what is needed is a willingness to give life and limb in the ascent and to never give up, to never give in!

If individuals look deeply, they will discover those attributes within and will overcome every obstacle encountered along the way. The path is strewn with aborted attempts, those who had too little of what is essential. Those are not lost expenditures of effort, though. Those climbers will one day resume their climb and the lessons learned from mistakes made will be deeply ingrained in the individual. Let us look at those vain attempts without haughtiness, lest we fall into a deep crevice ourselves. Rather, let us draw deeply from a lesson well learned by the example of another. Pride will blind us to the right choices; arrogance leads to misperception. But also, do not be dismayed by apparent difficulty. Our guide will see to it that our sincere effort will find fulfillment. Be of good cheer! Those who follow their Guru-guide, placing one foot in front of the other, will scale to that peak—keep your eyes ever glued on it, and your footsteps will naturally lead you closer.

At first, you may have to traverse through the trees of wilderness and only catch occasional glimpses of the peak. But then you will transcend the treeline and have continuous vision of the peak. This, however, is not the end of your journey. Continue up, moving beyond the beyond. Then is God seen without limit as the All in All. Be not afraid, but tread on and on and the goal must surely be yours.

This life in God, in service of God, in the love of God is the greatest life, and most interesting as well. I am returning to this abode of silence after a stay in Seattle, a trip to Victoria and Hornby Island, and a short stay in Maple Ridge. As usual, there is a slight twinge of fear on entering this solitude after being with devotees for awhile.

Upon my return, I had some lovely letters waiting for me. I sat down to read some, and it was nearly an hour later when I felt a powerful draw inward. I came in from the deck and settled in my chair. I felt a terrific, sharp pain between the shoulder blades. I closed my eyes and saw on that part of my body an astral creature. I have dealt with these before and entered into dialogue with it. This entity had burrowed its "claws" deep into my back, full of anger-hurt-pain. I thought at first it had come from someone who sent a letter, so I asked where it came from. It said it came from X, who I saw last night and had an interview with. It fit the feeling X sometimes has, so I accepted that as true. I thought to invite it to the Light, but it felt that it did not want to go. I said, "When you attached to me, you must have known I am only of Light; therefore, you must have wanted that." It said yes, that was true. So, I said, "Tell me your story; how did you become so contorted with pain?" It showed me glimpses of horrific scenes, terrible to see, easy to understand how the hurt turned to anger.

"Would you like to be held?" It said, "Yes." I held it and the pain in my back subsided some. "The same Light you feel in me is available by releasing yourself to the Light, but I will hold you as long as you live." Holding it as a mother holds a baby in her arms. "How long have you suffered?" I empathized. It relaxed a bit. I had a craving for a cookie and had some. It came to me these creatures crave stimulants like sugar, not for the taste but for the energy rush. How interesting. The pain is still a bit in my back; it does not trust me and thinks I might send it away. I will not. It is in need of love, acceptance. It was not in a very lovable form when it came, and its pain is tremendous, but I know that love and acceptance will heal all wounds.

It has come to me for this purpose, and I will give it what it is craving, like a mother gives a bottle to a babe, until it can imbibe the Light directly; then it will be free in God. If I had rejected it, it most likely would have gone back to X. In this way, God has me do this work for Him. You never know from one moment to the next what form that work may take: praying for one, counsel to another, momentary help, being playful, loving, understanding, or healing an astral entity. "Oh, for the love of God," say some. Yes, indeed, for the love of God all may be redeemed and brought back to the Light. Victory to God, victory to the Light.

Om Sri Ram Jai Ram Jai Jai Ram

May 28, 2001, continued:

The pain came back doubled! This sentient form that has been attached to me for its salvation wishes for me to know of its suffering. And great was its suffering. Torture, humiliation, helplessness is all part of its history. To have patience and equanimity in suffering is a key to gaining self-mastery; then the affirmation came: "Pleasure and pain are the same to the yogi."

After that came Papa's affirmation, "Bliss and pain are the same to the yogi." I realized with greater clarity how Papa raised the realization that pleasure and pain are the same to the yogi to a higher level. When the recognition that pleasure and pain are the same, one may view both in third person as an observer. But Bliss is in the nature of God. When pain and Bliss are connected through direct realization, one moves from the dual nature of the observer and the observed to a monistic view that Bliss and pain are the same and both are expressions of God's nature, therefore one with God. That is a tremendous truth to be realized. I encouraged this entity in the affirmations, and it began to loosen up. Throughout the afternoon, the stabbing pain came in torrents. Throughout it all, I was patiently letting it work itself out in me. Then the idea came that the next step was to open it all up to God. It is our self-imposed isolation that makes us suffer. I then encouraged the entity to say with me, "Lord, comfort me, help me. Lord, comfort me, help me." Over and again, we said this, and it provided much greater movement. Breathing became unified.

I then saw we were in a hospital setting, the entity in a hospital bed. I sought the agreement of the staff that I would be praying for this patient and that I might be there for an extended time, 16 or 18 hours, and they were not to disturb me; they agreed. Since that time, I have held the entity's hand, both of us breathing. At times I have felt the entity almost completely absorbed in the Light, which is what the hospital staff are there to help with. My commitment is to be there as long as it needs me, making this transition together. The hospital setting is responding to the need of the entity, seeing that its wounds have been properly cared for from its own human perspective. When it has received the caring it has yearned for for so long, then it will gradually, of its own accord, allow itself to enter the Light.

Om Sri Ram Jai Ram Jai Jai Ram

Carla (Gold) Hickenbottom, Honor (Wells) Baldigara,
Lois Hickenbottom, Jerry Hickenbottom on Hermitage deck.

June: The Masters Visit and Marriage

June 2, 2001

The one I have been working with to go to the Light merged last night into the Light. This has been a unique experience for me. I have delivered astral entities into the Light before, and I have helped individuals release parts, or aspects, of themselves into the Light, but the work of releasing parts of an individual in their relationship with that wounded part of themselves is new. In other words, I acted as a guide or a midwife for the individual and the part they were working with. In this case, an agreement was made that I would take that part from the individual. In this case, the part was too much for the individual to work with; the pain was too much, the psychology was too much, yet that part was ready to merge with the Light. It was not a conscious decision on my part at the time, yet I know that I accepted this on an inner level. Now the part is merging, and it merged into the Light. There is still a shadow, a memory-idea, that hovers about, but this will gradually dissipate. God's work! How wonderful.

Yesterday, the deep drone of the bee reverberated throughout my body; simultaneously, the higher-pitched flute emanated from the left side of my head, on the back side just above the medulla. That high-pitched sound is traced to my left shoulder blade area from where it seems to emanate, at least what I am aware of at this time. The bumblebee has been shaking my whole body to the core. Tremendous power has been moving through. Inwardly, the voice of Babaji tells me I must expand my consciousness in response to my questions. I have done the Clearing Breath with the affected area, the aura of this body, and I see the Cosmic "Breath" as alternating Light and dark. This is the razor's edge.

How are we to understand humans? Are they worms, devoid of light and understanding, clinging to the dark moist earth? Nay, humans are not worms, ingesting dust and muck and excreting the same. Humans are Divine. It is none other than the Divine Spark that animates their being—never to be full of darkness and error. Rather, the Divine Spark climbs in realization from the vantage point to the nest. At first seeing a narrower representation of truth, then climbing to a new vantage point and seeing with greater clarity.

Thus, from lesser to greater, Truth grows in understanding. Look not at the narrowness of view, but see yonder spark of brilliance! Slowly, perhaps haltingly at times, do they climb, but climb they surely must; must we all. O sons and daughters, see what makes you Sons and Daughters of God! When you accept the anointed One of God, that wonderful Light of realization into your heart, mind, and soul, that spark turns into a blaze. That blaze not only guides your way, but will be the guide for others as well. See the sparks all over the world ignite into blazes until a conflagration lights the earth and thrills of ecstasy makes of this a heaven on earth.

Om Om Om

June 5, 2001

The purification has been terrific over these past days. Intense pain with tremendous power running through me. It feels as if every cell is on electrical fire. I have been reading *The Life of Swami Vivekananda*. He was truly one of the greats in India. He reminds me so much of Master, both Bengalis, both fired with an energy I can only marvel at. Both brought fundamental changes to the West. I feel the power of his vision upon me, a freedom and universality of religion. It seems that my circumference is expanding beyond my own realization and that of select devotees, but it also includes the universalization of religions. It is a broader, more encompassing work than before. I stand at the doorway, and I glimpse at something much larger, larger than any individual, but a movement in consciousness. To universalize Christianity would help set this world free. I don't know what part I may have, but I feel my Gurudev's footprint on it. I surrender to the Infinite; I surrender to Divine Will; I surrender at the feet of my blessed Gurudev. Hari Om, Tat Sat

It has been said by some in the East that Christianity has many great truths, but no truths as great as the Vedas. While the Vedas are, no doubt, the most complete teachings on the full range of spiritual experience, nevertheless, Christianity, and in particular Jesus' sayings and life story, have every great teaching embodied in them.

Bhakti Yoga may be summed up in his quote of the old testament, "Hear O Israel, the Lord our God, the Lord is one." (Deuteronomy 6:4) "Thou shalt love thy Lord thy God with all thy heart, with all thy strength and with all thy soul," and the next commandment, to "love thy neighbor as thy self." (Matthew 22:37–39) These are the two greatest commandments.

Karma Yoga may be summed up in the saying: When you fed the poor man, visited one who was in jail, what you have done for the least of me, you have done for me. Not only service to all, but this saying speaks to the universal vision of God being in the heart of all. (Matthew 25:38–40)

Jnana Yoga was spoken of when separating the goats on the left side from the sheep on the right side, and only the sheep enter the Kingdom. Right discrimination is necessary to live life. (Matthew 25:33–34)

And Raja Yoga is spoken of when Jesus said, "Make thine eye single and thy whole body shall be filled with Light." (Matthew 6:22) As well as when he said, "Even as Moses lifted up the serpent in the desert, so must the son of man." (John 3:14) Raja techniques of awakening the kundalini and keeping the focus on the ajna are key to Raja Yoga.

In this brief summary, we can discuss the breadth and beauty contained in these few sayings. They are but a small sampling of what is contained in the sayings and life of Jesus, the Anointed One.

A new life is coming to Christianity, a universal vision that recognizes the fundamental unity of all the major religions. No longer will humanity be many divided rooms of religion, each saying I alone am right, all others are wrong! A new Light of understanding is on the horizon. The day is dawning, and it promises unparalleled peace and harmony.

June 7, 2001

Pain and ecstasy, pain and ecstasy. Some lives are like that. Not lived for themselves alone, they pay the price for others. Why a price? Why does a price need to be paid? There is the exacting Law of Karma, and the balance has to be accounted for before one can leave the transaction behind. So, the price must be paid.

My dearest Mother, my Gurudev, paid such a price. Ramakrishna Paramhansa paid such a price. Many are the great masters who paid the price. And what did they want in return? For devotees to hear the call and make the effort; in making a little effort, a lot of progress can be made, for the price has been paid. What a gift. What selfless service. What love.

I was drawn in and made to pray: "O Lord. I would dedicate this year of tapasya to X, for him to keep the purity of his soul. The world needs pure souls. Where else will they find one such as his? You have put the prayer into me." This answer came back, "Yes, be it so, as you have asked."

I have some rest now from that past torment.

June 8, 2001

Staying connected to a devotee: the devotee is able to flower when hanging on the branch of a tree. The branch is the Guru-teacher; the tree is Universal Life. There are many branches in the tree that bring forth fruit, of this there is no doubt, and the fruit of one branch is as sweet as another. After the initial flowering, the honeymoon stage, the flower drops off to reveal a little green nub. Through the season, that green nub grows in size, but remains hard. Towards the end of its cycle, it becomes very soft and sweet. The longer it hangs there, the softer and sweeter it gets. For any who taste that ripened fruit, there is nothing better in the world!

June 14, 2001

The thought: "There are thousands of Shivas, thousands of Krishnas resounding in me."

Lately, the last few days, I have been lifted into a clarified vision. It does not come in a trance-like state, but fully conscious, although material and energetic realms and thought realms recede to a great extent. The force of attention is from a great height, not above this world, but above all created worlds. Looking down from this height, I am also aware of All-Consciousness, so I have a focal point of consciousness and feel myself to be one with all, simultaneously. The clear realization is that down below are the forms of Babaji, Shiva, Krishna, and many pure manifestations of God-incarnates.

Those forms are as so many dangling puppets, expressing the will of the All-Consciousness. It is very matter-of-fact in my mind in recognition of how this all works, yet I have a sacred reverence for this wondrous expression. It is awe-inspiring in its breadth of expanse and purity. For the matter-of-fact feeling is one of total clarity and stillness—a stillness felt even as the activity of expression is also felt. It is the Unmanifest looking upon the manifest as its very own, yet aware that the unmanifest resides separate and apart—Nirvikalpa-Sankalpa.

June 16, 2001

This evening from 7:30–9:00 p.m., I had a supernal visit from Mother and Master. I was looking out the window, seated in my chair. It is the window above Mother and Master's images. With eyes open, I "saw" Mother at the window as if she had walked up the steps and looked inside. It was not seeing with these two physical eyes, but with the third eye. I could see there were others with her, but there was only a sense that they were para-param gurus, as if they had come for a visit. The thought came: "How thrilling it would be if that really happened!" and then thinking, "Would I talk?" and I knew I would keep my vow.

Thinking in this manner, a strong thought came to me, "They are here." Again, I "saw" Mother out the window. I focused on my third eye with the two physical eyes yet open and there she was. Oh, what Bliss to bow at those feet! I needed to settle my mind a bit to have a clear connection. If I had too much mental excitement, my mental warrior would become jumpy. What joy, what mirth she has. When she laughs, I feel it in my own belly like rippling water. I asked her about many things; she confirmed all my experiences, including the Alpha Centaurians. She indicated it was my advancement here in silence that made the connection possible, as well as my connection with her now.

She said as long as I was in harmony with my Self, she was happy. She also confirmed that she had sent Carla to me, and she sanctioned the marriage. I seemed to be anxious about mistakes I had made. She reiterated that when I am in harmony with the Self, she is happy. I sensed there was someone with her; it was Master. At first, I could only see the hem of his orange robe and his deer skin shoes; he was so vast.

I wondered whether I would be able to see him, and then he assumed a "normal" size. Again, I had to work to make my mind still, so I closed my eyes to help me focus to see him clearly. I asked him many questions. He confirmed I had his sanction to initiate others into Kriya; he had given Mother that sanction, and she had given it to me. He was pleased. He said that the organization had made mistakes, but it was necessary to reform it, and it had played an important function. He showed me his Autobiography and all they did, and indeed I could see all the good.

In their present forms, Mother and Master are pure joy, and the little bumps of the world are very little to them. Indeed, although their compassion is there, and clarity of thought is there, they are focused and are bringing others into that joy. When that joy erupts, as it often does, it starts to vibrate in the belly and goes out from them resonating in the belly region of all others. It is delightful and spontaneous, quite hard to describe but a unique experience. Oh, the joy of these moments. Occasionally, I thought, "They are going now," but they seemed quite leisurely in their visit. Mother was quietly on my left side and Master was right in front. A few times, I directed myself to Mother but she seemed to fade when I focused on her, and when I focused on Master, he was very clear. I got the message that with Master being there, he was to be my focus. They both were very reassuring to me. I was to keep my mind on God and all would be well. I felt so insignificant before them; but then I straightened myself up and came into my full self and the whole picture came into much clearer focus.

It was clear to me they did not need, nor want, me to assume an inferior position. My love and respect are automatic, and I had no temptation to be over-familiar with either one of them, so everything went on smoothly. Overall, I felt them reassuring me on every major point, and encouraging me to continue. I asked Master about Swamiji, who instantly came into the picture and Master said he liked him very much. I asked about Sai Baba, and said I felt some reservation (as he has been a test for me) and Master said to listen to my intuition. Just now, as I was writing, my solar plexus was becoming very painful and I had to set down my pen and go inside. Master wanted to give me a blessing. He said, "As I initiated, so do thou initiate," and he put his thumb on my third eye point.

I spent some time absorbed in his blessing (about the last hour).

I asked about Kriya and he assured me that what we had was more than enough, and we knew the power of Guru-shakti (my words, he was just showing it to me). I asked whether to go into the other Kriyas or initiate others into them. He looked into the distance for a while and said there may be occasions in the future.

I asked about my current Kriya (that I am too full already and can't do more) and he said that was fine and I was being shown alternatives by Babaji.

I asked about the painful, difficult time I have had in all the spiritual experiences I have undergone and if I was doing something wrong. He said, no, that was the path I chose, and I was helping others by going that way. He showed me individuals who have advanced as a result. I said I thought those who advanced were due to Mother's great sacrifice. He beamed and said that she had helped the whole world, and the fall of communism came to my mind.

I said, "She suffered so." He said he had been there; he knew, but the benefits to the world were great.

So many answers, so much joy! What perspective, wisdom, and Bliss. My cup runneth over. What blessings. What blessings pour upon my head. I feel baptized in their holy spirit. The body sanctified, if not just a little worn out!

Om Master, Om Mother, Om Infinite Spirit, and Papa dancing in delight! Om Amen

June 23, 2001—Silent Satsang

Dear Satsang Friends: Greetings, David asked me to read this to you.

Good Morning everyone, I am filled with joy to see you here. The fact that you have made the effort to be here today demonstrates your sincerity for realization. Only the utmost effort will bring us to that sacred goal. That reminds me of a story.

During my days as a Boy Scout, I had a Scoutmaster I loved very much. His name was Gordon Rausch. In fact, he owned the house where Jerry and Lois live now. He was a veteran of WWII and in combat, a strafing Luftwaffe plane fired a bullet that hit his eye. After his recovery and ensuing partial blindness, he went back to the front. Amazingly, his other eye was also shot, creating partial blindness in that eye as well. He went on to get a college education and was a civil engineer with the most beautiful printing I've ever seen.

Anyway, back to my story. Mr. Rausch went hunting one time for bear. He had a guide for this trip to help him to bag a bear. They spent several days camped out and scouting the woods to find a bear. For over a week they went out daily, and finally the time to return had come. No luck for the hunters; good luck for the bears. On the way back, Mr. Rausch was lamenting the fact that he had not been successful in getting a bear. The guide kindly explained, "You have to remember, you are just a part-time hunter; he is a full-time bear!" I don't know how much consolation that was, but it was the truth!

In order for us to be successful in getting our realization, we cannot be part-time hunters/devotees; we must become full-time in order to bag our prey! Nothing less will do. The nature of what we hunt will allow for nothing less. Do not be discouraged if you go out hunting a few times and are not successful. It is better to set a trap; we should use some bait and wait, rather than running all over the mountainside. Inside that trap, place your sincere desire and your full-hearted attention. God cannot resist such delicacies and will come and eat you up! But when he digests you, you will become Him! And thus, when your prey bags you, you will have Him. This is the easy, simple way to your realization.

So, become a full-time hunter in your aspiration for realization. Divinize your whole life and let your body-temple become a house of prayer. You will know un-ending, ever-new Joy. Wisdom will cross your threshold in search of you! Never will you regret the effort you make at realizing your oneness with your Infinite Beloved.

All goes well here for me. With the completion of nine months, I am three-quarters of the way in my time here. At a certain point in our journey to God, all becomes a constant unfoldment of Divinity within and without. Every cell of our Being becomes saturated with a Divine nectar. Every experience, both common and sublime, is embossed with certain knowledge that all is sacred. Good and bad, high and low, pleasure and pain are inextricably connected with one Consciousness, one Life, one intelligence, and one love. Nothing stands apart from that beatific knowing; thoughts come in a steady stream from hidden springs of intuitive inspiration. What remains as the individual "I" stands in awe as a conscious witness to Higher Forces at work. Yet, that separate self feels intimately, nay lovingly, connected to the Whole.

Then the separate "I" effortlessly blends into the Universal "I" and expands the identity of "I" to a boundless nature. No boundary or circumference is noticed in ever-expanding, ever-motionless Spirit. The tiny human heart seamlessly becomes infinite Divine inebriation. The little human mind becomes still, and its contents flood out into joyous purity. At one and the same time, one is the same as ever, and yet totally transformed. No stranger in a strange land here; a homecoming to a beloved child makes one at ease and in sacred awe.

My friends, my beloved, be not a stranger to your real Self. Make the effort today and every day that you may know Who and What you really are. Do not tarry on side-roads. Make straight your way to the Infinite, claim your inheritance as your very own and enter your

Father's Kingdom. You will not regret it; rather, you will be amazed you dallied so long.

Thank you for coming today, for bringing your part of God and helping us to be whole and complete. You are ever in my heart and soul, yet our joy is increased when we come together in body and spirit. May God and the Master's blessings be upon us today as we strive to know their Presence. May they be present with us today and share their joy, making it our own joy.

Hari Om, Tat, Sat, David

We will follow the same pattern as before: chanting at the top of the hour and meditation for the rest of the hour. Lunch from noon until 1:00. Since the weather is nice, we can all eat on the deck of the hermitage cabin, if you like. We will circumambulate the property with Ram Nam and close with Oms and prasad on return. For those who would like—we can continue some quiet time at the hermitage cabin from 3:00 to 5:00 p.m.

Om Namaste

June 29, 2001

I have eyes only for my Guru's feet. The straps of her shoes are of purest gold, the hem of her robe is of the darkest blue, and the color of her feet are pure white. O Divine Mother, focusing upon your feet, I become absorbed into your Being. No beginning, no end! You are the All in All. Your doorway of gold, blue, and silver is my entry into heaven. Your blessed grace has given me eyes only for your sacred feet.

THE CROSS AND THE LOTUS JOURNAL —JUNE 2001

Dear Friends,

Once again, Silent Sacred Greetings. How lovely to be able to connect with you once again through the pages of the Journal. The month of June is the completion of nine months of this time of mouna, silence. I cannot tell you what a sense of privilege there is for me to be able to serve God and Gurus in this way.

During the month of April, we had our three-day retreat. I want to thank all who came for making it a wonderful success. It has long been my wish to have a retreat in silence and meditation. One of the advantages of group meditation is that it stretches our capacity for sitting in concentration. I remember early in my sadhana days sitting with a small group in Bellingham for an hour each week. The discipline of sitting for that hour helped me to stretch out the times when I meditated on my own. To have those times when we have satsang, when we sing and meditate together, really acts to support us in going deeper into those interior spaces.

It was with great joy that I anticipated making the Clearing/Charging Exercises available during the retreat. While these breathing techniques are simple, it is their design of integrating the breaths to the three bodies and the nadis and their integrated use in meditation, that makes them especially powerful tools for change. The observation sheets filled out by participants confirmed my view that these Breathing Exercises will make significant differences in the lives of sadhakas. This confirmation made the joy complete. We will have Clearing/Charging classes on Hornby Island in October and in Prince Rupert in November. If there is interest, we can plan more Clearing/Charging Classes in other locations for the future.

As I mentioned before, this month of June is the completion of nine months in silence, leaving just three months here at Cloud Mountain. There have been times when this period of silence has seemed long, other times very short. Both of these notions pass like clouds overhead, noticeable, but not dominant. What is dominant is the inner Self. As a silent sentinel, it watches the coming and going of all events. In the Self lies the knowledge of the Ever-Existent (Sat), a depth of Peaceful Joy (Ananda), and an awareness that never sleeps (Chid). This awareness, of course, is not unique to me. This is the verity known by saints and realized beings of all religions; it is universal and equally present throughout the world. The realization of the Self is available to all and provides the solid ground upon which we can build our life.

One often hears, "This is a time of change." It really does seem to be a time of change for many. The oppositional force always figures into times of change. This oppositional force creates temptation, destruction, and challenge on every front.

As with the dual meaning of the Chinese character for crises, which means danger and opportunity, so do these times represent potential for growth as well as a time of temptation. Temptation calls forth from us strength and clarity of vision in order to stay on the path; destruction sweeps away past negativity and moves us to build anew with purity of purpose; challenges make us turn to the One for our sole source of strength and guidance.

Creation, we are told by the wise, is always in flux. When the foundation stones of our life are built solely on things of the world, then we are truly standing on shifting sands. The moment there is a change in our outer world, we are thrown into imbalance. Whether that shifting foundation is built on changing body conditions, relationships, or physical surroundings, we find that the instability of that foundation creates tension in us, between hoped for gain and fear of loss.

Does this mean, then, that to build a solid foundation we strip our lives of everything material: no possessions, relationships, that we pour ashes on our food and avoid all the world? The answer is no. Our guru lineage has shown us that we can lead a spiritual life and live in the world: marriage, children, home, and business activities, all are left intact. In fact, as Mother has taught us: living a life of balance, we may enjoy the fruits of this world.

Because God is life, all of life, we can enjoy beautiful things, our friends and family, career, and work in the world. So, what is the difference then, between those who have built their life on a solid foundation of what is permanent, real, and true, and those who have built on faulty ground? The difference is most clearly evident in the nature of our thoughts. The solid foundation comes from seeking God first, loving God first, and seeing God as All in All. When these attributes have become our state of mind, then we will know we have built our lives on the solid ground of spiritual principles.

To seek God first means we yearn for realization of God more than things of the world. As humans, we have our desires. We naturally desire happy relationships, success in worldly interests, and material plenty. The test is: can we say in our heart of hearts that we yearn more for God than we yearn for those things of the world? As we move through the world, can we say, "O God, not as I will, but Thy will be done?" Our gateway to freedom is in our seeking out and surrendering to Divine will and guidance.

To love God first means that the treasure of our heart is always in God. Attaining many of the worldly things we yearn for, we find our love goes to our feeling of possession; we have love for people, places, and things, even ideas. But, do we love God first? Does our mind dwell on God: as a lover's mind dwells on his beloved, a miser for his money, like a driven man's passion for power? Love brings commitment, that is why so many stand hesitant to fully enter the spiritual path; they sense the all-consuming power of that commitment. To love God first connects us with the fount of love itself, and it is limitless. Limitless love will be the indication we have put our love of God first.

To see God as All in All means the practice of the Universal Vision. In our journey to God, we have to begin with an idea, a vision of where we are going. We know in the beginning the mental affirmation that God is All in All is not the same as the reality of realized experience. But, we must begin this way to steer the mind in the right direction by seeing God as the All in All, and affirming His attributes: He is all wisdom, all love, all light, etc. Realized masters have told us the world is God; it is the living substance of God-stuff. To practice seeing God first is to mentally affirm and see God in every person, place, and situation. Seeing God first will help attune the mind to the Universal Vision and usher us into the Kingdom of Heaven. Gradually, the mental practice of affirming and seeing God as our All in All gives way to the Reality of the Universal Vision for which we long. Knowing our oneness with the Divine Life that pervades all creation and beyond will make us know we have the Universal Vision.

In these times of change, we are assured we have a secure place on which to stand and live a life of balance. Through seeking, loving, and seeing God first, we will be directed and comforted every step of the way. Through putting God first, we will be guided through temptations, find peace and surety in times of destruction; we will possess the highest-quality materials for new construction after the destruction of the old, and we will have the strength and power to meet all challenges.

May you be blessed by God and the Masters to have the clarity of purpose to always make God first and live your life in perfect balance. In God, Christ, and Gurus.

Out of India (and back again)

During my first visit to India, Swami Vishwananda predicted I would return to India many times. Since that trip, I had not felt any calling to return until now. It seems the land I think of as the place of my spiritual roots is drawing me once again. This intended trip is planned for January through March of 2002. The two pilgrimage sites of Anandashram and Dwarahat (Babaji's cave) are on the agenda.

As my life is not my own, if called I must go. Of course, I will take you all with me in my heart and soul (a trip for you without the heat and humidity!). One thing about living this life in God, I am never at a loss of surprise or wonder about what is to come next! I feel in my bones that God is preparing the way for something wonderful. Let us all hear the call, "Prepare the way, the Kingdom of God is at hand!" David.

Carla (Gold) Hickenbottom.

Yogacharya David and Carla (Gold) Hickenbottom at Cloud Mountain.

Happy Birthday, Michele.

July: Universal Consciousness

July 1, 2001

I had a moment of nostalgia for the familiar company of friends and past times. What is nostalgia? I reasoned sometime afterward that it is the longing for a feeling from the past. Past, present, and future are all within me; when focused on such a feeling, why should I feel separate from it? Separation is an illusion; therefore, a fallacy. All thoughts, feelings, and sensations are consciousness that exist now; therefore, there is no separation, no longing, and no nostalgia. I connected with loved ones in my consciousness, felt their perfect love, which is not often duplicated in outer reality, and felt complete. In ten months, having this nostalgia is extremely rare, as most times I have no sense of separation. This came for a moment, but it is good that it came. Like rooting up an underground weed, it gives me a chance to throw it in the fire!

July 4, 2001

THOUGHT FOR THE DAY

OM SRI RAM JAI RAM JAI JAI RAM

Solitude is an invaluable help to keep the mind ever in
tune with the indwelling infinite Reality.
It is something like recharging the exhausted battery of life, so that
life's mission in the world may bear ampler and more glorious fruit.
May the Lord make you a supreme instrument in His
hands for the magnificent service to humanity.
In fact, service is the keynote of a selfless and dedicated life.
The spirit of love and service daunts every
danger and boldly faces and endures hard toil and
great suffering, which it meets on the path towards
its fulfillment. Trials and obstacles only steel the will
for the purpose.

—SWAMI RAMDAS

Swami Ramdas (Papa).

July 6, 2001
When two souls come together, they are as two flames. The flames throw out the "Light," the light intersects and comingles, intermixing their light without claiming whose light is whose, only illuminating. This mixing of one another's light goes on uninterruptedly at the point of their meeting, yet the two flames remain ever separate and unique.

July 7, 2001
God's song rings throughout eternity. O Lord, I am no scholar, for my mind dwells only on You. I am not a doer of great deeds, for my body sits in rapt attention, caught in Your embrace. I have no words, except the ones you say and write through me. I am an idler, without movement, thought, or desire. If there is any merit in me, it has come about by Your Grace; I have placed myself at Your feet. That alone is of worth and that is all due to Your Will.

July 9, 2001
Sweet is your remembrance. You make Your Presence known in innumerable and indescribable ways. Your vibration touches on etheric nerves that quiver in delight. The Being's cells begin to vibrate in a delightful harmony that spreads to more and more cells, and then is gone. You cannot be contained or controlled, only

observed with keen appreciation, then a wave of peace flows over the body cells, akin to physical pleasure, but vastly more varied, subtle, intimate. The music of Aum rings localized on the back-left side of the head through a large opening there; the sound-vibration pours through. When the mind focuses its attention there, that sound becomes Limitless in dimension. Thrill after thrill plays through the body cells, the astral nerves, and the Idea Body sweeps and swirls, explodes and becomes as finite as an atom in an amazing and delightful dance of subtlety.

Constant is the play of Bliss and its many-faceted expressions. Yet, for all its beauty and delight, One beyond that Bliss, is the Observer, ever-conscious but never attached to the ever-changing ever-new play of Divine delight. Aum Aum Aum Amen

July 10, 2001

One week ago today, July 3, 6:00 p.m. I was suddenly in the midst of some tremendous grief. It enveloped me for some time. It came from no discernable source, and I believed it was not mine, but came from some outside source. Today, in the early afternoon, my solar plexus became very painful. Again, no discernable source within me, but the pain has been excruciating. It lasted in its full intensity until past 6:30. I was doubled-up in pain most all that time, I lay down for some time. The idea came that this pain belonged to the world. When this thought came, I perceived the world contained in my stomach cavity. As soon as this occurred, I had relief from the excruciating pain for the first time in six hours. I then wondered if there was some connection between the occurrences on the 3rd and today? Nothing is clear about that, only the question is there. I write only what I experience and what I have realized and do not embellish or say more than I have realized. Many would say these are imaginings, and if I did not have these experiences, I might be one of them! I only say what is true; that is enough.

July 10, 2001, continued:

Today in America, a version of Jnana is what is popular. American Buddhism is focused on self-awareness without any connotations of God or religious commitment and with some implicit promise of tantric powers. Compassion is an empathic feeling of sympathy for suffering. Much of this movement is high-minded. However, the power of transformation often falls short of human capacity. It is a relatively "safe" path, promised without the deeper notions of surrender. The Bhakti Spirit is noticeably less a part of the current popular wave.

The popularity of Krishna Das' devotional music is the first hint at a popular swing towards Bhakti. The power of Bhakti has yet to see an ascendency. I believe when it does, its power will eclipse the Jnani movement of today. Surely the heart must respond in a way that the mind alone cannot. It is a lovely thought to think of thousands in Kirtan feeling the uplifting vibrations lifting heart, mind, and soul like a rising tide, lifting all boats and making all to float in a Sea of Bliss. O Ram, will we live to see that day? How lovely to contemplate when God's names are sung with devotion and change this world!

I have often thought of the large sporting venues filled to capacity: all singing God's names. O Infinite beloved, what a world this would be to have such events widespread, and then to empty such arenas for all to go out and perform seva, selfless service! I go mad at the thought of such a world. Love, laughter, high-mindedness, self-restraint, purity, holiness all emanating like an aura of purest Light! What beauty, what change, what perfection! What is to stop such a thing? With the Divine Will, a sweep of Divine current goes out and touches hearts, minds, and souls everywhere, awakening them to their true life's purpose. Bewildered at their own past emptiness and misdeeds, they see clearly now their goal of sacred living. Dedicated now to living and realizing the fullness of their spirit, they become as new, fresh-born, innocent. The lion lays down with the lamb in peace. All Power to the Infinite, all-pervasive Spirit. All glory to Its Name.

Hari Om, Hari Om, Hari Om

July 10, 2001, continued:

Pure Spirit sports as the three qualities of creation: sattva, rajas, and tamas. Just as a king, his prime minister, and the king's messenger are all part of the royal house, yet each displays different functions to the world. The proper king is always acting for the good of his subjects and the kingdom. He is the father, ruler, judge, statesman, and friend to one and all. Everything good about being king is embodied in a righteous ruler; he is sattva.

The proper king is the repository for all virtue. Not only does he stand for all that is good, but he opposes that which would bring degradation to the kingdom or its inhabitants. The king remains regal and unmoved by those with selfish motives; his view is always to the health and well-being of his kingdom. Thus, he remains unentangled with petty jealousies and always points to the higher way. He is sattva.

The prime minister is involved in running the administration of government. He exercises his power, gives his judgment, and dispenses favors or punishments. He is all activity and efficiency but does not require the softening attributes of father, statesman, and friend that the king has. He is rajas.

Next comes the king's messenger. He is a fellow of low ambition and yet lower expectation. If sent on an errand, he finds every way to dawdle, borrow a smoke, and gossip about the king and court. He complains endlessly about the hardships of his life. He is tamas.

Spirit sports at all three qualities and enjoys the play. The king, prime minister, and messengers all see their roles as distinct. Each prefers his own role and each is secretly envious of the others. Only the eye of wisdom knows all to be expressions of a singular source; only the eye of wisdom knows its connection with all three and knows how it resides separate and above all three.

July 12, 2001

I read in the *Gospel of Ramakrishna*, the description of a minister for the Brahmo-Samaj by Ramakrishna. He was getting married for the second or third time. Ramakrishna was saying, how could such a one teach with any authenticity that the world is unreal, God alone is real. My soul was shaken; I inwardly saw Ramakrishna. My soul wept. "Is all lost? Am I such a one in a decrepit state?" I felt all my life to be a loss, a complete waste; my heart ached so.

Ramakrishna said, "Never mind, this saying is not meant for you. You are alright." What sweet words. They lifted my soul. I picked up the book the next night. I read the same passage again. The words rent my heart again. "Have I no value, no worth? Should I not get married? I place the matter at your feet, Ramakrishna. You were married; you ate fish, yet I know your penance of twelve years was with unceasing intensity; you remained pure in all that time, even in a tantric ceremony. I am not such a one. Is my life then for naught? Tell me only the Truth, no matter how it may shatter my heart."

Again, I am at Ramakrishna's knee, my head on his lap. Tears pour down at thoughts of those I have hurt, at impure living. Then various sensual scenes arise. I am simple, childlike as I look to Ramakrishna, saying, "I know as the saint of Dakshineswar, you may be shocked by such scenes, but as all-pervading Spirit, you are that which has projected Prakriti as all of that, and more. I am a child; You are the singular Power. The purity, simplicity, and total surrender I feel now is my Reality. The images filled with lust and attraction are Yours. By Your will, you may leave me in my pure state of Being, or You may draw me into Your Mayic drama. I love the purity, simplicity, and beauty of residing in Spirit alone. I surrender to Your Will: Thy Will be done! Leave me in my innocence or cast your Mayic dream and drive me out with unfulfilled desires. You are the Master; I am the machine, your slave."

As I say this, I feel myself residing in the purity of His Being. I place all power of attorney in God's Hands. There is no power other than that power; there is no will other than that Will; there is no reality other than His Reality. All outward desire is absent here, only He, only He, blessed Spirit only He! This moment is all I know. This Presence is all I experience. I am not in a battle; if there is a battle, it is His. I am but His instrument. My task is to keep my surrendered attention upon Him alone.

Consciousness is always moving through our field of awareness. What we choose to focus upon in our awareness acts as a filter to the subconscious mind. The subconscious mind acts as a reservoir that feeds back into conscious awareness, adding to world-consciousness that is always moving through. Remove the world-consciousness, such as when we close our eyes in meditation, and we continue to have the subconscious mind move through our field of awareness. When we choose to focus the mind on tamasic qualities, our mind acts both as a magnet to, and a filter for, those negative qualities. Even so does the mind act as a magnet and a filter for rajasic qualities when we focus on them. Finally, the same holds true for sattvic qualities. When we come to the point in life when we are fully focused on God, then the mind acts as a magnet to, and a filter for, God alone.

God-thoughts not only attract God to us, but filter out all other qualities. The more refined the filter, the purer the thoughts fed into the subconscious mind. The subconscious mind thus gradually becomes a pure reservoir that feeds the conscious mind. The conscious mind, purified, becomes a stable and clean mirror that perfectly reflects the superconscious mind, and the individual self becomes a clear channel for the Self and Spirit. These higher aspects, the superconscious mind and the self, are pure radiations or reflections of God-absolute. Through releasing all sense of I, the Self and the Superconscious dissolve and become the all-embracing Spirit of God. The ultimate freedom and unity of such a state defies all description. Sadhakas begin it all with putting their minds on God, filtering out all other tendencies, and magnetically drawing to themselves God's Grace.

Om Sri Ram Jai Ram Jai Jai Ram

July 14, 2001—Silent Satsang

Dear Satsang Friends: Good Morning everyone, David has asked me to read this to you.

Silent sacred greetings. Once again, we have the privilege of coming together for the noble purpose of gaining our Self-realization. One thing that has been driven home to me over these last weeks is what a rare thing it is to be drawn to the path of realization. So often, we are caught up in the whirlwind of life, trying to squeeze our meditation into the day, feeling pressure from so many different areas of our life, and not believing we are doing all that well living our spiritual life. And, we should always strive to do more, that is the best attitude. However, we should also recognize that the fact we are drawn to this path of realization is, in itself, a great boon and something for which we can give sincere gratitude.

Simple things on the path are oftentimes the most difficult to achieve. A purity of soul is simple; it has been compared to being childlike, it is so simple. Yet, how rare it is to see that purity in manifestation. Instead, we aim for cleverness, for being either in the crowd or out of the crowd. The ego of separation takes so many forms. But to be simple, straightforward, unconditionally loving, this is what we see so little of in the world. To make the heart and soul soft toward God, to enter into that inner silence where we can commune with Him alone, purifies the soul as nothing else will; then we must have the courage to manifest that in our life.

That means to not have elaborate self-defenses, to not spend our energy on being clever or getting one over on the other guy, to feel that you are a part of every living thing, and what is considered non-living as well, as it lives too. A childlike nature makes you simple, free of constraints. But if you become childlike only in a human sense, then you become childish, self-centered, and without self-control. But to become the Infinite's child, then you take on the nature of God. Your heart becomes soft and sweet; you see the world, but you see it as so many manifestations of the Divine. You may feel righteous indignation or anger, but it disappears as fast as it appears, especially when you encounter one who is truly sorry and is reforming their ways. You cannot look upon any part of this world and not see yourself as part of it, yet residing beyond it. All these things reveal a purity of soul.

As with many things in life, we can read a description or even see a demonstration, and we think, "I could do that if I really tried." But this is the crucial question, "Who really tries?" Who puts their whole heart and soul into the effort? We tend to be inconsistent, and that will not yield the results. One thing that masters of their art or craft do, they make their efforts look effortless. They make anyone think that they can do that as well. When we read or see the lives of real masters, like Mother, Master, or Papa, we think, "Yes, that is right; it is so obvious and true." Then we go to put those truths to work in our own lives and we bump up against some pretty tough walls. We have to decide then if we are willing to put ourselves entirely into the effort, or if we are halfway there, or not at all going to try. If we see uneven results, it is most likely we are giving uneven effort!

Sometimes, it is the simplicity of faith, the purity of being open and honest, and the quality of being a Divine Child that eludes our understanding, our way of Being. It means having the courage of faith, the sacrifice of openness and honesty, and the surrender into being the Divine Child. Perhaps in our meditation this morning, we may have some thoughts on this matter. (Not thoughts for how the person sitting next to you ought to live up to these ideals better! But thoughts of how *you* measure up.) It is a life of courage, sacrifice, and surrender, but oh, what a life it then becomes. We stand naked before the world, stripped of outer defenses. We not only stand revealed before God, but God unerringly stands revealed before us.

It is with great joy that I see you here. It has been a time for me of stripping the old away, a time of purging. Imagine, if you will, that you take a hammer and chisel or a pickaxe to your own insides that are as hard as rock, and really go to work on getting rid of that rock. That is how it has been for me, but there is great joy as well in the purging, the breaking away of old, ancient places of hardness. All happens according to God's design, and when we have perfect resignation and faith in that fact, then we have peace and perfect accord with the Divine.

And for you, I pray that you will have that softness to God, that simplicity and purity that comes with courage, sacrifice, and surrender. In all things, make God your All in All.

Peace and blessings, David

We will have our usual routine of Ram Nam at the top of the hour. I do ask that you keep your coming and going to those times. If you would like, come down to the hermitage cabin; it looks to be a beautiful day outside, and we can lounge on the deck. Also, it was suggested that we all go out to dinner this evening, so for all who would like, we can go out and eat before you head back. Perhaps we can leave here around four or four-thirty, so it does not make it too late to be driving back. Om Namaste

God Morning Carla!

Such a wonderful morning, I hope it is for you as well. The cool marine air has moved in with gray cover. It feels refreshing to have the moist cool air. I have always thought that bird watchers were people with too much time on their hands! But watching the birds here, I have grown to appreciate what diversity and wonderful characteristics they have (the birds that is; I have not seen too many species of bird watchers here!). One feature that has really struck me is the variety of ways in which they fly. Some flap their wings for all they are worth, some stutter their flaps, and some seem to float on the air, needing hardly any effort at all for that privilege. I do not think I will be an ornithologist any time soon! But it is all quite fascinating to not just see the birds, but to get to know them through their habits and the ways they get through the air. I think that has been the difference. I could never be interested in just seeing a bird, but to get to know them is different. For that, it seems one has to "live" with them a bit. To know how feisty a hummingbird is, to see the beautiful sweeps an eagle makes of its hunting preserve, to see the flash of a goldfinch (the state bird of Washington), has shown me a different aspect of Divine Consciousness and Its countless ways of expressing itself. It is mind-blowing, really, when there are scientists who spend an entire lifetime on one little aspect of creation, finding new depths to its nature, and this is just one tiny little planet in a vast creation. It is humbling and awe-inspiring.

And so must our lives be, always to be exploring the depths of God. What a privilege to know that we are on a grand tour of His Being, and with Him as our guide to boot! Worlds inside and out, and as fascinating as the outside world is, how much more fascinating is the inner world. I think the real kicker in it all is: we miss the inner bliss when we are attached to the outer world. When we are connected with His Being through that inner Bliss, then we continue our journey of exploration secure in His Presence. Then come what may, we are always with Him; in this is all the difference. Ah, what joy, what inner rapture to know that Presence. And yet to be unattached to the Bliss as well; so that whatever direction He gives, we easily, pliantly turn and move and bend to His will like a sensitive control panel to the smallest nuances of its operator. Ah, that is true Bliss, to be completely at His command and let Him play through us in all ways. Then pain is bliss, high and low are the same, everything is an expression of the limitless nature of the Divine.

I was reading the article you gave me on Oprah. I noticed she used a small case "d" on the word Divine. How can the Divine be regarded as a small case? To be chic or fashionable in the way we are approaching the Divine seems to me to be hypocritical.

One may say, "Well I don't want to turn people off by using strong images of language."

This seems to me to lack humility, not turning the mind over to God's will. To become child-like means to give up the calculating mind, to have the courage to be simple, open and honest. It is not easy to live in such simplicity. Then she goes on to say, after hiring two yoga retreat teachers to lead her weekend retreat for herself and three friends, "I have always believed that as helpful as a teacher can be on that path, you really need no gurus, no teachers, no guides—just yourself." It is all quite revealing in the way the mind plays with us to keep the ego in control and just "ahead of the game." Thank you for the article; it shows me that no matter how well-intentioned the ego is, it is not capable of being the guide we need. Of course, it is true, the Self is what we need, but who knows the Self in its fullness? And how can the Self be known without a guide, a teacher, one who is awakened to the Self themselves?

Her statement caused me to go within and ask God, "Is it true that no guru is needed?" This is what happened as a result. I found the words coming from me to Oprah, "Yes, for the level of work you are doing, no guru is needed. But, to go the final mile and attain the fullest liberation, then a guru must be present." The words came spontaneously to my mind, and I felt them to be truth. After this spontaneous inner response, the sayings of the great masters stating that same thing came to me: a guru is necessary for full realization. This certainly matches my own experience, as well. Of course, it has been popular to say, "Be your own guru." But is this not the blind leading the blind? I have never wanted to be dogmatic about anything I have ever been taught. Rather, I have wanted any truth I teach to come from my own realization. I have always striven to separate that which I have learned from another or read somewhere, and that which I have realized through my own experience. I feel satisfied with this truth, "The fullest realization can only come with the guidance, grace and protection of a realized guru."

When I think of my own years of sadhana and the teachings, grace and the power infused into me by my Guru, it not only fills me with awe, but with a deep appreciation for who and what the Guru is. The world is aflutter with so much information, so many ways of seeking out God. The word "guru" is bandied about in popular press in such diverse ways. It is common to hear, "The Wall Street guru, so and so, has predicted..." and then we have the examples of popular gurus who have come and have been found to be wanting in their behavior. The word guru means one who brings you into the light. The word guru can be a teacher or mentor of any kind in the human sense; anyone who gives you light on a certain subject is a guru, a teacher. Then there is the specialized meaning of the Sat-Guru. The Sat-Guru is established in the Self and has come to bring you from the darkness of ignorance to the Light of your oneness with God. To find and have the acceptance of such a Guru is, of course, rare and wonderful.

Because the realization of our oneness with God has not been held out as a goal, here in the West, so the role of the guru has not been known of or held out, as a living reality. Who would deny that Jesus of Nazareth was a guru to his disciples? They called him Master, Rabbi; he was their teacher, the source of God's power here on earth, the one who would lead them from being the sons of man to Sons of God. Later in their organization, priests were substituted for the role of guru. They took away the notion that the priest would have to be operating in the same consciousness with which Jesus operated; rather, Jesus would use their imperfect form. So, the idea that one was to be "perfect," even as your Father in Heaven is "perfect," was discarded in favor of a watered-down version of those original teachings. (Matthew 5:48) It is ironic that Jesus was judged a heretic for claiming a human could be equal with God; that is, he or she could be a manifestation of God through human form. Within a short amount of time, the church that was started in his name persecuted anyone else who would dare to make the same claim!

Most of the Christian world is convinced that Jesus will come in a blaze of glory from the sky and will dispense justice right, left, and center. Therefore, there would be no chance of mistaking who he is and what he looks like. I am sure they will expect him to look like one of the paintings where he looked Europeanized, with long hair and beard and robes as well! Yet, He said, "What you have done to the least of these, you have done unto me." (Matthew 25:40) Anytime we feed a beggar, visit someone in prison, treat the lowest of society with kindness and consideration, we do it for Him! Did Jesus not look like any of his contemporaries (they needed Judas to find Jesus and pick him out from the disciples)? So, if one looking like a modern-day one of us were to say, "God has come in this form to manifest His Grace on earth," who would be willing to recognize such a one? Would he or she be recognized as a Christ? Would he or she not be found wanting in the court of world opinion?

It is very interesting to see all the ways we "protect" ourselves from the knowledge of our own Divinity. We put up a wall of separation between the human and the Divine. If it is judged to be human, then it cannot be Divine. If it is judged to be Divine, then it cannot be human. A funny line in a movie came: a live-in couple went to see a popular guru, like some would go to see a rock star. As they were waiting, one said to the other, "Look, there comes God out of the bathroom now." Could those of the Christian world imagine their Lord performing human functions of the body? You see, it is difficult for us to put those things together because we are split apart ourselves. This attachment to the body as separate from the Divine is a way to keep ourselves from knowing our own Divine Nature.

This schism gets reflected in the guru as well. We may well think that such a Divine manifestation is impossible, or if possible, it is relegated to some personage(s) of the distant past who we can construct in our imagination in any way that suits us. Is this sentiment not reflected when the townspeople said of Jesus, "Is this not the man we know, the son of the carpenter, that ordinary fellow who lives down the street?" You see, wearing robes and sandals is what everybody wore; it would be like wearing blue jeans and shoes today. The Jews were expecting a great king, a great teacher. This fellow had not even been to university, or been to the great rabbis of his time; what was he talking about? *He* was the Messiah? Can you imagine being a townsperson of that time? What would you think? How would you react? You see, it is not such an easy thing. The disciples were filled with doubt. Jesus' teachings were enigmatic, difficult for them to understand, and vague. On the one hand, he looked very human; on the other, he seemed extraordinary. Was he human? Was he Divine? What could they trust? What could they know?

So, gurus come as instruments of the Divine. They have realized their oneness with God. This certain knowledge is not based on university degrees, social standing, or holding a position in an organization. Then how may we know such a one? Jesus displayed a miracle and that was offered as proof, but Jesus himself said that that was done because they were an unbelieving generation. And even those who saw the proof through the miracles were many times unconvinced, or unsure what to make of it all. If you have ever been a witness to a miracle, you will know that part of the mind cannot deny what has happened, but part of the mind does not, will not, accept what it has seen. It looks for other explanations or to somehow minimize or put away what it has seen. All the disciples of Jesus saw miracles, yet which of them stood with Jesus at the time of his trial?

In order for the disciple to become a real disciple, he or she must struggle with the doubts of the mind. In my own case, I had an immediate and sudden recognition based on an experience Mother gave to me, but it was many years before I worked through the layers of doubt and wondering. It is safe to say that I still am exploring the vast subject of the guru-disciple relationship and all that it means; it is vast, deep, and as wonderful as our relationship with God. There are those who say, "This is idol worship." But that is not right. For a guru is not an idol. The guru is one who has realized his or her oneness with God, and in that they are unknowable. Think of the ocean, and then see its many waves. Each wave is part of the ocean, yet each wave has an individuality and life to itself. Each of us is a wave in God's Ocean. The guru is here to awaken us to this fact. But this awakening is not just intellectual acceptance. It must be a deep and ongoing realization in order to become fully awakened. The power of who the guru is, which is the power of the ocean of God, along with specific teachings, helps to awaken us to our true nature, the nature of the vast ocean. The more we see the vast ocean of God in the guru, the closer we come to the realization of what we have within. The more we realize that vast nature within, the more we see it in the guru. The guru awakens that knowledge within; the knowledge within lets us see God everywhere about us. The transcendence of doubt comes with this full realization. Therefore, a part of the role of the guru is to be the battleground of the opposing forces of doubt and realization.

That is why the guru is such a powerful concept and why it triggers such passion for and against the whole notion. The guru manifests the human and the Divine, doubt and realization, our attachment to being separate from God and our desire for union with God. Whether that one is called guru, Messiah, Bodhisattva, Prophet, or any name that may represent that one who has come to bring us to the Light, they will be a lightning rod of hope and fear. But for those of us who are sincere in our desire for realization, nothing can take the place of an awakened one who has come to usher us into the Light. No watered-down version of an intermediary, no distant figure from the past, no false prophet of one who says he or she knows and does not know will be able to provide us with what we need. And the guru will come into our life with all the force of a lightning strike. For some, it hits all at once, others it is a more gradual recognition. However it happens, the guru will certainly be a battleground within our own soul, and most likely have its counterparts in the world around us as well.

When I think of my own Guru, the battles of my soul pale into insignificance. The place she has in my heart and soul is irreplaceable. And what has been the result of her being in my life? Every battle won has led to my greater realization of God. Every battle lost in the moment has led to further efforts to overcome doubts with realization, to heal the wound between the human and the divine. With this greater realization of God has come a deepened realization of my Guru. The description, the glory, the wonderful nature of the guru can never be exhausted with words, for it is as God is, ever-new, ever-conscious, ever-blissful. To some, this may sound like heresy, but for me it is the fulfillment of all the world's scriptures. For some, there may be only disbelief, but for me there is only profound awe, mystery, and certain knowledge of its truth. At whatever cost it has been to me, and at whatever cost that may come in the future, I count it as little for what I have gained for this tremendous realization of which I speak. I pray that this will be your realization, as well; that you may go deep into the laboratory of your soul and find the Eternal Guru ever dwelling within your heart. I pray that you know your everlasting oneness with the Infinite Divine ever dwelling within you and ever about you.

Om, Om, Namaste Om,

In Eternal Love and Blessings,

David

July 16, 2001

It is ignorance that makes us blind to the intelligence that permeates every particle of creation. When we see with the eye of wisdom, we see that Intelligence operating in every action. Not a leaf falls, not a centipede's leg moves without the will of that Intelligence. Every part of life is filled with wisdom and Divine Will. Think of it! Not one thing is devoid of this wisdom. How blind and ignorant is the unsuspecting mind to these Divine movements. How glorious and awe-inspiring the realization of this truth. There is no such thing as an empty space, a meaningless gesture; boredom and fear are removed from our vocabulary. Wherever we are is our ashram—our holy abode—every person we meet is our Infinite

Beloved, masquerading behind diverse masks. A holy vibration scintillates in the very air we swim in. O Blessed Infinite! Bless us with this Universal Vision for all time, in all space. We are bereft and bereaved when absent even a moment from Your Presence. Make us know this universe is Your body. Being in Your body, where can You be absent? The universe is Your body, what is there to fear? The universe is Your body, but the universe does not define You, even as the pattern of the whole body may be found in a single cell, yet the cell does not encompass the body. Vast, Infinite, boundless are You.

How do I know this? I sense it, but with a sense that extends beyond the body. I know it, but with an awareness that goes beyond the mind. I feel it, but with feeling of giant stature. It is intuitive, but an intuition that is more real than any of the senses. It is thrilling, and that thrill vibrates in every cell of the body. Infinite majesty, make this awareness undying for Your devotee. Operating a body, through the senses and mind, let the Spirit ever comingle with omniscience. Ten percent dedicated to the body, ninety percent residing in You. O Infinite splendor, You wear the universe as a loose garment; teach me to wear this body in the same way. O Infinite grace, freely You roam throughout all creation, be my ever-present captain and guide every move, thought, and any word that comes from this form. As Rama roamed free in the jungles, yet ever aware of who he was, let devotees ever more freely roam through the world, never forgetting their true nature.

Fulfill this prayer that You, Yourself, have prayed through this form. Let all devotees who take their refuge in You find You the never-failing Presence that lifts them into the supernal Universal Vision. Let devotees everywhere thrill to the Intelligent Bliss that permeates the All in All. Praise for Your Infinite glory, may it rise spontaneously until all is suffused with Your radiance and All merges into a Oneness of ecstatic Being. All is You! Your Spirit pervades the All.

Om Namah Ananda
Om Namah Consciousness
Om Namah The Eternal Self
Om, Om, Om

July 17, 2001

It is the glorious purity of kutastha chaitanya—Highest Consciousness that vanquishes all foes of lower consciousness. The multitude of mind, ego, ignorance, and the senses of the subtle and physical bodies vie to reign as kings over the atma, the soul. The attention kept upon the Highest Light may receive many blows and battles from the lower forces. Onward the terrific battle goes. Above and beyond the battle, yet directing and giving power to the forces for upward evolution, stands preeminent Divine Consciousness. The purity, power, and light of that Consciousness are never stained or touched by those lower forces. Like the sun, clouds of war may blot out its appearance at times, but when the clouds dissipate, as they must, the sun returns to all its glory. All hail the magnificence of the Eternal Nature. The power of its purity overcomes all darkened nature. The atma stands in the radiance of the Paramatma, the Light of Being reigns as unchallenged Perfection.

Om Namah Om

Om Sri Ram, universal, formless, Infinite creator and protector of all who seek Your Grace.

Om Namah Om

Pure Love, Light, and Grace, ever shine upon all who take refuge in You alone.

Om Namah Om

Herlwyn Lutz: a forest welcome.

Ruth Lamb
in Stillness.

Peggy Baker and Al Cone:
a reflective moment.

Elaine Cone on forest path.

August: Fire of Renunciation

August 2, 2001

A fire for God has been raging through me. It is a consuming fire, a fire of demand, a fire of rage. The demand is for the opening of closed doors. A spontaneous vision of two large bronze doors, rising high over my head, stands in front of me. With a large mace, I pound on the door. An adamant demand comes for the doors to open. I know it is God who has put this desire into me, this raging fire; it is also He who keeps the doors closed. Finally, after exhaustive attempts, the doors open and a flood of living water rushes past. Even though the reservoir of water is huge, the water passes by me. I fall to the green meadow, exhausted. I am spent; I am at God's feet. The burning has been intense; my whole body is aflame. Now, at God's feet, I surrender it all to Him. From my stomach come seven coals of fire. They come out of my mouth and I lay them at His feet. I wrap them in a nice package, which starts to smolder!

"Oh, Infinite Spirit, I surrender to You what You gave to me." This fire of renunciation yet burns within me. Is it for myself? For others? I can no longer discern a difference. "All is one, all is You! You are the solitary life, Consciousness, and Doer of the entire creation. Do with me as You will, for any purpose You desire. All is You; all is You."

All through the day, the fire has raged off and on—inner visions—pounding on open doors—1 door, 2 doors, 3 doors—all opened and the Living waters flooded out; the third door opened, and in this strange state, I collapsed in front of the doors. The water poured all around and over me. I had not the strength to move; not in the vision—not in my physical body. Then—in vision—came out of my mouth the coals. The other doors, after they were opened, and the coals ejected, they were red hot. This third time they were smoldering, seemingly they were burnt out. Then it seemed I had no life-energy left—none at all. I was ready to die, to leave this body. I reflected on all those I love and surrendered them to God. I thought of the work. I thought, "This has not been my work from the beginning; it is my God and Guru's, and if God wants to take me now, that is His will. His will be done."

I felt this body to be a burden and it felt good to leave it behind. I thought of those who would feel pain at my passing. I gave that to God. One tug was there, but, I reasoned, all will leave their body someday. Today is just as good as any to leave.

It truly felt I could leave my body now. Life in the body felt like a dream; the only thing that felt real was God. That felt the same with or without a body. I saw my blessed Divine Guru and bowed at her feet. My body had no Life; I had labored breathing and felt my heart could stop at any moment. I felt the pathways of subtle nerves in the head, the ajna, and a point in the center of the head that I would need to snap to consciously leave the body. I waited on God, but had no command to proceed. I waited in that state for some time. The thought came, "The only reason to stay is to serve, but I have no will around that. You know all, You decide." After some period of time, my breathing became more regular, my heart steady, and life-force gradually re-entered the body. Thus ends an intense, interesting, and unusual day. This life is but a dream, life beyond a dream. God alone is Reality.

August 4, 2001, 4 a.m.
Sri Yukteswar's Hour.

God showed me how, by acknowledging all detachment, He set my Life's barque free in the ocean only to be drawn back. Then after it was drawn back to the familiar shore of friends, it was set free again into the ocean. As a result of the second renunciation, all consciousness, all freedom, all power became available without attachment. Like Narayana, wandering heaven and earth—above the human drama, but playing a part in it. God then reminded me that the death happened on a Thursday, (8-2-01). Thursday is considered an auspicious day to worship the Guru. I have not thought of that in a long time and God made me think of it this morning. The thought also came to me: these are like the days for Mother when she was having so many revelatory experiences.

I am God's puppet. He pulls the strings and I move at His behest. This body is like a dead man; the mortician moves it here and there. The body has no will of its own. My only knowledge is: "All is He; All is He."

August 4, 2001, 8:30 p.m.
Bodies are nothing but urns
Waiting to be filled with dust!

August 6, 2001
Bhakti Yoga is the absorption in the overwhelming love of God; Jnana Yoga is seeing God as the Reality that is immanent and transcendent to all creation, and that the idea of separation is false. Karma Yoga is seeing God in all creation, and its creatures, and

serving the Light in every action, every breath. Raja Yoga is being absorbed in the Light and the sound of God, and the realization that God is the All and All in All.

God-experience is our only real teacher—all else is commentary!

Reverend Larry Koler in Silence.

August 9, 2001

O Lord, You have given me the greatest human privilege: the ability, desire, and need to meditate on Thee. Like a jealous lover, You demand me to come. I drop all that I am doing and come to You. If I tarry, You become insistent and make all else impossible. Thus, the One I cannot do without, cannot do without me! What a happy arrangement. You are my All and All; I never tire of singing Your glories. Not because You need me to, heaven forbid! But, to sing Your glories makes me thrill to Your Being. This is the hidden secret to singing angels: they sing Your glorious vibration which enraptures Your devotees everywhere. Where are gloom and sorrow when such splendor penetrates every cell? All darkness flees before the Light, powerless to stop its illuminating rays. O Infinite Splendor, illuminate this heart temple, and all heart temples with Your gaze, and make us feel the universal throb of life that permeates all, animates all, and alone makes life something to savor.

Hari Om Tat Sat

August 9, 2001, continued

Why do I write? The words flow from the pen without preconception or a clever plan. My words are like the boy who is infatuated with a beautiful girl. He pines for her daily. One day she looks at him and smiles. That's it. Just smiles. But, oh the effect of that smile. All the way home he walks, each step two feet above the ground. He sings and whistles the whole way. That is what I am like with my Cosmic Beloved. But you may say your Beloved has no body; how can you receive a smile? But I say my Beloved smiles to me through all human smiles, and when the golden sun first peaks above the horizon. My Beloved sings to me through the songbird and whispers Love through the breeze. I find my Infinite Beloved caresses me in Bliss and loves me through the flow of love in my own heart. Oh, but for in that glance of my dearly Beloved, what I would not give, for in that glance is my salvation.

Shall I go on singing the praises of the One I love? My pen moves of its own accord, for it is my Beloved who is singing these praises! And, loving me as my hand moves, and I feel my Beloved wrap the arms of Bliss all about me.

God Morning Carla,

All is well here, although there is a heaviness in the air of strong opposing forces. I have felt the struggle of so many devotees. Acknowledging that what God is and does is the only way out. He has given me work to do, and do it I must. But, in reality, it is He who does the work. My part is to follow explicitly His inner direction. In that is freedom. To take on the responsibility of success, for myself or others, leads to bondage. Of course, as I write this to you, I am really writing it to myself.

I say it so you may know my mind at this time. God, the all-powerful, gives us a limited role to play. He says, "Here, do this for me, will you please?" Like the mother asking the child to do some small role for her in the kitchen. The mother wants the child to take his or her role seriously, to do a good job. But, if the child were to look at everything to be done in preparing the meal, he or she might faint! The child could not imagine how a small child would know what to do or have the power to do.

Of course, the mother never expected the child to prepare the whole meal. She was giving the child a sense of participation and an opportunity for learning, something about what the mother does. She would never expect the child to take on the whole responsibility of the meal. And she watches the child. If he or she has some difficulty, the mother may not intervene too soon, for she knows there is value in the child trying to figure it out. But if the child is in danger of hurting him or herself or others, she comes to help right away. And if the child says he or she cannot do the task, then the mother puts her hand behind the hand of the child and helps. Then the child stands up straight and tall and says, "Look what I have done!" The mother smiles with pride and softness of heart at her child; how cute it is the child thinks he or she did it all themselves! Ah, it is all God's play. And is this not the way it is?

The father says, "Let the boys be boys when they play rough." But if there is any call for help, the mother cannot stop herself from rushing to him, cleaning off the dirt, kissing away the booboos, and making the child know he is loved and cared for. Ah, to have the pride of the father shower on us, to have the love of the mother caress us: such are the privileges of the devotee!

Well, these are my thoughts in the moment, and I send them to you in all love and devotion.

In the Ocean of Prem, David

Yogacharya David with Reverend Jill Hough.

August 11, 2001—Silent Satsang

Dear Satsang Friends: Greetings, David asked me to read this to you.

Good Morning, everyone, it is good to see you. Well, this is our second-to-last Silent Satsang here at Cloud Mountain. The adventures of this last month have been quite interesting, and I will share with you one experience that is having a profound influence on me. But first, let me welcome you here this morning.

As you know, we are a group of kindred spirits who come together for the greatest quest known to humankind, the realization of our oneness with God. There are no other side benefits of name, fame, or fortune that result from being attached to this group, which keeps the purpose very pure. Of course, this is the way Mother designed it, and I quite love the personal character we have, without the difficulties of a large group with monies and power, etc. The tradition of yogis is to practice in solitary haunts and come together in groups with their teacher from time to time. As long as those who come are striving for their realization and growing in God, then the purpose for our coming together is served.

A few words about the next and the last Silent Satsang. We will not be meeting here, at Mist Haven, but at Diamond Hall. I requested this as I think we may have a few more people at that time. There is no other retreat scheduled here for that weekend, and I thought it would be more comfortable. I thought for this final time we would have a potluck lunch and I will ask if we can use the dining hall, or if it is nice outside, we can set up a table and eat outdoors.

For those who would like to, you may stay here that Saturday night. The catch is, those who stay will help to move my things from the hermitage cabin and help with a final cleaning of the cabin. Now, I imagine none of you have had the experience of cleaning a hermitage before, and this may be your only chance, so sign up early! Really, I don't think it will entail a lot and it should be fun as well. I thought Saturday night we would go out to eat at a Chinese restaurant that I have been to a few times that has wonderful food. Sunday morning, we can prepare breakfast at the hermitage cabin. On Sunday, we are planning an open house potluck at Larry and Cate's house in the mid-afternoon. This will be open to all friends. I may be all talked out after the first three words, but who knows! And knowing this group, others can readily fill in for any lack of words I may have.

This next description comes from my journal. It is of an experience I recently had, and it has had a deep effect on me. I continue to marvel that God and Guru have instructed me to write about my own experiences for all to see. But it is my conviction now that there is only one life, one consciousness, and one witness. So, it is now more like writing something for my own satisfaction, then reading it out loud and seeing how I, as all of you, like it! When you hear this, you are various aspects of myself listening, evaluating, and absorbing what is said. This is not grandiosity on my part, but recognition of the universal nature of life. The old thoughts of, "Who will like it and who will criticize it?" have been replaced with the great joy of fulfilling His will, and then the fun of watching the various reactions, which are none other than my own self:

From Thursday a.m., August 2, 2001

A fire for God has been raging through me. It is a consuming fire, a fire of demand, a fire of rage. The demand is for the opening of closed doors. A spontaneous vision of two large bronze doors rising high over my head stands before me. With a large mace, I pound on the doors. An adamant demand comes from me for the doors to open. I know it is God who has put this desire and this raging fire into me for these doors to open; it is also He who keeps the doors closed. Finally, after exhaustive attempts, the doors open and a flood of living water rushes past. Even though the reservoir is vast, all the water passes by me and is let out.

I fall to the green meadow, exhausted; I am spent. I am at God's feet; the burning has been intense. In the vision, my whole body was seen in flames. Now, at God's feet, I surrender it all to Him. From the bowels of my stomach come seven coals of fire. They come out of my mouth and are purged at His feet. I decide to wrap them in a nice package for Him, which then starts to smolder!

O Infinite Spirit, I surrender to You what you gave to me. This fire of renunciation yet burns within me. Is this for myself? For others? I can no longer discern a difference. All life is one, all is You! You are the solitary Life, Consciousness, and Doer of the entire creation. Do with me as You will, for any purpose You desire. All is You; all is You!

All through the day, the fire has raged off and on—inner visions—pounding on doors—I door, 2 doors, 3 doors—all opened, and the living waters flooded out, but in no case did I drink of those waters. The third door opened, and in this strange state, I collapsed in front of the doors. The water poured all around, and over the top of me. I had not the strength to move, not in the body in my vision—neither in my physical body! Then out of my mouth came the seven burning coals at God's feet. In the previous visions when the doors were open and the coals ejected, they were red hot. This third time, however, the coals were smoldering, seemingly burnt out. With this, I had no life-energy left—none at all. I was ready to die, to leave this body.

I reflected on all those I love and surrendered them to God. I thought of God and Guru's work and all that is left to be done. I thought, "This has not been my work from the beginning, it is my God and Guru's, and if God wants to take me now, if that is Your will, Your will be done!" I felt this body to be a burden and it felt good to leave it behind. I thought of those who would feel pain at my passing. I gave that to God, but that was one tug for me. But, I reasoned, "All will leave their body someday, and sorrow is felt at that passing. Today is just as good as any to leave."

I was on the verge of leaving my body. Life in the body felt a dream; life beyond the body felt a dream, and the only thing that felt real was God; that felt the same with or without a body. I saw my blessed Divine Guru and bowed at her feet. My physical body had no life; I had irregular, labored breathing and I felt my heart could stop any moment. I saw and felt the pathways of subtle nerves in the head, the ajna, and the point in the center of the head that I would need to snap to consciously leave the body. I waited in God, but had no command to proceed; I waited in that state for some time. The thought finally came, "The only reason to stay is to serve, but I have no will around that; You know all; You decide." After some period of time, my breathing became more even, my heart took on a steady beat, and the life-force gradually re-entered the body. Thus ended an intense, interesting, and unusual day. This life is but a dream, life beyond a dream. God alone is Reality.

Also, I want to share this with you from August 4, 2001, 2:00 a.m.:

Sri Yukteswar's hour on a full moon night: God is showing me how, with acknowledging all detachment, He has set my life's barque free into the ocean, only to be drawn back. Then, after it was drawn back to the familiar shore of friends, it was set free again into the ocean. As a result of the second renunciation, all consciousness, all freedom, and all power became available without attachment: like Narayana, wandering heaven and earth—above the human drama, but playing a part in it. God then reminded me that the "death" happened on a Thursday. Thursday is considered an auspicious day to worship the Guru. I had not remembered that association in a long time, but God made me think of it on this early morning. The thought also came to me; these are like the days for Mother when she was having so many revelatory experiences.

I am God's puppet. He pulls the strings and I move at His behest. This body is like a dead man, the mortician moves it here and there, and the body has no will of its own. My only knowledge is, "All is He; All is He."

Afterword

A few days after this experience, a clear intuition came that this "death" was the culmination of the work I have been doing during this year-long silence and seclusion. It feels to me like some heavy burden has passed from me and I am in a glow of peace, stillness. This year of silence and solitude has not been a passive year by any stretch of the imagination. It has been a time of difficult work, sometimes of great suffering along with powerful upliftment, in God. For what purpose and to what end, I do not know: the slave's only task is to carry out the will of the Master.

Some other thoughts come to me as I write this. As I progress in this exploration of God's Infinite Body, some realizations get reinforced again and again, making the knowledge deepen in my whole Being.

One: every experience we have is an experience in God; nothing lies outside His province;

Two: the sense of purity and joy that is spontaneous to our nature when lived in harmony with God is deep and profound, beyond the reasoning mind's ability to fully comprehend or understand; and

Three: there is nothing to fear in all the three wide worlds, other than a sense of separation from God, and that can be cured by Grace and a determined effort to erase the self-imposed barrier.

I know there is nothing new in writing these thoughts. I have never thought I would be saying anything new, except perhaps offering my particular way of expressing it. When I write, I feel in full communion with the Infinite. Perhaps others, in reading it, will feel the same. Truth has ever been with us; it is a matter of making it our own. The key, when we have yet to make Truth our own, is to turn the mind to the Truth again and again. Whatever inspires us to do this, whatever points us in the right direction, is deemed helpful. Whatever takes our mind away from God, Truth, is seen to be in opposition to the Light. But even the opposition serves the Light, for when we go with the oppositional force, our lives become so miserable that we eventually turn to the Light once again with greater intensity. So, what turns our mind to God, to the Light, is our Dharma. Whatever turns our mind away from the purity of Light is adharma, unrighteousness.

My prayer for you is that you will ever be guided by the Light of Dharma, in perfect attunement with that which makes you one with the Light. You are a child of the Light. That has always been true, and it will always be.

My love and prayers are with you always, David

Cloud Mountain Waterfall.

Cloud Mountain: deer visit.

Editor's Note: From this time forth, from all the journals and papers we have found, it seems David immersed himself in a time of reflection and deeper teachings as he prepared to re-enter the world. There were no further diary-type reflections. David's continued August reflections follow as Summer Teachings.

Chapter Four
Summer Teachings

Jnana-Wisdom

The development of Jnana wisdom requires the ability to focus the mind on what is unreal and what is real, separating the two and attaining the real.

Our life is the training ground for learning this wisdom. We may start our practice with our life as it is now, guiding our intellect through the maze of life's choices. The beginning of Wisdom is the recognition of the importance of the choices we make. Each choice made builds a pattern that becomes our character.

The foundation for character is the adherence, or lack of it, to the essentials of virtue. Virtue is made up of those qualities or behaviors that are known to all as positive traits. Qualities such as telling the truth, integrity, logical thinking, compassion, high-mindedness, humor, fun, etc., are those attributes that are admired in a friend, loved one, business partner, etc. Each choice we make founded upon virtue creates an engrained habit pattern—a trait that becomes who we are.

In order to identify and adhere to such virtues, we should approach with a calm mind. Some of the great minds and characters of history have, early on, developed lists of virtues they most wanted to live up to. Benjamin Franklin and George Washington both come to mind, having created lists of character virtues and actively worked at actualizing those virtues into their lives. Clear-minded values will be the guide through muddy waters of daily life where clarity in choice, temptation, and virtue can all be lost sight of in murky situations.

A lesson may be drawn from pruning bushes and trees. The first thought in pruning is what overall shape we want the plant to have. Once the overall shape is established, taking into account the nature of the plant's strengths and weaknesses, then taking away all branches not in keeping with that shape. Then one looks for all crossing branches and removes them. By this time, we have reduced all major branches to those that support the overall shape, and have removed all crossing branches. So too in our life. We determine the overall shape of virtues and values we want, remove all other branches and tendencies, then look for crossing branches; we want to encourage those daily habits that cross over the healthy branches of behavior.

There are many people of less talent and intelligence who suc- ceed more effectively in life than their superiors, primarily because they have learned to set priorities and keep to them. Life is full of interests and fascinating aspects, but unless we narrow our focus and learn to see things through to the end, we will not achieve much success.

This ability to focus the mind and energy on positive goals and virtues is the beginning of wisdom. It is essential that we have sharp pruning instruments to cut away what is not part of our goal. Each successfully completed goal that is in keeping with the overall shape we want for our life is one more step in shaping our tree of wisdom. This includes our ventures in business, family, social cir- cles, personal habits, marriage, children, etc. Our active spiritual life used as both nutrition and the intended fruit of our wisdom tree will make our life one of peace and joy, through all the ups and downs of worldly endeavors.

The development of wisdom in worldly life and matters becomes the tool we use for gaining spiritual wisdom as well. Our ability to identify what is within us that is not in keeping with the highest spiritual truths, the shape of our spiritual tree, and removing those branches working at cross purposes, uses skills transferred from daily behaviors inconsistent with a spiritual life to our dealing with worldly dreams and goals.

The fast, efficient use of mental discrimination cuts away all that is not of God and focuses the mind on that which is of God. The life, light, beauty, joy, and wisdom of the Superconscious mind illuminate our understanding with increased clarity as we use discrimination in our thoughts, words, and behaviors. Wisdom from the Superconscious mind is not learned but self-illuminating—Direct Intuition replaces learned mental projections of truth. These learned laws of spirituality have their time and place, to begin with, in our journey, but with the purification of the mind, a flow of wisdom and discrimination comes naturally from hidden springs of spiritual consciousness.

The attainment of Wisdom is the spontaneous knowledge and understanding from the Superconscious mind, or the Self. As notions of a separate "I" gradually lose appeal and one can discriminate the little "I" from the Superconscious Self, God-consciousness, or the state of Being of the Eternal Self, All-consciousness and then Ever-New Bliss, becomes established.

One passes beyond the idea of the jnani, who identifies the Real from the unreal. All is perceived as part and parcel, so the real and the passing shadows of creation are known to be nothing other than the play of the Real, or God Absolute. Light, Beauty, Joy, and Freedom ring throughout all and all! All is seen to be so many movements of one undivided Life and consciousness. The Universal sports as the individual, and the individual sports with the Universal. No separation or isolation exists except where it is voluntarily assumed and clung to. Through wisdom's sharp sword of discrimination, one and all who have assumed separation may cleave to those attachments which keeps the shroud of separation intact.

What clarity and perfection come with that wisdom! An efficiency of cutting away of that which is untruth reveals Truth, the unvarnished Jewel of the Soul, resplendent in all its glory! Ah, Wisdom, servant of the wise and master of its servants, may you start us on our journey and ever illumine our way until the way and the goal unite in the perfect Wisdom of the One.

Breaking the Binary Code of God

A binary code can be defined as all information consisting of a code of digits, each digit being either a one or a zero, pertaining to the power of two.

The jnani yogi is involved in breaking the binary code of God. Through the selection of one ishta, or a symbol of God; in the jnani's case, this will be an impersonal quality of God. He or she will measure each thought against that chosen quality. Either the thought will be a 0 or a 1; it will either be in correspondence to the chosen ideal or will stand in contrast to it.

The chosen ideal will be derived from a teacher, a guru, or will come from scriptural lore that describes various qualities that are intrinsically God. These conceptions of intrinsic qualities are understood from the beginning to be but vague reflections of the Reality from which they are inspired. But through those reflections, one may be led through the maze of information flooding the brain at any one time by selecting and deselecting information based on that reflected ishta, the chosen aspect of God.

All externally and internally-generated information is thus reduced to a one or a zero, selected as a reflection of one's ishta, or deselected as not of that intrinsic nature of God.

For instance, if one's ishta, chosen aspect of God, is the Eternal Self, there are specific qualities that are associated with that Self. The Eternal Self, according to the Sanatana Dharma, the Eternal Religion of India, is unchangeable, immutable, ever-existent awareness. All information can be run through this filter of qualities and only that which meets the criteria will be selected; all else will be deselected.

In examining one's thoughts and perceptions, a rigorous test is set. Body sensation and sense stimuli are noted to be in constant flux and change. Not only that, but the body is seen to go through birth, growth, maturity, gradual gain, and is subject to illness, old age, and death. This does not meet the previously described criteria, ishta, and so is deselected.

Going beyond body sensations and stimuli, one becomes aware of emotions. It is observed that emotions are also in a constant state of change, coming and going, up and down, pleasurable then painful, etc. Nothing of the sort of unchangeable or immutable here; emotions are deselected.

Next, thoughts are examined. Most thoughts, when examined, are transitory. What is thought to be the truth today is discarded tomorrow. There are some thoughts that seem to show some promise. Are there not laws of science that seem immutable?

In examining the many laws of science, they are seen to be contingent on certain criteria being true, and these underpinning criteria are subject to change. This becomes problematic in a physical universe that is known to be in constant change and not well understood in a complete way. Not only that, but it appears that the physical universe, upon which these laws are based, is subject to what is analogous to birth and death. This means that physical laws must also be subject to the rule of change, as at some point the whole known universe may not be in existence, at least not in a recognizable form congruent with the current laws of science; therefore, these laws must also be deselected.

Are there not thoughts of wisdom that stand the test of time that would meet our ishta, our criteria of the Eternal Self? Well, certainly what is considered wisdom in one culture, time, and place could be thought to be nonsense with a change of context. But, what produces happiness, a sense of freedom, for an individual or a society? Are there not verities for the ages here?

Again, it becomes problematic as the goals of the individual and a society are not always the same. But surely survival, say, would be a constant? But that is not true as we can cite many examples of individuals and communities sacrificing themselves for an ideal beyond survival.

What about ideals? Well, there are those ideals passed down through time that, while not agreed upon by all, certainly seem to stand the test of time. Valor, bravery, idealism, sacrifice, overcoming obstacles, adherence to virtues, these come to mind. Even if the specific ideals that drive people should vary through time, surely the act of valor, perhaps not always the motivating reason for that valor, but the action itself, could be universally recognized as a lasting truth?

The problem here is that the human race is subject to change—that will result in the eventual extinction, death, of the race. Therefore, as noble as these sentiments are, they too would have to be deselected.

Body, emotions, and thoughts have all been deselected by the jnani, the seeker of wisdom. So, what is left?

There is the theory of the Soul, an aspect of life that survives the death of the body and presumably the death of the universe as well. It is said to be an aspect or reflection of God. The key here is that we have described this quality as a "theory," some mental projection subject to birth and death, and also used the word "presumably," which indicates a mental projection as well. Those thoughts were already deselected, as previously stated.

In India, there is a little story used to illustrate a point that perhaps can be of use to us here. A man walking barefoot on a path got a thorn deeply embedded in his foot, causing him great pain. Looking around, he spied another thorn on the ground; he picked it up and used it to dig out the first thorn. The analogy pertains to the field of thought. Even though thoughts have been deselected from being intrinsic to the process of Eternal Self or God, nevertheless, thought can be used to help us transcend the field of thought and have some experiences of that which is beyond thought, the Soul.

The limitation of the field of thought is that we can say what is *not* of the Eternal Self, but cannot say what *is* of the Eternal Self. And, as previously mentioned at the beginning of this writing, the qualities of the Eternal Self, as conceived in the mind, can only be vague reflections of the Reality. The compass of the mind can be used to keep us pointed in the right direction, so to speak, but the direction north is not the same as the area we call the North Pole, or magnetic north. In order to arrive at the North Pole, we have to travel beyond any area described as not the North Pole.

At this point in our dissection of what is of the Eternal Self and what is not of the Eternal Self, we are faced with a difficult task. All languages are but symbols for thought. We have to transcend thought to get to our goal, but here we are trying to describe the indescribable.

The task of the jnani at this point is a relentless cutting away, deselection, of what is not of the Eternal Self. Whatever is in the field of awareness will be analyzed as to its nature. In this practice, all body sensations, all emotions, all thoughts will be cut away, deselected, not this, not that. This mental dissection, the use of the thorn to remove the thorn, must be swift, decisive, and exact.

The premise that we are operating under is that if all of that which we have determined not to be of the Eternal Self is banished from the field of awareness, then what is left will be the Soul awareness. This presupposes there is something called the Soul that exists beyond the body, emotions, and thoughts. Therefore, while we are not involving blind faith, we must have enough anticipation of reward that we are willing to make the effort to clear the field of awareness of all that which is said *not* to be unchangeable, immutable, ever-existent awareness.

One way of thinking about it is that all that which is not of the Eternal Soul is number 1 with a power of 2, or pertaining to the dual nature of creation, I and thou. All that pertains to God is the infinity of 0 and has no dual nature to it.

This reduces the equation to its simplest value. Constant rejection of what is deselected will eternally result in the revelation of what is inherent in the Soul, beyond relative values.

As you, perhaps, see at this point, the essential principle is amazingly simple. In fact, the clever mind, looking for increasing complexity and obtuse formulas will quickly find itself bored by such a focused discipline. Children and those of a simple spirit could practice naturally what would take a complex, active mind much effort to achieve.

An illustration may help to clarify this. A scenario is presented to an ethicist, a lawyer, and a child (no this is not a joke in the making). A wallet is found with money in it. What to do with the wallet? The ethicist may reason, "Is there an ID in the wallet? Were efforts made to find the answer? How much money is in it, etc.?" The lawyer will have some of the same questions as the ethicist, plus he will examine the motives of the one who picked up the wallet, what would constitute a reasonable search for its owner, etc. The child says, "I know I am not supposed to take what is not mine. That would be stealing. I will give it to my mommy (an authority)." The child adheres to a simple rule of justice: does it fit into the category with a one or a zero?

The point is (who gets the cash?), the clever mind can very often miss the primary point through a convolution of facts and reasoning. Very often, great leaders are not great intellectuals. Great leaders have clearly outlined a way of identifying the primary principle involved. They are by training, or by nature, a jnani. Jnana, as sometimes described, is the path of intellectuals, and certainly, the discipline described here takes great mental discipline. But all those who have a chosen ishta that reflects the Absolute will have a jnani's knowledge of the Soul.

And one who persists in great love for God, in selfless service of God, who learns to direct all life-energy to God, as well as those who learn to discriminate between the unreal and the real, will attain a state of jnana, wisdom. In this state of jnana, the intuitive perception of discerning the Real will be every bit as acute for the Bhakti, Karma, and Raja yogis as the practicing Jnani who rises to that of a great saint.

This path will not be for those who insist on being clever, cleverness being a mind's focus on obtaining products of I, me, and mine. This path will be for the sincere, those truly desirous of knowing the Truth. As Jesus would say, "Thank you, Father, for not revealing this to the clever, but to children." (Matthew 11:25 adapted) In becoming simple, we become child-like. Reducing the equation to a binary code of what is unreal and what is real is approaching the child-like nature of a child and will break the code that has sealed us from knowing God.

Whatever the path, jnana is needed. To apply the simple formula of zero or one gets to the heart of the matter. The Mind unguided will run in infinite circles: "Could be this, could be that?" The jnani-mind says: "Not this, not that," and cuts like a surgeon's scalpel to rid one of ignorance.

When faced with a situation, let us go to the heart of the issue, quickly, using God as our guide through sincere prayer—that is, a sincere focus of mind. Determine what is of God. Is this 0 or 1? Then act. If nothing is clear, then wait; wait until you have that clarity. Whether our path be of love, service, or lifting the life-force, all will require decisions, all require jnana. Sincerity, dispassion, and calmness are the best attitude for a listening mind. Otherwise, the clutter of passions and chatter obscures the higher teachings. Break delusion's binary code—break through and know the Infinite Oneness of God through wisdom's door.

Detachment: The Way to Freedom and Harmony

Detachment is living in the world but not being of it. It is holding a thing without grasping it.

We have all played the game with small children. They approach us with some small object they have been carrying in their hand. When friendly contact has been made, they hand over the object. They momentarily turn their attention elsewhere, then stick their hand out, expecting us to give them the object back. And on goes the game as they experiment with the notions of possession, giving, receiving, and attachment.

Attachment is the opposite of detachment. Attachment starts with an idea. The idea is, "This is mine," or "I would like this to be mine." It is the notion of grasping, as opposed to holding. These two concepts of grasping and holding may seem to be very similar, but actually, they are worlds apart.

When we grasp something, the intention is to continue to hold the object. When the child "gives" you their object, it is done with the expectation that it will be given back to them. If we withhold it from them when they ask for it back, we will have a most unhappy child. The idea of possession and attachment is implicit in their giving and receiving. If we give the object back on demand, they may give it right back to us. But if we tease them by holding it, or if it is not their mood to give it, we find they fiercely grasp the object in their hands.

The material world tends to teach us to grasp: "Go after what you want and hold on to it!" The nature of grasping, born of attachment, is tension. Grasping is an active expenditure of mental and physical energy. Not only are we expending energy in maintaining what we have (with a background of fear that we may lose it), but we are usually in active pursuit of getting more. Of course, there is the satisfaction of winning at the game, gaining more and more, we hope, and growing in possessions faster than the next fellow.

The spiritual perspective teaches us that the cost of all the grasping runs counter to spiritual awareness. The sadhaka comes to see the cost in terms of the background of fear and of loss. It is the never-ending desire nature that keeps us forever running after that elusive fulfillment and brings loss of the life-energy invested in grasping.

Yet, with all these costs, the body must be maintained, and unless we move into a cave and beg for our food, we need to have things in this world to live. So, how to do this without this notion of constant pursuit and grasping that destroys peace and spiritual awareness?

The answer is a shift of attitude more than changing our circumstances. When the child hands us the object, we may tease him or her by grasping it and not giving it back, or we may simply hold it, surrendering it on the child's demand. This shift from grasping to holding starts with a mental attitude. It gets reflected in the willful energy we project. The kind of willful energy projected gets reflected in how we physically hold the object: in tight, contracted tension or in relaxed, watchful holding.

In addition to how we hold what we have, we find that the mental attitude gets reflected in our pursuit of objects. This mental attitude has, at its most fundamental assumption, the notion of who is desiring this object. Ego consciousness, rooted in the body, says, "I want this." The spiritual attitude maintains, "I (this ego-sense of individuality) am the instrument, and God is its operator. Therefore, my thoughts, my wants, my actions are not my own, but are the result of Divine Consciousness expressing desires through me."

We cannot serve two masters; either it is God or mammon. The operator of the machine, the human mind and body, will either be seen to be God, or it will be seen as mammon. The way of seeing that it is God desiring through us does not negate that there is a higher and lower nature, and that the goal of the spiritual aspirant is the attunement with the higher nature, or God. This is the goal, in fact, of the spiritual aspirant.

However, in this dualism of lower and higher nature, it is often assumed that God has no dealings with the world at all. And this is where perceiving God's will at work, both in the spiritual and what is thought of as worldly matters, is seen in a new light. In this emerging universal vision of the sadhaka, God is known to be active at all levels of existence. There is not an area of life that is devoid of God's will or presence, nor is there any area that is devoid of the dualism of higher and lower nature that does not demand sadhakas to pay attention to their higher calling and break with their lower nature. God, being all-pervasive, prompts sadhakas in every aspect of their life.

Initially, this prompting comes from the principles or laws as enunciated by realized beings. These sometimes come to us as scripture, sometimes as the teaching of a living master or guru. Central to these teachings is the attainment of a still mind; through the stillness, the revelation of Divine Will may be received. As the allegiance of sadhakas gradually becomes focused on that inner direction, a struggle is encountered. The struggle is a result of the attachment to the body and things of this world that draws the mind out of the stillness and into the hurly-burly activity of the world. The outward focus of the mind, that is the mind glued to its own attachment to the body and the world, makes the inner focus on stillness well nigh impossible. This is why it is said that one may not serve two masters; it is to be either God or mammon. The universal laws of behavior spoken of by realized masters are guides to sadhakas to help them through the confusion created by these attachments.

If sadhakas remain sincere in their practice, the mind gradually becomes purified of its attachments. Desire for action in the world is felt to come from that inner stillness. Trial and error teach sadhakas how to distinguish between the inner peace that results from being the Divine instrument versus acting from attachment to the body.

Then all possessions are seen to be in the hold of the sadhaka, but not in his or her grasp. Like custodians for their wealthy employer, sadhakas look after all the employer's possessions with care, making sure everything is maintained perfectly. But all the while, the custodians know that none of the things watched over are theirs. Living on the premises, they use the furniture, the vehicles, and all else available to the custodians. But, at any time, the owner may say to the custodians that their time of watching after these things is up, and custodians then leave the premises without even one piece of furniture. Like custodians, sadhakas keep all the possessions in their hold, ever willing to relinquish it all at one moment's notice.

And what is the result of such a strict inner discipline? One may have vast wealth and possessions, or have very little, and in either case, the sadhaka is at peace and in perfect harmony with Divine Will. One may be in the world, but not of it—may hold possessions without grasping. With this inner detachment comes freedom and inborn wisdom. One may be a multi-billionaire, or own nothing, and both stand on equal ground. In short, through inner detachment, one can know God; no possessions can match that. No position of prestige or authority in the world can bring what knowing God brings to the sadhaka.

Detachment is the way to freedom and harmony. May you know the blessings that come with such inner freedom. May you always be in the world but not of it.

O Ram, Thou Art the Infinite

All-Pervading Presence
How can I hold even a drop of world-knowledge
When my cup already overflows with Your Presence?
You, who wears the stars for Its crown
The Milky Way is but a path of a few steps
The burst of all creation but a twinkle in your eye
What cup could contain you?

When a man thirsts,
He goes to the river with sweet running water
He drinks a little and is satisfied,

He does not need the whole river
Nor does he care for how long the river is.

His need is to quench his thirst
And would he say:
"The river belongs only to me, only I may drink of it."
Surely, we would call that man a wretch, a scoundrel.

And what of other rivers with sweet-tasting water?
Would we say, "Only my river is worthy;
Your river is polluted, and those who drink it
Will die, will not be given life?"

Surely, they drink of their water
And they find it sweet and satisfying.
Is not the value of the river known by this?
We would say of those who say,
"Only my river is good" to be provincial?

Why do we argue for names?
Are not all names of God equally sweet?
Do not all who drink of those names
Derive its qualities and find satisfaction?

Let us not argue names,
But sing of the virtues of the living Water
And rejoice when another does the same.
A brotherhood of the one Living God.

How can ants measure the sun
Other than to say, "It gives out warmth and Light."
How foolish for the black ants to say to the reds,
"Our sun is true, yours is false."

We need not know how many stars are in the crown
To be in awe of its splendor.
And the cup that measures the ocean

Will say, "The ocean is the size of a cup."

We, the children of the Infinite
May rest in the Peace of the Stillness
And melt our boundaries to flood out into
The unfathomable sea
Until there is no cup, only sea.

Come, my brothers and sisters
Be not small-minded
See the vast carpet of starry crown
And be in awe of the majesty that created all.

Master I

Recently, a newspaper, *New Times of Los Angeles*, published an article about a man's claim to be the son of Paramhansa Yogananda. The man making the claim, Ben Erskine, says his stepfather abusively made the statement that he, Ben, was the son of that "Swami up on the hill." He said his mother never verified what was said by the stepfather, but he felt it was accepted by all in the family as true. Ben, with brown skin and distinct features, was a contrast to his fair-skinned nuclear family.

The article goes into some detail about DNA testing (said to prove Ben is not Yogananda's son) and statements by the children of some close associates of Yogananda's that would support his lack of celibacy.

For many of us who follow these teachings, such allegations are both shocking and upsetting. If there is truth in Yogananda's lack of celibacy, it contrasts with the image we have made of him. Part of the swami's vow is to be celibate, and our teachings also state that transmuting sexual energy is a goal for aspirants and will help one to realize God in His fullness. Some spiritual masters say complete abstinence is necessary for God-realization. Therefore, to think one of our swami gurus in our lineage was not abstinent would naturally come as a shock and be upsetting.

The other side of the coin is, if the allegations are not true, it is upsetting to have those allegations printed and for the impression to go "out to the world." And leave the impression in many people's mind that Yogananda had a child. It would not be the first time that a newspaper "got it wrong," but the result is that many people are left with the impression that the allegations are true.

Paramhansa Yogananda, as my Param Guru, my Guru's Guru, is in-as-much my family, my grandfather. As a disciple's disciple, I want to say, "No, that is not true!" But these are events that happened seventy years ago. I was not there. I don't know any facts about this man from the article or who his father is.

So, how to respond? One response came from a disciple of Yogananda's. Unfortunately, his reputation has been rather sullied with lawsuits and many allegations of sexual misconduct. His written response was a combination of, in the first two pages, speaking of the beautiful personality of Yogananda, and, in the last four pages, counter-attacking some who were quoted in the article. Some of his worst attacks were against Master's own disciples who had made no such allegations, apparently using his opportunity to defend Yogananda as a time to settle some old scores.

Well, what to do with all this? It is common when a system is under stress for it to attack itself. In families, this can be for parents to argue, pick on their children, or for the children to fight with each other. None of this ever leads to productive ends. What can be done in contrast? In a healthy system, all individuals can say what is true for them and then establish some idea of how to proceed.

What is true for me? The first thing: this article has had an impact on me; at least, the day and day after I read the article, I felt the force of it in my body. I will not say, as did the author of the counter-attack, that it had the effect of a "gnat at a picnic." It has been a bigger effect than that. My preference would be for such a controversy to not exist. However, it does exist, and it does have an effect.

So, what did I do with the feelings? I took them within. I took them into my Self, to God. I asked myself what I knew to be true. I searched for a solid foundation upon which to stand. I did not want some mental foundation. "What I believe, but something deeper— what I know through my own experience."

I found myself spontaneously asking my self (and my Self) what I know. The answers centered around: I know what I experienced with Mother, the truth, power, and beauty of God within her; I know the truth of the God-experiences I have had. Mother said she was the product of two Masters, Yogananda and Swami Ramdas. Parmahansa Yogananda was Mother's Guru. What I have received from Mother comes from Yogananda. The beauty, love, truth, and light of God are beyond any gift I could have hoped to have gained in this life. Master Paramhansa Yogananda is a direct tributary source of this; I have no doubt.

Soon after I asked my self (Self) these questions, I closed my eyes and focused on the third eye point. I saw, there, the deer skin shoes of Master that I saw in a vision not so very long ago. His body was huge, of cosmic proportions, in fact I could see no more than his feet, beyond that was outside my vision. To me he was the Purushottama, the Godhead or the Universal Divine Personality. At his feet, I felt sanctified, purified of any upset. In that state, I had no questions, no doubt, no judgment, only God.

How, then, do I (we) proceed? In an age of permissiveness, is this a free license for behavior? I think to read the story of Ben, his mother and family, one would have to conclude, whoever Ben's father was, a very high price was paid by all the family. Knowing a little of the inside story of the organization Yogananda founded, I think a high price has been paid by them, resulting in a change of the spirit and letter of what Master created. And, whatever may or may not be true in the story, the effect of those allegations will touch the lives of many people yet today. I think what is clear from all of this is a reinforcement of the idea that what we do matters; it matters a great deal.

The lessons that I draw from this story are as follows:

- I may use any information, any incident, to draw closer to God, to truth.
- I do not need to arbitrarily deny or counterattack something said, but I can use it as a focus to clarify my own cause and spiritual path.
- This world is, and always will be, of a dual nature. Highs are followed by lows, good by bad. The only sure refuge is in the Self. Here, the ups and downs of duality are seen as God's play. We may be called on to defend or attack at times, to reflect and meditate deeply at other times.
- Loyalty to my Guru(s) means taking the "good" with the "bad." Since this world is of a dual nature, that means the Guru-lineage will also reflect a dual nature; human and Divine. When I look beyond (not deny) this dual nature, I see only the Divine.
- I can draw lessons from everything I see, everything I experience, to further clarify my own values, to guide how I conduct my own life.
- I learn to love, and to see God, beyond the passing shadows of the world; this is the singular lesson of life. My Guru(s) have taught me this central truth and are constantly calling me to keep my thoughts dwelling upon God alone.

Master II

Recently, a newspaper article was about a man from Oregon who grew up believing he was the son of Paramhansa Yogananda. The lengthy article described the man's abusive stepfather hurling this accusation at him during his years in the family home while his mother was silent on the issue. The article also quoted some other sources, mostly reports supporting the idea that Yogananda was not abstinent during his time in America.

Such lack of abstinence runs contrary, of course, to being a swami, and raises questions regarding his self-control and even his state of realization. It should be noted that there was no evidence presented in the article such as might be required in a court of law, but second-hand rumors and stories from some sources close to Master during his early years in America. It should also be noted these sources all had differences with Master that entailed hard feelings on their part and even lawsuits. I am sure we will hear more of this, as the story unfolds, regarding the DNA testing of the man said to be possibly Yogananda's son.

It brings the question to mind: what are the qualifications of a realized soul? One of the aspects of India's Yogic science is the gradation of the various stages of realization. Self-realization is viewed in progressive states of consciousness. In Mother's language, there is a point where you "go over the top and there is no possibility of a fall." Until that state is reached, a fall from God-consciousness is still possible.

And, what is a fall? To know that, we must know what a realized state of consciousness is. Knowing the presence of God is a definite state of Consciousness. God-consciousness transcends normal human consciousness, yet physical consciousness is an extension of God-consciousness. To be in a God-conscious state is to feel that Presence as the source of one's Being; for the purity of that Presence to inspire all thoughts and actions, and to feel that Presence in every part of creation, within and without.

This elevated state of Consciousness is contrasted with the human state. The human state of consciousness is driven by needs and habits of the body; by and large, it is unconscious of a Divine Presence. It is self-centered in its desires versus the Divine prompting of a realized soul acting for the highest good of all.

With very few exceptions, souls, even great souls and avatars, progress through gradual stages of development that vacillate between the human and the Divine. At one time, even for extended periods of time, one may feel entirely in God-consciousness. Then, all of a sudden, or gradually, desire nature of the body takes hold. Some chemistry stirs passions, a feeling of loneliness, a desire to escape the stress and strain of sadhana may all head to this downward turn.

The example of Jesus falling under the weight of the cross—the body—is given as an allegorical description of this truth. Of course, it is upsetting to devotees who have put their trust and faith in a spiritual master only to find out the master has been subject to a fall or falls. That is, the master has been driven by body desire nature versus pure God-consciousness.

A devotee may ask, "Are there times when God-consciousness would direct a spiritual master into behavior that would look the same as a desire from body consciousness?" The answer would have to be, "Yes." This represents dangerous ground as the actions of a realized master and one who is pretending or is self-deluded about their mastery can look the same. How is one, then, asks the devotee, "To know the difference between a charlatan or a self-deluded master and a genuine spiritual master?"

The answer is that it is difficult to tell. One answer was given by Jesus; "A tree is known by its fruit." (Matthew 7:16–20) A genuine master will draw devotees closer to God, closer to their fully realized state. Human-based desires produce further enmeshments into the human drama and desire nature. These results may take time to unfold; fruit initially tasting sweet may turn sour when digested; other fruit begins as stringent when coming in, but has the most wonderful long-term effect.

Paying attention to the fruit of one's own experience further reinforces the Guru within, the sweetness of God-experience, and it can be more and more our guide. The outer Guru has come to help reveal the inner Guru. To the extent God awareness is awakened within us, the Guru has fulfilled his or her mission. In order for that to occur, the Guru must be awake in God.

Also, as one ascends the spinal stairway of Consciousness, a soul may attain great heights, have tremendous experiences, yet be subject to falls. It is called a fall because the consciousness falls from the purity of spiritual Consciousness in the higher regions of the spine and brain to the realms of body consciousness in the lower part of the spine. Falls can occur in many areas of human desire. They can be of a sexual nature, money and greed, psychic powers, wielding power from a position of authority, addiction to alcohol, drugs, etc.

These falls can run different courses, and this is a crucial part of the story for soul development. Because falls cover such a breadth of human experience, not every fall will be of equal weight. The measurement of a fall may be known by the depth of the desire nature in the soul.

A fall can be a seed of desire that is triggered by some experiences and the desire is released. This brief experience leads to a renewed focus on the higher regions of Consciousness and the soul moves forward in its progression toward the Infinite. Even highly realized souls are subject to these.

Another kind of fall can occur when the soul has episodic struggles with some desire nature. This represents a deeper pattern that requires a more constant struggle. The soul works hard to free itself of the desire; at times, it is successful and other times, the desire runs strong.

It must be understood that a soul can have tremendous spiritual experiences and revelations and still be in the clutches of this see-saw battle.

The third level of fall represents one whose desire nature is always just beneath the surface. The battle is constant and the behavior is chronic. This compulsion will drive the thoughts and behavior. One can even be, what is called in the addictions field, a dry drunk. That is, one keeps from doing the behavior, but the desire is always there.

The three categories demonstrate that not all falls are of the same nature. In our way of thinking, we would like to believe that if one is a spiritual master, a spiritual teacher, that they are not subject to a fall at all. When one meets an individual who has awakened their spiritual potential, it may take a form of rose-colored glasses for the devotee who does not recognize that the spiritual teacher is struggling with some desire nature themselves.

If knowledge of this fact comes to the devotee, it may create some disturbance. To compound this illusion by the devotee, spiritual teachers and/or followers of the teacher may hide the fact that falls have occurred or the fact that spiritual teachers have struggles with desire nature at all.

In the *Gospel of Swami Ramdas*, Papa was reading about Ramakrishna Paramhansa. Papa once commented that there is a quote that would not be found in any literature put out by the organization of his followers. This lack of "full disclosure" is not necessarily motivated from bad intention. There are times when a spiritual master wants to paint a picture of utmost purity to inspire the devotee to reach out for that highest nature.

However, intentions for covering the truth are not always that pure. In addition, an unrealistic picture can make the devotees feel bad about themselves. If they feel any desire nature, they feel they must be terrible sadhakas on the path! This can result in negative self-esteem and hurt spiritual development.

The worst cases are those spiritual teachers who give themselves over to debauchery, all the while holding out a picture of themselves to devotees of a being quite different from that; maybe even going out of their way to condemn others for doing exactly what they are doing!

We have seen many of the most famous spiritual teachers, both Christian and Eastern, publicly exposed for misuse of sex, money, and power. From a distance, it is difficult to see whether the allegations are true, and if they are true, what category of a fall: a brush with a desire and it was released, an episodic struggle, a battle waged with pure intention, or a wholesale giving-in!

What are the lessons for us? And what do we make of a spiritual hero who falls?

These questions really lead us back to ourselves. We can be like children when embarking on this path. A child does not know what it is like to be the parent, so they infer from what they see and guess a lot. As they grow older, the child-becoming-an-adult goes through many stages. From idealizing their parents, they may now become rebellious; or they may imagine all the ways they would be a better parent. Eventually, they become parents themselves and they understand their parents in a more realistic way. When they see their own children, they now know that the life of the parent is both *more* and *less* than what the child imagines. A spiritual master is also *more* and *less* than what the devotee-disciple imagines.

Learning to see who the spiritual master really is means growing to the same level of development the master has achieved. Everything that happens in our life is meant to awaken our true spiritual nature. This being true for mundane occurrences, how much truer for a spiritually-charged master?

We must struggle in order to grow. This is true throughout all of nature, and it is true for the spiritual path as well. Therefore, we must struggle to attain the Divine Consciousness our Spiritual teacher and the great masters have attained.

During that struggle, we too will be on a see-saw battle between our human and Divine natures. We will confront ourselves again and again. At times, there is value in seeing our gurus in their perfect state. We draw strength, inspiration, and imbibe the purity of their Being into our own. At other times, we may be confronted with their humanity. This may include what, from a human perspective, appears as shortcomings, biases, lapses, and even falls.

With touching humility, Sri Yukteswar asked Yogananda that if he, Yogananda, ever found Sri Yukteswar in a fallen state, would he promise to bring him back to the Divine? Sri Yukteswar went on to explain that is when a friend is needed as never before; this, coming from such a highly realized soul and Guru to Yogananda! You see, humility is not calculated for effect, it comes from child-like surrender.

To see the Guru as they truly are means to see them as both human and Divine. Part of the idea of being separate from God means we have separated our humanness from our Divinity. We rebel at the thought that God is also our human nature. We cannot truly understand the reality of this truth until we have transcended the human nature and become united again with our Divine nature. There is a paradox in that; it cannot be avoided.

We must struggle to overcome the magnetic pull of human desire and habits. Only by struggling to direct our attention to God will we rise into God-consciousness. This polarized struggle is intense. In fact, it would be impossible to win this struggle without the inherent Christ-nature or Krishna-nature within us. The Christ or Krishna-nature is the perfect reflection of God's nature. Even with that Christ or Krishna-nature, the struggle is not over in a moment.

Spiritual teachers, if they are who they really should be, have established themselves in that higher nature. But, they may not necessarily have gone over the top. Papa said it was years after establishing the ashram before he was perfectly established in that highest consciousness, Sahaja Samadhi. Before that, he was teaching and playing the role of Guru. In fact, some teachers have said an aspirant must have accepted and helped some devotees as disciples before attaining the highest state themselves.

How then do we balance the ideal of gaining absolute purity of God-consciousness and the possibility of a fall—either in ourselves or in a guru? To have a mature view, we must see that for most souls, full realization does not happen in one jump. We must see that to the degree we stay focused on God will be the greatest determinant of our realization. We must also balance this with a human understanding of the powerful forces of human desire. Masters have emphasized the divine because that is where they want our minds focused. This focus is required for the great struggle. But, we should not create an unrealistic picture of making one giant step out of the human to Divine.

When we know this struggle is part of the path, and what we encounter is what every realized master has had to encounter in their soul's evolution, it balances our perspective. Human desires will challenge us; this is the horizontal cross aspect to the upward vertical movement of spiritual desire on our human cross. Keeping our minds glued on God, we will struggle; we may stumble, and yes, we may fall. Knowing this is a possibility, we will also know what to do if it should happen. We will get back up, brush the dirt and blood off, and continue on our way. If we fall again, we will get up again. We will never give up; we will never give in until we reach our goal!

Duplicity, cover-ups, and hypocrisy are not part of this road to Golgotha, the hill of the skull, or highest realization. Not everything needs be broadcast to the world, a world eager to denigrate anyone striving for something higher. But, also, one should not lie or do harm to another in an effort to deny something that happened. It is now part of the history of that soul, and if that one continues on to fullest realization, even the falls can be an inspiration for those making their own way to the top.

Of course, there is the concern about those given over to desire nature but propping themselves up as spiritual teachers, those who are compulsive in their desire and have really, in their hearts, "joined the other side." They can use this more liberal attitude to justify doing whatever they want and play to the good nature of disciples.

What can be said of such ones? God will surely protect sincere devotees. If one does not go against that "still, small voice," then God will surely deliver them from the clutches of one given over to wantonness. Even as cream always rises to the top, so will a sincere devotee rise to the top, so will a sincere devotee rise up to God, surpassing even their unrepentant Guru.

It is in this crucible of worldly experience that the soul is purified of dross, leaving the essence of God alone in the devotee. In the

East, it is described as a battle; in the West, as a crucifixion. Both describe the same process of purification. It is the way of the cross and the Christ; it is the pearl of great price. Only the courageous and intrepid will enter. Our integrity and sincerity are our compasses, courage our shield, discrimination our sword. Our driver and guide, the Christ-like Krishna of pure light within. The Guru comes into our life to awaken that sleeping Christ and bring us to that fullest realization of God.

May that awakening be yours. May sincerity, courage, wisdom, and integrity ever be yours to lead you straight away to your Infinite Beloved.

Om Tat Sat Aum

Vision Illumined

Like a blind man first gaining his sight, so do spiritual devotees only see the light for a short time before desiring the darkness and a rest. Gradually, the eyes get accustomed to the light and grow more desirous of the light and averse to the dark. Now, the sadhaka glories in the light at all times and never cares for seeking out the dark. His or her Soul awakened, vision illumined, he or she is ever residing in the Infinite Beloved.

O Lord, teach us to see with equal vision that All is an expression of Your play, high and low, good and bad, ever springing from Your Eternal Being.

In that equal vision, seen by Your Grace, give us a heart of compassion for all alike, high and low, good and bad, knowing all comes from Thee and all returns to Thee as well.

From that compassion, let understanding bloom, seeing that actions beget like results high and low, good and bad, and that all action takes us back to Thee by long or short routes.

Equal vision, compassion, and understanding are the components of wisdom and make us know You are the Sole Doer. High and low, good and bad, all resides in Your expression of Love and Bliss!

O Infinite Divine

O Infinite Divine
Beloved Friend of friends
Source of love, wisdom, and joy
All creation is in search of You.

Yet where are You to be found?
You grant a glimpse of Yourself here
Then You withhold Yourself there
You tease with a promise, but withhold with all.

You enjoy Your Game,
Anticipation burns in Your devotee
Yet You hide behind a veil
And smile at Your own jest.

Is it cruelty or love that motivates You?
Oh! It cannot be cruelty, so it must be love
A love born of anticipation
Knowing the joy of finding will be multiplied many times.

You play Your game
But do You never tire?
When at last, Your devotee, in sad repose,
Surrenders all, then You come as mother to child.

You embrace, caress, and sing sweet songs
Then You are gone again
With echoes of Laughter following
You play Your game.

I tire of the game
I want to find, not seek
I want union, not anticipation
I want You.

O Infinite Splendor
Open my eye to see You shining everywhere
I don't want to behold You in one form
But in all forms.

I want to swim in Your Ocean
Of Sat-Chit-Ananda
And explore the vast being You Are
Not in separation, but in the Oneness of All.

You are with me now
Answer my wish
And let Your Grace
End this separation and end in Bliss.

Full-Time Awareness

The goal of Life is complete God-realization. Complete God-realization is full-time awareness—it is God alone who animates this body, mind, and soul as well as every aspect of creation. This Omniscience, Omnipresence, and Omnipotence is One, without a second. When consciously realized, the body, mind, and soul are purified of any self-will directed by body-consciousness; the body is the machine and God is the operator.

The Way of achieving this complete union with God is the subject of all great religions and the teachings of realized masters. In a few rare instances this realization comes without visible preparation, complete, whole and in an instant. Other examples include brief-but-intense sadhana, others are years of intense sadhana. The length of time and the exact circumstances of a soul gaining complete realization covers a broad range and is of absorbing interest to many sadhakas.

The complexity making for this variety is partially due to the fact that souls have different starting points. It must be understood these starting points are states of mind only but may be illustrated by a physical analogy. If one were to go to New York City, the journey would be quite different depending on the starting point. If one was in New Jersey and only needed to cross a river, the way would look quite different from someone starting in Los Angeles. And for one starting from Tokyo, the way would vary even more. So too with sadhakas, depending on their make up based on their karma, or their prior actions, the starting point, and what the path looks like will vary a great deal for aspirants.

However, all are free to start their journey at any time. It is possible for one starting in Tokyo, making a sincere, determined effort, to arrive at the destination before someone with lackluster motivation starting in New Jersey. The goal is available to all. The length of the way can vary by a wide range. The last point is that will and determination play a critical role in the success of the aspirant.

Krishna

Toward the end of Krishna's life, the city he built was becoming corrupt. His own children began to lose their adherence to Dharma. As a result, Krishna led his sons and their retinue to a sacred river in order to purify their minds. They had seen signs of terrible things to come, so they were amenable to trying to stop it.

Earlier, Krishna had brought forward some honorable sages for the benefit of his citizens. As a joke, one of the sons dressed as a woman and the other son told the sages that this "woman" was pregnant and asked what the sex of the child would be. The answer was, "This birth will not be of a boy or girl, but a pestle." Sure enough, the imposter-mother came down with a great pain and a pestle was found in his stomach. That pestle was pounded into pieces and spread all around. One larger piece could not be reduced and was thrown into the sea.

All these scattered pieces continued to play a part in the story. Some of the grains of that powdered pestle became a weed that grew by the water into which it had been thrown. The weed was very hard and very sharp, like a sword. The larger piece was found by a fisherman in a fish he caught. That piece was made into an arrowhead and given to a hunter.

Now Krishna and his sons were camped by the river doing purification rites. All was going along all right for a while. Even though alcohol was forbidden by Krishna, the sons had brought homemade wine. One night, as they were drinking and the purification rites had slowly slipped from their minds, some words were said in jest. This led to a fight.

Now some of these weeds that were hard and sharp as swords grew near the river. Soon the fighters resorted to using those weeds to slit each other's throats. It was a wholesale massacre, and none were left alive in the end. Krishna, returning from this failed attempt at saving his sons, sat down in the forest and became absorbed in the Infinite Nature. A hunter, mistaking the sole of Krishna's foot that crossed his leg for prey, shot him with the arrowhead made from the pestle.

Now, what is the meaning of this story? One lesson to derive from it concerns a spiritual teacher and his children, his spiritual sons. The Master, having constructed a great spiritual city, takes the role of father to many. Eventually, the disciples become slack in their spiritual practice. Their desire for name, fame, position, and the like, supersede their love and childlike adherence to the Dharma and God.

The Guru inspires them to purify their minds, leading them to the river of life. However, old habits take over. Wine is made of fermented fruit. The fruit the guru gives us becomes rotten and the guru ferments in an unleavened mind. A war of words ensues that leads to the slitting of each other's throats. That is, the tongue becomes hard and sharp, contrasted to a devotee in tune with God whose words are sweet and healing.

A war ensues and the disciple's children get busy slaying each other, each thinking they are in the right. As a result, the spiritual gifts of the Master are destroyed; they may outwardly look to be spiritual children, but in reality, they have died to the Spirit.

As a result, the Master too is killed, and his city sinks back into the sea. The question is asked, why did Krishna leave nothing, not his children, not his city, not even his body, which he took with him. This answer given: he wanted to show that when the body had fulfilled its purpose, it was no longer needed. In other words, the outer form would become an obstruction rather than a help.

In our own lifetime, we have seen this story played out by the disciples of several masters. Is there no avoiding this implosion made by disciples? I think the story is told to say, "Yes, it can be avoided." How? By maintaining one's intensity of sadhana. That will make the fruit given by the guru ever-sweet. The lack of striving for name and fame, pride of position, etc., will ensure the ego maintains its position as the lover of God and the servant of God.

May God and Guru's blessings shower all devotee/disciples everywhere with sweet, healing words and the ongoing intensity of sadhana to ensure adherence to Dharma and the long life of Para-Param Gurus.

Freedom In Action: Prem-Ananda

The Guru is ever anchored in the Divine. Due to the ever-existent connection, the Guru is able to be at one with all devotees who seek shelter. The Guru may feel the devotees' pain, stand by their side as they face the dilemmas of life, and live in the devotees' hearts.

It is the devotees' sincere call that brings the Guru into their heart and soul. In their communion with God, Guru and God are one, and the devotees come to know that God has become their Guru, and Guru is ever-existent in God.

If the Guru was not thoroughly anchored in God, he or she would be caught in the whirlwind of the devotees' karma. Caught up in that whirlwind, the Guru would over-identify with disciples and lose balance. Through oneness with the Infinite, the Guru may stand with devotees through thick and thin, taking many of the karmic blows for the devotees, yet remain unaffected due to union with God.

These karmic blows may come in dark clouds of causal doubt, tortured winds of emotional turmoil, or heavy knocks to the body. Never does the Guru flinch under such conditions. Only love of the Divine, in all of its purity, can provide the mettle for the Guru. For every knock that comes, devotees may nary give a glance to the Guru and may even allow themselves to be carried off by the forces of their own karma.

What then, the fate of the Guru if he or she were attached to some outcome, expecting gratitude or understanding from the uncomprehending disciples? Would the Guru not be filled with disappointment, seeing ingratitude and worse, become bitter? Only by being anchored in the Divine, devoid of attachment, can the Guru not be swept away in separation from God.

Where then, is the source of this superhuman perspective? Why, the Guru sees it in God's expression in all nature. The sun shines on the just and the unjust the same, not withholding its life-giving rays to any. The rose wafts its fragrance to all who avail themselves of a whiff, whether they are the ones who tended the garden or neglected it. And the cedar never releases so much of its perfume as when the unmindful axe fells it to the ground.

The Guru sees countless examples in nature of how God gives without thought of reward or the merits of the receiver. Are we, who are made in the image and likeness of God, to think we should be any different?

And what reward is there for such unbounded giving? God gives through nature because it is His nature to give. To withhold would mean it would no longer have the nature of God; so, with us. We give because it is our nature to give. And for our giving to be sweet like the rose, or permeating every cell like the cedar, it must come from the heart and soul.

When giving in the spirit of God, we feel ourselves to be in union with God. We become God in action. The love and joy that permeates our being from that giving perfumes the gift with the loveliest of vibrations. If the gift is lost, unrecognized, or misused, it does not turn the gift or giver bitter. Rather the sweetness continues to permeate the air. If a perfume bottle is broken, the fragrance continues in the room more than ever. Even so, the giver of God's bounty. That beauty, love, and light going out from the giver will find its recipient.

How many saints have lived in obscurity in their own lives, only to have their sweet vibration go out and permeate all of history after them? And, how many saints faced persecution and misunderstanding only to have their influence gain in power and beauty, while others faded into obscurity? Surely, some may have thought they lived their lives in vain. How could they know that the essence of God they distilled from their own lives continued to intoxicate generations afterwards?

Saints, gurus, and devotees have hearts that beat with the same light. The essence of what they distill from life will leave its imprint on all those who follow. Whether it be the vibration of Jesus or Judas, Rama or Ravana, the effect of how a life is lived exists long after the physical life is gone. Whether it be of the famous or the obscure, each leave their print. Could the famous have lived their lives if not for the sacrifice of countless ones playing their parts in obscurity?

Each one of us has a part to play. As in a theatrical production, a minor part may turn out to be the star performance when played to perfection. There are no minor parts, for each must play their part well to make the play great.

The greatest way to play our part in this Divine drama is to anchor ourselves to the Divine, then we play the part with all our heart and soul. We do not hold back, neither do we become attached. Bliss comes from knowing we are the Divine playing the role. We give without thought of reward; we act for the sake of the role assigned. We remain in freedom even amidst activity.

O Sadhaka! This is our time on the stage. Let us savor our role, but never forget our Divine heritage. We are God in human form, here to fulfill a sacred purpose, even in mundane activities. All come from Ananda, Bliss; all return to Ananda. And when looked at through the lens of God's Light, all is love—our eternal treasures, attributes. Prem Ananda, Love and Bliss. May all sadhakas ever be filled with Prem Ananda, now and always!

Jesus: Blended Thoughts of the East

Two great Lights shine from the East. Krishna and Buddha continue to illuminate the hearts and minds of millions worldwide. Jesus too, came to illumine the world. In studying the lives of the Avatars, it has been my conviction that Jesus traveled to India and studied with the great masters there. Having access to their scriptures, living masters, and modes of worship, Jesus, and perhaps John the Baptist, as well, clarified the vision for the upliftment and salvation of humankind.

There may be those who don't care for the idea that Jesus was influenced by others. In viewing Jesus as an "original issue" from God, it is also interesting to see how he compares to other world teachers. This is not an academic study, rather it is a view from a devotee of all three Masters.

John the Baptist immersed aspirants in the River Jordan for remission of sins, even as Hindus are immersed into the Ganges for the remission of sins.

Jesus and John practiced fasting, prayer, and sought out seclusion in the wilderness and mountaintops to commune with God, even as yogis perform fasts, prayer, seeking out seclusion in the wilderness and mountaintops for the realization of God.

Jesus traveled without money, begging for his food and drink, wandering from town to town. He instructed his disciples to do the same, to travel with simple cloth and sleep on the ground, even as yogis-sannyasis and the Buddha in India.

Jesus was a renunciate, unmarried; he had no possessions and advocated for at least some disciples to do the same, even as the Buddha and sannyasins renounced all in search of the Truth.

Jesus was a pacifist, preferring to sacrifice his own life rather than take another's life, even as the Buddha was—and the view of ahimsa is in Yoga, harmlessness.

Jesus had love for nature and its creatures, even as the Buddha and Krishna had love and compassion for nature and its creatures.

Jesus was openly confrontative to religious leaders of his day who betrayed the principles they were supposed to be upholding, even as Krishna was the open opponent to secular kings who betrayed the righteousness they were charged with upholding.

Jesus identified himself with the Godhead, or the Supreme being even as Krishna identified himself with God. Jesus identified himself as a shepherd even as Krishna is identified as a cowherder.

Jesus performed various miracles and healings even as Krishna and Buddha are identified with many miracles and healings.

Jesus said that to look upon himself and his name is the same as seeing God, even as Krishna did the same.

Jesus used bread and wine given in a sacred ceremony, because transformed food and drink become spiritually charged, even as Krishna and Hindus observe the giving and taking of prasad.

At death of the body, Jesus' physical body disappeared, returning in a transformed body, even as Krishna dematerialized his body at death, and the Buddha is said to have ascended to Nirvana.

Jesus is undoubtedly the greatest spiritual influence in the West. It is astounding when you think of his origins, coming from a carpenter's family and growing up in a small town. One marvels at the spiritual power that began as a seed, from one of his parables, and grew into a great tree.

The teachings of Jesus stand on par with the greatest religions of the world. It is purported he taught but for three years. Even in this short span of time, he was in seclusion for various lengths of time and traveling by foot in remote areas.

In my own study of spiritual teachers, Jesus' life stands as unique, yet the comparison of his life with other great avatars—perfect

Spirit descended into flesh—is natural. The two lives and teachings that come naturally to my mind for comparison are Siddhartha Gautama, the Buddha, and Krishna, both in India.

It is thought by many that Jesus traveled to India, studying with, and teaching many of the great spiritual masters there. If this be true, Jesus would have easily been exposed to the scriptures of both Krishna and Buddha. As I study the lives of the great masters and teachers as a devotee, not a scholar, I am struck by the similarities I see in Jesus' teachings to Krishna and Buddha. To my mind, he took aspects of both the magnificent avatars and blended them with his own native Judaism.

To followers of Jesus, this may be heresy, but to me it is a devotional study. To those who insist on the unique differentiation of religions, this will be the mixing of oil and water. But to those who see the profound traditions as expressions of the same source—transcendent truth—then the comparison will seem natural and possibly illuminating.

Introduction To Peace Pilgrim

In 1978, I met Peace Pilgrim when she gave a talk at the college I was then attending. I was captivated by her straightforward, clear-thinking message of peace. "Peace begins with the individual," she said. "If enough individuals live their life in peace, then world peace will surely follow."

Her message, as she said, was not new. The truths she spoke are timeless and all people already know them. What would be new is for people to live according to these truths! True to her message, she lived her words. At a time in life when most people are thinking of their financial security, she set out on foot to walk 25,000 miles for peace. The year was 1953. Courageously, she walked along the highways of America, alone and with only the clothes on her back.

Peace Pilgrim carried her message as she crisscrossed the continent, "This is the way of peace: overcome evil with good, falsehood with truth, hatred with love." She had only the clothes she wore, no money, food, or other belongings. She vowed to, "Walk until given shelter, fast until given food, remaining a wanderer until mankind has learned peace." In short, she lived her message. I felt privileged to have met this Western saint and woman of high realization.

I had a desire for her to meet my Guru. She said she would like that, but had to travel from Seattle to Bellingham by that afternoon for a radio interview and then to give a talk at the Bellingham Unity Church that night. For the first 25,000 miles, she had accepted no rides. But that time was long past, so I offered to drive her to Bellingham. She accepted. A fellow devotee, Michael McCurley, and I drove her the one-and-a-half hour trip to Bellingham.

On the way, she spoke of her life as an American "sannyasini" (my word, not hers). She traveled with only the pants, shoes, socks, and sweatshirt she wore. In her sweatshirt, she had two pockets that kept the correspondences she had received. She had a permanent address for mail and the letters would be forwarded to her.

She spoke of a time traveling in the Midwest. A sudden snowstorm hit the area. She was alone, walking in the bitter cold. I reflected on hearing this that I had known a young healthy man whose truck had broken down in such a bitter cold. He had to walk a little over a mile to a truck stop and literally wondered if he was going to make it! So, I knew this was a dire circumstance for this woman without even a jacket.

Peace Pilgrim found a large cardboard box in the middle of nowhere in which she found shelter from the subzero winds that were threatening her life. Due to that shelter, she survived the storm, which she considered nothing short of God's Grace.

Her talks tended to focus on universal principles of sound psychology and practical wisdom. But clearly, she had the solid foundation of an active spiritual life in God. I know that she and my Guru would have had much common ground.

I hope you enjoy this unique American story and will derive insight into living your own life of peace from her inspiring story and teachings. True to a Karma Yogini, one who finds union with God through selfless service, she died with her boots on (tennis shoes in this case). She left her body during a car wreck. She was traveling to her next engagement to speak of peace. Now, free of an earthly body, she is free to travel all creation to broadcast her time-less message of peace to all.

The Guru's Glory is God's Glory

The Guru's glory is God's glory. To surrender to the Guru brings his or her mantle down upon us: it is the mantle of light, purity, and love. The Guru's mantle is God Itself. What is beyond good and evil? God alone—His love, light, and all-knowing wisdom. With compassion and equality, God sees all His creation as original innocence, because He is original innocence itself. Every body is a temple of light and purity to the all-comprehending intelligence of God. When we see creation as God does, we shall be as God: all bliss, ever-new joy, in peace, and with unerring wisdom and equal vision.

The word of God is not stale, stagnant, or old fashioned. If we think so, the error is ours, not God's. God is you, me, and this entire creation. In fact, God is not only this fascinating creation but is the unlimited potential beyond it as well. I say, "Don't find a new word for God; change your understanding to match the grandeur that is God!"

God is your Friend of friends. He resides in your heart. God is not man, woman, or any other thing. God is the life and intelligence that gives you the power to live, breathe, move, think—everything is done by that power and intelligence. God is not far off, but is the breath behind your breath, the feeling behind your feeling, the thought behind your thought. Eliminate all ideas of separation now! And God is yours.

Freedom, real freedom, is not the capacity to do anything you want. Real freedom is the result of self-mastery. Self-mastery results in total surrender. Total surrender brings about the annihilation of the ego-self. Annihilation of the ego-self produces a rebirth in God-consciousness, and that is real, absolute freedom.

Recognize the sole power of God as humility. When I first started giving talks at my Guru's request, I was subject to other people's projections, as they saw in me what was actually in themselves. A spouse of one of the devotees said, "You must feel real power when you give talks." His comment made me feel soiled, unclean. Yes, I felt the power of God flow through me; no other experience compares to that. But it is not an ego thing of feeling powerful. It is the complete reliance on God and feeling His power and intelligence acting through me.

Another situation came about when I first gave talks. People would come up to me and say, "I saw Master (or Mother) in your place while you were talking." Of course, it is wonderful to think the Masters are near. One woman who thought of herself as highly advanced once commented after a talk, "I saw all the Masters on either side of you when you were speaking." God prompted me to reply, "That is a reflection of your own consciousness." She was quite vain, and said, "Yes, yes that is true." And I saw her ego take in everything. It is a fascinating play.

When I meet people, I immediately see their state of mind. Whether they feel guided in uplifted states of mind, or they can be leading an immoral life headed for trouble, it is all written on their brow.

I do not comment on most people's development. Sometimes I build their ego a bit because they are in need of a boost; sometimes, I ignore them because they need their wings of ego clipped a bit. The Infinite does it all; I am merely the machine. God is the operator. He does all, for the highest good of all.

As I have grown, I have become more direct. It is an art to be direct without being blunt. Some people are blunt and say they are only speaking the truth. But it is not really truth; they are speaking because their motives are not pure. One must have pure motives to speak the truth; otherwise, what they say may be factually true but built on a lie.

God is purity itself. To realize God, you must be pure, but if you are filled with the impurity of the ego, only God can make you pure. Only Grace can be your salvation.

God-realization is not seeing or hearing something in a vision. God-realization must be the total transformation. You do not become someone else, but, for the first time, you truly become yourself.

Having outer purity without the corresponding inner purity is hypocrisy. Love of God, of truth, and desire for realization must outshine desire for the things of the body or the world. Without that burning desire, you will not achieve your goal of realization.

The Mystic Light Within

Feel that mystic Light within you. You may live in the city, dress in normal fashion, but in your heart beats the same Light that animates yogis of Himalayan peaks and the desert prophets of old. You do not need to be of the desert or the mountains to know what they know, to feel what they feel. Turn your mind to the same Source of life, purity of Spirit and Light of Being they focus upon. That Light is in your heart; it is not far away but as close as your breath!

True knowledge does not come from books or lectures. True knowledge comes from the crucible of experience. It is in this crucible that you strive, yearn, and work for the impossible. It is impossible, but for the ingredient of grace. Grace is the all-powerful force within you that transcends your doubt, weakness, and ignorance. The crucible produces heat, pressure; it dissembles and rearranges the atoms of your being. Do you think that kind of change comes with just some passing interest? Passionate yearning for Truth, Freedom, and Light must take hold of your whole self. This kind of yearning is a result of Grace. You can open yourself to that Grace by praying for it. When you create an opening, then Grace will fill you up and make the cauldron crucible to boil, producing in you a Divine Being.

This life in God is like no other; it demands all from you, physically, mentally, and spiritually. This life in God will take what you give and transmute it from dross to the gold of Spirit. It demands your all, but it gives back so much more.

Scriptures like the Bhagavad Gita and the Sermon on the Mount do not appear out of thin air. These sayings are the distilled wisdom of intense practice, yielding a profound wisdom. Who can understand the power behind these words that has inspired God-men and women for thousands of years? Twenty or thirty years of meditative study will certainly result in priceless gems of realization. But to say one has encompassed the depth of these scriptures would be tantamount to saying one has circumscribed God! Use the scriptures as guides to take you deeper until you become a creature of the Deep. Even then, these glowing words will move you as no others can.

There are many today who object to the notion of religion or God. Instead, they talk of spirituality and the Self, or nirvana. This distinction is, in reality, artificial. There are those of orthodox minds in every religion. Their mind-set is concrete. They tend to think they are right and all others are wrong. This is as true of those who speak of religion as it is of those who speak of spirituality. It is a form of ignorance and pride.

God does not care about what name He is called, or whether the reference is to a He, She, or It. God looks to the heart. If the heart is sincere, soft, and yearning, God is pleased. If the heart is full of pride, ignorance, and I, me, and mine, He becomes a stranger. It is not a matter of education, which religion one belongs to, or even a belief system. It is a matter of the attitude of the heart.

Krishna, speaking as the Infinite, says, "I do not care what you offer me, it can be a leaf, a drop of water, anything offered with a sincere heart is acceptable to Me." (Gita 9:26) You see, God looks into the heart. A great devotee said, "And if I am wandering about and do not even have a drop of water, what then?" Krishna replied, "As long as you have even one drop of water in your eye as a tear for me, I consider that a more valuable gift than gold, jewels, or money given by others!"

So, you can take all artificial divisions and throw them into the ocean. Speak to God with your heart, no matter what name or mental concept, as long as it pleases you and purifies your heart. Those with a pure heart shall see God.

There are many teachings and techniques you can use to get over interior hurdles. They are given to be of help. Like a craftsman uses tools to create something beautiful, when the project is done, the tools are put away. Even so, the spiritual techniques; when God is realized, the techniques are no longer needed. Some would-be craftsmen collect many tools, but remain unskilled in their use. So, it is with many would-be spiritual aspirants. They read books, listen to lectures, but refrain from real, deepened practice. Only those who sincerely practice will make progress towards the goal.

It is time to put away artificial divisions made in God. All religions strive for the same ultimate goal, to bridge the gap between individual humans and God. Through love, support, and understanding, you will come to see there are many sincere devotees in every religion the world over. This universal recognition will help heal divisions among people, and therefore help heal the division between individual humans and God. With love, faith, and sincerity, may all live according to their highest creed and attain their goal.

Affirmation for Meditation

I am a loving child of God;
Rich ideas from God are now pouring into my consciousness.
God gives me dominion over fear, hate, weakness, poverty,
and in harmony,
I am continually protected by God's love.
Disturbances cannot annoy me, because I abide in God's presence.

Through the help of God, I am master of my emotions.
No disappointment can disturb or discourage me.

Deepening Kriya

The microcosm of the body is a perfect replica of the macrocosm of the universe. The Kriya breath replicates the purity of creation, preservation, and dissolution. Through individuals identifying with the body and the world through the five senses, they lose that original purity, or innocence, and as a result, lose conscious communion with the Infinite Creator.

The pre-Kriya breath, the first inhalation, is the enactment of drawing all scattered, disparate forces of life-energy into the main channel of the spine, the shushumna, and offering it to the feet of God at the ajna. This sets the stage for creation, in all its purity, to be enacted from its pure source, the kutastha chaitanya, emanating from the ajna.

God breathed life into humankind, it says in Genesis. Through focused attention, the life-energy is circulated over the head, offering it first to the unmanifest, formless, beginningless and endless Spirit, Sat at the Sahaswara at the crown of the head.

The Breath of God, or the pure life-force, is then passed down the "outside" of the chakras of life-force, thus keeping the life-force in its "virgin" state and creating a positive charge in each chakra.

The breath comes to rest at the base of the spine. Here the magnetic current of the life-force is reversed.

Through the individuals' misuse of free will, this life-energy is normally expended out through the afferent and efferent nerves. Of itself, this is not a problem. But when individuals identify fully with the body, they forget their spiritual origins and "fall," or become conscious primarily of the three lower chakras only.

This identification with the body finds its most powerful expression through sexuality. Physically, sex produces great pleasure in the body and "roots" the whole attention at the base of the spine. And from there out to all other subtle bodies. The life-force is expended and creates a desire to be fulfilled again and again. Psychologically, the mental energies become focused on finding a mate, or mates, and the mental energies are expended in this search. The result of this activity is the production of children, as God-as-nature designed it to be, which draws more attention to the body and the maintenance of the family.

The remembrance of the spiritual nature is lost, and one becomes completely focused on bringing the body and its relationship to the world. In reality, there can be no actual separation; without the spiritual power, intelligence, and creative forces, no life could exist, not even for a nano-second. However, the mind of the human becomes separated, creating a mental barrier to this greater reality. The goal of Yoga is to re-unite the conscious mind of the practitioner to its Spiritual Nature, or God.

Since the life-force has been used to create an imbalance, a negative charge in the spine, that is an imbalance of outward flow to the senses, Kriya Yoga is then designed to create a balanced equilibrium of the main powerhouses, or chakras, along the spine. By "deposition," or activating positive charges on these centers, the life-current is then reversed—drawing it back up the spine, the balance is restored.

Normal usage of the life-force in the fallen state is to positively charge these chakras unconsciously and use the life-energy through the senses.

The Kriya Yogi, however, doesn't expend the life-force out through the senses, but reverses the flow and draws it back up through the spine. The negative charge in the chakra is "collected" and guided up the spine. The chakra is charged, balanced, and purified through this upward and downward movement.

This balancing action of Kriya is represented by the up and down movement of the life-force, the warm and the cool sensations, and the outside and the inside charging with the life-force along the spine and in the brain. This balancing also purifies the chakras, creating a still, calm state. With each chakra in a charged, but still, state, equilibrium can be easily brought about.

The inhalation brings the life-force up the spine and delivers the "virgin" life-force, unspent through the senses, to the ajna, or the inner sanctum-sanctorum of the body temple. This inner offering of the pure, unused, virgin life-force is reflected in the human and animal sacrificial rites. These useless and destructive sacrifices do not release humanity's obligation to make the true sacrifice, the return of the unsullied life-force to God.

When the chakras, body cells, and blood are sufficiently purified, a magnetic force draws the Kundalini life-force and full attention of the yogi to the ajna. With the attention fully fixed on the ajna, the yogi surrenders all desire, even thoughts of spiritual experiences, at this inner door of heaven.

A prayer may issue from the yogi at this point, "Lord, if it be Thy will, reveal Thyself, reveal Thyself." And then the Kriya Yogi resides in the inner silence and stillness, content with leaving all in the hands of the Infinite.

This Kriya path is the most direct way to realization as it works with the life-force, the spine, and the brain in an integrated, balanced way. Some put great emphasis on practicing a higher number of repetitions of Kriya to gaining enlightenment. But who properly practices each Kriya breath with full attention now? Of what use, then, to seek to do more when one has not mastered what is already given? For a realized soul, very few Kriya breaths result in total stillness, or no breaths at all. Practice perfectly what one has been given, then reside in the equanimity that comes as a result.

Since Kriya is not practiced all through the day, we also have been initiated into chanting God's name. This chanting, whether with the lips or in the mind, is a great purifier of the mind and chakras as well. Whenever we feel the Presence of God, this is the fruition of our practice. If we reside in the Presence, even while active in the world, we will quickly realize that God is our indwelling source of life, intelligence, bliss, and joy.

Where does our reality come from? Physical scientists will tell us that some unknown cause resulted in an explosion of mighty proportions that eventually resulted in suns, planets, celestial movements, and somehow biological organisms that eventually found expression as the human. Ask most people and they would agree with this or a similar summary.

However, what makes us think that this is true? Well, we can take measurements, analyze data, form hypotheses, and test these through experiments to the best of our ability. In this way, we continue to disprove what is not true, and hopefully come closer to finding out what is true. Besides, I can look around, touch, smell, and hear this world, and it all confirms it is real.

One question: when we dream, do we not generally suppose that the dream is real as long as we are dreaming? It is usually upon waking from a dream that we say, "Oh, that was only a dream!" Until then, we believe that the dream is reality. "Yes," comes an answer. "But that *is* only a dream, something in the mind. *This* is reality." Well, mystics from ancient times say: what we call reality is a sense-play with the senses, and has not more, or less, reality to it than a dream. They say they have awakened from this dream to a greater reality, and we are no more than sleepwalking.

All of this outer reality is actually a projection of ideas generated by the inner human.

Silence—a paradox: "But here I can die: if I hit my head on a wall, it hurts; it damages my body. This is real!" Does that not all remain true in a dream?

September: Journey of the Soul

September 7, 2001—Silent Satsang

Dear Satsang Friends: Greetings, David has asked me to read this to you all.

Good Morning Everyone. Welcome to our last Satsang here at Cloud Mountain. This Saturday marks the completion of my one year in silence. I have felt it to be a great privilege to have spent this time here. It would not have been possible without your love, prayers, and support. Thank you so much.

Today we will follow our regular program. At the top of each hour, we will sing Ram Nam, then meditate during the rest of the hour. With the configuration of the room, I think we will be able to sit so that we will be able to circumambulate the room during our chanting.

I will ask you to come and go only at the times of singing. At noon we will have a potluck lunch in silence out on the deck by the dining hall, where there are picnic tables we can use, as it is a beautiful day.

At 3:00 p.m. we will leave Diamond Hall and assemble up at the Babaji Grotto site. There we will have an installation of the Babaji statue and add the power of our vibrations to that spot. After the installation, you may want to stay and meditate for a while or walk the grounds. Between 4:00 and 4:30 p.m., we will leave here, drive into Longview, and eat at a Chinese Restaurant where we have reservations.

Thank you for coming today, and helping me to make this a sacred day, and a fit conclusion to an eventful year for me.

Om Namaste Om, David

Reverend Peter Schultz building
the Babaji Grotto.

Yogacharya David with Babaji Statue.

Yogacharya David with
Babaji Statue.

Yogacharya David offering
Babaji Arati Blessing.

Yogacharya David offering
Babaji Arati Blessing.

Yogacharya David offering
Babaji Arati Blessing.

Babaji Statue.

Reverend Peter Schultz and Reverend
Larry Koler on Grotto Meditation Bench.

Babaji Statue.

Babaji Statue.

Babaji Grotto.

September 9, 2001:

Silent Satsang Completion, David reads:

Om Jesus
Om Babaji
Om Lahiri Mahasaya
Om Sri Yukteswar
Om Paramhansa Yogananda
Om our Divine Mother

Om—From the unreal, lead us to the Real; from darkness, lead us to Light; from death, lead us to Immortality!

Dear Satsang Friends,

Thank you for coming. These are my first words in one year. Why did I take this year in silence? It was God's will. He did not tell me why, and as the post says, "Ours is but to do and die."

It has been a multifaceted journey in this past year. Some of which I have written to you, some of which I will speak to you; most of which will remain with me.

I had two intimations before entering silence related to what this intense sadhana was for. First, my time in seclusion had come. The subtlety of thought renunciation was upon me for some time, and it was appropriate to remove myself from outer activities for this purpose.

The second reason had to do with the world. The trends in the world, and particularly this Western Culture, have disturbed me. With the unparalleled wealth and freedom in the history of the world, what have we done with it? The tendency has been to accumulate more wealth and spend it on entertainment. The entertainment industry has tended to play to the lowest and meanest in society. Where are the great thinkers, those who enable humankind?

Instead of ennoblement, it has been degradation. Instead of sacrifice for upliftment, it has been spend, spend, spend. And spend on what? On time watching television, movies, theater, art that appeals to the "want" in people. Additionally, we live in a world where our political leaders spend their time in a spoils system that silences men and women of principle.

What makes a society great? When we look back on history, the first thing that stands out are the great religious leaders through history. Krishna, Buddha, Lao Tzu, Jesus, Mohammed, just to name a few. What was common to all is their transcendent vision of Ultimate Reality, God and their willingness to sacrifice their lives in pursuit of this vision, and their full-fledged commitment to serving humanity. This is the first and greatest mark of a great society, to have ones such as those leaders in its midst.

What are the other marks evident of great civilizations? To name a few: advanced science and education, architecture, art, entertainment, and philosophy. These fields, when they achieve excellence, are viewed with awe and glory. In so many cases today, these areas are either downplayed or are simply achieving nothing of note. In each of these categories, the will to sacrifice to achieve is where?

What is missing today is that willingness to sacrifice, that willingness to renounce the payoff of the moment for a greater ideal. In the East, this ideal is called Dharma. Dharma calls on the individual to know that they are here for a purpose higher than eating, sleeping, working, and fornicating. It must be, for either a society is growing and being elevated, or it is shrinking and being degraded.

One of the greatest barriers to the establishment of Dharma—doing the right thing—is the division that exists amongst religions and their sects. This division that says, "I am right and the rest of you are wrong" must go. Obviously, we hold a belief because we believe it to be right. But we can hold a belief while, at the same time, respecting the other person's right to believe in another way. The key to finding a unifying ground in all religions is to search for the same thing, lasting happiness. Humanity searches in such a variety of ways, it really boggles the mind. But search it out we do.

And this highest expression of that search is when our feet are put on the spiritual path.

God is not a religion. Rather, all religions are so many roads to the same City of Light upon the hill. Most recognize that the search of the Hindu, the Christian, the Buddhist, the Jew, the Muslim, the non-affiliated searcher, all leads to the same ultimate realization. Without that recognition and support for the other to hold up the Dharma—the true way—this world will not realize peace or its true potential. When there is respect for all, then peace will reign.

It is possible to recognize universal principles upon which all can agree. Whether it be the compassion of the Buddha, or the sacrifice of the Christ, love is the expression of the ideal. And that love must find practical expression towards all humankind to find its fullest expression. Inner peace, founded on a transcendent premise, whether it be called God, the Tao, Paramatman, Allah, or Jehovah, it makes no difference in the name. The definite indication of light and peace as an aura around that one speaks a universal language.

Going beyond name, beyond form, and identifying what is universal and true will quell the collisions of differences and establish an undercurrent of harmony. As we grow more and more into a world-community, we must establish these basic principles rooted in a transcendent state of Being that will tie humanity together with a bond of goodwill and common purpose.

Darkness and error thrive in the world split by division and petty differences. In that striving, jealousy, fear, and hatred all gain strength and seek to destroy the good. Bound in fundamental principles, Spiritual Purpose can stand as a united bulwark against those forces that seek to hinder and even destroy the good.

Many souls are left in the vacuum that religions leave when they play small, splitting into smaller and smaller factions. Each individual has the right to worship in the way they feel inwardly directed. It can be truly said that there are as many religions as there are people: for no two people will share every idea, every ideal. But when the fundamental principles are agreed upon, then individuals are given a tool to measure their own ideals and make adjustments.

The second purpose for my year of seclusion and silence has been focused on this lack of Dharma in the world. To what end will this year of one person's sacrifice serve? The answer: follow the inner direction and do it!

One thing has rung true for me, even as a resonant bell or gong that goes on reverberating—that is my love for God, and for you my dear friends, has only grown stronger, deeper, and more secure. As I have gone deeper into this Journey of the Soul, it seems that the trademark of love is what grows the most. It is truly said that God and love are one and the same.

The deep mystery of *all that is* cannot be plumbed with a single sounding. But, we can touch the essence of that which we call God, and in touching it, we gain access to where it exists—in all places. And this is my prayer, my deepest desire for each of you is that you seek to plumb the depths of God, and in the existence of that Infinite Ocean, you lose yourself in that love, joy, and Wisdom of that pure Light of Being.

Thank you, my friends, again, for coming. All my love and all my blessings; I bow to the Infinite who resides in your heart.

Om Tat Sat Om, David

THE CROSS AND THE LOTUS JOURNAL —SEPTEMBER 2001

Dear Friends,

September will mark the completion of one year in silence. How did the idea for this year start? It came about as a chance comment that seemed to carry great potency and truth to it. I continued to inwardly confirm the truth of it, as well as to ask some others. Every person I mentioned it to felt that it was the right thing to do. As usual, the final authority came as an inner sanction from the highest Source. I will tell you a secret, now that the time has drawn to a close. I do not remember ever spending even one day in intentional silence before this year-long period.

Feeling that it was God's will for me, I fearlessly entered into this year. I also felt it should be a year of seclusion. After a search for a place in which to spend this year, I came to know of Cloud Mountain Retreat Center. David Branscomb had just completed a hermitage-cabin at Cloud Mountain, especially built for long-term silent retreatants. Also, David's early spiritual influence on the path was from Paramhansa Yogananda, having taken Kriya Initiation many years ago. It proved to be an ideal fit for both of us. The retreat center is open to those of all faiths. They have been all love and kindness, and I have greatly appreciated their openness and generosity. Also, Chad Hickenbottom came to Cloud Mountain for over eight months in order to be here with me, working most of that time as a volunteer at the retreat center for room and board and a small stipend. He sought to serve me in all ways and I very much appreciate all he did for me. I am sure it is a time he will never forget.

In my list of gratitude, Carla Gold needs to be mentioned. She has been invaluable in managing many tasks for me and has been the contact person for my time here. She does all this cheerfully and efficiently. Elaine Cone also does wonderful work helping with written materials, tapes to Center Leaders, and many other unseen tasks. I would also like to thank Larry and Cate, Peter and Laura, and all the Center Leaders who have kept the Light aloft. You graciously open your homes for all who wish to come and share in the Light; my love and gratitude go to you all. Finally, to everyone who has supported this work with your efforts, love, prayers, and donations; thank you, thank you. My heart melts with gratitude.

We gather together in worship for one reason only: to realize the real goal of life, our oneness with God. In the West, the tendency is toward large institutions, with impressive buildings and grounds. In the East, for thousands of years, the one-to-one Guru-disciple relationship has been the emphasis. Kriya Yoga has the tradition of the

Eastern model. The notable exception to that in our lineage is the work of Paramhansa Yogananda, who had a special mission from Babaji that was destined to influence Western Culture. For that, an institution was needed. However, with that accomplished, the traditional method for handing down initiation and the teachings by word of mouth, and one-to-one instruction, is securely in place thanks to Mother, my great Guru. Thus, in homes, in small groups, without fanfare of advertising or need of dues or paying attention to who's who, we come together with our attention on one thing alone, the realization of God.

It is a beautiful and sacred privilege to be a part of this continued flowering of the Kriya lineage, which has its origins in Jesus and Babaji. It has been recorded that it was Jesus who asked Babaji to send someone to the West to teach the soul awakening techniques of Yoga. It is evident from the teachings of Master and Mother, that these techniques were part of the original teachings of the prophets of the Old Testament, and of Jesus, and of the disciples of the New Testament. Through time and the darkening influences of the Kali Yuga—the dark ages—these original teachings were lost to the West. The beauty of Bhakti Yoga, the love and devotion to God, and the goodness of Karma Yoga, the path of action and selfless service to God, are very much left intact in these scriptures. What was lost was the power of Raja Yoga, the methods and techniques for entering into deeper states of meditation and communion with God. This is the missing part in the West that has now been revived through Yogananda and this Kriya path.

In India, the Yoga tradition has been traced back at least five thousand years. Anthropologists have found artifacts dating back to 3000 B.C. in the Indus valley showing figures in meditation pose. This tradition rightfully makes India the cradle of all religions. Their spiritual scientists have entered the inner sanctuaries of the soul and discovered the indwelling Light of the universe. Through specific techniques, the methods for this realization have been kept alive these many thousands of years.

In the West we have entered, in relatively recent times, a scientific era of incredible advancement in science and technology. With all the advancements in science, we would expect the satisfaction level of those enjoying the benefits of this progress to be growing by leaps and bounds. But many surveys show that isn't so. Stress, dissatisfaction, and a sense of foreboding are prevalent among many people. Modern Western Culture, with all its time-saving devices and equipment for making life easy, is failing at the task of making people happy. With the emphasis on the scientific technology for making life easy, the culture has virtually ignored the inner spiritual "technology" that taps into natural joy, balance, love, and wisdom.

There are some signs that the tide is changing. Even in the traditional scientific communities, there are movements towards the study of the mystery that lies beyond technology. Recently, there have been scientific studies on the power of prayer. The National Institute for Health has funded its first-ever study on the effects of prayer for patients in recovery from operations. Both mantra meditation and prayer are being looked at seriously now by scientific study for their health benefits.

It is high time the antipathy between science and religion became a thing of the past. The spiritually minded should embrace the scientific as the systematic study of God's remarkable expression of Creation. Scientists, noted for an atheistic bent (some polls have noted that over 90 percent of scientists say they are atheists), should embrace God's magnificent design they see inherent in a cosmos operating through intricate laws of balance and precision. Together, spiritual science and natural science promise the greatest human happiness for future generations.

It is wonderful to think of the blending of East and West, science and God. Anchored in spiritual science, humankind will be guided to fulfill its potential for material and spiritual happiness in balance. Without adherence to those truths learned in the spiritual sciences, the natural sciences will remain rudderless, like a powerful engine with no pilot. Without the balance of inner wisdom, all of us are without the guide that will bring us to the port of soul-joy, soul-wisdom, and soul-fulfillment.

I look forward to seeing you all once again and sharing in this exploration. For an exploration it truly is, with limitless horizons waiting for us when we attune our mind with the Divine Mind.

May you ever be guided by the Light of your own Being. David

Feel the Mystic Light Within

Feel that mystic Light within you. You may live in the city, dress in normal fashion, but in your heart beats the same Light that animates the yogis of the Himalayas and the desert prophets of old. You do not need to be of the desert or mountains to know what they know, to feel what they feel. Turn your mind to the same source of Light they focus upon. That Light is in your heart; it is not far away but as close as the air you breathe!

Yogacharya David in Silence.

Babaji Grotto

At David's request, Peter Schultz has designed a shrine in honor of Babaji to be given to Cloud Mountain Retreat Center. David Branscomb, the owner of Cloud Mountain, has given over a little hollow in the hill above the Hermitage and below Mist Haven for the shrine. David Hickenbottom has done most of the clearing, digging, and land preparation for the shrine and David Branscomb has prepared the steps leading up from the main path.

Below is shown the lettering for a plaque to be placed on the seating bench's support post:

Babaji, Divine Himalayan Yogi
In Commemoration of One Year of Silence
at Cloud Mountain Retreat Center by
Yogacharya David R. Hickenbottom

From the December 2001 Cross and Lotus Journal:

David Breaks His Silence

On September 8th, we were all treated to the extraordinary experience of being with Yogacharya David Hickenbottom when he broke his silence at Diamond Hall at Cloud Mountain Retreat Center, where David spent this last year during his seclusion and silence. It was a very holy occasion. The first sounds that issued from David's lips were: "Om . . . Om . . . Om . . ."— which he sang in a nice baritone. After that he sang Papa's mantra: "Om Sri Ram Jai Ram Jai Jai Ram" a couple of times. David then gave a short talk after which he led us in a round of group chanting of the mantra. There was a powerful, spiritual feeling in the room.

After chanting and circumambulating within Diamond Hall, David led us all up to the new Babaji Grotto, to attend a dedication ceremony for the installation of a statue (called a murti, in India) of the great Mahavatar, Babaji. This ceremony took place at the grotto (just below Mist Haven Meditation Hall) that was developed over the preceding months by David, Peter Schultz, Larry Koler, and David Branscomb (the owner of Cloud Mountain Retreat Center).

David spoke for a few minutes on what inspired him to take up the task of donating this temple to Cloud Mountain. He spoke of the great service and contribution that David Branscomb has made to society by creating Cloud Mountain Retreat Center and how grateful he was for the warm and loving support he received from David Branscomb and the staff of the retreat center. Then, David spoke of the great inspiration that he had felt from Babaji during his year of silence. The grotto seemed a fitting place for the remembrance of this great year in God.

Babaji, the Great Himalayan Yogi.

CHAPTER FIVE
RE-ENTERING THE WORLD

Editor's Note: David Re-enters the world, emerging from retreat and silence. We close this section with a selection of insights: one David quoted from Papa, Swami Ramdas, and three teachings David gave in 2004 as his time of silence continued to manifest results within his deep cosmic sea of consciousness:

Silence

Silence is the first step when entering the inner temple.

Just as in a home there are rooms dedicated to different purposes, so in the mind and consciousness we can find walls of separation that define the purpose for which they are designed. For instance, when we enter the kitchen with the purpose of preparing a meal, we move into a mindset that allows access to all the skills and knowledge of what it takes to make that meal. When we enter the bedroom in order to sleep, we go through various rituals that make us ready for bed and then to drift off into sleep. Different environments help the mind to shift into different modes of consciousness. That is why it is beneficial to have a dedicated space for meditation.

When we enter into verbal silence, this helps to shift the mind from the world of the body and senses. We do not always realize how much energy goes into speaking. Like preparing a meal, when we speak, we have to think first of what we are going to prepare, either what to make for the meal or what to say. Then we have to put the energy into the action itself, making the meal or projecting words. We then consume what we have made, either by eating the meal or absorbing the thoughts and vibrations of what we have just said. Hopefully, we have carefully made a tasty meal, so we do not get indigestion, gastronomically or verbally! And then comes the clean-up: either cleaning up after the meal or trying to clean up mis-understandings from what we have said. Whew! That can be a lot.

To withdraw life-energy from the act of speaking allows for that mental and verbal energy to return to its Source, Divine Spirit. However, this amount of energy is more than most people are used to channeling within. Many people are actually afraid of silence, as if their very existence will come to an end. So, this simple act of not speaking is very powerful. Verbal silence can take us to the portico of the inner Temple.

Once arriving on the portico, imagine entering into a temple sanctuary where there is a hushed silence; the very air seems charged with vibrancy. Mental silence allows us to enter into the hushed, vibrant air of the Temple. Our whole Being is alive in a powerful, inner environment that is full of potency. There are many who run right back out from this inner state of being because it is so full of awe-filled power; the descriptions of mystics who were sore afraid when standing in the Presence of God speaks to the human mind being overwhelmed with the power and majesty of that Presence.

If, in that moment, we can hear the inner voice saying, "Do not be afraid. I am your Father God," and we remain in that inner Temple, then we will deepen our inner silence to the next level.

By residing in that inner Silence, our Temple within, we commune with our Infinite Spirit. In that communion, we feel the peace, joy, and unlimited expanse of our Spiritual Nature, our Heavenly Kingdom. Grace then takes us into the inner Sanctum and lifts us into our eternal oneness with God. No trace of separation exists, Bliss (Ananda), Consciousness (Chit) and eternal Selfhood (Sat) are realized to be the real Source of our Being. In the awareness of these eternal natures, three in One and One in three, we know in truth who and what we are.

Master used to say that the price of greatness is solitude. Inner solitude is our inner oneness with the Infinite Spirit. Today, let us climb the steps to the portico of our inner Temple, enter into the room of Silence, overcome our fear, and enter into the inner Sanctum of our oneness with God.

Observing Silence

Maintaining silence is a powerful tool of self-awareness. Typically, days are filled with activity that draws the mind outward. Even if you are not engaged in speaking in the moment, you are often thinking about what you will do or say, or are remembering what has been done or said. By stilling yourselves, first outwardly then inwardly, you make available the tremendous power of Spirit that resides in all. This power of Spirit has the capacity to transform your lives, heal your bodies, and lift you up into transcendent states of Consciousness.

Self-awareness can begin with self-observation. The ability for self-observation is a critical developmental stage, both psychologically and spiritually. Without the ability for self-observation, you will identify completely with whatever thought, emotion, or sensation that is present in the moment. This identification with the thought, emotion, or sensation limits awareness to what you identify with. Since the Self resides beyond thought, emotion, and sensation, you will remain ignorant of the Self without self-observation.

The more purely you can observe your thoughts, emotions, and sensations, the more you disidentify with them. For instance, you are now reading the words on this paper; perhaps, like me, you are also hearing the words you are reading in your mind. You also have some mental commentary on what you are reading, "Yes, I understand that," "No, I haven't a clue as to what he's talking about," "I like the way (or don't like the way) he has written this," etc. You also have anticipation, some excitement, and some anxiety, about a time of silence with others. Others are making some noise in the room that slightly draws your attention. You have the ability to observe all of these things about yourself, related to thinking, feeling, and sensing.

The more you observe these movements of mind, emotion, and sensation, the less you identify with them as the absolute definition of your Self. For example, when I observed that there was some feeling of anticipation for that time in silence, some anxiety, and some excitement, I became less identified with those feelings. The more powerfully I can take the observer's stance, the less identified I am with what is being observed. When the sense of being the observer becomes dominant, then the feeling of excitement and anxiety continue to be experienced, but almost as if they belong to someone else. In other words, there is a field of separation between the knower and the known, the observer and the observed.[14]

When the observer can be completely aware of the feelings of excitement and anxiety, a new, additional awareness comes. Behind the feelings of emotion, one becomes aware of a great sense of stillness. This stillness is a quality of the Self. The Self resides beyond all thoughts, feelings, and sensations. This Self is the Purusha of the Vedic scriptures. It is the Light of God residing within you. Therefore, in the Psalms, David said, "Be still, and know that I am God." (Psalms 46:10) In this stillness is the Almighty Presence of your Divine Self.

In order to attain to the Self, learn to disidentify with the thoughts, feelings, and sensations that keep you bound to a limited, restless self of the body. For many, there is complete identification with the body. The body includes sensations, drives, and desires—an identity created around body consciousness: "This is my name, occupation, social status," etc., and its relationship to the world: "This is my mother, father, wife, husband, child," etc. These attachments to this limited identification of the body are cramped quarters when compared to the vast, limitless expanse of the Self. Therefore, you

---

14   This detachment is not dissociation that occurs during a traumatic time. Dissociation brings none of the qualities of the Self forward, such as peace, joy, and enlightenment. Rather, dissociation makes one feel detached from thoughts, feelings, and sensations as a numbing action reduces consciousness rather than expands it.

need to release yourselves from this self-imposed exile in order to experience the unlimited nature of Spirit.

The way of the Jnani is through self-inquiry and self-observation. The Jnani uses the scalpel of the mind to dissect "That which is God" from "That which is not God." A simple but powerful exercise for the mind is to observe that which is in the field of awareness. The observation of thoughts, feelings, and sensations creates a separation between the observer and the observed. This field of separation can give one an experience of the true Self. Implicit in the ability to observe is the fact there is an observer. The observer is not identical with that which is being observed. The deeper the observer is aware of the self who is having thoughts, feelings, and sensations, the more the observer will be aware that that which observes is separate from what is observed. This awareness frees the consciousness of being attached to the body.

This non-attachment occurs through simple observation, not by tying to create separation from attachments. Oftentimes, what occurs when efforts are made to be non-attached is a struggle between the attachment and a part of yourself that is determined to be non-attached. The battle, far from leading you to Self-awareness, makes you more enmeshed with the ego that is attached to being non-attached. This can only be of help when the ego admits its failure at being able to do such a thing. In that moment of surrender, the real Self can be revealed. The way to avoid such a battle and still get the results, the revelation of the Self, is to simply observe what is in the field of awareness, moment to moment.

There were many lessons I learned during my year of silence and solitude. When I took up time for silence, I knew there would be some obstacles along the way. Moving into Cloud Mountain after maintaining a busy schedule would surely mean a period of adjustment. Getting settled down meant not only arranging my new living quarters and creating a new routine, but also letting the energy body settle down. I was used to having places to go, people to see, a routine of activity—but now, nothing of the sort. The energy body was geared for action, but now I lived a life that did not need that kind of active energy. I suspected, and it turned out to be true, that it would take some weeks for the energy body to adjust to its new way of being in the world.

Not only did I have the habit of being busy, but there was something deeper that disturbed my becoming still. When I stopped the outflow of energy into the world, it could only have one place to go, it would be turned within. This life-energy stirred the inmost parts of my subconscious mind. Residue from the past inevitably flowed into the conscious mind. By observing these events, I was able to let them flow through, out, and be gone from my consciousness. Neither attached to them being there nor not being there, my mind became a Teflon-like surface to which nothing stayed attached. This is not to say that I was not disturbed by any of it. But through the practice of observing my reactions to powerful inner events, they would pass in a relatively quick manner.

The passing of such memories and reveries of the mind gradually allowed my mind to become established in the greater Self. With this establishment came the qualities of the true Self. An equanimity stemming from the inner stillness allowed me to see all passing phenomena of the world as a play. Both inner and outer reality was then placed subordinate to the peace and joy of the Self. Even sensations of the body assumed their rightful place in the hierarchy of the soul.

Fear of pain and difficulties intruded no more upon the sole authority of the light of Being. No graven images, even in thought, were placed before the Supreme Being of God.

My path has been of a four-fold type, relating to the four forms of Yoga: Bhakti Yoga of love and devotion, Karma Yoga of service-full action, Raja Yoga of Kriya meditation, and Jnana Yoga of being the observer. All four have played a role in my movement from the human to the Divine. Here I lay out some of the principles of Jnana Yoga. You may choose whatever practice that calls to you today, but you may like to deepen your practice of this Jnana Yoga method of being the observer.

Simply observe what is in the field of your awareness: sensations of the body, emotions, and thoughts. Observe your thoughts; notice how the ego tries to control the practice. Become simple, quiet, observing all that is. If fear comes, observe it coming and going. If judgments come, simply observe that you are having judgments. In this practice, your whole objective is to observe what is— whatever is in the field of your awareness.

You may notice that as you observe you will begin to experience an inner quiet. You may like to sit still for this practice or go for a walk, but whatever you do, keep the attitude of the observer. As you move your body, become aware of the minutest movements of your body. As you extend your hand in action, feel the movements of the muscles; be aware of the controlling brain orchestrating those movements. As you sit, observing your thoughts, be aware of the thoughts behind your thoughts, the constant commentary going on in your mind. Be aware of self-consciousness, fear that others may judge you, whether you feel better or less than others. In your feeling nature, be aware of heaviness, sadness, elation, or joy; observe them all. Do not observe only the negative emotions and identify with the positive, even if you associate those feelings with being close to God. Observe them all.

I think you will find this practice useful and one that you can engage in anytime, anywhere. Through this practice, you will find you have better self-awareness, self-control, and a ready access to your true Self.

The Doorway of Consciousness

Papa says:

> Worldly things or God can be had if you intensely long for them. After intensely longing for them, you must let go the longing. Leave the matter to God and then your

desire is fulfilled. So long as you are longing and longing without allowing God to play His part, it will only be a protracted struggle. You place yourself always in a state of anxiety and fear as long as you feel that you yourself can get things done. Stop worrying and leave everything in the hands of God: immediately the result is attained. You set an arrow to the bow, pull the string, and let go. Instead, if you go on pulling and pulling, the arrow won't be shot at all. Do you think that by worrying you can achieve anything? No. You must leave it to Him after doing your part. The trouble is, you do not allow God to do His part.

When your mind is silent, it does not come in the way of God playing His part. This is the secret of success. Churning the curds is all right, but after having churned for some time, you have to stop doing so and allow the butter to be formed. Instead, if you go on churning and churning, butter can never be obtained. So also, when you have a problem on your hands, you must think about it, work hard for the attainment of your object, and then sit silent, leaving everything to Him, without thinking any more about the problem. Keep the mind still, calm, and serene. It is in the still mind that divine power, light, and joy act and reflect.

— *The Gospel of Swami Ramdas* (PP. 457–8)

To Enter Silence

To enter silence means to quiet the body, energy, and most of all, the mind. Silence is not a nothing state, rather in it all creation is held in potential. It is void of form, but filled with Spirit. It is actionless, but vibrates with the vitality that creates this universe.

Thoughts are alien to this deep silence, but conscious awareness never lives more brilliantly or with greater aliveness.

The yogi in the cave may appear dead and removed from life. But his or her looks are deceiving; inwardly, a vital life is born. This vital life expands in unlimited Spirit. Native wisdom comes unbidden from intuitional wellsprings; the very source of life is known in reality. Incarnations of lifetimes seem to be tiny bubbles of existence and the puny concerns of this world fade in this grand perspective.

The price of admission to this wonderful promise held in stillness is your effort to direct the mind, and thus your life-energy, within. It is in the subtle spine and brain that the doorway of Consciousness is awakened. The struggle to open this door is the overcoming of old habits of constant activity and lethargy. Use your time today and work to open that doorway. Become quiet, still, and let God reveal to you what may be—indeed, what already is!

Yogacharya David: one year
of Silence complete.

CHAPTER SIX
CLOSURE

Editor's Note: We have completed our journey with David through his journal, *Silence: Entering the Cosmic Sea of Consciousness,* where he writes of his subjective experiences as he dares the deeper dive into silence and the inner realms of consciousness that test and purify the intrepid seeker. David is candid and trusting of his reader as he shares his journey of the soul.

Part Two, Notes to Sadhakas, consists of a series of reflective teachings David wrote mainly in the autumn of his silent retreat. It is as if he was synthesizing and sharing his state-of-being so he could explore his core inner nature as the inner stillness deepened.

We close this section with a poem that David wrote while in Anandashram sometime after this silent retreat. This poem is published in *Climbing the Sacred Mountain: Poems and Prayers of a Western Yogi.*

In the next book to follow in this series, we reconnect with David. He has now left Cloud Mountain. We are fortunate to share in a love story. After David leaves the mountain, he formally proposes to Carla. She says, "Yes!" By Christmas, David and Carla are married, and very shortly after, they pilgrimage to India. David and Carla, now together, enter the *Householder Yogi* life—our next volume, following David's journals, speaks to their love story and adventures in God.

David shares:

It is in this crucible of worldly experience that the soul is purified of dross, leaving the essence of God alone in the devotee. In the East, it is described as a battle; in the West, as a crucifixion. Both describe the same process of purification. It is the way of the cross and the Christ; it is the pearl of great price. Only the courageous and intrepid will enter. Our integrity and sincerity are our compasses, courage our shield, discrimination our sword. Our driver and guide are the Christ-like Krishna of pure light within. The Guru comes into our life to awaken that sleeping Christ and bring us to that fullest realization of God.

Silence

Silence is Stillness,
Stillness of body, speech, thought,
All comes into a quiet
Quietness becomes stillness.

No past intrudes here,
No future stretches ahead,
Only the present
In all of its fullness.

If activity survives,
It only plays on the surface
And leaves the vast ocean
Unaffected in its depth.

Being replaces doing,
Awareness is absent of thinking,
Stillness is eloquent
And denotes silence.

All the worlds come
From this potent Stillness,
And they reside in it
But stillness is not contained by the worlds.

It comes with practice
But as a spontaneity
Of its own making

We can be its servant,
But not its master.

Be still,
And know that I AM God
Be quiet,
And know that I AM of your Being.

And in the I AM
Know you are forever one
With the Eternal
Without Beginning or End.

Be still
Enter into the quiet
Become one
In the silence of your soul.

Yogacharya David.

PART TWO

CHAPTER SEVEN
NOTES TO SADHAKAS

How Dharma Works in Everyday Life

YOGACHARYA DAVID R. HICKENBOTTOM

Written From Cloud Mountain, 2000–2001

Sadhaka's Homecoming

O Sadhaka,
Have you heard the inner music?
Have you seen the lightning flash?
These, O Sadhaka are leading you home.

Your home within,
Your home in eternity,
Your home, your very sweet home!
Won't you visit it, not even once?

But, be warned!
On that journey of a million and no miles
Storms will wreck you
And shaken will you be.

But, take heart!
You are not destroyed.
Sun replaces darkness,
And you know your true Self.

Ah, and that homecoming!
Stars twinkle their welcome, moon glows warmly;
And O, the sun, like a thousand suns it shines!
Yet neither burns nor scorches.

Angels sing thrills of joy!
When coming to your home of eternal bliss.
Once there—the way will seem as nothing,
All sorrows transform into haloes of peace.

O Sadhaka, let us journey home together,
For each is born and dies alone;
But here, we have the glad privilege
To walk hand in hand.

And once knowing our joy,
And finding it a boundless fount,
Drinking deep to our fill and more,
We gain even more joy when sharing it with all!

So be glad, O Sadhaka!
The journey may be long and difficult,
But you journey in the right direction!
And we will yet live to see your homecoming.

—YOGACHARYA DAVID R. HICKENBOTTOM

INTRODUCTION: LIVING A SPIRITUALLY CENTERED AND PRINCIPLED LIFE

Notes to Sadhakas is my way of sharing thoughts about leading a spiritually centered and principled life. A spiritually centered life is the substance of our interior workings—it is feeling God's Presence as the central part of our being; it guides, comforts, and protects us. Through inward stillness and deepened prayer, we grow in our ability to perceive that Presence.

A spiritually principled life is the outer structure or form of living: the principles we apply. The laws of the scriptures and the teachings of spiritual masters help elucidate how we should live—principles that inform us how to guide our life. Abiding by these principles purifies our mind and we become qualified for knowing the Presence of God.

The form and the substance must go together. With all form and no substance, our life may look outwardly perfect, but inwardly we are spiritually dead. The spiritual Presence without the corresponding outward congruency leads to the imbalance of the physical, mental, and spiritual bodies.

My intention and my prayer are that *Notes to Sadhakas* will help stimulate and deepen our spiritual life. It is true for most of us that spiritual growth occurs gradually—going to deeper and deeper levels of realization. One day, we may awaken to a much more profound awareness of Truth through a powerful inner experience. It is then that the same words we have heard, and we have even spoken ourselves, suddenly take on a new and insightful meaning. A devotee once said to me after having one such experience of the omniscience of the Infinite, "You have always said that God is everywhere, but God really is everywhere! Why didn't you tell me? Well, I know you told me, but why didn't you tell me!" With the principle of gradual awakening in mind, we may read the books and scriptures of realized masters throughout our entire life and continually get richer, more profound meanings—for growth continues even after we realize our oneness with God.

This reminds me of when I sat at the feet of my Guru. Mother Hamilton would many times repeat a story. She had a very particular way she would tell a story, using words as an exacting craftsman—carefully creating a marvelous and beautiful structure. If I ever repeated one of those stories back to her, getting the words even slightly wrong, she would instantly correct me. As I listened to her repeat something I had heard her say before, and down through the years it may have been several times, I would think to myself, "I want to be able to hear this story from the same level of consciousness that Mother is in when she is telling it." Needless to say, I never plumbed the total depths of even one of her stories.

In the spirit of true sadhakas, let us go deep, drinking from His unfathomable well of *living waters*—those *living waters* of Truth, Consciousness, and ever-new Joy. Let us thirst to drink them dry— but we will never be able to! His well, brimming with *living waters* enough to fill the thirstiest soul to overflowing, continues to flow as long as we are open for more. For it is His great joy to give of Himself to us through His never-ending reservoir. Never let any words or concepts take us from that prime simplicity of direct God-perception. Rather, let us use these sayings only as a means of expanding our ability to drink from that holy well.

A word on why I use the word "sadhaka" and other words of Sanskrit and Indian origin in these writings. The word sadhaka comes from India, where the science of realizing God has been brought to wonderful fruition. Here is the definition of sadhaka from the encyclopedia (Wikipedia):

> In Jainism, Buddhism, Hinduism, and Yoga, a *sādhaka*
> or *sādhak* (Sanskrit) is someone who follows a particular *sādhanā*, or a way of life designed to realize the goal
> of one's ultimate ideal, whether it is merging with one's

eternal source, *brahman*, or realization of one's personal deity. The word is related to the Sanskrit *sādhu*, which is derived from the verb root *sādh-*, "to accomplish." As long as one has yet to reach the goal, they are a *sādhaka* or *sādhak*, while one who has reached the goal is called a *siddha*. In modern usage, *sadhaka* is often applied as a generic term for any religious practitioner. In medieval India, it was more narrowly used as a technical term for one who had gone through a specific initiation.

Hindu, Jain, Tantric, Yogic, and Vajrayana Buddhist traditions use the term *sadhaka* or *sādhak* for spiritual initiates and/or aspirants.

Sanskrit is the language of Eastern spiritual science, as Latin is the basis for many technical words in Western physical science. Many Sanskrit words simply do not have English equivalents. Also, there are nuances of meanings that are reflected in these words, which according to yogic science are conveyed through the vibration of the words when they are thought or pronounced. So, I have occasionally used Sanskrit words to add significance to these writings.

Sadhaka means one who is seeking God through sadhana, the practice of certain methods or disciplines; sadhana, sadhaka, and sadhu are all related to the word root sadh: *to accomplish.* Sadhana is the methodical search for God, whether through love and devotion, selfless service, wise discrimination, or meditation. To have the explicit goal of realizing God, merging and becoming one with Divine Consciousness, has found some of its greatest exponents in the scriptures, saints, and realized masters of India.

I would also like to say something here about how to read this, or any writing meant to take us deeper into our practice of sadhana. Words also have both form and substance—these writings have outward, practical principles, and they hold the power for awakening the Divine Presence—to connect us with our spiritual center. To get the fullness of both, I encourage listening on three levels.

First: listen with your mind. Use your reasoning mind to understand the concepts, and when you find they have merit, translate them into action in your everyday life. Not putting these ideas into action is to abort their very purpose. A principled life must be the first step in realizing God—practice is the core of sadhana. To confine yourself to philosophizing without changing your life is virtually useless.

Second: listen with your heart. Your heart is a place deeper and closer to who you really are—your spiritual essence. It is the *you* who is behind the outer mask of ideas and projections you wear for the world. To enter into the heart of its meaning is to find that place where it is intimate and personal to you.

And third: listen with your soul. That is the part of you that is connected with the universal intelligence of all that is—God. Through knowing that connection, your soul may take wings, not made of earthly wax but of heavenly inspiration, and soar in oneness with the omniscient Spirit of God.

As you listen in all three ways, I pray that we may take winged flight together, fulfilling the prayer of the great Master that reflects leading both a spiritually centered and a principled life: "Thy will be done on earth, as it is in heaven." (Matthew 6:10)

Dharma: How It Works in Everyday Life

The word "dharma" comes from Sanskrit, and like all words in Sanskrit, it has multiple meanings—for Sanskrit is the perfect language for subtle abstractions. Many times, dharma is translated as religion, righteousness, duty, or law. Early Buddhism gives slightly different shadings by defining it as truth, the *saving doctrine*, or *the way.* Later, Mahayana Buddhism translates it as the essential quality of any reality.

The short definition of dharma is **do the right thing:** abide by your morals and principles no matter the cost. In the movie, *A Man* *for all Seasons,* Sir Thomas More is placed in a terribly difficult situation in which his king, Henry VIII, wants More's support for the annulment of yet another marriage, and for the king, not the pope, to be the head of the church. As a result of holding to his principles, Saint Thomas loses his head! It is a story of a dharmic life.

Milarepa, the great Tibetan yogi, gives us his definition of dharma in his rebuke to a learned priest. As in the life of Jesus, the priestly class tried to entrap Milarepa due to their fear and jealousy of him, attempting to ruin his reputation. Milarepa answers the priest's sarcastic question on the *logic* (scriptural authority) for his way of life in this manner. I am paraphrasing:

> My dear scholar, you should try to rest yourself in the inborn Dharma-Essence instead of in words and talk. In daily life, you should always attempt to subdue your desires. Correct understanding and merit can only grow from within; otherwise, you will be driven into miserable realms by jealousy and the five klesas (poisonous cravings). So please do not ruin yourself! I do not understand the logic of your School. My own "logic" is that of the Guru, of the Pith Instructions (key instructions of the Guru), of diligence and perseverance, of remaining in solitude, of producing the Realizations and true understanding within, of the sincere patrons (teachers) with true faith, and being a genuine and worthwhile receiver of patronage. Being bound by the "logic" of jealousy and evil cravings, one is liable to experience the "logic" of hell and suffer the "logic" of pain; I do not know of any other "logic" than this.

Of course, the realized Master was pointing out that genuine dharma is drawn from following the teachings of one's guru; this leads a sadhaka to direct perception of the truth (Dharma-Essence). Direct perception of truth informs him or her on how to live his or her subsequent way of life. So, the realization of truth is at the very core of dharma—is both the way and the goal. True dharma may be said to have three aspects: 1) It has its origins in knowing that truth is derived through Self-realization. 2) This truth manifests as the universal principles and methods taught by a realized master. 3) In following these principles and methods, the aspirant realizes God through the dissolution of the ego-self (atman) and is raised into the consciousness of the Supreme Self (Paramatman). Having realized the Supreme Self, Dharma-Essence is realized and expresses itself in right action through a spontaneous flow from God.

Sadhaka—to act correctly in this world is to act upon the spiritual principles you have been taught and make yourself a living example of dharma. This begins with clarity: the real purpose for taking birth in a human body is to attain Divine-realization. This purpose requires that you do service in the world to resolve your karmic debt, and simultaneously, you make every effort for achieving Self-realization by diving deep in meditation. Direct perception of God transcends the law of cause and effect and leads you to live life as a spontaneous expression of your Dharma-Essence, or God's will.

By creating a positive influence in society and staying inwardly detached from the results, you free yourself from the web of karmic ties that have kept you bound. You do this by first learning to sail the skies of divine perception through deepened meditation, then loving and serving God in all that you do, and in all whom you meet. You practice discrimination to correctly guide your thoughts, words, and deeds—this is the sure path that leads you to inner glory and freedom.

In practical terms, you make the realization of God first in your life—before the demands of this world. By establishing your life on the *solid rock* of putting God first, you practice those spiritual principles and techniques that harmonize the inner and outer life with the highest truth you know.

Thus, you establish the basis for living that helps you to determine a good and positive work to do in the world. With a focus on highest truth, you will have guidelines and principles on which to establish lasting happiness in work, relationships, marriage, raising a family, and recreation. Like a hand in a glove, attunement with your inner life (Dharma-Essence) guides, inspires, and makes possible a successful outer life.

Your life is your religion, your dharma. To integrate your spiritual realization with every aspect of your life is your goal. You do not need to leave living a *normal life* in terms of work, family, and fun. Rather, Self-realization spiritualizes the entirety of your life—your mundane life, your spiritual life, and all that is! Your real purpose is to realize this great truth; that is the essence of dharma.

Implementing this plan to becoming fully realized is all-powerful, and applying it to your day-to-day life is, as they say, *where the rubber meets the road.* It is the practice of this religion—dharma—that must take possession of your soul. Practice of this sort does not simply mean reading "The Good Book" once or twice a day and saying your prayers at night. It is the employment of these highest of principles and techniques at all times and in all places. As you can imagine this is a commitment of a lifetime, and one, when it really comes down to it, few are relishing to take. But when you do, you are on the most fantastic journey of your life.

As Milarepa said, "My dear scholar, you should try to rest yourself in the inborn Dharma-Essence instead of words and talk." Do not be a scholar of the word only, rather seek out inspiration for right behavior from within, and in deepened meditation set sail for new horizons—persevere till you reach that which is beyond description. May God and the Masters' blessings be with you on the journey of fulfilling your Dharma-Essence.

Babaji On Faith

Yesterday, Chad[1] and I meditated in the future Babaji Grotto here at Cloud Mountain. While steeped in meditation, I began to petition Babaji with a prayerful mantra, "Om Babaji." This phrase came again and again. A desire rose up in me to see Babaji face to face—and for Chad to see the same. Babaji appeared before my inner eye. "Babaji, please come," I requested inwardly. "No, I shall not!" came the terse reply. The inner voice quoted the *Autobiography of a Yogi*, "It is easy to believe when one sees, there is nothing then to deny." He continued with a Biblical quote, "Now faith is the substance of things hoped for, the evidence of things not seen." (Hebrews 11:1)

This quote from Paul rang in my consciousness. My searching mind opened itself to know its meaning.

David: "Is there something special to be gained by going in faith?"

Babaji: "Yes."

David: "Does faith open doors of receptivity?"

Babaji: "Yes."

David: "If you came in physical form, would it add nothing to the development of needed faith?"

Babaji: "Yes."

David: "And with this perfected faith, you, or anything else, would be manifested naturally?"

Babaji: "Yes!" came the answer.

Inner consciousness has long been working on deepening my understanding of faith. Jesus emphasized it as a central theme of his ministry. I have often wondered over this fact and the doors of understanding have slowly opened through the years. The essential problem to the ignorant mind is that a veil of separation, obscuring the Light of Spiritual Consciousness, covers it as a shroud. The solution to this dilemma is the most pressing matter for the spiritual aspirant.

---

1   Chad stayed at Cloud Mountain for part of the year I stayed in residence.

All great religions and enduring mythologies speak to this separation of the soul from its Divine Source. The ultimate resolution of this knotted point is to pierce the veil of separation in order to directly perceive the Divine. It is observed that for the accomplishment of any great goal, faith is required. It may be the faith of self-confidence, faith in a great principle, or in a higher ideal, such as liberty, justice, or faith in the supreme governing Intelligence of God.

Faith in one's self is good, faith in a higher ideal is better, but faith in God creates a link between our self and the omniscient and omnipotent Consciousness that is the *All and All in All.* This link to God is the greatest accomplishment of faith. Faith literally multiplies one's inner and outer resources by many, many times. In fact, corresponding to the degree of faith, the individual may be a clear and open instrument for the Almighty to operate in any way the Divine wills—with unlimited potential.

Like a laser, deep faith makes the mind singular and rends the curtain of separation that directly connects the soul to the infinite Source of Being. But the mind is stubborn in its adherence to the world of matter. Deep subconscious associations to the limits of the world work against knowing Spirit. The shortcut of using faith in God to surmount attachment to matter is of great import to the sadhaka on the spiritual battleground.

Some materialists say, "If I only saw a miracle, then I would believe." But is it so? Let that one be witness to a so-called miracle and the mind would weigh, measure, and dispense with that miracle in a hurry. "It's a hoax," declare some. "It's an anomaly," say others. "It can be true for them, but not for me." Or: "They have a special gift, a power, unexplained by science, but it does not prove anything beyond a simple new discovery!" Thus, the skeptic wipes his or her hands clean of the miracle, puts it into a comfortable box, and continues on the materialistic way.

When the inner calling draws us deeper into Spiritual Consciousness, oftentimes in spite of the mind, not because of it, we come to a belief in something deeper than the ego-self and physical nature. Through our deepened communion with Spirit, the negative influence of a matter-drenched mind is gradually dissolved.

Communion with Spirit takes us beyond the human mind alone. Belief, a thought of the mind alone, is the weaker cousin of faith. **But faith is an inner knowing that transcends a belief. Faith directly connects us with a deeper reality and brings spiritual power and understanding to the fore.** The tiny firefly of human belief is easily eclipsed by the stupendous solar power of faith. Babaji, Jesus, and all the great spiritual Masters are constantly drawing our attention to the superior power of faith.

Through faith, awareness of Spiritual Consciousness deepens. We perceive a world of potential opening up. This world of infinite potential is all about us, but unseen by many. With this opening, spiritual power vibrates with new possibilities made possible by faith—bearing fruit in a changed consciousness. We realize this world is brimming with spiritual Power and Intelligence. We see clearly the Light of our own Being is connected to the very same cosmic Light that is God and which illumines all creation.

In this illumined state, we have perfect faith that this unlimited spiritual Power is working on our behalf. With deep faith and inner surrender, the supreme Power and Intelligence guides, protects, and reveals our ultimate destiny. Faith, then, becomes a transfiguring lens that sharpens the mind to be a fit instrument of Supreme Consciousness. Faith takes us to the threshold of realized knowledge through direct experience. All this, faith does when we open ourselves to its unlimited potential.

"If you have faith as a grain of mustard seed, ye shall say unto this mountain, remove hence to yonder place; and it shall remove; and nothing shall be impossible unto you." (Matthew 20:17) This is no idle promise. The fact that the demonstration of that promise is only too rare in this world does not mean it is not true. It only means that, as aspirants, we have work to do. Through prayer and deepening communion with God, we grow in our understanding and experience of faith. The disciple Peter represents the personi-fication of an intuitive perception of truth. But even he fell short of perfect faith when he denied the Christ. Yet, he never gave up, and eventually came to have that perfect faith. Through the same kind of tenacity, we perfect our faith that leads us to be consciously one with our greater Reality, God.

My friends, receive the blessings of Babaji. Through oneness of Spirit may our faith be perfected into complete Self-realization. May that perfected faith result in manifesting the purity of Light in all we do and in every part of our life.

Om, Peace, Bliss, Amen.

Tithing[2]

Tithing dates as far back as there has been a recognition that man is subordinate to something greater than himself—God by whatever name. The tradition is to give the first fruits to God. This presen-tation of a gift is made to a place of worship, a deity, or a teacher. When you enact the giving of *the first fruits* to God, then you set into motion several blessings.

First: Giving the first fruits to God creates the right attitude for you in life. Through your offering, you humbly acknowledge that God is responsible for your prosperity and your ability to succeed—that He is the source of all *good fruits* that come to you.

Second: You support that which brings Light into your life through those offerings. If you receive value from a teaching or place of worship, it is incumbent upon you to support it.

---

2   The word "tithing" comes from the old English *teogotha,* meaning "tenth." To tithe means to give one-tenth of your agriculture or income towards the support of the church and clergy. Although the word tithing only goes back to Middle-Age Europe, the giving of support to a church, deity, or teacher has dated back to the earliest recorded history.

Third: You bring direct blessings to yourself. The spiritual principle says, "As you give, so shall you receive." When you give of your time, your abundance, your love, and service, then you receive accordingly in return. Life becomes dry and constricting if it is all about me, mine, and more. You open a circuit when you give in mindfulness to God; this mindfulness opens channels of connection with the Source of all that is. "Give, and it will be given to you: good measure, pressed down, shaken together, and running over will be put into your bosom. For with the same measure that you use, it will be measured back to you." (Luke 6:8) When you see someone in need, when you give to them as you would give to God, then it is very pleasing to God and His saints. Let all such giving come freely from your heart, and your heart will know the blessings of both giving and receiving.

Fourth: Has to do with putting your attention on God. Give God the "first fruits" of your thought. Chant His holy name, breathe Hong Sau, keep your morning and evening Kriya appointments, think of Him as you serve Him in others, give Him at least ten percent of your attention—the first fruits of thought going to Him all through the day. In truth, there are very few tasks that require your full attention, and even then, you can precede the action by invoking God to be your strength and to direct your efforts. With the first ten percent of your attention always on God, you can never forget Him, and by the virtue that it is your first ten percent, you will always choose to go *with* Him, never against Him.

FOUR LIONS AND THE DIAMOND LIGHT

(A ~~TAIL~~ TALE THAT ENDS WELL)

Going to the inward Mind
Four lions lie in wait:
Fear, lust, greed, and wrath.
Waiting, waiting, waiting, they wait!

For a moment, a weakness is perceived...
Then upon their hapless victim
They pounce to devour his very life!
The life that will make the lions to live again.

Four lions lie in wait,
Looking for a moment in time
When they catch a look, a glimmer,
Of lack of resolve gleaming in the eye!

Or doubt, it is, that creates a chance;
Perhaps loneliness, it makes them lick their chops!
They lie in wait in darkened dale
Where self-pity makes its prisoner an easy prey

But wait! The lions scurry for cover
When like-minded aspirants join in on the stroll.
And oh, how those lions detest and are sickened to death
When melodious words are sung to the Most High.

Ah! Here comes a chance, a lovely trap
When ego of pride makes stilts for legs.
Yes, pride places the head high on wobbly peds
"We will not attack 'til the moment is right,"
say those wily lions in wait!

Oh, here he comes, that aspirant riding high
Round corner too fast, head and chin tilted to the sky.
Lions on the wait on either side
For unwieldy stride to bring that one down with a crash!

And when the crash comes, as it certainly must come,
The trap of shame is sprung.
The game is theirs, the lions have won!
They suck life's blood down to its very marrow.

And when the gorging is done, (but it is never truly done),
They seek to devour corpse and all!
But deep down inside, close to the heart,
Resides a spark they can never touch.

It is a spark, a glowing Light
That is oft' clouded by gray and dark.
Is hidden, really, never dimmed;
For once uncovered, it shines brilliantly as ever again!

The lions, if they could (and they would if they could),
Take away that little diamond of Light
And devour whole: life, ego, and corpse.
But they can't, they can't! As much as they would like.

For that Light, that brilliant shining Light,
Cannot be bartered, sold, nor stolen away.
No, not even tarnished, corrupted, or even a dent will it know!
For it is forever, and that cannot be changed.

That is your treasure O aspirant!
Gems of realization and spiritual Light of gold
It is your inheritance that, no, not even you can give away.
It is a gift, and it pleases It greatly to give Its Self to you.

So those lions may be there, they can lie in wait,
But you've a secret weapon they cannot devour;
no, not even in their dreams.
You've defeated those rascal lions, you've beat them square,
You need only claim ... (shall I say it) your lion's share!

Blessings from the Guru

Through the all-pervasive, all-knowing consciousness of God, time and space become principles without absolutes. Therefore, sadhakas who call on their guru in full faith, wherever that guru may be, will receive help both visible and invisible through the God-tuned Guru.

Just a small incident with my own Guru has stayed in my mind for over twenty-five years. I was traveling in the Sahara Desert, riding through a military zone on an army truck. Nothing but sand dunes for as far as the eye could see in any direction. Suddenly, there was the fragrance of my Guru's perfume she wore at that time. It came without any particular thought of her—out of the blue, you might say, and it stayed with me for many minutes. It made me know that although I was halfway around the world in a war zone, she was ever with me.

It is God Himself who has set up residence in the guru-teacher. That is, through the spiritual perfection of a devotee, God is able to use that one as an instrument of His will as the guru. Because spiritual aspirants, ignorant of their oneness of the all-beneficent Presence of God, are in need of a human example of that Oneness and these teachings, God commissions that one to serve as the guru to all whom God brings to him or her.

The faith of a devotee may be awakened through the guru, and love and devotion may be channeled to God, in part, through the teacher. The guru, being absent of ego, acts as a conduit to awaken the Living God within the devotee—therefore fulfilling a pattern set down through history. Even Jesus, coming as an Avatar, required baptism by John the Baptist, his Guru from a former lifetime.[3]

When the devotee of God calls upon the guru with awakened faith, then virtue, the healing power of God, goes out from that one. Sometimes the guru is fully conscious of this fact, sometimes

---

3   *Autobiography of a Yogi* (p. 35).

partially conscious, and sometimes not at all conscious. It makes no difference, for it is the Superconscious action of God that performs what is necessary. When Jesus walked through the crowd and many were touching him for his blessing, he stopped and asked, "Who touched me?" The disciples were confused by their Master's question because so many had been touching him. He said, "I perceive that virtue has gone out of me." (Luke 8:45–46) This is a case of Jesus being partially conscious of being used as a medium of God. Isn't that marvelous! He felt virtue go out. And indeed, out of all who were reaching out to him, one had full faith and was healed.

Lahiri Mahasaya said, "If you deem it (my picture) a protection, then it is so; otherwise, it is only a picture."[4] The faith of the devotee makes it so. And, it is in combination with the God-tuned nature of the Master that it becomes a very powerful connection to Divinity indeed! The protections I have received from my own Guru are too many to count.

One time comes to mind when I was protected on the spiritual level. A popular "Guru" from India came to town sometime after I had met Mother and taken her initiation. I had gone to see him speak before I met Mother and felt nonplussed by him. It came to mind that it would be interesting to meet him now, after having met my Guru, to see how he would seem to me now. After his talk, which did not impress me any more the second time than the first time, he was leaving the place. All the devotees stood as he left. As he walked out, he stopped and looked in my direction. He was about twelve feet away. There was a parting of all the devotees and there was a straight line of sight between us. I could clearly sense him psychically rummaging around in my psyche, feeling a definite invasion. The thought of Mother came to me and immediately I felt surrounded by a wonderful aura of Light. The Guru's head snapped back and he proceeded out of the hall. Sometime later, I heard that he practiced many occult powers. I gave a prayer of thanks

---

4   *Autobiography of a Yogi* (p. 31).

to my Omniscient Guru for her protection. It also made me aware that although Mother had access to the most intimate parts of my psyche, I never felt invaded by her, and this gave me a newfound appreciation for the purity of her Light.

Through his or her own realization, the guru has dissolved his or her ego of separation from God and has realized Oneness with the all-pervasive Spirit of Consciousness. Then God may commission that one to play the role of the guru. That is, the guru will teach the methods for devotees to practice in order to realize their greater reality; the guru will stand as the devotees' protector on the spiritual plane; the guru will be the example of a realized person; the guru will impart the essential spark of Divinity required for devotees to become fully realized.

Even after I had several Kriya Initiations with Mother, each one had special significance, as in my enlarging consciousness I could absorb more of what she had to give. Mother had been quite ill at the time I received my last initiation. Kneeling in pronam before her, she touched me on the ajna in blessing, and the power that radiated from that touch I can still feel when I think back on that time. Such are the blessings God gives through the guru.

Because the living Presence is consciously moving through the guru and the sense of ego has dissolved, if that one is who he or she should be, then God may fully express Himself through that personality pattern. It is often the case that God uses a spiritually evolved human instrument in which the human ego is not fully dissolved, Lahiri Mahasaya, Yoganandaji, and Mother being prime examples of this in their earlier years of teaching. Highly developed in their realization, but not yet perfected in consciousness, they assumed the role of Guru by God and their own Guru's commission. In fact, by assuming such a role, it helped that one to dissolve his or her own ego by fulfilling these karmic ties. They did not assume the roles out of ego, but by inner direction and the request of their own Guru. Mother told me at the time of making me a minister that Master making her a minister and giving her permission to initiate others had helped her attain her own God-realization.

As long as the guru is not yet perfected, but making progress toward the goal, God may use that one to full effect.[5] In fact, it can be encouraging to devotees to find common ground with a highly realized guru treading the path ahead of them. The devotee will think, "I can do this also; it is not only for perfected Beings to achieve this goal!" One advantage of the guru-disciple relationship is that it keeps the devotee's attitude humble before God. Always feeling the desire to please the guru, always knowing the guru went to his or her own realization before the disciple, the aspirant keeps a humble attitude before God and Guru. This helps to prevent egotism from taking a foothold, even in the higher realms of consciousness.

Following a path or a spiritual master should not lead to narrow sectarianism, nor should it be treated as a business enterprise. As Mother used to say, "God can neither be bought nor sold." In the same way, those who teach and promote themselves as an exclusive way to realization fall short of the full truth. And there are those who follow a true Guru, and then, after the Guru's passing, treat the Guru as a product that only they are entitled to copyright and have the exclusive right to sell! True devotees are attracted to the honey of realization. They will pass the glittery show of the spiritual marketplace and be drawn to the Truth of a realized master. In this way, they will find fulfillment of their one true desire.

The guru-disciple relationship is personal. I always had a twin sense of wonder around my Guru. On the one hand, I was so amazed that there were others who were as interested in Mother as their Guru as I was, and on the other hand, was amazed that the whole world was not at her feet, so great was she in God. But whether a guru has one or two devotees they take to God, or thousands or

---

5   Meher Baba wrote that one fully established in the fifth chakra may be commissioned to be a Guru.

more, the Light is just the same in each true Guru. They come as a blessing to all, even those who are not conscious of it. The guru then is a source of blessings to all whom God puts into their hearts to make it so. As a teacher, role model, and source of invisible virtue, the guru becomes a blessing in our lives that is without comparison. Realization of God being the sole aim of the Guru for the devotee, they yearn for real devotees on whom to shed the Grace and blessings of God.

Of Will and Surrender

Will

Will, or volition, is the basis for all creation. God the Father resides in His Self as formless Spirit. This Pure Spirit, transcendent to all creation, is called the nirguna aspect of God. In this aspect of God, will is at rest. When pure Spirit takes form as creation, It is called Prakriti, Mother Nature. The Shakti power of God expresses its will through the laws that govern spiritual and material creation. This created form of God and its laws is called the saguna aspect of God. Sown in every particle of creation is the perfect Light of Spirit known as the Savior or the Son of God. The will of the Savior is the preservation of Light and Its attributes in nature's creation. This makes up the trinity of the One God. For God is both manifest and unmanifest, with form and formless.

We, as human beings, are said to be made in the image and likeness of God. (Genesis 1:26) The image of God is God with form, saguna, and the likeness of God is Spirit without form, nirguna. The Supreme Being of God is the All in All. The first of these Alls is God as Spirit, nirguna, and resides as a hand in a glove in the second All, God with form, saguna. Thus, as in the inner, so the outer. As God expresses Himself in a vast cosmological sense, so does God reflect that same pattern in humanity. Since humans have the same pattern as God, they are endowed with free, creative will.

From our first movement and cry as a baby we manifest will. The cry of the newborn is *automatic physiological will.* From the beginning of this birth, children have their own distinctive personalities. This is due to vasanas, subconscious patterns from previous lives. These vasanas, combined with new patterns developed in this lifetime, create our *unconscious will;* that is, will that comes spontaneously from the unconscious mind.

As we become more conscious of the world, we learn to copy and obey those around us. This develops *unthinking will* because it is responsive only to the environment around us. The next stage can be characterized by the "terrible twos," when we learn to say "No!" We exercise *blind will* against authority, as this will is reactive only.

As development continues, and our ability to reason progresses, we manifest *thinking* or *Reasoned will.* We can observe this Reasoned will in even young children who start a creative project and reason their way through to completion. Each developmental stage adds another ability to the whole but does not usually completely replace the developmental stages of will that came before. For example, a carpenter is using *Reasoned will* to build something but misfires his hammer, nailing his thumb by accident! He reacts with automatic *physiological will* and draws his hand back with a yelp.

We can analyze our own behavior to help determine for ourselves if we have successfully developed all these stages. Many people are not fully developed in their *reasoning will* and are dominated by a lower developmental will. For instance, one may be an adult and still be ruled by *blind will* and remain eternally rebellious, automatically reactive to any authority figure. When confronted with someone who has authority over him or her, this individual will all too often quit his or her job or try to get revenge, acting out of *blind will.* Persons dominated by *unthinking will* may specialize in conforming to what is expected by others without even knowing what they themselves want and never dream of going against an authority figure.

Also, a later stage of developmental will can dominate over an earlier stage. For instance, a *blind will* may not show any *automatic physiological* response to an authority figure: i.e., a defiant child will not cry when spanked. Or a well-developed *Reasoned will* may overcome a *blind* reactive will by learning to *think* before acting instead of just acting.

Will has come under criticism due to a perception that it is used to suppress feelings. Will, in this scenario, is seen as a ruthless dictator and it is deemed necessary that it be dethroned. True, an unbalanced will can try to rule as a dictator. Of course, there are rebellions by disgruntled "subjects." These battlegrounds of the psyche often manifest in the offices of doctors and psychologists. Reason should be a wise king who listens to all subjects and then does what is best for the higher good. The rule by feeling nature or less developed wills makes for poor decisions and sometimes disastrous consequences.

When one is drawn to the spiritual path, these various types of will are usually in diverse states of development. Under different environments, each may predominate in its influence. For instance, given a predictable set of circumstances, a *Reasoned will* may be that benignly just ruler. Suddenly a threatening circumstance, real or perceived, and it triggers a *blind will* reaction that becomes rebellious and angry in a tense situation. Most aspirants on the path come with wills that are in a flux with various states of development.

Due to the fact that spiritual development represents the most powerful dynamic in human development, it is no small wonder that it represents not only the greatest hope for the individual but the greatest threat as well. The proper development of will becomes integral to the spiritual development of the aspirant. The human ego's highest form of development comes as a strong, balanced *Reasoned will.* It may have been honed in earlier development through sports, business, and artistic or intellectual pursuits. There are a number of areas in which this balance can be partly or wholly achieved.

As balanced *Reasoned will* strengthens, it brings its subjects *automatic physiological will, unthinking will, blind will,* and *unconscious will* into a happy balance. This state of affairs is rarer today than common, so a large part of sadhana, spiritual discipline, is bringing this inner kingdom of wills into balance. Any personality ruled by lower wills cannot maintain a steady state of mind required for higher spiritual advancement. Fortunately for those of us entering the path, there is also help in developing this balance by following the light in deepened prayer and meditation. Our willingness to work on *Balanced Will* is greatly enhanced by the strength gained through repeated contact with the Light within.

The next stage in the development of will comes as a transpersonal or spiritual development. Paramhansa Yogananda prayed this way:

O Father, Mother, Friend,
Beloved God, I will reason,
I will, I will act:
but guide Thou my reason,
will and activity to the
right thing that I should do.[6]

Buddhi, or higher reasoning of intellect, may be turned downwards to things of the world, or focused upward on things spiritual. When spiritualized, it becomes illuminated by the Purusha or the Son of God. This spiritually charged will may be termed, *Dynamic Will.* In the beginning, leading a spiritual life means learning and obeying the laws of God handed down by prophets, spiritual masters, and the scriptures of religion. Using human reason, the seeker brings his or her life into harmony with a set of dos and don'ts designed to purify the consciousness from material desires and bring it to Spiritual Consciousness. The use of reason to bring one's life into alignment with true spiritual principles plays a real and valuable service for soul development. This alignment of spiritual principle and outward action is like creating the solid foundation for a skyscraper building. It prepares body, mind, and soul for

6   Paramhansa Yogananda. *Whispers from Eternity* (p. 93).

deeper God-communion. If these essential principles are not exempli-fied by sadhakas, their attention will always be drawn back to the missing step, often with difficult consequences.

With this proper preparation, individuals are readied for deeper association with the Divine. With the indrawn attention of the intellect, Buddhi, the rays of the Light of God enlighten the con-sciousness. Through deepened prayer and meditation, this enlight-enment may come in the form of a realization through feeling/intuition, an inner vision, a strong insertion of an idea, a voice, or a dream of the superconscious dimension. It may also come as rec-ognition of receiving the truth from an outside source: i.e., from another person speaking, reading a book, or by observing nature. The enlightenment clearly comes from a source beyond the normal conscious workings of the mind. The entire Being of individuals can be uplifted, bringing them into contact with a sense of purity, clarity, and truth. At these times, the will is charged by *Spiritual Dynamism* and a feeling of power that transcends any of the lower wills, mak-ing one feel in touch with a vast storehouse of will and potency.

At this stage, the upliftment comes and goes. When the Light of upliftment recedes from the intellect, individuals notice a definite difference between normal thought processes and the illumina-tion that has just occurred. An afterglow of the clarity, purity, and truth may still be hovering in their consciousness, but it cannot be fully maintained. The unillumined rational mind must then use *Reasoned will* to approximate harmony with the revelation. This is contrasted with *Dynamically Charged Will* experienced in the uplifted state or when surcharged through prayer.

When in the uplifted state, individuals feel so natural and free that it cannot be imagined to be any other way. But, because the mind has yet to be fully purified, past patterns act like gravity to pull them down, back to earthly consciousness. Returning to human consciousness from that heightened state of consciousness cre-ates a battle between harmonizing old habit patterns of the mind with the new state of Being experienced while uplifted. A battle often ensues between lower natures of will and the enlightened *Reasoned will* in this aftermath. Maintaining a true parity will not be possible between the *Reasoned will* and the purity of revelation, since *Reasoned will* is inferior to Superconscious Realization. In the beginning of sadhana, these experiences of upliftment will seem all too rare for sincere seekers and *Reasoned will* must do its best to live according to its own highest Light of Truth. Sadhakas are tested again and again, striving to attain the higher consciousness, and experiencing the pulls of vasanas, past habit patterns. Through prayer and meditation, they are able to access the *Dynamic Will* of Spirit to overcome all limitations of the past. Sadhakas combine what they have learned of spiritual principles with inner revelation to guide their actions for further purifying of the mind. Gradually, the mind and will become more purified of lower tendencies and can grow into the greater life of *Dynamic Spiritual Will* and beyond.

Rising to the next step of will in this long journey of the soul, individuals are initiated into the mystery of the Presence of God. A spiritual master may awaken this Presence in sadhakas when they are taught the methods of deeper spiritual communion, such as Kriya Yoga, chanting the name of God, dedicating actions in selfless service, and divinely loving God. This Presence takes an active role in guiding the life of the sadhaka through *Intuitive Spiritual Will*. This will guides aspirants even in minute matters, resulting in the acceleration of mind purification, which is necessary for higher attainment. It is superior to *Dynamic Will* in that sadhakas feel as if they are but a witness to the workings of *Intuitive Spiritual Will* versus the feeling of a powerful *Dynamic Will* being operated by the individual. It is at this stage that surrender takes on an even deeper meaning.

Surrender

From the beginning of our spiritual journey, surrender plays a role. At first, surrender means subjugating the whims and desires of the ego to the Ten Commandments or the Yamas and Niyamas, those dos and don'ts of spiritually principled living. We gradually increase *Reasoned will* to bring the lesser developmental wills into conformity with these principles. This surrender of the ego through *Reasoned will* to higher virtues teaches the intellect the practical value of surrendering to a higher order than to desire nature of the ego. It also strengthens the focus of our spiritual purpose in life.

Going beyond learning and obeying a principled life, individuals open themselves to a greater interior life. This means surrendering their exclusive focus on things material to the intense desire for Spiritual Awakening. This is more demanding and exacting of them, mentally and emotionally, than following the commandments of principled living. They are indeed of greater faith now moving from the relatively safe confines of leading "a good life" to the bewildering jungles of inner enfoldment. Deeper lessons of attunement to an inner knowing become, moment to moment, vitally important to their spiritual survival. Prayer and meditation must be the precursors to this enfoldment for it to go normally. The inner laws of attunement are even stricter in the governance of behavior, and paradoxically, sadhakas feel greater freedom through surrendered servitude to the Infinite One.

Through intense sadhana, the mind and its various levels of will are brought into line with the *Intuitive Spiritual Will*. The *Reasoned will* surrenders itself completely to the higher order of *Spiritual Will*. The training previously gone through in obeying spiritually principled living is a necessary preparatory period for this greater demand of the Spirit. The soul at last has come face to face with its evolutionary destiny. Total submission of the egoistic human will to *Intuitive Spiritual Will* allows for the total transformation from the son of Man consciousness (the ego consciousness) to the Son of God Consciousness (the Spiritual Illumined Self). During the sadhaka's life, they will experience three stages of surrendered will. The first is to know and obey spiritual principles such as the Ten Commandments or the Golden Rule by *Reasoned will*. The second, through deepened prayer, gaining access to *Dynamic Will* surcharged by spiritual power. The third is the total sublimation of individual *Reasoned will* to *Intuitive Spiritual Will*, resulting in the elimination of human will as it was previously known. At this final stage, the volition of sadhakas comes spontaneously from the Divinity through *Intuitive Spiritual Will*.

These three stages of spiritual development can be likened to three ways of knowing the sun. Following spiritually principled living by studying the scriptures, reading the lives of saints, and praying to a distant God is like standing on the earth looking at the rays of reflected sunlight in the full moon. When revelation comes directly to the mind and individuals feel more and more guided by an inner light, it is like standing on the moon, looking directly at the sun. When total transformation comes into the Being of the Soul and *Divine Will* flows spontaneously through every thought and word and deed, then it is as if that Soul becomes the burning orb of the sun itself. No longer is that one looking for the Light, or being led by that Light, but that one **becomes that Light Itself**. This is the whole meaning of Jesus' life in giving up the ghost, the human individual self, and resurrecting in the Holy Ghost, the illumined one!

Individual will disappears and one becomes a witness to the *Divine Will*. The seesaw battle between the lower developmental wills and Divine Will is over. The lion and sheep lie together in peace in this united kingdom. Individuality sees itself as but a witness to *Divine Will's* play, both within and without. Free of internal struggles, the soul is a fit instrument to carry out the Divine Father's Will. Then, with Jesus, that one may say in full awareness, "Of myself I am nothing, It is my Father who doeth the works." (John 14:10)

And what works are these? Everything! Every thought, word, and deed, comes from a singular Divine Source. This same state of consciousness may say, "I make no judgment, but if I judge it is true." (John 5:30 adapted) Does this statement contradict itself? No, not when seen in the light that the "I" is the witness, who has no judgment, but observes the flow of universal Christ Consciousness that discerns very clearly Light from dark.

The drama of Jesus' life depicts going the final mile to that total surrender. The son of Man represents the ego. The Son of God represents God Consciousness. Jesus had temptations along the way, such as in the desert after his illuminating experience with John the Baptist and his forty-day fast; the pleading temptation by Peter for Jesus not to go to Jerusalem and be crucified; and, the greatest temptation was in the garden of Gethsemane depicting Jesus' absolute submission, even unto death, unto *Divine Will*. Even while carrying the cross, Jesus fell three times, indicating the tremendous load he carried, buckling under its weight in carrying out his mission.

These are all indications of what the sons of Man can expect on their way to transformation. With unswerving passion, individuals must rise through these opposing forces. In times of temptation, they must use strong *Reasoned will* and *Dynamic Will* anchored in prayer and meditation to guide their way. It is in these very times, caught in the clutches of the opposing force, that they are least likely to feel the inner guidance. But through pure faith, they assert *Reasoned* and *Dynamic Will*. At other times, they feel the Divine Presence, a flow of Divine Guidance, and surrender to that movement. In the upward ascent, sadhakas will have occasion for the right use of *Reasoned will*, surcharged *Dynamic Will*, and full surrender to *Divine Will*, depending on the inner fluctuating states of consciousness at the time—like a dance responding to the partners they find themselves with at any one time. This dance goes on and on in sadhana until at last the beast, the ego, is dead, until *Divine Will* is enthroned as rightful sovereign.

When the human ego has been fully sublimated into the Divine Ego, called Sahaja Samadhi, sadhakas are purified of all vasanas, past habit influences, and the sense of dual wills is no longer present. The fresh spring waters of *Divine Will* then continuously feed the Atman-Soul. Like the thieves on either side of the Christ, the legs are broken of self-will and the sacred *Self-Will* of God reigns free, without a second. Sadhakas then fully realize the three natures of God's Will: **Sat,** the Eternal Self (God the Father), **Chid,** conscious awareness (The Witness, the Son of God), and **Ananda,** bliss that flows as joy in all creation (Divine Mother). All in All is seen as a Divine expression of the Universal Will of God, eternally springing from Joy!

Balanced Sadhana

Balance is a beautiful and delicate word: delicate, and yet enduring from ancient times. The Buddha, when yet performing severe austerities, heard the words of a musician instructing his chela. The musician said, "The strings of this instrument, overly tightened will break, and too loose produce no sound."

Those words changed the Buddha's life and helped him formulate the "middle path."

Once in meditation, a simile made itself known to me. The balance needed on the spiritual path is like the skill needed to sail a boat. The sails must be adjusted just right to get the best speed. Let the sails billow too much and there is a loss of speed, made too taut, again loss of speed. Constant adjustments to the wind and water must be made. The course must be set and kept in line with the rudder and the depth and weight of the keel are essential to keeping the boat upright.

Just so with the spiritual aspirant, the proper tension must be maintained in one's spiritual practice. Too little effort, little progress. Too tense, again, little progress. And the conditions are always changing, so no one rule always applies. The course too must be set. The captain sometimes sails according to the polestar to keep on track. He goes according to the maps and logs left by those who have gone before. So too the sailor on the sea of consciousness: the sadhaka goes according to the Guru, that one who has sailed those seas to his or her ultimate port. Sound reason and intuition of the

Divine is the rudder, deepened spiritual practice is the keel. When all is kept in balance, ever-new joy and intuitive soul knowledge become the hallmarks of progress.

In Japan, a craftsman was in apprenticeship for twenty-eight years! Can you imagine, twenty-eight years as the apprentice? Think of the care, the diligence, the patience, and attention to detail that must be required for that apprentice, and the master! The master craftsman may do his or her craft with speed and proficiency. The novice can have one or the other, not both. The tension produced by the master may look effortless to those who don't know, but would break the novice.

It has often been said that the spiritual path is *the* most difficult undertaking known to humankind. How much more so, then, must we take a balanced, proper approach. This balanced approach comes about by creating **pure intention, commitment, loyalty, and an intensity that defies human expectation.**

And, what may we expect in return? Birth into a realized state of Being, to become awakened to, and ultimately one with, the Divinity latent within us all!

> To reach the port of heaven we must sail sometimes with the wind and sometimes against it—but we must sail, and not drift nor lie at anchor.
>
> —OLIVER WENDELL HOLMES (1841–1935)

Intention

From the beginning, every conscious being practices **intention,** whether it is choosing food, a mate, clothes, starting a career, or setting the goals of a government. But many people live their lives led by unconscious motivations. The work they do came about because family members or friends got them started in that direction. They had children because their friends were starting families. Guided by social norms, they work, live, dress, and talk as their peers. There is nothing inherently wrong in this, but it does limit a soul's expression only to what is accepted by the crowd.

At some point, the soul yearns to be more conscious of its deeper self and to express it outwardly. The requirement for this deeper expression of the self is breaking out of societal norms and becoming consciously intentional. This produces clarity of who we are beyond social norms and speaks directly to who we wish to be. Immature souls define this as becoming counter-culture. But that merely defines us as, "I am not that!" We then join a group with those who are also counter-culture, then an even *stricter* code of behavior is formed regarding the mode of dress and language.

To know who we are spiritually and to create pure intention from that deep sense of knowing requires courage, effort, and self-awareness. The most efficient way to do this is through quieting the mind in deep prayer and meditation. Gradually, an inner life emerges from the burnt ashes of old patterns. This inner life produces a clarity that prompts us to action. These actions emanate from the clear soul-springs of intuitional knowledge. These emanations are in harmony with those eternal Truths that saints and mystics have enunciated with one voice throughout time.[7] This is the product of pure intention.

When prompted to action through this inner knowing, we become clear on the object of action. With a calm mind, we enact the inner prompting. It may come to us as a complete picture of what is to be, or it may be a step in faith where we know only the next step and no more. In any case, we seek to harmonize the outer action with the inner knowing. The same vibrational pattern we feel inside is put into the outer manifestation.

Pure Intention requires being consciously mindful of each step we take. No detail or aspect is beneath our awareness. When this flow has been fully activated, we feel as if the Divine Presence Itself is acting through us. We realize the reality of pure intention as outlined in *The Lord's Prayer:* "Thy kingdom come, Thy will be done, on earth as it is in heaven." (Matthew 6:10) The fulfillment of this prayer

---

7   These truths are not harmonious because of some need for conformity; rather, it is because they are universally true.

comes about when we have harmonized our thoughts, words, and actions with the highest intuitional wisdom of the soul.

God the Architect

Who Thou art I know not,
But this much I know:
Thou has set the Pleiades
In a silver row;

Thou has sent the trackless winds
Loose upon their way;
Thou hast reared a colored wall
Twixt the night and day;

Thou hast made the flowers to bloom
And the stars to shine;
Hid rare gems of richest ore
In the tunneled mine—

But chief of all Thy wondrous works,
Supreme of all thy plan,
Thou hast put an upward reach
Into the heart of Man.

—HARRY KEMP (1883–1960)

Commitment

Now, to realize the enactment of pure intention requires **commitment.** Once we decide to move in a certain direction, we bring all the forces we have available to bear to make it manifest. Whenever we make the choice for one action, we rule out 99.9% of the other possible actions. If I choose to live in Seattle, Washington, I will be excluding every other city in the world to live in at this time. Rather than be preoccupied with the idea of living somewhere else, better to be fully focused on where I am now.

The same is true with a moment in time. I can daydream all day of a time in the past or time yet to be, but what a difference when I practice being present to this moment. These may sound like self-evident statements, but most people are not fully present in the here and now! So, commitment means to be fully present to our choice in this moment. And, it means to bring our full sense of being into the fray.

I remember a time when I really became aware that "This is *my* life," and it was up to me to live it! This is my time on the stage and if I do not fully commit myself to it, I will be the same as the player on a sports team who is seated in the spectators' bleachers during the game, wondering why the game is not going well! Our time here is limited and if we do not choose to fully live now, then when? Full-hearted commitment means to take our life seriously and make it count.

Dare Greatly —
It is not the critic who counts; not the man who points out how the strong man stumbled or where the doer of deeds could have done better. The credit belongs to the man who is actually in the arena; whose face is marred by dust and sweat and blood; who strives valiantly, who errs and comes short again and again; who knows the great enthusiasms, the great devotions, and spends himself in a worthy cause; who at the best knows the triumph of high achievement; and who at the worst, if he fails, at least fails while daring greatly; so that his place shall never be with those cold and timid souls who know neither victory nor defeat.

—THEODORE ROOSEVELT (1858–1919)

Loyalty

In order for our commitment to count, we need to cultivate **loyalty**. There are those who are sparked by an idea, commit themselves to it, then fade before the finish line. Like the gold diggers who shovel their way down five feet into the ground in search of the treasure, only to start a second dig that penetrates the ground ten feet. Again and again, they begin new holes. All the while, the mother lode is at a twenty-foot depth! Never loyally committing themselves to dig to twenty feet at any one place, they dig countless other holes that add up to hundreds of feet in depth. In defeat, they cry, "There's no gold in them thar hills!"

When we find a path to God-consciousness we have faith in, we should stay with it until we reach our destination. Practicing loyalty in friendship, work, marriage, and parenting is all part of building a pattern in our life. This does not mean going along with something that feels absolutely wrong out of so-called loyalty. Short of that, loyalty will build our character and will get us over those little and big bumps that inevitably occur in any commitment.

When I was traveling in India, a western woman asked if I would teach her a higher Kriya technique. She said, "I have a teacher here in India, but he won't give the higher initiation. Indian time and my time are just different." She was telling me right there and then why she wasn't ready for higher initiation! Loyalty should not be given lightly, nor should it be withdrawn easily. In previous generations, "A man was as good as his word." And, if he shook hands on a deal, he was loyal to his commitment. The world suffers today from broken agreements and disloyalty. The practice of loyalty, too, makes for good relationships, good business, good government, and a healthy society. And finally, loyalty is a key to all spiritual progress.

> The kingdom of God is a society of the best men,
> working for the best ends, according to the best
> methods. Its law is one word—loyalty.
>
> —HENRY DRUMMOND (1851–1897)

Desire That Defies all Human Expectation

Great minds have purposes, others have wishes.
Little minds are tamed and subdued by misfortune;
but great minds rise above them.

—WASHINGTON IRVING (1783–1859)

Great, high-minded goals always come at a cost; oftentimes the greater the goal, the higher the cost. In spiritual transformation, the cost is the life of the ego, which is identification with the body. Since the ego is who we have come to think of ourselves to be, it translates into a willingness to give our ego to God. Naturally, this would require a **desire that defies all human expectation**. Human expectation will do much for the anticipation of wealth, fame, security, or pleasure. All of these are thrown into the fires of renunciation! So human expectation cannot play a part in this journey. And what about desire?

What explorer, scientist, inventor, or anyone with a worthy goal became successful without the intensity of desire? How much more so then for the spiritual scientist/explorer. Krishna says that out of many thousands there is one, here and there, who seeks out realization in a real way. (Gita 7:3) And, out of those rare seekers, one here or there becomes fully realized. Why? Is it because of a capricious god who whimsically grants this one entry and not others? No! Humankind is born with free will. No one else determines our direction in life.

We choose! We choose to get up in the morning and meditate or roll over and go back to sleep. We choose to keep our mind on God in service during the day or identify with ego desires and attachments. We choose! And in that choosing, we determine the course of our life.

If we find lukewarm desire for realization, or any worthy goal, then we must pray deeply for greater intensity, and *not* to stop that prayer until we get what we need! We are born with potential in the ready, but we must make ourselves receptive. Divine Grace is always in and around us like a boundless sea. Prayer is not to make a god of a fickle mind—it is to change us! In some distant past, we closed and locked the doors to Grace. Only one person is in charge of changing that condition. We must exercise the same intensity in opening our own closed and locked door to God's Grace as we expended in closing it in the first place.

> Our duty to God is to make ourselves the most perfect product of divine incarnation that we can become. This is possible only through the pursuit of worthy ideals.
>
> —EDGAR WHITE BURRILL (1883–1958)

How many times does another New Year's celebration find us repeating halfhearted resolutions for the next? Let us create great desire to open the door to Grace and supercharge our will with Divine Will! United with Divine Will and surrendering ourselves to it, we become spiritually balanced. We weigh the anchor of indifference and set sail at best speed to our Heavenly Goal. In order to make the goal of Self-realization, and all worthy goals, cultivate today pure intention, commitment, loyalty, and that intensity that defies all human expectation.

John the Baptist proclaimed the kingdom of heaven is here, now! (Matthew 3:2) Jesus echoed that and boldly taught that God and the kingdom of heaven are within you. (Luke 17:21) It always has been. Their voices call to us from down through the ages in concert with realized Beings from every part of the world and from every age. The time is now! The place here! And, if we proceed on the balanced middle path, with high-mindedness, we will discover gold, not of the cold ground, but of the all-embracing, never-ending Spirit. May that realization be yours *now* and *always*.

Awaken O Divine Mother

O Divine Mother
In purity, You have inwardly called me to Yourself.
But also, in outer beguiling forms
You come to tempt me away.

You are the sacred Power within
And secretly You yearn to rise
Through subtle channels that flow,
To awaken Divine experience itself!

But age-old patterns strive to divert
That steady minded approach
And seek to worship lesser gods
In vain pursuit of carnal happiness.

Awaken in me, O Divine Mother,
Pure love for Thy Divine Form alone.
Burn those puny tempting idols in fiery sacred flame,
And free me, now and always, in Thee alone!

God: With and Without Form

Is there only one God? The answer is, unequivocally, yes! "Hear O Israel, the Lord our God, the Lord is one." (Deuteronomy 6:4) God, being omnipotent (all-powerful), omniscient (all-knowing), and omnipresent (everywhere present), is the only force and intelligence there is. Therefore, God really is one, without a second.

Now, how to explain multiplicity, which is God appearing as the separate forces, beings, and perspectives that we see in all creation around us. In India, the yogis have a concept called Maya. Maya is God creating an apparent separation where none truly exists. In deep sleep, we unconsciously experience ourselves to be one with

God; all separation ceases to exist. To consciously be in that state (which yogis call samadhi) we would know ever-new bliss, be fully conscious, and know ourselves to be ever existent.

However, that conscious awareness is rare amongst most of humankind. The veil of Maya keeps us separate from this knowledge. Nevertheless, realized Beings, from ancient times to modern, have attested to its veracity through their direct experience. The history of religion is also the history of the evolution of consciousness. Early humans, intimately acquainted with nature, worshipped the spirits that live in and control those elements. As humankind evolved from hunter-gatherers to agrarian, the power of the sun, seasons, and celestial movements took on greater meaning and resulted in the worship of God in those forms. Gradually, as we know from recorded history, the development of higher consciousness occurred. Mystics began to experience deeper insights into what we call God. Transcendent visions revealed more refined states of Being beyond this physical reality.

Spiritual scientists, exploring the laboratory of their own consciousness, came to understand this singular Reality called God. The names and rituals regarding this understanding of God's nature vary throughout the world, according to language and cultural differences. But the principles remain unchanged as to the nature of God and the seemingly ephemeral nature of this physical reality. Ancient records reveal the earliest affirmations of this central truth coming from the East in India and in the West, with Judaism. A monotheism evolved in India that recognized a unified field of consciousness that permeates all creation yet stands beyond that which is created. Through careful mapping of consciousness, a new inner cosmology appeared. In Judaism, a singular creative cause was revealed to its early seers, and came to be known as:

I AM THAT I AM

These two impersonal concepts of a universal Divinity, one from India, one from The Middle East, moved theology forward in our recorded history. This was not, and has not been, a smooth progression. Resistive forces of tribalism, privileged classism, unwarranted dogmatism, divisive sectarianism, corruption, and the influence of lesser minds took their toll on these truths. No religion and no area of the world were left unscathed during these past dark ages.

Saints and realized Beings have stood as spiritual bulwarks to keep alive the true spirit of religion. Transcending institutions and privileged classes, these brave souls were often persecuted in their own times. But the sweetness and purity of their lives and the truths they taught spoke to those in need of spiritual example and upliftment. Spiritual Truth, like all universal principles, transcends the small-minded and vindictive. Although Spiritual Truth has been crucified innumerable times in millions of hearts, still the Light finds fertile soil in those who are yearning and receptive. Some religions banned the worship and veneration of saints or symbolic deities. Often, the practices of worship of these deities were crude throwbacks to earlier developmental stages in religion. These forms of worship were discouraged, many times with the sharp edge of a sword. Impassioned believers came to see the worship of a deity as an affront to God.

In other religions such as in India, these symbolic deities were seen as so many expressions of the monotheistic Supreme Being. Recognizing a human need to focus on images, saints, and deities, this form of worship was fostered as a legitimate avenue of approach to a singular Divinity. Stories of these saints and deities are charming, emotionally engaging, and instructive. Passionate prayers, songs, and rituals evince a lasting value to these expressions of Divinity. There has, however, been much quarreling over the matter of what is appropriate worship of God. Is worship of forms in keeping with the highest truth?

Moses first knew God through direct perception as a voice in a burning bush. Later, he built a simple stone altar to worship God. When the people of Israel reinstituted an older worship of Baal, the response was swift and severe. It was at that time Moses gave instructions for the creation of an elaborate temple that was made of gold, silver, and cloth of purple and lavender. An ark was created that depicted twin seraphim and a priestly class was formed to conduct rites of worship, including animal sacrifice. The people had an object on which to focus their attention.

Christians have no representation of God the Father, but the crucified Son of Man is in the front of most churches, or at least a cross; there are pictures of Jesus in homes, and Catholics use pictures of Mother Mary and the saints. Islam prohibits any human depictions of saints or of God, but those of Islamic faith have put their creative talents into the architecture and construction of the mosque. And, although the Buddha forbade the use of images, I doubt if any image has been more reproduced than the Buddha's!

We can see through these examples that the human mind, in many cases, needs objects of adoration and worship. Finding it difficult to focus the mind and devotion on a God who is beyond form, beginningless and endless, devotees are very often attracted to holy places and personages to whom they can relate. Again, is this in keeping with the highest truth?

In the Bhagavad Gita, Krishna holds out the Universal Vision[8] as the supreme attainment. He, speaking from that Universal Consciousness, says that those who worship God's lower forms sincerely, He accepts that worship as well. (Gita 9:23) The true essence is the purity of heart in worship. That is, loving God for God alone and not for what we can get from our worship in terms of material success, power over people, or nature. This expresses my conviction also. I think most of us need a focus for our attention and for inspiration. In order to progress more quickly to the Universal Vision,

8   Universal Vision: the realization of God as the Supreme Being manifest as all creation and beyond creation as formless, beginningless, and endless spirit.

however, we should always affirm that the Light we behold in the visage of a realized master or deity is a manifestation of the Universal Divine Light. As a stained-glass window cannot illumine itself, so no spiritual master or deity can be anything but a conduit of God. Constantly bring to mind the Universal Light in what we are worshiping in form. Let us pierce the outer form of the image and go straight to the inner source of our adoration.

If our mind is focused on an individual aspect of God, then practice seeing that aspect in all people and all creation. If our chosen ideal is Jesus or Krishna, then practice seeing Jesus or Krishna in the hearts of everyone we meet. Many years ago, I was blessed with the experience of seeing Mother's face in the heart center of every person I met. For twenty-four hours, I was in this experience and all the walls of separation crumbled between others and myself. This was my first glimpse that God resides in the heart of all people, each one a shrine of the omnipresent Spirit.

From the beginning, my attention was drawn to that indwelling formless Presence of God. The one universal principle in religion is the path of the spine and the brain. Through my focus on the ajna and feeling the Presence in my spine and brain, the transformation of body, mind, and soul continued. Over time, the spiritual masters revealed to me their unique signature of Light that is at once personal and impersonal. Now I hang their images on the wall to remind me of their sweet presence and protection. All who enter my home also have this uplifting influence.

Mother was very focused on her own Guru, and that focus took her all the way to the feet of God. As a final gesture, she even threw that into the ocean of God Consciousness. Later, when she set her altar, it was with the simplicity of flowers, candles, and some incense. She did not display pictures, although she had a large picture of her Guru, Sri Yoganandaji, on the wall opposite her chair in her home. Every fully realized master has overcome all limiting forms of worship, but many continue on with veneration for God in certain forms as an example to those who follow after them or for their own purposes.

Worship of God with form or without form is all due to personal preference. Ultimately, all worship should take us to the Universal Vision: the realization that God is nirguna, formless spirit, and saguna, with form, having taken form ultimately as all creation. The Vision of God as both formless and with form is the highest realization.

There is a fascinating account of two highly realized souls regarding this subject. Ramakrishna Paramhansa was living at Dakshineswar, a temple compound near Calcutta. Ramakrishna worshipped God in the form of Kali, the Divine Mother. One day a wandering monk, Totapuri, came to Dakshineswar and recognized Ramakrishna's great spirit and decided to initiate him into Vedanta. Vedanta holds that the world is an illusion and God is only to be found in transcendent Spirit. Here I will give a brief account of Totapuri's initiation of Ramakrishna.[9]

> Totapuri began to impart to Ramakrishna the great truths of Vedanta. "Brahman," he said, is the only Reality, ever pure, ever illumined, ever free, beyond the limits of time, space, and causation. Though apparently divided by names and forms through the inscrutable power of maya, that enchantress who makes the impossible possible, Brahman is really one and undivided. When a seeker merges in the beatitude of samadhi, the seeker does not perceive time and space or name and form, the offspring of maya. Whatever is within the domain of maya is unreal. Give it up. Destroy the prison-house of name and form and rush out of it with the strength of a lion. Dive deep in search of the Self and realize It through samadhi. You will find the world of name and form vanishing into the void, and the puny ego dissolving in Brahman-consciousness. You will realize your identity with Brahman, Existence-Knowledge-Bliss Absolute.
>
> ... Totapuri asked the disciple to withdraw his mind from all objects of the relative world, including the gods

---

9   *The Gospel of Sri Ramakrishna* (pp. 28–31).

and goddesses, and to concentrate on the Absolute. But the task was not easy even for Sri Ramakrishna. He found it impossible to take his mind beyond Kali, the Divine Mother of the Universe. "After the initiation," Ramakrishna once said, describing the event, "Nangta began to teach me the various conclusions of the Advaita (God without form or attributes) Vedanta and asked me to withdraw the mind completely from all objects and dive deep into the Atman. But in spite of all my attempts, I could not altogether cross the realm of name and form and bring my mind to the unconditioned state. I had no difficulty taking the mind from all the objects of the world. But the radiant and too familiar figure of the Blissful Mother, the embodiment of the essence of Pure Consciousness, appeared before me as a living reality. Her bewitching smile prevented me from passing into the great beyond. Again and again, I tried, but She stood in my way every time. In despair, I turned to Nangta: 'It is hopeless. I cannot raise my mind to the unconditioned state and come face to face with Atman.' He grew excited and sharply said: 'What? You cannot do it? But you have to!' He cast his eyes around. Finding a piece of glass, he took it up and struck it between my eyebrows. 'Concentrate the mind on this point!' he thundered. Then with a stern determination, I again sat to meditate. As soon as the gracious form of the Divine Mother appeared before me, I used my discrimination as a sword and with it clove Her in two. The last barrier fell. My spirit at once soared beyond the relative plane and I lost myself in samadhi."

Sri Ramakrishna remained completely absorbed in samadhi for three days. "Is this really true?" Totapuri cried in astonishment. "Is it possible that he has attained in a single day what it took me forty years of strenuous practice to achieve? Great God! It is nothing short of a miracle."

With the help of Totapuri, Sri Ramakrishna's mind finally came down to the relative plane.

Totapuri, a monk of the most orthodox type, never stayed at a place more than three days. But he remained at Dakshineswar for eleven months. He too had something to learn.... He ridiculed the spending of emotion on the worship of a personal God.... About this time, Totapuri was suddenly laid up with a severe attack of dysentery. On account of this miserable illness, he found it impossible to meditate. One night, the pain became excruciating. He could no longer concentrate on Brahman. The body stood in the way. He became incensed with its demands. A free soul, he did not at all care for the body. So, he determined to drown it in the Ganges. Thereupon he walked into the river. But, lo! He walks to the other bank. Is there not enough water in the Ganges? Standing dumbfounded on the other bank he looks back across the water. The trees, the temples, the houses, are silhouetted against the sky. Suddenly, in one dazzling moment, he sees on all sides the presence of the Divine Mother. She is in everything; She is everything. She is the mind. She is pain. She is death. She is everything that one sees, hears, or imagines. She turns "yea" into "nay," and "nay" into "yea." Without Her grace, no embodied being can go beyond Her realm.... She resides in Her Transcendental, Absolute aspect. She is the Brahman that Totapuri had been worshipping all his life. Totapuri returned to Dakshineswar and spent the remaining hours of the night meditating on the Divine Mother. In the morning he went to the Kali temple with Sri Ramakrishna and prostrated himself before the image of the Mother.

God, being both with form and formless, is both personal and impersonal. His Form is filled with the formless. The formless Spirit always has form.[10] One cannot separate the one from the other. The potential problem for a sadhaka comes when there is an attachment to form that precludes them from gaining the Universal Vision. In India, they say a thorn in the foot, deeply embedded, can be removed by using another thorn. That is, to transcend the realm of limiting thoughts, we can use a thought, a mantra, or an image of God, in order to ascend to overarching Spirit. With that transcendence, we come face to face with the Universal Consciousness and come to realize that all is God, One without a second. Placing the attention on God, with or without form, seek out His very real Presence, and let Him usher us into His Universal Vision.

Gardening with God

Three Gunas, or qualities, associate themselves with human life.

The first quality is sattva. Sattvic qualities are those attuned to the spiritual, such as search for truth, devotion, selfless service, a loving nature, meditation, and other spiritual practices. These lead to a refined personality that is saintly in nature.

The second Guna is rajas. Rajasic qualities are activating, stimulating of desire for the things of the world. Desire for name, fame, fortune, dominance, and emotions such as anger all result from the rajasic nature. It tends to be restless, always on the move.

---

10   Sri Yukteswar's delightful description from the *Autobiography of a Yogi* (pp. 404–5): "Joyous astral festivities on the higher astral planets like Hiranyaloka take place when a being is liberated from the astral world through spiritual advancement and is, therefore, ready to enter the heaven of the causal world. On such occasions, the Invisible Heavenly Father, and the saints who are merged in Him, materialize themselves into bodies of their own choice and join the astral celebration. In order to please His beloved devotee, the Lord takes any desired form. If the devotee worshipped through devotion, he sees God as the Divine Mother. To Jesus, the Father-aspect of the Infinite One was appealing beyond other conceptions. The individuality with which the Creator has endowed each of His creatures makes every conceivable and inconceivable demand on the Lord's versatility!"

The third Guna is tamas. Tamasic qualities are depressive in nature, drawing our mind into smaller spheres of awareness. Examples of tamasic qualities are: depression, jealousy, fear of loss, and pettiness. These can lead to a degradation of the personality, even to the point of suicide.

Much of life in the world today is a play between the forces of tamas and rajas, with a little sattva. Of course, for the sadhaka to progress spiritually, cultivation of a sattvic nature is the goal. But when we as sadhakas are confronted with habits, stemming from past actions of the rajasic and tamasic natures, what do we do?

One method is to graft the rajasic or tamasic desire or habit onto a sattvic root. To do this, we change the root cause assumption behind the drive of a lower nature. For instance, if we have a strong drive for worldly success, which is quite appropriate at certain times in life, then, Sadhakas still wants to have the right relationship with that drive rather than have it carry them off to even more worldly desires and attachment. So, the sadhaka changes his or her mind-set about that drive for worldly success by seeing it as God who is expressing Himself in that desire through the mind of the sadhaka. In other words, it is God who desires success in the world. By constantly bringing to mind the root association of God, the prior ego association of, "This is my desire," is lessened and finally becomes resolved in the new thought.

An example would be a rajasic desire for name, fame, and fortune as an entertainer. It feels to the sadhaka that his or her entire world revolves around that one desire, even though he or she has been given the desire for Self-realization as well. By constantly thinking, "This is God who desires to be a successful entertainer," the relationship of the self to the desire changes. Gradually the sadhaka becomes a third person watching God moving through the outward personality as the entertainer. With this third-person perspective, attachment to results lessen, as the results are surrendered to God. An inner calm begins to emanate from a deep place within, moving the sadhaka from restless rajasic nature to an inwardly calm sattvic nature. An additional advantage to the sattvic nature is that the calm mind's acuity for observation is heightened, critical for any art, craft, or intellectual pursuit.

Beyond these boons in performance, the tamasic natures of depression and jealousy are eliminated, sadhakas can become more balanced, more professional, and less prone to excesses such as drug and sex addictions.

This grafting technique can also be used with tamasic nature as well. For instance, we may tend toward depression, sadness, despondency, feelings of hopelessness and helplessness, etc. The way to graft those qualities onto God is to associate all those thoughts and feelings to God Himself. The feeling of sadness and loss is the feeling of sadness and loss at having lost connection with God, the source of all Joy and Love. In the past, those feelings were connected with the loss of a person, place, or situation that is no longer in the sadhakas' life. Any or all of those connections are switched to one category: inner loss of connection with God. By the constant new association of grafting this feeling to God, we open our heart to the healing Light that can come only from God. This opening to the Light adds sweetness to our sorrow and eventually changes it to a mood of Joy and a Love stemming from the new internal root association with Spirit.

The idea of helplessness gets grafted on to the new root by mentally knowing that the ego is helpless to give true happiness. Only by surrendering the idea, "I am the doer," and admitting the ego is helpless, do we connect with the real source of power that is God. With that connection comes the realization that Grace is the real power of accomplishment and regeneration. In that recognition, the power of Grace begins to transform sadhakas into something new, something sattvic in nature.

Any quality not of sattvic nature can be grafted in this way. What about sexual desire? Sexual desire is the desire for union, oneness, which is turned outward; that is, finding one's counterpart in the world. By affirming the intense desire for union by grafting it onto desire for Cosmic Consciousness, we utilize that powerful energy for upward propulsion into sacred realms. It is in this Cosmic Consciousness the desire for union is truly fulfilled, versus a relentless search on the outside punctuated by occasional fulfillment.

By this positive grafting approach, we actually utilize the energy of the desire by giving it a new rootstock. This is far superior to surrounding ourselves with the negations, "Not this, not that, can I do." A concern may come, "Won't this focus on a desire increase that desire rather than change it?" If we do it properly, the results will let us know we are on the right track. Confirmation will come by increased calm, inner joy, and a love that comes spontaneously from the heart. We will find ourselves less attached to the outcomes and get joy in the sheer doing of the activity itself. And, if the activity is not suitable to sattvic energy, it will lose its attraction for the sadhaka. Like oil on water, the two will not mix. In these ways we can judge for ourselves our progress.

Cultivating sattvic qualities will necessitate letting go of some old activities. But the inner joy that comes as a result of attunement to our good, will more than fulfill the empty promises of outward enjoyment of wrong activity. A feeling of inner purity will rise up within sadhakas that no worldly gain can duplicate. Expansion of Spirit-awareness and a renewed sense of who and what the sadhaka really is will be the growth, blooming, and fruition of a life rooted in sattvic nature.

Brahmacharya

The word brahmacharya is a Hindu word denoting celibacy. In the Vedas, the ancient sacred writings of India, four stages of life are laid out.

The first twenty-five years are categorized as the student phase, or being a brahmachari (brahmacharini, feminine). Traditionally, youths (male) left home when they became eight years or older. They lived at a hermitage or with a teacher. Here, they were taught how to live a spiritual life and received an education in reading, writing, math, astronomy, etc. During this time, they remained celibate and were often taught by teachers who also observed celibacy. Most then moved to the second stage of life, that of the householder. A very few, who felt called, would continue as celibates, but this was rare. It was during the time of Adi Shankaracharya, who became a renunciant at a young age and reorganized the order of swamis, that becoming a renunciant while still young became more widely practiced in Hindu culture.

When we take a survey of religious traditions around the world, we find celibacy, abstaining from sex, is observed in all major traditions in one form or another in regard to living a spiritual life. Why? The inward reason has to do with physiology, psychology, and spirituality.

The physiology of the body and the pranology[11] of the astral body reveal the true nature of sexual energy and sublimation. Sublimation comes from the Latin root *sublima*, which means to elevate. Its Webster's definition is: "Psychology: to divert the energy of (a sexual or other biological impulse) from its immediate goal to one of a higher social, moral, or aesthetic nature or use." It is well known that artists and intellectuals, when consumed with their chosen field, will oftentimes be abstinent. Far from feeling this is a sacrifice, they know the inward pleasure of transformed energy. What Webster's definition leaves out is the spiritual element, not yet understood in most of Western thought.

In India and other cultures of the East, it has been long understood that the transformation of sexual energy, called kundalini, is essential for Spiritual Realization. Yoga calls life-energy "prana." Prana is the essential stuff that allows us to move, think, and operate in this body. It is the indefinable "something" that leaves the body at the time of death, along with consciousness. It is intelligent, yet is responsive to individual will. It is primarily of the astral body, too fine an energy for human detection on a physical realm, but nevertheless can be experienced, and is experienced by all. This energy carries on the building and maintenance of the body. Good health is dependent on its

---

11   Pranology: the study of prana or life-force.

balanced functioning. It should not be too surprising this energy has not yet been discovered by Western science. Since it is not detectable by instruments, it remains hidden. How many laws of nature do we take for granted now, but at one time were unseen by uncomprehending minds of science? Yogic science tells us there is coiled-up potential life-force at the base of the spine that is normally dormant. Under certain circumstances, this energy in potential can be released and becomes a transformative force for evolution of the consciousness. When this occurs the condensed life-force at the base of the spine streams up the astral spine into higher regions of the consciousness. It is here that the real work of the kundalini takes place. These higher centers of awareness are activated, changed from their previously dormant status to being active and alive with energy and awareness. This leads to the gradual ascendancy of consciousness to becoming fully awakened, or illumined. For such a one, the titles of Christ or Buddha may be rightfully applied.

The psychological aspects of this awakening concern the changes the mind goes through in this unfoldment. In order for complete awakening to occur, a total change in thought process is required. Yoga science has two categories for normal mental functioning for human beings. The first is manas. Manas may be thought of as the more developmentally primitive part of the mind. The second category is the Buddhi. The Buddhi is the higher realm of reasoning that is said to be unique to humans. Through abstractions, humans may philosophize, create more complex tools, etc. This is the power of Buddhi when focused on human endeavors. When the Buddhi is spiritualized, it has the capacity to perceive spiritual consciousness.

When the transformative energy of the kundalini is activated, a battle ensues over the domination of the human psyche. The manas traits of the animal mind and the Buddhi-intellect, focused on human endeavors, carry on with the momentum gained over many lifetimes. This lower mind of the human lies in direct contradiction to the spontaneous flow of Divine consciousness ever streaming to the sensitive brain when it has been awakened. The psychological and physiological battle that ensues is the stuff of which so many scriptures and myths concern themselves.

In this way, we see tremendous changes occurring on the physiological, pranalogical, and psychological levels of existence. If the sadhaka feels besieged at times, this is a ready reason why! Understanding all three levels of this battle will help illustrate the power of sublimation, so closely akin to the word sublime.

Sexuality has often been associated with the fall of man. When we look at the physiology of humans, it is obvious in design that human beings were meant to be sexual in nature. Why then the emphasis on sex as the apple of temptation? If you imagine a person's nervous system running from the base of the spine to the top of the head, and in that image, think of the brain as the roots of the tree, turned upside down, then the trunk of the tree is the spine, running down the back of the torso to the tailbone. All of the afferent and efferent nerves running to and from are the branches of this nervous system tree. Each branch of this tree represents some sensory experience in the body. Each of the sensory experiences calls for the attention of the brain. All these nerve centers operate simultaneously, each with their own messages for the center of experience, the brain.

What we know from oriental pranalogy of the subtle astral body, with its seventy-two thousand nadis (astral nerves), reveals powerhouses all along the spine and brain. The three powerhouses located toward the base of the spine control functions of the body and human will as they operate in the world. The chakra powerhouses from the heart up to the top of the head, are mostly sleeping. Humans, in their full capacity, have those upper regions awakened. The highest region is at the top of the head, called the Sahasrara, and when this center is fully awakened—illumined—the knowledge of our oneness with the omniscient, omnipresent, omnipotent Spiritual Consciousness becomes a fact. What this means for the potential evolution of consciousness cannot be overstated. This awakening is the real purpose behind religion and all great philosophies.

As we imagine this upside-down tree, with all of its fruits of experiences, seeing, hearing, touching, smelling, tasting, we can easily see how our attention is drawn to these captivating sensations. What about those higher centers, why don't we know more about them? The myths of all the great religions depict "the fall of man," or the entry of humanity into a delusive nature. This is always associated somehow with the body, and usually has something to do with sex consciousness. Physiologically the sex organs reside at the most distant point from the roots of this tree of consciousness, the Sahasrara, or the crown of the head. Pranalogically the sex organs represent a great magnetic pull away from the higher centers of consciousness. Psychologically, the sex urge focuses the attention for union on oneness away from an interior union of Spirit toward finding a complementary soul "out there." Symbolically and functionally, sex energy and sex consciousness represent the furthest extreme from oneness in Spiritual Consciousness.

A revelation showed me the inner meaning of the Adam and Eve story when the serpent was "sentenced" by God to crawl upon its belly. This is symbolic language for a natural cause-and-effect consequence of entering into this mundane world of experience at the expense of our fully awakened Spiritual Nature. The serpent is the kundalini force, designed to feed the upper regions of consciousness with life-force. When consciousness is directed by the will to flow to the exterior world, and most powerfully through the sexual organs (the fruit in the midst of the garden), to the exclusion of the higher centers of consciousness, the vast kundalini power becomes mostly dormant. There is sufficient life-force to enliven the lower centers of consciousness; nothing more is being utilized. The more highly charged energy of the kundalini would prove harmful to the soul focused on the outer events of the world alone. So, the serpent, the kundalini, crawls upon its belly, or remains dormant below the belly button within the spine.

The kundalini and the higher regions of consciousness wait for their awakening. In order for this awakening to occur, the redirection of the will from outer worldly consciousness, with its all-consuming attraction, to the inner world of Spirit is needed. As long as

the attention is focused purely on the sensory world and its preoccupations, so long will the inner nature of Spiritual Consciousness
remain dormant. Brahmacharya is not simply abstaining from sex.
Brahma is the Self, or God in Its absolute form. Achari means he
or she who lives in—so, a Brahmachari is one who lives within the
Self, or is God-realized. By transmuting the life-energy that is normally spent on worldly pursuits, raising it up the spine, and activating the higher centers of consciousness, we advance spiritually.
When the kundalini, the coiled-up life-energy at the base of the
spine, becomes activated, then the whole spinal system becomes
charged, electrified with this dynamic evolutionary force. This is
the fuel for the awakening, to become a Buddha.

For the sadhaka on the path, this upward ascent is the goal of the
aspirant. But is it necessary for the sadhaka to abstain from all sexual
activity? There is a time in the sadhana of an aspirant when all the
forces, both human and divine, are focused on this upward journey.
For the sadhaka, there may be a variety of circumstances in which
they find themselves leading a brahmacharya life. A devotee may be
unmarried; a couple may choose to be leading a celibate life while
married, or circumstances may result in abstinence beyond the control of a married couple. Mother taught that to lead a normal sexual
life as a married couple was the best for the vast majority of aspirants. It is better to experience the fullness of marital love and know
what it can offer and what it does not offer in order for the aspirant
to see it clearly for what it is. Mother often said that the love shared
between the married couple in the sexual act represented the highest experience on the human level. This is especially true when the
relationship is spiritualized. Mother described a time in her own
marriage when all desire for sex dropped off. With this spontaneous
dropping off of sexual desire in her own ascent to the Divine, she
held out as a model for married couples. No doubt this is a sensitive
subject when this dropping off happens for one of the partners and
not for the other. However, if love and caring are present, all such

difficulties can be managed. Eventually, for all, the time will come for the complete focus to be on God alone.

We who have not been acquainted with the potential that can result from this interior union may eye celibacy with some suspicion. The focus of our mind may be trained on what is being given up, versus what is being gained. We have been so conditioned, especially in modern Western culture, to think of sex as the "be all, end all" of human experience. Without the idea of the transmutation of the energy and the awakening of these higher centers, this concept would be all about denying ourselves what comes naturally for no obvious gain. Those who have had some experiences in uplifted consciousness may get a glimpse of what is possible. Others may have an intuitive hunch of its value, and others may have an intellectual grasp of the potential. We are in fact struggling with eons of programming regarding the sexual impulse. Take away the subconscious programming from other lifetimes, and we are still the result, biologically, of thousands of years of sexually driven parentage. It is in our genes to reproduce! To redirect this energy is no joke, and should not be taken as a given to happen so easily, or that if we struggle with it there is something wrong with us. This is a momentous shift of will, and while very possible, it should be thought of soberly, in the light of day.

The process of working our way through material creation as a conscious entity may be thought of, to this point, as evolution. We have been involved with knowing this material creation from the ground up, literally. We have experienced ourselves to be matter of minerals, matter of the livelier vegetable kingdom, matter of the mobile animal kingdom, and finally, matter of the higher reasoning faculty of human beings. From evolution, we now move to involution: the shift from exterior consciousness, the exterior world of the five senses, to the interior world of inner awakening and intuitive Divine perception.

Our long journey into this material world and exile from our spiritual home is coming to a close. When we are ready, we will start this new journey and awaken to this inner reality. For those still focused and intent on the outer reality, there will be incomprehension and disbelief in this inner reality. But what of it? They are satisfied with their current experience. But for those ready to awaken to this world of Light within, nothing else will ultimately do. Thus, we shift our attention from evolution to involution.

The Means of Brahmacharya

The Nature of Sexual Energy and Sublimation

First, recognize that sexual energy within mankind is one of the most powerful forces there is. That is why the human race continues: the miracle of new life is spawned as a result. It is also the reason sex is used to sell so many things, and when it is out of control, why the effects can be so devastating. Next, there is the idea amongst many religious schools that sex is bad, a terrible thing. However, since sex produces babies, one of life's most precious gifts, how can that be bad? Sexuality brings the union of husband and wife closer together in love and intimacy; how can that be bad? It is not the use, but the misuse of sexual energy that creates positive or negative conditions. Since it is such a powerful force, its potential for good and bad consequences is also powerful.

Given that it is powerful, and that the life-energy within sexual energy is power itself, you must use wisdom in the expression or transmutation of this energy. To begin the discussion on the means of sublimating sexual energy into spiritual-creative energy, create a positive goal in your mind. Since mind is the beginning of all creative processes, create a picture in your mind of what you would look like as a brahmacharya. As a realized brahmacharya, you have gained full self-mastery of yourself and raised that powerful force into the higher regions of your Being. Begin with looking at yourself as another person would see you in that transformed state. Inwardly, the fuel that comes from sexual energy is streaming up your spine; it has opened the heart, throat, ajna, and crown chakras (the consciousness powerhouses in the higher spine and brain). Although the invisible energy is not seen with the two physical eyes, nevertheless it produces an effect on the physical body and subtle bodies that is perceptible. As that third person looking back on your illumined self, do you see a glow on the face? Do you notice a shine in the eyes? More subtly, do you feel a vibration of peace and love emanating from that one? When that self speaks, do you sense a vibration in the voice that "awakens your better angels?" Take some time to fill in this picture in your mind's eye before reading on.

Now, enter the body of yourself as the realized brahmacharya. What do you notice about the way you stand, the way you carry yourself, the way you breathe? Next, notice the flow of your thoughts, the activation of creative centers, and access to higher consciousness. Now, notice the flow of energy within your body. And now all around your body. Take your time. Breathe into this picture and be careful to notice everything about this state of being. This is your future potential self!

Now observe how the sexual organs operate and life-energy flows into the spine and to these higher centers. In your imagination, as you see these centers fully open, ask yourself, "Am I missing anything essential by using this energy inwardly rather than outwardly?" If you really follow through on this exercise, you will realize that the life of a brahmacharya has its advantages.

I am not intending to sell you on the idea that being a brahmacharya is the only way to live your life. I am in hopes that you may get an inkling of the richness of the life possible through sublimation, what may have been before, unseen possibilities. You have been so indoctrinated into thinking that sex is the "be all, end all" of human experience, that to consider a life of brahmacharya as fulfilling is a rarity. You can now dispense with outmoded caricatures of the celibate as stilted, prudish, and life-denying. The potential for a life as a brahmacharya is unlimited, fascinating, and open-ended beyond our current imagining.

Moving Into the Life of a Brahmacharya

Self-mastery begins with mastery of your thoughts. Jesus is quoted as saying that to even desire another man's wife is adultery. This is a very strict criterion indeed! But it speaks to the power of thought. Thought is the primal creator of all that is. *When you think, you create.* That is why I had you paint a picture in your mind of a complete brahmacharya; you may want to do that often, every day, several times a day, and especially as you go to sleep at night and when you first awaken.

When you realize that thought is creation, it begins to dawn on you how important it is when you create intention. Thoughts can be spread all over the place, with little power to create. Or, they can be focused like a laser that can cut through all obstacles to find fulfillment. **Self-mastery includes the creation of pure intention; that is, those focused intentions that are for the highest good of all.** When I started my life as a sadhaka, I accepted the idea that I would be a celibate, at least for the time, since I was not married. It was a terrific struggle for me as a young man, much of the trouble was brought on because I did not have the means to control my own mind.

There was another part that worked against me. I wanted to be in a relationship with someone. Of course, this is natural for most people, but since there was no one in my life in those years, I surrendered the idea to God as to whether it was to be my lot to find someone that was right for me, or not. I say I surrendered the idea, but what I should say, is that I worked to surrender the idea. I really wanted to have that special someone, but where was she!? This mixed nature in me, part surrendered, part holding on, made for mixed results. I was my own worst enemy in that I did not create in myself a pure intention. Really, I had mixed intentions. It is not that I did not try; I worked with all that I had to do it right. **As long as you have mixed intentions, you will get mixed results.** Much of spiritual sadhana is creating the pure intention that what you want is God-realization above all else. Sadhana is the purification of the mind toward this single intention.

To control the mind is to control the imaging, or imagining factor, in the mind. The mind constantly creates pictures: of the past, the future, what you want, what you desire, thoughts from the subconscious mind, all of it passes on the screen of your imagining mind. When intruding desire-thoughts come, and they will, what to do? Having created the intention of purity of mind, you will strike out every thought image not in concert with your goal.

X it Out

Whenever an image comes onto the screen of your mind that is contrary to your goal of brahmacharya, put a big black **X** in front of the image. Immediately replace that prior image with an image that is in concert with your goal. For instance, you may have an image of someone to whom you feel sexually attracted, immediately, put an X over that image. Then you bring to mind the image of yourself as the fully illumined one you created before. Then step into that picture and feel what it is like to be that illumined one, the freedom and bliss of that expansive Self. Or, you may see yourself sitting in a circle with the Masters all around you, feeling their influence and spiritual vibration. Never leave a blank screen after erasing the old image, for that invites the old desires to express new images on the screen of your mind. Be sure to feel what that new Self is like, for feeling creates the desire nature, and you want to desire God alone.

Avoiding

Everything felt in the body is a reaction to a stimulus and your inter-pretation of that input. Stimuli may be external, something you directly see, hear, feel, taste, or smell, or it may be an internal stim-ulus, a memory, projected idea, or dream. If you are dealing with external stimuli, you see someone attractive, smell something that creates desire, hear a stimulating voice, etc., you can avoid the stimulation or create a new association for it.

Sometimes avoiding is thought to be a bad word, but it can be very helpful when used correctly. Avoiding someone who stimulates desire is a good strategy. You know when you are playing with fire. When you have sexual energy for someone and you go out of your way to play with that energy, it goes against mental purity. When you find someone visually stimulating, you can look to the side or down to avoid visual contact. If you have good concentration, you can also be looking at the person with these two eyes but your greater focus is upon the ajna, the third eye. Also, you can avoid situations that bring you into close contact with someone you find attractive. Avoidance can be a very good tool to keep your mind on the right track.

Creating New Associations

In India, the men in the ashrams call all women "mothers." The new association is, "This woman is my mother" (a rather cooling thought to sex drive, warming to the heart). Or, "This woman is the Divine Mother," a sacred thought. And for women, "This man is my father, my baba, or papa." When you see all those of the sex you might have an attraction to as mother, or father, it changes the association.

When I worked in an antique store as a retail manager, I practiced mentally bowing down at the feet of all women who came into the store, seeing them as the Divine Mother. It became an automatic thing to do and helped me create new associations for all women.

Another way of using associations is to visualize a picture that produces a cooling effect. For instance, you might imagine someone without any skin! See that person as organs, bones, muscles, and blood vessels, all without any skin covering at all. Or, you can imagine him or her getting older and older, until very old, shrunken, wrinkled; and then to see the person die and turn into worm-infested bones as the body gradually turns to dust! This is all-out war!

Transmuting Physical Sensations

What creates desire nature is the feeling of pleasure that comes with an experience. When you feel the Bliss of God and recognize its superior nature over sensory experience, you have a desire more and more for God alone. For most sadhakas, desire is mixed. Part of you aspires for the higher nature of Bliss. Part of you is pulled to fulfill the desire nature of the senses. Through spiritual practice, you feel the Bliss of God more and more, and this becomes the predominant motivation for you. But bodily desires do not die overnight! The struggle over the psyche of the mind is terrific. All the great masters assure—persevere and you will reach your goal.

When physical sensations stemming from the sexual plexus get stimulated, either from exterior senses or interior images, the drawing power toward fulfilling sexual desire becomes very strong. Combining the power of imaging with the power of feeling, you can transmute this energy and then feel the wonderful results. Repeated practice of this begins to convince the mind of the wonderful qualities of Spiritual Nature.

Imagine, at the base of the spine, a series of nerves that lead to the sexual organs. In your mind's eye, trace those nerves back to the base of the spine. Imagine in the spine a switch that turns on or off the flow of life-force to the sexual nerves. Repression is when the switch is left on, stimulating the nerves with sensations, but the desire is not acted upon. Transmutation occurs when the switch is turned off and the energy is released to flow upwards into the spine and higher centers.

For example, you become aware that there are feelings of arousal in the sexual plexus. Mentally bring the focus of your attention to those nerves and trace them back to the spine. When sensitive, you can feel and "see" exactly where those nerves go and feel the energy being fed by the spinal powerhouse. When you locate the connection between the powerhouse in the spine and those nerves leading to the sexual plexus, you can imagine flipping a switch from the on-position to the off-position, or you can imagine a "Road Closed" sign (you can use any imaginative signal to the brain that your creative mind can come up with to indicate that the outward flow of energy is blocked). Now, just above that point in the spine, see a trapdoor that is closed, blocking the passageway further up the spine. Then, see that trapdoor suddenly spring open allowing the flow of energy streaming up the spine.

Now the subtle astral spine, the sushumna, is continuous from the base of the spine to the medulla oblongata. Realized yogis and spiritual masters know this through their own experience. You are taught to focus your attention on the heart center, the ajna, or the crown chakra. Bring that flowing energy to any one of these three points. See and feel that energy come upwards and express itself as love through the heart, merge into the Light at the ajna, or bring you into absolute union at the crown chakra.

In this way, you feel the superior joy of the soul expressing itself in these higher planes of consciousness. This positive joy and fulfillment create an association in the mind the soul would like to establish as a regular feature. Through positive attraction then, rather than by negatives alone, the transmuted sexual energy finds a new source of fulfillment. Complete union with God has been described as ten thousand orgasms happening at once! This powerful positive feature of transmutation opens new vistas, new frontiers.

And from the heart center and the ajna, creativity can flow in whatever way the Divine wishes to flow in you. Whether through words, art, voice, craft, healing, or silently loving the world, Divine life flows spontaneously through you to all. Without fetter or restriction, it uses your talents and abilities and raises them to their highest form. And the fulfillment comes not just with the outer expression of some art or science, but an inward joy is experienced through the action itself. Every moment lived in this way is a fulfillment to itself.

And when your life is filled with such moments, a spontaneous flow of Divine life, then you fulfill the real reason for which you were born. You no longer earn your living by the sweat of your brow—although your brow may sweat, you imbibe God's goodness, and by expressing it to all, He looks after your every need. You find yourself walking in the Garden of Eden, at one with your God, at peace with yourself, and in the knowledge of the oneness of spirit in all things, created and uncreated.

This, then, is the fulfilled life of a brahmacharya. No loss, do you feel. No separation or barriers, but oneness of Soul and Spirit are yours. This can be yours through the practice of brahmacharya.

The Body

There are means of doing exercises with the body that can also help in this transmutation. The Clearing Breath can be focused on the sexual plexus and base of the spine with good results.[12] Also, the Mahamudra in Kriya Yoga is designed to help transmute this energy. The Shoulder Stand and Candle Stand and exercises of Hatha yoga are good for reversing the usual downward flow of sexual energy. If one has the flexibility, one can sit in the Hero Pose,[13] then shift the weight to one side, placing the anal passage on top of the heel. Feel the energy moving up the spine.

Diet can also be important. In yogic thought, a spicy diet is not good for brahmacharyas—perhaps that is why the spicy Indians have a large population! Onions, peppers, and other spicy foods are to be avoided. You may notice other cause-and-effect foods: for example, too many creamy foods increase desire nature. Experiment with yourself, noting any cause-and-effect links between the foods you eat and your body consciousness.

I think it does not need to be said, but I will say it anyway: provocative pictures, performances, movies, and fantasies all go against mental purity. Even if it doesn't have any noticeable immediate effect, it goes into the subconscious mind and comes back later. If unavoidably caught in such circumstances, you can just look away

---

12   See Appendix for full description.

13   Another version is to sit in Hero Pose, bring one knee against your chest, then shift your weight and bring the heel in place.

and chant. Besides, by having God on your mind, you will probably have a better time of it than the attentive audience!

High Frequency Energy

All these practices and the transmutation of this energy can cause a high frequency of energy to flow up the spine. If it is not channeled properly, it can cause disturbances and imbalances. As mentioned earlier, the heart, ajna, and crown chakras are the best to focus on. Be responsible with this energy. If it is used for the wrong purposes, you will pay for it with karmic consequences. The safest way is to stay focused on God. Make that your goal and mantra. Create goodness and upliftment for yourself and others. If this transmuted energy is used to strengthen a rebellious will, if used to create ugliness and mischief, if used to promote ego-driven spiritual powers, then woe unto you. You will be the creator of your own self-made hell, as you will have to face the effects of everyone your thoughts and actions have reached. Let this only be for good and for God. If nervousness or increased mood swings occur, then seek to purify yourself by chanting God's name and finding positive creative outlets. If problems such as these are occurring, of course, you may contact anyone with an appropriate background to help in these cases. These words are not said to frighten, just guidelines for the "what ifs." I pray that God's blessings be upon you, that He lift you up and bring you to the realization of who and what you truly are through deepened prayer and meditation upon God alone. May it be so!

Spiritual Powers

From the beginning of time, humankind has sought to gain advantage for the promotion of its survival, comfort, some plan or ideal, or the domination of others. Through physical power, mental power, or spiritual power, this has been the way. Generally, one thinks of spiritual qualities such as universal love and service, experiencing joy, bliss, and surrender to the Higher Will as the qualities of a saint. But few of us can read the stories of great saints or spiritual masters and the apparent miracles that occur in their lives and remain unaffected. To be honest, it has to be said that this is an appealing feature in any anecdote of a spiritual master.

There may be one thing said in regard to spiritual powers. The difference between fully realized masters and those of some realization who use powers from an ego standpoint, is the fully realized master is indifferent to having such powers and only uses them by Divine command. No taint of pride, personal agenda, or attachment goes with any display of a mystical power.

It is proclaimed by all the great scriptures and masters that powers are to be eschewed. The temptation to delve into the world of powers is very seductive. High-minded souls can be drawn into thinking they can be of help to others through the use of extraordinary powers. The reality of such thinking soon shows itself; the powers are not serving us, but we are serving those powers. Emperor ego delights in having more than the fellow next door. And who are we to know what serving a good is? If we heal someone who is working out past karma through that affliction, do we not risk only postponing the inevitable, creating future difficulty for that person, perhaps with interest?

Only through God-given intuition may we know for certain that a certain act is the right thing to do. That is why Swami Ramdas said: "You can do no good until you are God-realized." This is an astounding statement, but true, at least in terms of us doing a predictable good. Because no one has sufficient information to be able to determine what will lead to a good. Does this mean we cease to act? No, of course not. But in our prayers, we should ask God to lead our reason, will, and activities according to His will, and then do our best to attune ourselves to that will. We do this until that time comes when we have dissolved the little self of the ego into the vast universal Self of God, and then even the ideas of "I" and "Thou" are no longer present, and going against God's will is not even a possibility.

If we take the attitude of the child when it comes to spiritual powers, then we are all right. "O Father, Mother, God, you do all through me. I know nothing of these powers; if it happens, it will happen automatically through me without my doing." Thus, will think the Bhakti, the devotionally minded aspirant. The Jnana yogi, guided by discerning intellect, will think, "O Infinite Spiritual Consciousness, all activities in this world are an illusion. Why would I trade one illusion of being helpless for another illusion of being powerful? I abjure them all!"

The Karma yogi will think, "O God, I serve all as your form. In fact, it is You, You, in this form who serves all as You, who exist in other forms. Therefore, I know of myself, I do nothing. It is You who doeth the works." And the Raja yogi proclaims, "O Infinite Self, powers come naturally to the yogi. It is an anathema to real spiritual progress. You may use this body as an instrument of Your will. I am neither attracted nor repulsed by the powers. What are they in comparison to You, the magnificent Existence both in this world and beyond?"

In this way, all four personality types of real sadhakas will strictly avoid egotistic use of powers. It may be said, there are two broad paths when it comes to the mystical. One is spiritualism: that is, contacting dead spirits and the development of occult powers. The other is spirituality, which is the cultivation of a surrendered ego for the purpose of realizing the ultimate Being, God. The two paths are polar opposites in where they lead the sadhaka. Many get involved in a spiritual path due to enticing stories about the development of occult powers. Through this interest, they come to a path whose focus is on Self-realization. So, they may have a mixture of attraction for spiritualism and a draw to spirituality. The beginner may fail to distinguish between the two! Of course, needless to say, the ego would like both! But since they lead to opposite goals, this is not possible. Cultivation of powers leads to the aggrandizement of ego. Spirituality, on the other hand, leads to the end of ego-consciousness and involution toward Divine Consciousness.

A decision must be made by the sadhaka. The more we rise in spirituality, the bigger and more tempting become the powers.

There are very highly realized yogis who become derailed by the seduction of powers. So do not be deceived by progress on the path or a feeling of oneness with the Infinite, thereby above temptation. Become neutral to powers, neither attracted nor repulsed, for repulsion may be hiding a latent desire for powers. Rather, let's see ourselves as the indifferent instrument, and if it is His will, He will effect the change through us, with or without our knowledge. With this kind of surrender, we will be blessed with perfect peace and secure knowledge that it is indeed our Heavenly Father who doeth the works.

Dragons at the Door

A sadhaka has God-experience for some time, then gradually, or suddenly, falls from that high experience of peace or bliss and is immersed in worldly affairs. Like someone who has taken ill and cannot remember what it is to feel well, so the devotee becomes enmeshed in the world and either completely forgets God, or feels as though it were a dream. How does this occur, and why?

We have all come from God, the bliss, peace, and all-pervading Consciousness that is our natural state. The reason we become dissatisfied with the world is due to this deep subconscious memory of our oneness with God. I have talked to so very many people who have come from families that were like descriptions of hell. Yet, they held onto an idea that it should be different, and that idea (ideal) is so strongly embedded in them that they come to a spiritual teacher or a therapist with the idea of having something they know must be theirs, yet they have not had that experience. This ideal is common to so many, and yet most people do not even question why those with such a difficult background should think their life should be any different.

If we are a product of our environment only, then one would think we would be more accepting of the reality we have grown up with and not question it. Even if we were exposed to other families that seemed to be closer to that ideal, we might wish we had that, but we would not necessarily think, "That should be me." The reason for this ideal, this drive for something better, is because that ideal is fundamental to our makeup. At our core, the essence of who we are is resonant with that ideal, and we want our outer life to reflect that essence. It is the aberrant person, rather than the norm, who would not have a vision of something greater for themselves and their family: a life filled with light, peace, and wisdom. Even if we are not actively involved in creating this kind of life, and in fact living a miserable life and making others miserable to boot, yet this desire for light, peace, and harmony is pervasive.

But there are those who have a faith, an undying faith, despite all outer signals to the contrary (they may be called an idealist or an optimist), but they have not given up on this resonant thought, the essence of what we call Spiritual, or God. In faith, they start on a journey to find that ideal, to experience and live in Light and Harmony. Others whose faith has been shattered may jeer at those optimists, but the ones who have an undying drive go beyond what the world thinks of them. And because of that, they embark on a journey that takes them beyond the realm of the material. Their sincere desire brings them to a path that focuses their attention within. By going within they face their entire past. Those dark forces of the past are the dragons that stand guard at the door to the Eternal. Anyone who does not have the courage to face those dragons will not gain entry; every fear, every outward desire nature must be faced and overcome. This is not a journey for the weak of heart. One must have faith and courage, and a willingness to go on in the face of stiff opposition. Faith is perhaps the greatest weapon such pilgrims/warriors have at their disposal. This allows them to face these dragons (breathing their fire, casting their spells), using their faith as a shield and discrimination as a sword.

Layer after layer, they descend into the mountain deep. If sadhakas persevere, at last, they come to the lair of the dragon with the gold and gems of spiritual realization for which they have been seeking. But with each new discovery, enjoyed for a while, comes a new opponent.

Of course, in all of the opponents we are facing, it is really our very own self. On this journey of self-discovery, we must work to seek out those treasures of Spirit. Those treasures are ours already, but because we have, in memory dimmed past, placed obstructions along the way, we must face and overcome each obstacle. Through our past actions, we have set mind traps of negativity, greed, lust, jealousy, and hosts of other limiting and false beliefs. A narrow human view made us think at the time of their creation that there was no consequence to our actions or possibly no alternative to the way we lived our life. But once done, these thoughts, words, and actions of the past do not just disappear into the ether. They carry a life-energy with them, and they reside inside of us. They become a part of the sum total of our consciousness. Not until we rid ourselves of the idea of "I am the body" will these inner dragons be slain. When we realize, "I am Spirit, I am He," then all dragons will become nothing more than paper dragons. With a puff, these paper dragons may be whooshed away, carrying no more power than a fleeting thought.

Having discovered the spiritual treasure within, we make our ascent up the center of the mountain; there we will be lifted into the high realms of the Universal Vision. During this upward ascent, we are suddenly, at the speed of thought, dashed down to the ground; this is nothing more than the uncovering of other dragons jealous of their domain. Again, we make the ascent up, then something along the way captures our fancy, and like a helium balloon suddenly weighed down with a leaden basket, the upward ascent is stymied and brought back to the earth. These traps, sometimes subtle, sometimes frightening, sometimes tempting, run the whole gamut of human experience. Again and again, we seek to make that ascent. Again and again, we are brought up short. Only the intrepid, only the determined, only those who persevere beyond all obstacles may gain the goal.

Once we recognize that this up and down journey is part of the game and not peculiar to just us, we take away one of the most powerful dragon weapons: low self-esteem. This low self-esteem causes us to think, "I am the worst devotee because I have these thoughts, these fears, these desires, and all I want to do is hide!" And so, we hide away, away from our spiritual practice, our spiritually kindred spirits; we hide away from the Light. Of course, we cannot really hide, but we do try. All we succeed in doing in this hiding is to create more dragons, dragons of shame, and dragons of bad habits. We have just loaded more weight to the load we were already carrying. No wonder the world seems so heavy on our shoulders at times when we are carrying the weight of all those dragons.

Letting go of feeling worthless and letting go of avoidance, we proceed with faith that we are God's very own. We hold in our hands the sword of discrimination that cuts away that which detracts us from our journey to God; **eyes ever fixed on our journey's end, we will make progress and we will arrive at that ideal that has ever lived in our heart.** We are God's very own and no darkness, no obstacle, no dragon on the path will ever change that! Let us affirm our unity, our wholeness, and our all and all to that Divine Nature, and no obstacle will bar our path. Know, without any doubt, that at this moment we are the purity and power of absolute Spirit. If we do this with complete faith and surety, we will rise to the top of that mountain. And in so rising, we will behold that the whole world is nothing but a manifestation of that singular Spirit. We have ever been, we are now, and we will ever be completely and totally one with the Divine Consciousness of God.

The Razor's Edge

An inner fire of renunciation must burn clean and strong for the fullest God-Experience to be born within us. This fire of renunciation, coupled with a complete focus on God, will effectively purify the mind of attachment and make us attuned to God alone. The realization of God, however, is not usually gained in one jump, but is a process of purification. Even those who rise high in spiritual consciousness contend with dual forces, one going to God and one toward desire nature. Sadhana, the pathway to God, is walked, as the saying goes, on a razor's edge.

India, more than any other country or region in the world, has made a science out of realizing God. With clear descriptions of the various levels of consciousness in the divine realms, they give a roadmap by which we may be able to judge our progress. Along with seeking higher consciousness, these sages are giving the constant admonition to continue in strength and purity to the very end. The very end is what is called Sahaja Samadhi, a rare state of attainment where all opposing forces are once and for all absorbed into a unified state of realization. From this lofty height, the soul is free from a fall as it has attained a unity with the all-powerful and ever-pure Consciousness of God. This high goal is held out as the true purpose for taking birth and should be the supreme goal for all humanity.

When the soul is ready to make that final journey to God, a Sat-Guru comes into his or her life. This ancient and highly cherished tradition of the guru-disciple relationship is practiced all over the world, varying only in what it is called. Jesus acknowledged his past-life discipleship to John the Baptist when he said it fulfilled all righteousness that he should receive baptism from John. (Matthew 3:15) Krishna took instruction from his Guru, Sandipani. The guru is an instrument of the Divine to awaken the inherent Divinity within the receptive sadhaka. Even in the case of great Avatars, already perfected ones, the honoring of the guru tradition is evident.

At the point of entering upon this steep ascent of following the Sat-Guru, we are asked to sacrifice everything at the feet of God. Inner renunciation is essential to climbing these spiritual heights. This renunciation of the outer stimulation that once so attracted the mind allows for an inner magnetic draw of bhakti, or love and desire for God-experience, to take the sadhaka over. With growing desire for higher spiritual states, we feel ourselves to be in contact with realms divine. The oppositional forces, far from retreating from this field of battle, come on with greater intensity—fighting for life.

The path of realization is a series of ups and downs. Perhaps after a beautiful meditation, we float out of the door with feet barely touching the ground and the air has never smelled so pure, the flowers never looked so beautiful. Suddenly, a car angrily honks its horn, music blasts its raucous vibration from a neighbor's house, the crowd thickens and people are pushing to make their way through; the din of activity is crushing to the sensitized nerves! From that pure state of joy comes feelings of hurt, anger, and thoughts of revenge. Oh, how fragile that state, how easily we are drawn back into the world and even into negative states of thought and feeling!

Through dedicated practice, we gradually experience the higher states of bliss and expansion of consciousness, making us feel a part of everything that is. A broad universal love and empathy make us feel we are not just one body, but the bodies of all. Even while moving in the body, we feel in deep communion with this high state of consciousness. We have achieved some mastery of ourselves and are living more and more in Divine communion. At this point, we may feel we have made it—transcended the realm of duality and are living in the supreme state. This experience may last for hours, days, or extended periods of time. Then some desire nature beckons; something lying in the subconscious mind gets triggered. Continuing in the glow of this higher consciousness, devotees may come to see themselves above the laws of cause and effect, thinking that what they desire is what God desires through them.

This is a dangerous time for sadhakas. It is the time Jesus was referring to when false Christs will rise up and proclaim their pre-eminence. The sadhaka-master thinks, "Here is a desire, is it not the desire of God?" It is a great test to the sadhaka; back and forth goes the mind in trying to judge the rightness of the situation. The mind tries to reason, but reason sees both sides of the coin; perhaps there is reason to think that following this desire will do good for another or others. The desire is strong, and one feels strong in God; should the sadhaka follow the path of desire? This is the razor's edge.

The scriptures of the world and the lives of all saints are filled with the stories of temptation, of rises and falls. Even in the stories of such luminaries as Jesus and Buddha, times of temptation are narrated. Jesus fasted in the wilderness for forty days, then came a time of temptation. In the case of Jesus, the temptations concerned the power of performing miracles and having world dominion. Two very seductive temptations for the upward-bound master. The final temptation came for Jesus at the garden of Gethsemane when the annihilation of the ego, body consciousness, was at hand. Would it be human will or Divine Will? Jesus surrendered to Divine Will and the world has been the recipient of vast blessings as a result.

The Buddha too went through his night of testing. Mara came in the guise of young women to test the Buddha. Mighty soldiers came to threaten his body with war and destruction. He passed these tests, reposing in his Self, his true nature. As a result, he achieved Buddhahood, even as Jesus achieved Christhood. We know of their victories. Did they also have times of falling short of the mark, not overcoming the temptations? We are accustomed to stories of spiritual masters always making the right decisions. Of course, in the Old Testament, we have examples of those who made the wrong decisions and paid a price as a result. There are parallels in all scriptures where good, even great men and women of God, made the wrong choices.

What is tremendous about Jesus and Buddha is that in their over-coming, they attained the pinnacle of realization. With that Divine transformation, they achieved a wonderful Status—they went over the top, no longer subject to falls or making the wrong decisions.

But what of those masters, great in their own right, but who have not yet achieved Buddhahood or Christhood? What shall be said of them, and being tempted, do not make the right choice? Desires that lead to a fall can be in any field of human endeavor; they can be in the realms of gaining influential power, sex, money, psychic powers, gaining name or fame, even in the name of doing good. Whatever is most seductive, most alluring to sadhakas, will come with great power and seek to turn them away from advancing further in realization.

When this desire nature comes to sadhakas, reason, feeling, and all faculties may fail to help. It must be understood this can happen to souls in very high states of development. Having gained a great deal of self-mastery, they have moved into high states of consciousness. Others may look upon them as world teachers, spiritual masters, and they would be right to say so. But they have not gone over the top; they have yet to go to the supreme heights of Sahaja Samadhi, and they are yet in danger of a fall.

The fact that one who is recognized as a great master is subject to a fall can be disillusioning to sadhakas who have looked up to that one. They may feel betrayed, hurt, angry, lost, and forlorn. We have examples of some of the most famous spiritual teachers of our time, both East and West, subjects of scandal: sex, money, and power (both worldly and psychic) being the chief objects of temptation. Sadly, this has been one of the signs of our times. One cannot observe this without compassion for the innocent, those with faith in such teachers feeling crushed by such revelations.

And what of the master, what shall we say of him or her? Newspapers and gossips love some juicy news. They are willing to destroy anyone at the price of something to report, sometimes forgetting to note whether it is actually true or not! A reputation is thus destroyed, but rarely restored. The voracious appetite for scandal is really quite amazing. Others can then say, "See, none stand higher than any other," and in this way, they can support their own complacency. So, balance and fairness are not to be expected from such sources. We must have the means to make an evaluation, for we all make judgments of others, and when it comes to following someone's teachings, we should evaluate the one we follow.

Following the razor's edge is no small task. At times following that edge leads to a fall. Not every fall can be said to be equal. The complexities of the human mind and karmic patterns are wonderfully varied. Temptations and falls will represent a pattern of the subconscious mind. Temptation can be a lifelong preoccupation, or it can be some sudden eruption from the depths of consciousness. It is this polarized struggle through which each soul must pass. We have some brilliant examples of spiritual masters who shot to the top, but even they talk of spending years in becoming stabilized and balanced in that highest state. This is the great battle that all must wage, the crucifixion through which all must pass.

The outcome of such struggles, and falls, is not dictated so much by the power of the temptation, but by how the master deals with such temptations. A master may face a temptation and through the power of grace and self-mastery, not act on it, rising above it. This scene may be enacted again and again, but the master remains victorious. These virtuous ones are deserving of our highest praise. Others, attaining a level of mastery, may give in to temptation and become ensnared in its tangle for a little time, or a long time. The struggle is terrific. If the master emerges from the other side, he or she will have conquered the opposing force, and will become more stable in the refined God-Consciousness. These souls too, although temporarily tainted by their actions, end up victorious, gaining their complete emancipation.

Others do not come out of the struggle, but stay in it, not rising above, but not totally giving in to it either. Back and forth it goes with no absolute resolution. If they die with this struggle, they attain to the good reward they have earned, then return to another body to continue the struggle to gain total self-mastery. The other class of souls who struggle with darkness are those masters that do not rise above the struggle and turn from the light and lead the life of a lie instead. They no longer struggle, other than experiencing an occasional guilty conscience. The desire nature becomes institutionalized into their life. These individuals have given up any right to be called a master and are leading lives of darkness, not light.

It may come as a surprise to some that I would give the name master to one who has not attained total mastery. But the truth is, one can be in the realm of mastery and yet have more to pass through. Teachers may be a guru, a master, when they have become stable in the fifth chakra. This allows them the discernment for helping others to attain that exalted state. In fact, most of the world's teachers had yet to attain total mastery at the time they started their ministry to the world. "When such masters are in positions of authority, positions of teaching, should they not be perfect?" For many such masters, it is the fulfillment of their karma that they need to help others to their realization in order to become fully realized themselves. Hand in hand, the master and sadhaka walk the path to the Infinite.

There is a danger in the sadhaka misconstruing the truth of this teaching, thinking, "Falls happen, if I give into a temptation, it is no big deal." This would be a total misreading of the facts. One who turns away from the light pays the price; the law of karma is exact and immutable. Oftentimes masters, in their teachings, hold out only the highest, only the most perfect of realizations and do not mention recovery from falls when they are at high states of consciousness. The reasoning is, "Whatever is placed into the mind is what is then created. If only the most perfect attainment is taught, then the sadhaka will strive for and attain to that most perfect union." This is a great and noble teaching. However, there is a danger that the sadhaka, not being taught the nature of falls, will gain a false conception of the path. If sadhakas struggle with desire nature, even after attaining higher states of mastery, perhaps even having a fall, they may feel they are unworthy of spiritual realization; hence, the high teaching could actually retard the progress of sadhakas.

Sadhakas must hold the highest ideal and be realistic about the nature of the path at the same time. Like climbing a mountain, they constantly keep their mind on the peak, but remain also mindful of the ups and downs of the path through the foothills and the rocks on the path during the final steep ascent. Too much thought of the peak without paying attention to the path will lead to stumbles; too much attention to immediate surroundings and forgetting the goal of the peak will make sadhakas lose their way. **God is both the goal and the means to the goal.** So constant fixity of the mind on God, overcoming temptation, and seeing God as the absolute goal will keep sadhakas on the path in the best way.

We have the example of one guru who came here to the West and gained quite a following. He made it his specialty to collect very expensive cars. One of his ideals he put forward, in contrast to all the great teachings, was that if you have a desire, you should go out and fulfill it. I suppose one of his desires was for Rolls Royces and he was busy trying to get his fill of as many as he could. This abuse of his position, of course, was just the tip of the iceberg. He ended up going to further extremes to the point where his group was accused of attempting to poison the water supply of a nearby town, guards were carrying automatic weapons, and many other examples of adharma—unrighteousness. Some example of a spiritual consciousness!

It also must be clear that there are many misconceptions about mastery and the nature of being established in the fifth, sixth, or seventh chakras. Some teachers substitute being well versed in philosophy for being realized; others have some movement of kundalini, or some sensation in a chakra and say, "I have awakened that chakra," assuming they are then qualified to teach. Still others have some revelations, experiences in higher consciousness, or they gain some powers and think they are now established in the highest Consciousness. These are the many "false peaks" on the way to the pinnacle of realization. The true way of knowing we are growing in realization is the continuous state of joy and purity of consciousness we enjoy. Confirmation from a living guru, saints, and realized souls has the greatest value in these higher stages. The sure path to God is to keep our attention ever fixed upon Him and be in humble submission to His will. Only when communion with God is ongoing and perfectly established may we say we have attained the goal.

Another example of a fall from grace was some years ago when a young man from India came to America with an ability to reveal an inner light in the third eye to initiates. He attracted large crowds and grew in name and fame. Some scandal about him came into the news and his family started to quarrel about money and control; the whole thing fell apart. The seductiveness of power, name, and fame is quite intoxicating. Only through total renunciation and inner surrender to God and Guru may one safely pass through the maze of traps that lie in wait. Even with the best of intentions, teachers can fall miserably, hurting both themselves as well as many others.

So many aspirants have a sincere desire for spiritual awakening. There are many such instances where sincere devotees were willing to put their trust and faith in one, only to be let down. It is a crime perpetrated against their souls and is of the most serious nature for both teacher and student. Many teachers are quick to claim they are beyond the law of cause and effect and thus excuse their behavior. The fact is that in most cases, even when a genuine master has risen above the law of karma, they continue to practice right behavior as an example to those coming up the ladder. They know how easy it is to slip off the narrow way and they want to be the example of one who leads an exemplary life.

Until the time we are fully established in that highest state of Sahaja Samadhi, we are subject to falls. We may be best guided by the wisdom of saints and scriptures: the basic dos and don'ts. If we should have a fall, then our immediate response is to pick ourselves up, brush off the dirt and blood, make reparations where possible, and get going back on our path to God. If we fall again, we get up again; we never give up, we never give in!

We must strive with all our strength, heart, mind, and soul to "be perfect, even as our Father in heaven is perfect." (Matthew 5:48) If we have some question about an inner prompting, as to whether it is from God or from lower desire nature, then we should submit it to our living Guru or a living God-man or God-woman. If these are not available, then we guide our lives by the scriptures, or by going within and seeking out the truth. If we are sincere and miss the mark, our sincerity will guide us back to God and the truth will be revealed to us.

Spiritual masters are here to lead us and help us get to the goal. If they are sincere and fall on the way up, then we should give them our compassion and our prayers for strength and clarity, letting it be a reminder of the need for absolute purity on the path. From the *Autobiography of a Yogi*, we read about the touching humility of the Guru toward the chela when Sri Yukteswar asks Yogananda, "If you ever find me falling from a state of God-realization, please promise to put my head on your lap and help bring me back to the Cosmic Beloved we both worship."[14] When is a soul more in need of the strength and compassion of another soul than when they have fallen? Even highly realized masters can make errors; that is the time that all need to come together in strength, love, and prayer.

If we come to see that the master is not who or what he or she should be and has crossed over the line of deserving our respect or discipleship, then we take it again as a living example of what not to do and continue to strive for that inner perfection of God. Lest we be too quick to judge masters, let us look at the fruit of their lives. Do they lead others to God, or to themselves? Do they take full accountability for their actions and make sincere efforts to recover

---

14   *Autobiography of a Yogi* (pp. 94–95).

from a fall, or are they only stumbling from one fall to another? Are they humble, submissive to God and Guru, or are they arrogant and full of superiority? If the answer is consistently in the right direction, toward God, then they are leading us to the goal, even if with some faltering. If they are not, then better to shake their dust off our feet and continue on our way.

This life of the razor's edge is the most demanding we will encounter. Let us ever keep the highest goal in mind, while recognizing that human nature will be at play as the opposing force. Let us ever keep our purity of purpose, the fire of true renunciation, and real aspiration for God ever as our guide. The more perfectly we keep our mind on God, the surer and more direct will be our way to the goal. Let us ever strive with all our heart, mind, and strength, and ever pray for that all-powerful grace to lift us and keep us in that most perfect union with God.

Victory to God, Victory to Gurus, Victory to sadhakas everywhere!

A Songbird's Verse

My life is a dedication to God. In fumbling steps and in the precision of movement, I steer my life toward that precious Goal. My great Guru set the course, direction, and Goal; she beckons me still from Her deeper life.

God awakened me to that purpose when my own will would have taken me to self-destruction, or at best to a mundane, senseless life. I pretend no greatness, nor even goodness, for there is none other good than my Heavenly Father. Truly, I can say whole-heartedly that it is by God and Guru's grace that I have found my Self.

I suppose it is natural to want all the world to share in that sacred mystery that I feel, and it would be sheer arrogance to assume no others do. But there is the songbird within that bursts into Divine verse and aches to share that deepest Intimacy, yet finds that longing all the more painful as its song disappears into the void. The pain is nothing but God's constant yearning for His children to forsake their gloom-drenched dream of creation long enough to join once again in Divine Union.

Songs of angels are not just beautiful voices, but the thrill of vibration that resounds throughout all space and is caught, and finds resonance in, the receptive soul. Like strings and reeds of various instruments, the soul feels the thrill of that glorious vibration. Thrill after thrill moves the soul, then settles into a quiet pool of peace.

A whispered breeze of joy gently plays on the surface of that quiet water; then a giant whale of inspiration rises above the surface, coming from great depths, revealing a portion of its massive body; then it sinks down below the surface once again. All nature, all existence is seen to thrill in ecstasy as a single life in various motions.

The heart heaves under the burden of the fruit it bears; the little mind is stilled, and the great Mind encompasses all as its own. No boundaries are there, circumference melts into Infinitude; peaceful, gentle, powerful, intimate, and expansive states of Being exist simultaneously in total harmony.

The Divine Song moves in the ether in constant waves, but ears and eyes are dulled to its tune by muddy coverings of earthly preoccupations, those reeds and strings of the soul dampened by material desire. O children of the Infinite, awaken to your vast mansion within! Let your souls sing in mystic vibration the thrilling tones of your Soul's Song. To die to the vain preoccupation of separateness is to resurrect into your vast, dimensionless Self:

No birth, no death, nor body am I,
I AM HE! I AM HE!
Blessed Spirit, I AM HE!
I AM HE! I AM HE!
Blessed Spirit I AM HE![15]

---

15   Adaptation of verse by Adi Shankaracharya.

Let this be our anthem, our affirmation, and our realization. Die in our surrender to the Infinite Creator, our Heavenly Father, and resurrect in our perfect oneness with God alone.

What is in a Word?

What is in a word? Swami Sri Yukteswar wrote in *The Holy Science*, "The Almighty Force *Shakti*, or in other words, the Eternal Joy *Ananda*, which produces the world, and the Omniscient Feeling, *Chit*, which makes this world conscious, demonstrates the Nature *Prakriti* of God the Father."[16] In some later editions published in America, an enterprising editor decided that Sri Yukteswar did not know exactly what he meant in his own writing and interpolated the word "produced" for "produces." The variance of words represents two very different perspectives and demonstrates the beauty and sanctity of a Perfect Master's words.

In saying that God produces the world, Sri Yukteswar reveals a dynamic creation, not a static conception. In a dynamic sense, the world is constantly being created. Moment to moment, the Creator projects forth the idea of creation, keeping it aloft with His preservative power. One may ask, "Where does this creation come from?" The answer coming from realized saints is that creation is a manifestation of the absolute, unmanifest Spirit, sometimes referred to as the Void.

In order to grasp more clearly the relationship between the unmanifest Spirit and creation, we need only look to our own creative process. When we sit down to create, whether it be a writing, a drawing, whatever the creation, where does that creative idea come from? We can say, "It just came to me," or "I got the idea from seeing what someone else did." But when we are truly creative, original, where did that originality come from? Again, we may say,

---

16   *The Holy Science*. (1949). Jnanavatar Swami Sri Yukteswar Giri, Chapter 1, Sutra 2. Yogoda Sat-Sang Society of India, 3rd Edition.

"The idea just came to me," but where was that idea before that? Did it exist before it "just came" to you?

Yogic science tells us it did exist before; something does not come from nothing. This unmanifest Void is not an empty nothingness. Rather, it is all that is in potentiality. What is manifest today as this earth, the trees, animals, and people, may be said to be just a fraction of all that is in potential. An author can illustrate a simple example of this. An accomplished author may have penned many volumes of books. When an author is writing something new or looking over something written before can we say all those volumes written are from him or her? Can we say they are in the author, and even more volumes exist yet to be written? But in that moment of time, all the author's attention is reduced to a single sentence or even a single word. In that moment of time, all that potential of what has been written and what is yet to be written is in the invisible void of the author.

In the same way, God produces His creation. Focused on a moment of time, on one particular aspect, He creates in this moment out of the infinite potential of what He is. And that creation is us, as we read these words. The thing that is amazing to the human mind is that God is simultaneously aware of creating the billions of people who inhabit this earth along with all the animals, vegetables, minerals, and every aspect of all creation, and He is equally aware of all that lies in His unmanifest potential as well. As God writes His play of creation, of which we are a part, He does not create something and then leave it behind, such as the author may leave written works behind in leather-covered volumes. There is no "leaving works behind" for God; there is only what is.

God is actively manifesting all that is at all times; if He was not, it would dissolve back into the unmanifest void the instant He did not actively sustain it. This act of preservation is the second principle of creation. In Yogic thought, there are three such principles. The first principle of manifested creation is the creative principle that brings all that is into being. The second is the preservative principle, and the third and last is the destruction principle that withdraws all creation back into the unmanifest void from which it came. These three principles are constantly at work in all creation, and they are constantly at work in us as well.

It is from our human perspective that we can look about ourselves and see stability in the world. Day after day we awaken to a world that appears very much the same. If we have lived in the same house for a long time, we can see the preservative principle at work. Those valuable treasures we piled in the garage are still there after years of trying to forget that we ever put them there in the first place. The preservation principle makes it appear to the human mind that God must have created this world, put things into place, and then left them there. This concept is pure delusion. The preservative principle freezes the creative projection as a trick of the mind in sequential moments of time. It is like looking at the creation and destruction of the world in a slow-motion movie scene. The projection of the creative principle is constant, or it would not be appearing to us. Destruction is the withdrawal of that projected creation back into the void, and it is also constant. Preservation is the appearance of that creative projection maintaining stability as a static state. It is a fact that God "produces the world" constantly and it is, therefore, a misperception that He "produced the world" in the past tense as a fait accompli.

What does that mean to us in a practical sense other than making a fine philosophical point? In order to see this creative principle in its true state, we must awaken ourselves from the preservative complacency of mind. Because of the preservative principle at work, things become familiar, and we come to believe a thing is known to us because it is familiar. This familiarity is necessary so that we are not in a constant state of disoriented confusion. This same familiarity tends to breed contempt. Because something is known, is familiar, we grow complacent with it; we take it for granted. We cease to see the marvel of its newness and we cease to be in awe of its destruction. A mind-numbing sameness can chloroform the mind into sleepwalking in this life: "Oh, it's just another day, going to work, driving home, just the same old thing." This lack of active awareness at the newness of life, its vitality constantly at work as seen in the miraculous nature of a flower, a newborn life, blinding us to the withdrawing power of dissolution, makes us the walking dead. We cease to see God's hand working in every aspect of creation.

This creation is not something, as some suppose, that God produced and then left in the hands of the devil. And it is not, as many materialists suppose, a creation that came from inert exploding gases, a happenstance expression of nature, devoid of meaning. This life, our life, is a marvelous expression of Divinity, full of meaning, ever new and alive beyond the comprehension of the human mind alone. To awaken to the fact that God produces the world moment to moment is to be alive to the idea that God creates us moment to moment. We are an active manifestation of God, an expression of God—God living His life through us! This is not the "same old thing" of life. To awaken to this dynamic nature of God is to awaken to that creative principle within our Self.

So many people become insensate to this aliveness. To realize that each moment is an active expression of Divinity puts us in touch with the vitality of our own Divinity. Worry, preoccupation with the world, fears, and desire nature, all have the habit of putting us to sleep in this active creative principle. There are times when we will awaken to the idea that we are missing this aliveness in our lives. It is at those times when we wish to leave everything we've created and start out new. The sad fact is that unless there is a deep change in our mental nature, we'll sustain the newness of life but for a short amount of time, then recreate the old sameness with clock-like regularity. Radical changes do not often match the hoped-for outcomes.

Aliveness, divinity, is a part of everything that is, and is embedded in our life right now. To awaken to it is to awaken to the fact that God is creating in us right now. To connect to the power and intelligence of that potential requires our simple acknowledgment of the fact that God is producing us now. By actively looking for that connection in life now and making the moments of our day count, we will know that God is living in our heart. We no longer count ourselves among the walking dead—we woke up, became alive to the great Divinity manifesting within us and all around. We do not sleepwalk through our life only to awaken at the death of the body and think, "Why did I not awaken during my life? Why did I sleepwalk through it as if it had no greater meaning?"

God is moving in us now as the intelligence with which we are reading these words. He is creating in us this very moment. We are He in human form. Arise, Awake! Know this fact beyond any mind-numbing, outward, worldly fact that has been accepted as reality. In awakening, we will know that Life, that Intelligence and that Joy, which produces all creation through all time. May that blessing be true for us now, with every turn of the page, in every sentence, and saturating every word of creation that produces our life.

Unlimited Power

Obstacles come into our life but for one reason: to make us draw on and grow into the Infinite power within us and make it manifest. Whether the problem be one of the body, relationships, work, or any situation we are in the midst of, we must realize we are not of limited, but of *unlimited*, potential. Strength doesn't come by having power over others or access to a large bank account; true power is the manifestation of that inherent Spirit within us.

Tests come to us as a challenge to our faith. Those who lack faith repeat to themselves, "I have not the means," and so they don't. Times come in everyone's life when opposition rises up and enshrouds the soul as a dark cloud. At that time of darkness, the test of the soul reaches its greatest climax—a profound test of faith.

There have been many great souls who have faced that cloud of darkness and with faith in their own power to overcome, have gone on to do great things. There is even a higher class of souls who, when faced with that dark night, have submitted themselves to their Divine Source and manifested a higher order of Spiritual power. In our survey of history, it is plain to see that the most powerful men and women in society have relied on that Divine Source.

The reason for this noticeable difference of results, between reliance on humans alone and reliance on God, is due to the perceived source of power. When individuals perceive the source of strength as in themselves, it is by its very nature limited, no matter how grandiose their vision. When individuals acknowledge their source of power as Divine, then they know no limit to the resources upon which to depend. Divine power, being unlimited, makes the individual an agent of unlimited power.

The other limiting factor for human expression of power is the limit of human intentional will. When a person seeks the accomplishment of some task, some goal, it has a certain circumference of thought, limited by the vision and imagination of the individual. However, when individual will is surrendered to Divine Will, then the unlimited nature of the Divine Mind may be brought to bear with its unbounded vision. The third and most crucial factor is human acknowledgment of the Divine Source; this power provides unerring direction for the use of power. Human nature is self-centered and tends to cater to what is good for the individual apart from the whole.

Divine Consciousness is ever aware of the whole and Its interest is in the good of the whole. Therefore, Its guidance to the surrendered mind brings about conditions that are for the highest good of all.

The combination of unlimited power, will, vision, and unerring direction produces the greatest potential in human experience. Whether it be the life of Krishna, Buddha, Jesus Christ, or any of the many saints and realized Beings who have moved this world, and have the power to move it still, we observe that they stand as living testaments to the superior power of the Divine.

These examples lie in contrast to the many great rulers who led in their own names. These men and women, some of whose names are known to us today, do not have the power to move us today in the same way as the previously referenced illumined ones. Many of the great and good men and women of the past we may admire, but greater by far are those who surrendered to their Infinite source.

A greater contrast can be drawn between those fully surrendered to the Divine and those powerful leaders who worked contrary to the Divine Light. One such leader who showed great promise, but betrayed his higher calling, was Napoleon. Napoleon brought many enlightened ideas and programs to his country. Many admired his ideas and viewed him as ushering in a new, more enlightened, era. Then, upon his coronation as emperor, he took the crown from the Pope's hands and placed it upon his own head.

This act was not just a dispute between a church official and a self-made ruler. The statement made by this act went beyond the wrangling for worldly power; it acknowledged man the ruler, disconnected from Divine submission. Even though Napoleon was at the height of worldly power at the time of his coronation, with that act he sowed the seeds of his own limited rule. All truly great leaders have known the Divine as the source of their power and lived in a humble submission to this fact.

A leader from this same era who displayed that humble submission is George Washington. He knew his reliance on Divine Providence was essential to success and enforced this among his troops. After the war, when offered the crown of absolute power, he repeatedly refused it. Rather, he accepted leadership reluctantly and set the pattern for peaceful succession when he gracefully surrendered authority of his own will. He stands as a unique example in modern times, in humble service to the greater good of a nation and to God.

In ancient India, there are stories of Rajas as absolute rulers, surrendering their throne, wealth, and power and leaving their kingdoms behind in order to practice spiritual discipline and gain enlightenment under the guidance of a guru. These Rajas were not only kingly in worldly attainment but became Rajas in Spirit as well.

Each of us is a leader whether we have a position of authority or purely by the "authority" of our own example. Every life is an experiment in realizing unlimited Spiritual power. This experimentation takes place in the human and Divine fields of experience. The discovery that we have unlimited power in the Divine comes as a revelation to a disbelieving human mind. For most, the mind slowly grows in faith and humble submission to Divine guidance and power.

Few humans have had to face such hopelessness, despair, and tragedy as George Washington had to endure in eight long years of war. But when we, in our own dark night, face those moments of difficulty, we may firmly rely on Divine Providence as our source of strength to go through that darkness and overcome all obstacles. Affirming unlimited spiritual power, will, and vision, we may rise to new heights, realizing that in God we have power and wisdom beyond measure. Even as clouds covering the earth have no effect on the sun, so do dark nights of the soul have no effect on the inherent Light and power we have in God. With full faith, we know this truth of our being and claim it as our own!

At all times, and especially in times of difficulty, let us go into deep communion with Infinite Source; accept no limitation to that Divine power and see our "bank account" of Spiritual power as full. Then, in surrender to Divine Will, turn ourselves over to its power, direction, and workings. Let us renounce all thoughts of negativity and align ourselves with Light. Every experience takes us closer to God and His unlimited bounty. We are the reflected child of that unlimited Source, the All and All in All.

The World is a Reflection of Your Consciousness

The world you see and interpret is very much a mirrored reflection of your consciousness. A walk through the woods and hearing someone's description of what they see will tell much about their consciousness. A hunter will describe the game found in the woods, good places to hunt, places for the blinds, etc. A photographer will look at angles, lighting, and the framing of shots. A military man will see good places to ambush, areas to array troops. An engineer will observe the mechanics of nature, and an architect, the design. Each will see the woods through their own peculiar filter of understanding.

Sadhakas can tell a lot about themselves or another person by what they consider worth observing about life in general, how it is observed, and what conclusions are made. For sadhakas, a unique view of the world begins to emerge with their practice. Many of the familiar filters of the mind will remain intact. The architect continues to notice design, the engineer, function. However, a peculiar link is formed in the mind regarding the source and reason for the form and function of a certain thing. All form, all function, all activity is seen as having one source and one ultimate purpose stemming from the supreme creative Intelligence of God.

If you are in the market to buy a car, you will narrow your choices to a few models, perhaps one make and model only. Due to your focus on that make and model of a car, you begin to pick out that car wherever you go. Your interest drives what you observe. By focusing on the Divine, you will see it manifest everywhere. The sadhaka-businessman is not only seeing a product produced, marketed, and revenues generated, but sees the movement of God as the creativity, intelligence, and power that makes it all possible.

When you let go of the idea that you are the doer and are but a mere instrument of that Divine Source, then you see with amazement and childlike innocence all that occurs in the world. Without guile you can operate in the world: "Wise as serpents, harmless as doves." (Matthew 10:16) Far from rendering you useless to the world, spiritual life makes the best of whatever occupation chosen. Sensitive to the movement of God-Consciousness, you open yourselves to creativity, focused attention, enthusiasm, integrity, and loyalty that makes for excellence in your field. By fulfilling the purpose for which you are born, you work in the world not just for personal gain but also as a means of bringing your light of God to all.

This makes for good business and professional development. No artificial barrier should be placed between work life and spiritual life. As Mother used to say, "When you are in business with God you are in business with all of life," because there is but one source for all of life and that is God. Therefore, God is interesting—you know that because the world is interesting. God is complex, He has many nuances. God is fun and dramatic. The essential things of God are simple and close to the heart. In short, God is all of life.

God cannot be removed from the world; He cannot be relegated to dusty books or be confined to a Sunday service. Unless your spiritual life permeates every breath taken, every thought, every action, you have yet to fulfill your sadhana. Someone may say, "Aren't you being a little extreme here? It's all right to be religious but let's not go overboard!" But that is the voice of someone who has yet to realize that God is not remote and aloof from human affairs. When you realize that God moves, is responsible for, and controls every aspect of life, then you know there is no part of your life God does not affect.

Not only is God part of all life, but He is also bliss, and all life is permeated with that bliss. Spontaneous joy, peace, and freedom are to be had for one attuned to this great life. Spiritual Consciousness does not subtract from life, but only adds a wondrous dimension of happiness for which all yearn. Many only deny themselves access to this dimension of bliss, Light, and freedom by clinging onto the old notions of separation from God. It is time to gain that union with God and awaken to who and what you really are.

There are pictures that have faces and objects hidden in the drawing. In the rocks and trees, your mind gradually identifies a face, an animal, all sorts of images you realize have been hiding in the picture. Once your mind identifies the picture in a picture, you can no longer avoid seeing the hidden picture. Your spiritual life is like that. Once you see the hand of the Divine moving in all creation, proceeding from one image-experience in life to another, every scene of your life gradually becomes imbued with that sacred Divine Presence of the All in All.

With this, enjoyment of life multiplies by many, many times. No longer do you find life boring, empty, or mundane. The mundane becomes Divinity manifest in all of its beauty, power, and intelligence. Boredom could no more be a part of your life than stagnant water be a part of a waterfall. All of life becomes a movement of joyous expression. Even loss, tragedy, and grief are viewed in a new way.

With perfect knowledge that all happens for a purpose and is working for your ultimate higher good, lose fear and gain peace. Difficulties and hardships draw you closer to the Light within through deepened prayer and communion with God. Comfort, guidance, and sustenance for the soul are found in that communion; in deep faith know you are part of a Divine Plan of goodness, whatever the appearances of life's situations.

A charming and instructive story about Mataji tells us much about her wonderful personality. She worked from early morning straight through to late night, serving Papa and all sadhakas who came to the ashram. At night, Mataji would ask Papa to read the newspaper to her. Of course, newspapers then, as now, are filled with the world's woes and tragedies. Her head would be nodding to sleep as Papa read. Finally, Papa said, "Mataji, every night you have me read you the news. You are tired, why don't you go to sleep?" "Because," Mataji explained, "when I hear about these tragedies it is my only opportunity to pray for those people." Isn't that a wonderful attitude? It really changes the way you listen to the news if you employ that. It changes *you* as you hear the news. As you enter into deep prayer for those afflicted, it not only changes you and helps those being prayed for, but it also puts out a vibration that helps to positively change this world.

There are more and more studies confirming the power of prayer. One hospital study observed a control group of patients for whom no prayers were being offered; another group of patients was the object of a prayer group. The doctors and nurses were unaware that a study was being done, and thus had no idea who was being prayed for. Those doing the praying did not personally know any of the patients. The study showed that those who received the prayers spent less time in the hospital, had fewer medications administered, and recovered faster than the control group. The scientific community is at last gathering evidence for, and taking seriously, the power of prayer.

Behavioral psychologists like to say you are a product of your conditioning by the world. It is true, of course, that your experiences in the world color your perception and understanding. Realized masters call these samskaras, or conditioning from the past, including past lifetimes. Through stilling the mind, these spiritual masters have penetrated deeper into the psyche than has the influence of worldly conditioning. These sages intuitively perceived that the physical brain is an instrument of a transcendent spiritual consciousness. The brain is not the creator of consciousness, but is actually the result of the primary builder, God-Consciousness. This is a reversal of understanding of cause and effect from the physical scientist's point of view.

Your intelligence, and life itself, is the result of the Divine Source of your being. The material mind seeks life "out there," out in the world of the senses, but the spiritual mind seeks life and abundance within, within the being—not outside. The conscious mind is inhibited from an inward search by a glut of sensory experiences. When the eyes are closed in concentration, distractions continue to disturb the brain as an "echo" of worldly vibration. Only in stillness is the mind illumined with spiritual Light. This is why the material mind is seen as darkness, and in opposition to God, the intuitive Divine Mind.

By focusing the mind within and upon God, the brain becomes illumined with the Light of this Divine Consciousness. As your mind is illumined with Light, you see your inner world and this outer world filled with Light. "The light of the body is the eye: if therefore thine eye be single, thy whole body shall be full of light. But if thine eye be evil, thy whole body shall be full of darkness." (Matthew 6:22) A quick test will reveal the nature of your consciousness. When you close your eyes and go within, do you perceive the light of your own being, or are you engulfed with darkness? Look out on this world: Do you see the light of spirit shining in all?

In the *Gospel According to Thomas*,[17] purported to be the original sayings of Jesus found in some caves near Nag Hamadi, Upper Egypt, we read a very interesting description of the kingdom of heaven:

> Jesus said: "If those who lead you say to you: 'See, the Kingdom is in heaven,' then the birds of the heaven will precede you. If they say to you: 'It is in the sea,' then the fish will precede you. But the Kingdom is within you, and it is without you. If you know yourselves, then you will be known and you will know that you are the sons of the Living Father."
>
> His disciples said to Him: "When will the Kingdom come?" Jesus said: "It will not come by expectation; they will not say; 'See, here,' or 'See there.' But the Kingdom of the Father is spread upon the earth and men do not see it."

I once went to my Guru with a problem that was disturbing me at the time. I said, "Mother, I feel God greatly inside of me as a Presence, as peace and bliss. But I do not see Him in the world. In fact, I find the world disturbing to me." Mother said, "First, you find God within you, then as you grow in God, you find Him everywhere." That helped me to see I was on the right track but had not

---

17   *The Gospel According to Thomas* (Saying 3 and 113).

completely reached my goal. (The second part I knew already; it was the confirmation I was on the right track that was so helpful!)

As the mind is purified, it becomes filled with Light on an ongoing basis. First, that Light is seen within, then it is seen in all creation. The Kingdom of the Father truly is spread upon the earth and not seen. But when you do see it, you enter into that realm and know that you are the son of the living Father. The Light that fills your Being is then known to be the same Light that you see in all creation. It is the good news, the gospel, that John the Baptist and Jesus brought for one and all: the kingdom is here; it is now, within you and all about you!

Saints and mystics have understood this power of the spiritual life for thousands of years. They have known that the Universal Vision of God produces the greatest happiness for you, or any individual. It also makes you ideal for your chosen work and benefits all the people in your life. It has the power to transform how you see this world. As your mind is illumined with Light, you see this world filled with that same Light. You come to really know that how you see this world is a reflection of your consciousness.

Plateaus

In any sadhaka's journey, there will be plateaus. A plateau, in a physical sense, is an elevated level piece of ground. In spiritual consciousness, a plateau occurs after gaining some elevation, some higher consciousness, and then a feeling of flattening out; a kind of status quo is established. Now in all growth, there are natural plateaus: a vigorous building period followed by a time of consolidation and rest. This is true throughout all of nature.

In the natural cycle of building and growth, there comes a point where either the cycle shifts from rest and consolidation to building once again, maintaining the earlier momentum, or else if one stays too long in one place, one tends toward becoming inert, sluggish, not able to move. If you are out on a hike, for instance, and you have been scaling a fairly steep climb, the body will benefit from a certain amount of rest, recharging blood cells with oxygen and carrying away waste; having brought the overall system into balance, once again you are prepared to continue the climb. But, continue the rest beyond a certain time and the energy required to get the body in motion again needs to be multiplied many times. The one who works in physical labor knows he cannot take too long a lunch break for this very reason.

Inertia is a two-edged sword. It maintains forward momentum when in motion, but it is also the tendency to remain still when at rest. A strong man used to demonstrate his strength by pulling so many train cars harnessed to him by a chain. With great strength and will power, he would strain to break the inertia of the stationary cars. Once the inertia of the train of cars at rest was overcome, he found the momentum of the moving cars made the next steps easier than the initial steps. The hardest part of the demonstration was overcoming the inertia of the cars at rest; it was relatively "easy" to keep them going after that.

These outer examples help you to examine the less visible inner world of Spiritual growth. Plateaus can be a time of needed recuperation, or they can become a place of eternal rest! The negative aspect of a plateau is that it can become like a train of cars at rest to which you are chained, needing incredible strength to get going again. The law of mind states: *with your thoughts, you are always creating.* Every idea that crosses the threshold of thought carries a spark of energy with it. It may be a little or a big spark; it may be a singular thought or there may be a legion of them. A negative habit can be like the proverbial poor relatives who come to visit; suddenly, all their children and dogs and cats have invaded the house, all with the stuck inertia of *not* moving out! You may assess your current trend by asking yourself: "Am I putting real effort into my sadhana? Taking a bit of a needed rest? Stuck on a plateau? Or am I plunging into descent?"

With a little honest reflection, you can make this assessment at any time as to the nature of your thoughts and the power or energy behind them. The power of habit will be your default mode, so whatever your past habits have been, that will be what you return to if you do not stay focused on the new pattern you are working to create. Since an evolving soul is working to get free of samskaras (habits from the past that keep you bound), then without active spiritual effort, your tendency will be to go to those old habit patterns.

In most cases, your past is dominated by body consciousness and your psyche is oriented around the ego. You must then have sufficient spiritual spark, a drive and enthusiasm for spiritual growth. If you do not, then not only will you hit a plateau and stay there, but there will be a tendency to head back downhill. Attitudes such as, "Well, I know I should meditate more, but you know, my life is so busy and when I get home, I just want to watch some television (for 2 or 3 more hours). After all, I work hard, don't I deserve some rest?" The excuse-making may take a myriad of appearances; but as I say, a quick assessment will let you know if you are taking a needed breather, if you have overstayed your break time, or if you are running headlong back down the hill!

And if you have lost forward momentum, what then? One of the aspects of lost momentum is the associated thoughts that come with it: "This is all really too much; I have worked so hard and gotten nowhere. This old life is really not so bad. You know, I am just so darn busy now. Maybe later in my life, then I will make more of an effort." One idea that comes when we are really looking for an out is, "Well, I think that spiritual stuff and meditation was a kind of phase in my life; I have moved on to other things now." In response to this, I would ask, "How can your search for the source of your Being, the source of all life, beauty, love, creativity, and of everything there is, be called a phase?" Surely, nothing so important can be thought of as a phase. The honest truth would be more becoming to a one-time earnest sadhaka.

These thoughts creep into the mind and are soul-destroying. That is, they undermine your spiritual search and aliveness. Living in this world, but not being of it, is a terrific challenge. There is no one keeping score; there is no one to please but yourself, but you should be honest with yourself as to what you are deciding in any moment. Decisions are important, and they determine your future. You must be willing to face the consequences of your decisions, and by doing that consciously in this moment makes you more keenly aware of the importance of such decisions. One way to cut through all the noise of mental chatter, the pull of past tendencies, etc., is to project to the time when you will leave the body, the time of death. As you mentally project forward to that time and you look back over your life, make an assessment of your life. How did you live your life? What did you spend your time on? How satisfied are you with your decisions?

This perspective of the afterlife will be more closely attuned to your Soul's values. The pull of past habits can become intense and become even more so as you try to pull away from them. The reason that most aspirants fall short of the goal is not for any reason other than a spiritual indifference that creeps over the mind. This indifference is the plateau, and it has a great force to it. There must be a greater force exerted to overcome the past than the force the past has on you today. Where did that force of past habits come from? From yourself. Your own combined thoughts and actions have culminated in this great magnet of the past that pulls you back towards itself.

To remain oriented to where your soul's values are, you should associate with other spiritual souls. The magnetic field of one who is awakened, or is in the process of awakening, spiritually magnetizes your pull to things spiritual in a positive way; conversely, it weakens the pull of things worldly. Every soul goes through times of doubt, times of plateaus, times when the old life pulls with incredible force. The fact that these things act on you is not a sign of having fallen, or that the spiritual path is not right for you. This pull from the past is, in fact, a sign you are, like Arjuna, on the spiritual battlefield. You are caught between the opposing forces: one pulling toward God, one pulling you away.

Every day, deepen your prayer so that you will be graced with increasing desire for God alone. Even when enthusiasm burns madly for realization, pray for more. Why? Because every thought, every moment, is a creation; you are either increasing or decreasing. And while there may be the occasional rest, be like the first-string basketball player put on the bench: his whole attention is on the game and desire to get back into the game. Every thought and every moment are creation, so you must ask yourself, "Am I creating the intensity of desire to overcome the stuck places and ego tendencies?"

It is the ego's tendency to want to draw back from growth. With the ego's desire to stay in control, it chooses to hang back and not put itself totally into the effort. For so long in my life, I made efforts in the world, but I was halfway about it. Somewhere in my mind, I reasoned that if I did not put myself fully into the effort, and for some reason, it did not work out, I really didn't fail, because I had not put my full self into it. This may be true with many of you; you dabble at things. You do a little of this and a little of that, but you don't really get anywhere because you have not fully invested yourself.

There is an interesting phenomenon that I notice during most public lectures. When Mother spoke, I always wished to sit as close to her as possible, but in most situations, people will come to some lecture, perhaps after paying a lot of money for the privilege, then vie for the seats at the back of the room! The seats typically hardest to fill are the seats in the front. Why is that? The reason is: most people are reluctant to commit themselves. It is more comfortable to have one foot in the room, and the other next to the exit door.

This phenomenon of having one foot in and the other foot out, or at least close to the exit door, is common in the world. And it is the reason most do not get anywhere; their motives are mixed, their desires are mixed, and their emotions and thoughts are mixed. This is the single biggest reason for getting stuck on plateaus. People don't want to make a mistake, look foolish, to be thought poorly of by friends or family (or anybody for that matter). So, they stay in a "seasonless world," as Kahlil Gibran says, "where we laugh, but not all of our laughter, and cry, but not all of our tears."

It takes courage to commit to any venture a hundred percent. But unless you are willing to commit yourself, you will not gain the realization that will satisfy the soul. I think the great genius of Mother, Master, Papa, and the other great saints and realized masters is their clarity of purpose, thought, and feeling in committing themselves one hundred percent to the realization of God. For them, there was no sense of one foot in and the other next to a safety outlet. They were fully in the game. And that is the reason they succeeded in their quest. If you don't want to look foolish, if you are never willing to make a mistake, if you do not hold yourself responsible, then you will not reach the goal.

While leading this inner spiritual search, you must lead a balanced life; you can still do work in the world to support yourself and be a part of a family and social structure. But, as Sri Ramakrishna used to say, "When you work, keep one hand on God's foot and the other hand on your work. And when finished working, keep both hands on God's feet." Do you know what you will find when you do this? The inner communion with God, which is the rest and recuperation you have really been looking for. This is the true Sabbath day: you rest completely in your communion with omniscient consciousness when duties to the world are done.

Every day becomes a practice of letting go of attachments to the little and big things of life. Every day is a practice of orienting yourself to loving and serving God. Every day is a battlefield, destroying fear, greed, lust, moodiness, and dead inertia, and in turn winning victories of love, generosity, purity, and smooth temperament. Everyday life is your sadhana, the place where you surrender ego and are reborn in spiritual Self-hood. This is happening every day, every moment. And it is not tiring, although sometimes strenuous, and it is not defeating, although sometimes it can look overwhelming. Because when you are on the sadhanic battlefield, you are in the midst of life, and therefore life-energy. When you have Krishna as your charioteer, guide, friend, and your very Lord, then you can be assured of the battle won, no matter how dark things look. Know that always!

Throughout each day, you may assess at any moment, "Do I feel the Presence of God? Am I lessening my attachments to things of the world? Do I feel more loving and more in tune with selfless service now, today? Am I diving deeper into the ocean of God-Consciousness, into the peace, stillness, and all-pervading awareness?" No one day will look like another, and some days, despite your best efforts, the results will not seem to be what you would like them to be. But you can assess if you have made the "good fight." You do not control the results, but you do control the effort.

Therefore, keep your focus more on your efforts than the outcomes. The focus on your effort will tell more of the true story. And if you are making sincere efforts today, you will see results tomorrow. Break asunder all plateaus of inertia and negative tendencies with deepened prayer and meditation and know the Bliss that is the foundation for all creation! Know yourself to be one with that Bliss and be drawn up by the power of universal love into the all-embracing Union of Divine Consciousness. May it be ever so!

Om Sri Ram Jai Ram Jai Jai Ram

Becoming Poor in Spirit

"Blessed are they who are poor in spirit:
for theirs is the kingdom of heaven."
(Matthew 5:3)

Becoming poor in spirit means being dispassionate for the things of the world. Learning dispassion means being in a long process of learning, and relearning, all the ways we hang on to things of the body and the world. It has also been learning the means for releasing those attachments and letting them go.

In yogic thought, this dispassion is called vairagya. Unless one is an avadhoot, one who possesses nothing (not even a fig leaf), then we all have some possessions. The phrase *poor in spirit* means becoming *poor,* that is, detached or dispassionate about things of this body and possessions in the world, and *in spirit* means an inward renunciation, a mental and emotional letting go of attachment.

When the wealthy young man approached Jesus, saying he had followed all the commandments all his life, and asked what he needed to do to gain the kingdom of heaven, Jesus answered, "Sell everything, give it to the poor, and come, follow me." (Matthew 19:21 adapted) The man turned away sadly and walked away. And who today would make that choice? Who would sell everything in order to follow this command, *especially* if wealthy?

All of us have been born with a desire nature. In its simplest terms, desire nature is desire for happiness and cessation of pain. For one centered in body consciousness, that means comfort and security for the body with the least amount of threat. This can be sought in maximum body pleasure, a large bank account, a beautiful home, a prestigious job, power over others, world fame, etc.

For those of a spiritual bent, happiness means entering the kingdom of heaven and experiencing lasting Soul joy and peace, inner revelations of wisdom, and ultimate union with the Supreme Consciousness. As we make spiritual progress, it becomes increasingly clear that preoccupation with things of the body and the world interferes with spiritual experience.

In order to make spiritual progress, there is a need to become less concerned with things of the world and increasingly focused on inward attunement with God. The problem in carrying out that shift of focus from the world to God comes to the fore, "I still live in the world; how do I participate in it but not be of it?"

What it comes down to is our mental perspective. A young boy was sent to a saint-king for instruction in spiritual matters. The boy had no faith in King Janaka and his spiritual instructions, as the trappings of wealth and power of the world surrounded him. The king started talking to the boy about living in the world but not being of it when a fire broke out in the palace where they were sitting. Attendants rushed to and from them with news of the fire. The king sat unconcerned, saying to the attendants he was busy talking about spiritual matters and he was sure they could take care of the fire. The king was so caught up in his talk about God, he would not even evacuate from the palace as the flames leapt near! At last, the boy's few spiritual books he had brought with him, his only possessions in the world, were being threatened by the flames. The boy was tamping out the sparks as they landed on his precious books. King Janaka commented, "Here I sit, totally focused on our discussion of God while this palace burns, yet you are distracted by your attachment to your books." The boy realized he had never seen the degree of vairagya, inner detachment, the king possessed. Humbled, he asked for pardon and earnestly requested initiation by the saint-king. Although outwardly a king, Janaka was inwardly *poor in spirit*.

Poor in spirit means to have the kind of inner detachment King Janaka demonstrated. When a fire destroyed a building at Anandashram, Swami Ramdas danced and laughed like a child watching the play of fire. Others were naturally upset that valuable property of the ashram was being destroyed. When news went out of the destruction of the building, new monies came; the old building was replaced with a new and improved structure. Papa was ever calm, even delighted at the destruction of the old and the construction of the new.

Everything of the world will pass. In one hundred years, with few exceptions, all the people now living on the earth will be dead.

That is really an amazing thing when we think about it. We must realize that we rent, or at best we lease, our time here on earth; we are not buying! Yet, as I said before, we come with desires for happiness, and we have to maintain this body and any dependents we may have. How do we live in this world, take care of our body and our families, and yet remain detached? **One attitude is to see those desires we have in the world, for professional development, care of our family, etc., as coming from God. Let go of any sense of ownership of them.** As long as He puts the desire in our heart, let it be there by His will. If He chooses to withdraw the desire or to fulfill it, that is His doing. Inwardly, we are dispassionate witnesses.

If God chooses to create, build, or destroy through us, that is His doing. Be a pliant instrument for the Divine. Let the thrill of His expression run through our veins, yet hold no attachment for it to remain. He may choose to build a great empire through us; He may choose to remain inwardly withdrawn into our own Being with no outward activity; He may want to raise a family through us; He may want to be a dandy in us. **However He expresses Himself through us, let the focus of our attention be upon His absolute, changeless nature within us, and be a witness to how He chooses to express His creativity through us.** This requires our utmost surrender and detachment.

How do we test whether we are detached or acting out of personal motive? If detached, we will be able to stop any action at any moment and be carefree. With an inner command, we can walk away from everything and continue to reside in the presence of God. Whether fame or blame presents itself, we are equally unaffected. If all possessions suddenly left us, we would feel equally Self-possessed. In short, we find our completeness and fulfillment through an inner wholeness that is independent of exterior conditions.

If we wonder if such Self-containment is possible, it is only because we have not experienced the absolute Consciousness that is God. Sadhana is made up of practicing detachment to the body and the world, but just as importantly, it is the positive attachment to the Presence of God. With that positive attachment, we find the things of the world are long on promises of happiness, but short on delivery. While God-experience takes initial effort to achieve but delivers far more than it demands.

We can begin detachment by inwardly and, if possible, outwardly simplifying our life. We fill our lives with so many things to do. With all the "time saving" devices we have in modern Western civilization, we would think that we would have excess time galore, but find it is quite the opposite. People feel more pressed for time than ever before. Why? Because with all that is available to us, that has quite literally not been available before, our expectations have grown even faster. We now believe that so much more should happen so much faster. The resolution? Simplify. To simplify, we must be willing to say no. We choose more carefully, more consciously, as to what we let into our lives.

One way to inwardly simplify is to practice going half speed. "Half speed?" you might say, "I won't get it all done!" But it is amazing, when slowing down, being fully present to what we are doing in this moment, we make fewer mistakes and things get done as well or better than when always being in a hurry, distracted, and pushing. It is confounding to our mind when tasks go smoother and are completed by moving at a Self-possessed speed. We can also practice slowing the mind down. Rather than thinking of ten things at once and by becoming inwardly calm and focused, while letting go of thoughts of other activities or of all the things that might go wrong, we bring Self-containment closer.

These activities that we surround ourselves with are addictive to the brain. The noise and activity of television, radio, going places, and always running from one place to another keeps us going at a faster pace. To *think* of slowing down feels so good, but instead, we add to the load. Why? Because underneath all the stress is a fear that if all this activity stopped, so would we. We would not have any place for all that stirred up energy to go and it would drive us crazy, kill us, make us a mess, or make us sick; in short, our world would fall apart. We have quite literally become addicted to all the stimulation. This is the way of rajasic, stimulating energy.

To compensate for all this stimulation, we alternate it with trying to over-satiate the body. Through food, sex, sleep, and activities aimed at calming all that energy, we seek to find some peace. Through overdoing satiating activities, including alcohol and drugs, we hope to find relief for our overstimulated nerves. This is the tamasic, negative state leading to an unconscious stupor. Such mediums as television can be rajasic, passive stimulation to the nerves, such as the excitement of a sporting event, or tamasic, mind-numbing "vegging out."

For many people, one or both of these states of rajasic and tamasic is all that life is. Even a religious life can be just one more meeting to go to, another activity in joining the choir, being on the board of directors, teaching Sunday school, or perhaps a place to get that perfect nap during the sermon! In reality, these are not all that different in quality from the rest of our life.

A quality resides beyond the active rajasic and the numbing tamasic. This third state may be all too fleeting and rare in our life. It is the sattvic, uplifted, state of being. When in a sattvic state, we have spontaneously occurring joy and peace. It comes to us not by worldly activity or satiation of the senses, but through a flow from an inner source. "Sounds perfect," says the overly stimulated/satiated individual. But there is a catch. "Oh, I knew it, nothing comes for free!" says the rajasic merchant-thinker. We must learn to be still. "What, and waste my time doing nothing? What for? Can't I join a club or something and get it through activity?" says the activist. Well, yes, we can learn to be outwardly active but inwardly still. But first, **we must learn to be still.** A terrifying thought for many.

Let someone addicted to activity and satiated senses try meditating quietly for five minutes. "Well, that's it, time must be over. On to do some things I've just got to get done!" says rajasic thinkers after their allotted five minutes. Or the tamasic thinker says, "That was a quick five-minute nap, maybe I can get another half-hour nap before I get going!" Letting go of rajasic and tamasic states is another level of what it means to become *poor in spirit*. One renounces attachment to constant doing and satiation. No small task for those addicted to these twins. But, in order to enter the inner kingdom of heaven, this is the key: to become dispassionate towards things of the senses and things of the world, including the tamasic and rajasic states.

For such a one who willingly practices inner dispassion for the world and focuses on the positive attraction to the Spirit, an inner world of realization awaits. Currently, that Spirit may be slumbering, or at least partially slumbering, within us. But with outwardly slowing down, simplifying, practicing inner renunciation, and having repeated contact with Spiritual Consciousness we begin to change—with new eyes, we see the outer things of the world to be God's play. The inner states of Spiritual Consciousness are seen to be the transcendent Reality of lasting joy. No longer addicted to stimulations of the world, and no longer seeing the world as a source of our ultimate fulfillment, we live from the *inside-out,* instead of the *outside-in.* Living from the *outside-in* means things of the world and the senses are the primary focus for happiness and fulfillment and dictate our direction in life. Living from the *inside-out* means spiritual attunement is our source of happiness and fulfillment and direction in life comes from intuition that guides outward actions.

Through the inner dissection of outer attachments with the scalpel of wisdom, our minds become steady and are able to focus on inner stillness. The rajasic-tamasic twins come into their subservient roles as designed. Having become *poor in spirit* to the world, we enter into that inner kingdom of heaven, a mansion with many rooms. We explore the vast potential of who we are in Spirit. With the lower forces mastered, we participate in the world, but we are not of it. New hope for new men and women! True men and true women of a new age, finding fulfillment within and expressing it in all they do. May it come to be, even now!

A World Stood on Its Head

O Lord, I have had wealth
It bought me only misery with fleeting happiness.
I have had possessions, the best the world had to offer
Each was a burden on my back.
I had world authority, even unto life and death
Each decision ladened me with terrible responsibility.
I waged war and gained immense power
And it became an anchor to my soul.

And now, I have no material wealth
And possess immeasurable happiness.
I own little, and would happily relieve myself of that
And I feel the lightness of Being.
I have no authority in the world
But there are those who would lay down their lives for mine.
I now wage war on ignorance and wish all to have peace
And my soul is set free.

Spirit has turned the world on its head
Those things I thought would bring pleasure, brought pain instead.
Power that brought fame
Resulted in disturbance and disaster
Use of force made me a prisoner.
O Lord, free me of worldly gain
Make me poor in spirit
So I may be rich in You.

The Washerman—Washerwoman

Sadhana may be compared to washing clothes by hand. One begins with soiled clothes. Some detergent is applied and the rough work of squeezing, hitting, and pressing the clothes, along with some vigorous rubbing, brings the soil out and makes the clothes clean again. The clothes are then hung to dry in the sun.

The mind full of worldly desires and attachments is the soiled cloth. Detergent added is the grace of the guru. Squeezing the clothes is applying the directions of the guru, hitting is the use of one's own will, pressing is devotion of the heart, and the vigorous rubbing is the interactions in the world for sadhana's sake.

Even with the application of all the above, there may be stains left that seem part of the fabric itself. It is the Grace of God Himself that alone can remove these stains through complete surrender by the sadhaka. So, it is through following the directions of the guru, application of one's will, working in the world to resolve one's own karma, and by Grace of God and Gurus that one may be freed of a soiled mind and stand free in the pure sunshine light of God.

Sadhakas go to the Movies

Going to watch a film for a sadhaka is a test. The whole intent of the makers of the movie is to "pull you in" to the story line. Whether to make you laugh, cry, or tighten in fear, they wish you to identify with the characters in the film, in order to move you in some way. If the movie-goer gets involved with the storyline, they will find themselves laughing, crying, or in total fright. And, at what? Nothing but a play of light on a screen and some sound. Still, that play of light can evoke all the emotions and even sensations of physical world experiences. This proves that attachment to the word is mental.

If sadhakas can go to the movies, be in the movies but not of them, then they may have all the enjoyment of the movie but not be lost in the movie, that is, to forget who they really are. Laughter may be there, even some tears and fright, but not all the way. Always, inside, they keep some portion of themselves inviolate, pure, without identification with reactions to the play. That way, they stay aware of their greater reality and know it is just a play.

When you live life this way, in and out of the movie house, and know that you are really God playing a part in the vast drama of life, then you are free, even within the play itself.

Know a Gift's Value

Seekers of Truth, in meeting, and many who are initiated by a true Teacher-Guru are likened to children of a very wealthy father. The father lavishes gifts upon the children. He willingly gives them gives gifts of gold bonds, blue chip stocks, and silver certificates. Unknowingly and foolishly, the children redeem these treasures for things of little value. With unseeing eyes, they look upon these gifts, not comprehending their true worth. They go to the corner market and seeing shiny trinkets for sale, they dream of having some of those things. So, they consign themselves to the merchant, live in the merchant's basement, and abandon their father who loves them so. The father waits and waits with longing for their return, but they return not. Thinking only of their trinkets, they let languish their treasures unused or spent for foolish trinkets.

O Sadhakas, count not yourselves among those foolish ones who have eyes but do not see, and who have ears but do not hear. The eventide of this life comes nigh too soon. Let not your gifted treasure be for naught. For you are accountable for all things. And if you but bury that treasure, then like the man or woman of one talent, even that which was given is taken away. See that you are like the person given five talents, doubling their value, and therefore proving your worth to be given even more. (Matthew 25:14–30)

O Sadhakas, be like that one, and ye shall be inheritors of your Father in Heaven's vast wealth. Invest what you have been given into time, effort, and intensity, and your return will be realized many times over.

Be an Instrument of Joy

The Sadhana of service is not done for any particular outcome. No matter how sincerely we believe what we are doing is essential or doing a good, that good or need we are fulfilling could be wiped out in a moment. Then, one might ask, why act? We act because ultimately it is God moving through us in that action. Even in fulfilling so-called mundane desires of eating, providing shelter, or clothing ourselves, it is Divinity Itself that moves through us, as the creative idea, the energy in the doing, and the material/physical creation of all action. The Power and Intelligence flowing to us make us creative, give us energy, and manifest physical creation.

I am sure that people thousands of years ago performed actions they believed to be good or essential, but who remembers them now? To act as an instrument of the Divine means we become the observers of how Divine Intelligence directs us, how life-energy moves through our bodies, and how the material/physical aspect comes together. Through purification of the mind, we attune ourselves to the essence of Spirit in action. We feel the purity, the joy, the fulfillment in being the instrument. Just as a musical instrument, such as a flute, does not play its own music, but rather the musician plays its music through the flute, even so, we are the instruments of the Divine.

We play for the joy of being played. The more we surrender our individual will to the Divine Will, the more we become perfect instruments for Spiritual expression. Stubborn individual will is like keys of the flute that stick or become frozen. Pride and jealousy likewise make the instrument partially or totally unusable for sacred use. Making ourselves soft and pliable, sensitive to the most subtle of movements, we will be an instrument the master musician will find joy in playing; all who hear the instrument will find joy in listening, and the instrument itself will be in joy just due to the fact it is being played by the master.

Guru

Guru is in your heart. Guru is the glorious Light of God. Guru is sown into every part of creation. Guru is savior of mankind. Through the Light of Guru, darkness is dispelled. Guru is universal, without beginning or end. See the blazing Light of the Guru! Know ye not you are made in Its likeness of Spirit and It inhabits your image of the three bodies. Guru is love. Guru is Light. Guru is wisdom. Guru is power of Yoga. Guru is not man, woman, nor any one person or thing. Guru is savior to all creation. Guru uses man, woman, or any vehicle It chooses to transform souls darkened in ignorance into enlightened Souls of Realization. As loving as mother and father is the Guru. As desirous for union as newlywed couples is Guru to be in union with their beloved devotees. Union not of bodies, but of hearts, minds, and souls. Union to Universal Consciousness. A union to the Union of all unions. O glorious and ecstatic Guru! In form or formlessness, It burns ever within you and all about you. O sadhaka, purify your eyes so you may see Its glory. Make your eye of attention single so you may see Its Light. Quiet the mind so you may hear its entrancing voice. It is nigh to you now. Wait no longer but find your Guru now, now ever now! (Written in an ecstatic moment.)

Inner Renunciation

John the Baptist is the forerunner of Jesus and preaches, "Repent ye: for the kingdom of heaven is at hand." (Matthew 3:2) To repent means to turn away from, to renounce. This spirit of John the Baptist comes upon us and induces a spirit of renunciation from within. John lived outside of the cities of men; his clothes were not fine, his food sparse and wild. His was the life of a renunciate. As we know, it must be an inner life of renunciation, as outer acts do not necessarily correspond to the inner nature. John is the forerunner to the Christ, the Messiah. That is to say, before Christ Consciousness can come, a spirit of renunciation must be present.

Before Mother Hamilton started the inner Mystical Crucifixion, she and her husband sold all that they had in order to go to India. Both she and her husband were in their mid-fifties, a time of life when most people are very serious about retirement, pensions, the equity in their home, etc. Mother and her husband, Ralph, sold all to make the trip to India! When arriving at Anandashram, Swami Ramdas made it clear every attachment had to be renounced, thrown into the ocean of God. Mother had a fierce love of her children. With all her heart, she renounced special attachment to her husband and children. All this is in the spirit of John the Baptist, as a voice calling in the wilderness. The wilderness is a state of mind when the sadhaka realizes the things of the world will not bring fulfillment. Inwardly, the sadhaka has left the "cities of men," those attachments to worldly aspirations, but one has yet to enter the holy city of consciousness, so remains in the wilderness. The voice of one crying is the voice of intuition that tells it is time to let go of the things of this world, but that voice is not yet the Christ Consciousness; it is the forerunner of it.

In this spirit of renunciation, some aspirants get attached to the world of non-attachment. Becoming prideful in their ability to do without, they do not proceed further. Some of John the Baptist's disciples did not go on to follow Jesus because he was not following an outer life of renunciation as John, their teacher, did. Also, in the Buddha's case, there were those who practiced with him the outer austerities during the seven years he made those his sadhana. When he left that path of severe outer renunciation for the middle path, they did not go with him.

As mentioned, the spirit of renunciation is an inner one. Jesus' very first recorded saying in the Sermon on the Mount is, "Blessed are the poor in spirit, for theirs is the kingdom of heaven." (Matthew 5:3) To *be poor* of course meant to own nothing, and *in spirit* means inwardly. So, to be poor in spirit means to have inwardly renounced the world, body consciousness; the kingdom of heaven, Spiritual Consciousness, becomes your state of Being. Krishna, in the Bhagavad Gita, says it this way, "He who is unattached to every-thing, and meeting with good and evil, neither rejoices nor recoils, his mind is stable... The self-controlled Sadhaka (disciple) while enjoying the varying sense-objects through his senses, which are disciplined from likes and dislikes, attains placidity of mind. With the attainment of such placidity of mind, all his sorrows come to an end; and the intellect of such a person of tranquil mind soon with-drawing itself from all sides, becomes firmly established in God." (Gita 2:57)

The attainment of this inner renunciation is the heart and soul of Sadhana at this stage. In Jnana Yoga, the mind uses the sword of discrimination to cut out all attachments. The mind is in constant vigil; no attachment is allowed to reside in the mind. In Raja Yoga, renunciation is practiced through pranayama, life-force control, to draw all life-force, normally channeled into sense consciousness, back into the spinal nervous system up into higher Consciousness. John the Baptist was in the River Jordan where he washed sins away. The River Jordan inwardly represents the spinal nervous system. When, through the spirit of inner renunciation, life-force is drawn into the spine and lifted upwards, the sin of separation from God is washed away in the holy vibration felt there. The third Yoga is Bhakti. Through intense love and devotion for God, the mind is turned inward to attain union with the Beloved. And, in the fourth Yoga, Karma, all activities are dedicated to the service of God. Eventually, one feels that it is God Himself who is doing the work, and with this, the mind is turned inwards even while engaged in outer activities. All four Yogas lead to the same goal—an inward mind. Detached from the ups and downs of worldly events, the steady mind feels its union with the Sat Chid Ananda nature of God. The establishment of the individual consciousness of the soul in this all-embracing Consciousness of God is the kingdom of heaven.

In East and West, the message is the same. A renunciation of worldly consciousness and turning the mind inward reveals a Kingdom of Spirit residing within every soul. When the inner eye of Spirit is opened, it reveals that same Light, that same Spirit found within is also saturating all creation. Like people with closed eyes, once having opened their eyes see sunlight all around. At once they realize their darkness was self-induced. Before, when their eyes were closed, they would say to one and all, "The world is so dark!" Now they proclaim to all who still have closed eyes, "Open your eyes; there is light all about you." But something keeps those with closed eyes from opening them. They remain in their blindness. Such is the nature of world-bound souls.

In order to enter Spiritual Realms of Light, we must become inner renunciants to world darkness, to become poor in spirit. Then, through making the mind inward through Jnana, Raja, Bhakti, and/ or Karma Yogas, we attain to God Supreme. Let us listen for the voice of one crying in the wilderness, the voice of one leading us the way to Christ Consciousness, to "Repent ye: for the kingdom of heaven is at hand."

Kundalini

Many years ago, I sat in meditation pose as a part of a group in Bellingham, Washington, intent upon the kutastha chaitanya, the third eye point. Twenty-four years ago in the fall of 1976, I had been a student/disciple of Mother Hamilton for one and a half years. I came with a burning desire for God, although I would not have put those words to it when I first came to Mother. She redeemed the word "God" for me in my mind and gave me a living teaching for Who and What He is. Mother taught me that by meditating upon the point between the eyebrows, God might reveal Himself.

All of a sudden, as I meditated in that group, a "snap" was felt and inwardly heard. With that snap, an upward surge of energy directly and powerfully rose up my spine and curved from the lower part of my skull at the medulla, and shot across to the third eye point upon which I was meditating! In this sudden dramatic movement, I was a helpless onlooker. The energy at the ajna created a terrific heat. Fortunately, I had been grounded in Mother's teachings and knew of this force, though nothing can truly prepare you for it.

The heat became intense. The thought came to me, "I could fry eggs on my forehead!" Strange thought, but there you have it. I knew not what to do but to keep my attention on this spot. In fact, there was nothing else I could have done. Like a powerful magnet, it drew my whole awareness to this area, along with the feeling of power that was surging up my spine. The body was in the background of my awareness, but demanded no attention. It is difficult to gauge time in these matters, but I would guess for ten or fifteen minutes this powerful surge of kundalini continued unabated.

Slowly, the force subsided. I did not know whether to be sorry or glad. I was so grateful for this mystical experience, but a bit overwhelmed by its power, and the body felt it had been terrifically strained. Still, I wanted more. I wanted realization of the Self and was willing to do whatever I needed to achieve it.

Twenty-four years later, today, I can say that enthusiasm for this path and the realization it brings has not subsided in the least. As Yogananda's song extols, "Devotees may come, devotees may go, devotes may come, devotees may go, but my Lord, I will Love Thee always, my Lord, I will love Thee always." So as with the song, so with the devotee.

Earlier today at the Cloud Mountain Retreat Center, I was meditating in front of a shrine that is here in the cabin with a figure in it. The figure's lower part of the body is a serpent, the upper half, a woman's winged figure. Above her head, the heads of five serpents. The woman sits serene. Apparently, this goddess has its own traditions and meanings in Buddhism. But in my mind, I see her as kundalini shakti risen in full self-mastery of the lower five chakras and fully residing in the sixth chakra, or the realm of the realized Buddha, Christ, or Krishna Consciousness. "And as Moses lifted up the serpent in wilderness, even so must the son of man be lifted up." (John 3:14) Any attempt to be in a fully illumined state without the complete illumination of the ego is an unrighteous way and will result in boomerang karmic results.

As I prayed to God in the form of this goddess, memories flitted across my mental screen. Memories of my path since that first awakening. A sense of, well, not exactly regret, but a longing, a yearning deep down that I could have had a purer, more refined, more mature understanding during those years. I struggled, I did the best I could, and have somehow lived through it all. I had the perfect teacher and example in my Guru. This alone I am sure is what has made it possible to be where I am now.

But, this yearning to have been different, better, reminds me of a favorite story. The chief of a tribe approached a father and said, "It is time for your son to join the hunt." The father responded, "Yes, I have been thinking the same thing. Shall he be part of the next hunting party?" "Yes," answered the chief, and so it was agreed.

Now the father started thinking about the hunts. They were sometimes long, dangerous journeys that required physical endurance and mental stamina. Then he reflected on his son, not fully physically mature, sometimes like a little boy in behavior. He went to the chief and told him that he, the father, didn't think his son was ready for the hunt. The chief started chuckling, hardly containing himself. He saw straight to the heart of the issue. The chief, when he recovered himself, said, "Of course your son is not ready for the hunt; the hunt will make him ready for the hunt!"

Well, this is the spiritual path in a nutshell! We do not begin at the end. We must begin exactly where we are at, not at some idealized picture of ourselves that may not have any truth in it anyway. We begin with the rough stuff of what we are. We have aspirations, dreams, hopes, strengths, ideals, etc., all on the plus side. On the shady side of the street are our fears, angers, unresolved past issues, inadequacies, weaknesses—shall I go on? Get the picture? This is us. This is a snapshot of us at that moment. No getting around it, no denying it, or at least no good reason to deny it. Why do I mention all of this in relation to the kundalini?

Because the kundalini is all about purifying the very stuff of what we are made of. Jesus said the sheep that are on the right get in, the goats on the left are out! (Matthew 25:32–33) Now he's not talking about people, even if we think we know a few goats. He is referring to the individual. We are all made of mixed character. Can't be helped, that's how it is. But don't despair, and don't rest satisfied—proceed with patient expectation.

Now, kundalini is a response to an intense soul desire. (If you think the kundalini has not been awakened in you, you may be right, and this is a call to intensify sadhana.) But kundalini is not realization by itself, it is a necessary means to gain realization. Realization is a result of the purification of the mind. Purification of the mind comes from keeping the mind on God at all times. This focused attention comes through meditation, prayer, chanting, serving, and loving God.

Through this intense focus of attention on God, the kundalini is activated and purifies and strengthens the nerve pathways of the physical and astral bodies. It also awakens higher centers of Consciousness within the sadhaka. **But, unless the purification of the mind, through a singular focus on God, accompanies that kundalini action, the kundalini energy will be dissipated or will run in unnatural avenues.** If the kundalini is dissipated or misdirected it will not achieve its ultimate purpose: conscious Self-realization.

Some sadhakas will have a sudden or powerful experience of the kundalini and through fear will shut the transformation power off. Even as this intelligent force will guide and direct us, so will it respond to our strong will. Whatever is on the conscious or sub-conscious mind will be strengthened by this force. An ego-driven person may become even more so, and consequently misuse the energy. Others will have surface or latent desire nature activated. The energy channeled through sex nerves, desire for name, fame, wealth, power, and control can subvert purity of spiritual purpose.

And what is purity of mind? It is a total, one-hundred-per-cent, surrender to the Infinite. It is the realization, even as Jesus had, "Of myself I am nothing, it is my Father who doeth the works." (John 14:10 adapted) Purity of mind is surrendering to the highest inner workings of the kundalini shakti in order to scale the summit of Realization. And through this action, the old self, the ego, is dead and the resurrected Self, the Christ Consciousness, lives.

The inner fulfillment of the world's great scriptures requires this individual purity of purpose by the sadhaka. Those that would try to enter by "some other way" other than surrender of the ego will not attain their purpose. (John 10:1) The law must be fulfilled; the price must be paid. And those who choose not to pay the price should not be pretenders to the throne. Jesus' worst pronounce-ments were on those religious leaders who perverted their office for personal gain of name, fame, and fulfillment of ego gratifica-tion. Woe be unto them! (Matthew 23:13) For their penalty of kar-mic debt is much greater for this hypocrisy than any other. All who would enter must pass through the steep path and narrow gate. (Matthew 7:13–14)

And, if we are willing to lay down our lives, perhaps literally, in obeyance of this requirement for purity? What then? Then the kundalini will go about its high purpose. This means the purification of the body temple, a body made new in Christ. It means the kundalini will enter the seven inner churches and light the seven inner candles of Supreme Consciousness. (Revelation 1:20) The work of resolving the knots of past karma ensues from our conscious and subconscious minds in order to gain in purity of mind.

Latent tendencies are exposed in order to cast them into the purifying flame of Light. And if instead of casting them in the fires, we act on these desires, reigniting their dormant life-force? Then we find ourselves in a battle royal for supremacy within the consciousness. Each positive attention paid to past desires feeds the spark with the rocket fuel of kundalini. If we give in to this tendency, the mind will find justification for its action. It will reason: this fulfillment of desire is why I was born; I cannot live without that desire; things spiritual are false, a passing phase, for someone else but not for me, etc. The mind will find every possible trick to tempt us to go with the triggered desire. Why? Because that is the nature of desire, to fulfill itself. It takes no account of the cost to ourselves or others.

And what of that one who chooses this? They wander the path of self-justification. They deride spiritual law as antiquated. Some others perhaps feel that they have risen above such laws as the Ten Commandments. But Jesus said the God-man comes to fulfill the law, not destroy it. (Matthew 5:17) The mind is ruthless in its attempts to have its own way, though. Gradually, usually not all at once, that one loses their light and falls back into the ignorance of separation from God. Sadly, an opportunity is lost. The kundalini either retires back to dormancy or is manipulated into wrongful purpose.

The other possibility is they awaken to their error. Realizing they have made poor choices, they humbly retrace the steep trail back to their wrong turn. They make amends where possible, repent, or turn away from their error and get started back on the path to enlightenment.

I have known a good many souls seduced into subverting their experiences through wrong desire. In some cases, it resulted in death, in most it resulted in strong accusations against a moral path and the spiritual teacher. In some, a more moderate denial of their Spiritual Nature, substituting psychic phenomena that enhances ego, instead of the ego-annihilating spiritual path. In either case, the ultimate destiny of the soul will be fulfilled: that is, the consummation of the separated ego-self into the all-embracing God-self. In this lifetime, or in some other, the soul will once again awaken to its desire for ultimate realization. We may each wisely take from these examples the lesson that even for highly realized souls, the journey to Self is fraught with pitfalls. Unless we cultivate that pure desire for the complete realization of Self, we may very well suffer similar fates.

Karma and Kundalini

Karma is a result of our free will, revocable—never. There is no arbitrary God casting out judgments in anger or jealousy. There is nothing more difficult than the law of karma, the law of cause and effect. Mathematical in efficiency, it is the cosmic feedback machine that lets us experience the impact of all our thoughts, words, and actions. That is why to love God and all creation as yourself is not just a sentimental abstraction. It puts into effect a very exacting law. What you give, you receive.

There is the joke, "Why did God create time?" Pause... "So everything doesn't happen at once!" Well, in the realm of karma, not every effect comes immediately after its cause. There is a time lag and a build-up time. Individuals with very good metabolic health may have to work a lifetime to destroy the good health karma with which they were born. So, the full effect of past actions, good or bad, may take time to manifest. As we might imagine, karma is a complex weave of mixed patterns.

When we say to the universe, "I am ready to go to my spiritual home now," with pure intention, the operating Intelligence of all that is sets into motion all the conditions that are necessary for that desire to be fulfilled. That means meeting and resolving our past actions. "For verily I say unto you, Till heaven and earth pass, not one jot or one tittle shall in no wise pass from the law, till all be fulfilled." (Matthew 5:18) Like people who collected credit cards like baseball cards and use them to their maximum, there comes a day when the bill is due. All resources are then applied to paying previous debt, sometimes just enough to survive on now is used for present living. The sadhaka may complain, "My life seemed better before I set myself on this path!" Just as the credit card holder can say life before paying off this debt was "easy street."

But in all of this payment of debt, there is help. Just as those in credit trouble may go to an agency that takes over their finances and arranges all payments, so may sadhakas cast all the burden of the debt upon God. Now, if the credit-troubled man or woman gets help but secretly gets more credit and uses it, he or she breaks the agreement, and help is withdrawn. So, with God. But, if the sadhaka is sincere, then God truly lifts the burden and makes the load light. All we have to concern ourselves with is attunement with God in this moment and feel His Presence, unconditional love, and guidance.

The guru also is there to take the load. As the credit-troubled man or woman may win the sympathy of a wealthy individual, especially if the rich person sees the burdened individual really struggling to do the right thing, so the guru lifts burdens from the sadhaka.

One of the things Jesus got into hot water for was when he said, "Thy sins are forgiven you." (Matthew 9:2) Those who went by the law decried that as blasphemy. No one can forgive sins. But Jesus was a living testament to the fact that a human being can be one with the omniscient Spirit of our heavenly Father.

Through God-tuned thought, the God-man may project an idea that purifies the sadhaka from a darkened blot of the past, or take onto his or her own body the effect of some past actions of the sadhaka. Such is the grace of God acting through the God-man or God-woman. And Jesus came to show what was possible for all who would pick up their cross, their body, and follow him, the God-tuned life of complete surrender.[18] This all occurs for the purification effect that kundalini energy is creating in the sadhaka.

There is great comfort for sadhakas when they know that each knock received is another debt paid. Let purification proceed! We do not need to seek out trouble or pain in some vain attempt to pay off karma! For that would truly be vanity. Difficulties, if they are to come, can find their way to our door without our help. Rather than fixate on what debt there might be, let us get busy with liberating the mind now. Whatever comes our way, with God-thoughts centered in the mind, bliss, joy, love, and freedom are ours now! Let the body go through what it must, if it is to be. But we may know our oneness now by letting the mind be intermingled with the ever-present Christ Light within us. Such is the grace being offered. The father of the prodigal son ran out to greet him when he was a long way off, to make his peace with him. We may also know that peace now.

We do not know where we are, how near or far. Some sadhakas may have had experiences we've not had. But that may be because we have already gone through them in another lifetime. Do not compare—only look to that singular Light of Being and harmonize ourselves with that Essence. All else will be taken care of perfectly.

As I mentioned before, kundalini may come in dramatic ways or more subtle ways. Do not try to judge such things. Let us focus our mind on whether we are experiencing oneness with the all-embracing Spirit. We will know that through expanding, ever-new joy, a sure knowledge that we and our Father are one. We will feel ourselves to be an instrument or an expression of God in action

---

18   Jesus referred to the cross long before the crucifixion: "Then said Jesus unto his disciples, If any man will come after me, let him deny himself, and take up his cross, and follow me." (Matthew 16:24)

through service, and will feel universal love and compassion for all. These are the signs of oneness with God. These are the rooms of our inner Kingdom. When we have this purity of experience, without a second, as our natural way of Being, then God will confirm for us our oneness with Him.

Until then, more sadhana! That is to keep the mind firmly fixed on God, to allow Him to arrange all for our progress and purify our lower desire nature into transmuted Divine Nature.

Jai Shakti Kundalini, Jai Guru, Jai Ram

The String of Intuition

"How do we know what our intuition is telling us?" This question often comes up when speaking of following our inner knowing. It is both a subject that we can apply too much, and too little, thought to. This may sound like a strange contradiction, but let us reason it through together. If we apply too much thought to the field of intuition, then we will block our intuition. If we apply too little thought, then we will accept every passing thought and fancy for being true intuition. We must train ourselves to be both open to intuitive thought, and be willing to "Test every spirit." (1 John 4:1)

The essential ingredient for developing intuitive thought is to learn to be still, to quiet the body, emotions, and thoughts that normally occupy our everyday experience. In that stillness, a certain kind of knowing may come to us. It comes initially as "a still, small voice." We may feel it as a tug in a direction in our lives, or suddenly we come to know the rightness of going in a certain direction. It may come as a whole or complete picture of everything that is to occur, or we sense what our next step ought to be. In either case, following our intuition means taking the next step toward our ultimate goal. This movement is like picking up the end of a string and following it. It takes a certain amount of faith to do this: faith in inner knowing, faith in ourselves. Intuition coming as that inner knowing may stem from the mind's ability to unconsciously assimilate information, or to recognize patterns that present us with solutions. Or, that inner knowing may be the ability of our consciousness to reach beyond normal ways of thinking, giving us access to the psychic realm or the Superconscious realm.

Through intuition, we have information not derived through a sequential, reasoned thought process. We may test that knowing in several different ways—some using reason and intuition. Some reasoning ways of testing what we are getting is to ask, "Is this for a positive purpose for myself, my family, my community?" Also, "Will this be for the highest good of everyone concerned?" Thirdly, "Does it make common sense, or at least, can I see a logical sequence of events that will lead to a good?" If we can answer affirmatively to these questions, then we may feel we are on safer ground. In relation to the third question, intuition may outdistance the reasoning mind's ability to pull in all the rational information to know if it makes logical sense. Therefore, we may not be able to answer this question fully.

Intuitive confirmation can be sought by asking for a response from our intuitive felt-sense. For instance, we can ask, "Does this measure up to the highest Light of which I am capable of knowing right now?" Or, if we ask God, "Is this a true intuition of Your will?" When asking these questions, it is important to become still, clearing the mind and body of the flow of thoughts and feelings and to listen for the voice of God—that higher means of knowing from the Superconscious. From that stillness, is there a positive response? Ultimately, we can only be certain of what may be intended for us in the moment. Other confirmations may come by asking a fully realized Being, or if time proves the intuition as coming true, then it becomes a prophecy fulfilled.

When we first get an inner prompting and continue to follow that voice of intuition, we have picked up the end of the string and we are following it. That is, we respond to what we are getting intuitively in each moment. Then we continue on to each next step, all the while testing the intuitive prompts, both cognitively and intuitively. We may not know the whole of our journey, but we will always know the next step. And, if nothing comes to us? We then check, are we still in our feelings, and are our thoughts open to what may come? If the inner stillness reveals no prompting for action, then the direction is to not act. However, we stay alert, open for the next movement to action. It is by following each step in this way that will keep us focused on the moment and support our making progress toward the ultimate goal. It also keeps us focused on that inner Light and helps us to fulfill our Dharma—the reason we are here. **This method requires faith, a faith that replaces a need to know all the details of a journey before we take a single step.**

One example comes to mind of being guided by this inner knowingness. Once I was in a large department store. I had been shopping while a friend had gone to another part of the store; where, I did not know. I was done shopping and wanted to find my friend. I felt a magnetic force guide my movements up an escalator and then another. I felt my steps guided while in the grip of this magnetic force. I was made to turn in circles at times for no apparent reason. I had to suspend my resistance to being noticed by others for some strange movements on my part and release myself to this guiding force. Finally, I was made to stand in a certain place on the third floor and then to stare in one direction. The magnetic force kept me standing there. I wondered why I was staring at a part of the store that was empty of all persons, when my friend stepped out of a dressing room at that very moment!

Now, clearly, the force that guided me was more than anything I could have known through the five senses. As a receiver of this information, it was required that I open myself to such guidance through a calm, receptive mind. Second, that I be willing to overcome my self-consciousness relative to what others would think of me so I could stay attuned to this inner direction. Third, that I surrender to this inner prompting without knowing the final outcome before starting. Other cases of intuition may be more or less dramatic than this example.

Every day, intuition may come in seemingly very ordinary ways. We may be wondering what to do next in life. When asking this very big question about our life, no direct answer comes. An inner prompting suddenly comes to clean the bathroom! Now, what does that have to do with one's life's purpose? In this case, it can be picking up the end of the string and starting the journey. Getting our house in order may be the first step in getting onto our life's purpose. And so, we clean the bathroom. While cleaning, an idea comes into our mind about a book we once read and were inspired by at the time. Following the string, we find that book and open it at random. We read how the hero was inspired to do what he or she loved to do, following the greatest Light. It comes to us that we have followed a route of least resistance and have lost touch with that inner knowing of what we always wanted to do. Fear grips us. We ask, "Can I do that? Do I continue to follow the string, or do I let the fear stop me?"

Emotions such as fear and anger block our inner knowing. Also, desire nature such as greed and lust will overshadow intuition. That is why out-of-control emotions and desire nature are so destructive to making good decisions in attunement with our inner direction. The practice of meditation, quieting the mind through focused attention, teaches us to remain the observer of our thoughts and feelings, not denying or identifying with them. Free of distracting thoughts and feelings, we become aware of that still, small voice of intuition.

As we increasingly value being guided by intuition, then our receptivity increases. Grand visions of what can be may stretch out before our inner vision. Even with these grand vistas must come the steps to gaining these vistas. By honoring this inner stillness and gaining the rich harvest of inspiration and Divine direction, our life is founded upon the hard rock of realization of that kingdom of Light. May we all come to grasp firmly that string of intuition that leads us to fulfill our life's purpose and further bring the fruits of that kingdom of Light, both within and without.

Meditation as Renunciation

The sadhaka gains strength from acts of renunciation. Renunciation may be thought of as any turning away from the world and focusing on God. Turning away from the world means turning away from the sensory stimulations and striving nature of desire for things of this world.

One of the greatest extremes of renunciation is meditation. In meditation, we close the eyes; we are in a quiet place; we are in a relaxed posture without touching or being or being touched; we have the mouth closed and we are not actively smelling our environment. All five senses are brought to a quiet standstill.

Next, the mind, which runs after things of the world, past, present, and future, that active mind with its constant commentary on everything, hopping all over the place, is slowly trained to become still. Either we learn to be the observer, the stillness behind the thoughts, or we learn to become one-pointed in our focus. Either way, the mind becomes still, and we renounce thoughts of this world.

Having renounced the senses and thoughts, and having come to a stillness, we make ourselves attentive, but without desire. This means we also renounce desire for enlightenment or any spiritual experience. This is the final stage of the renunciate.

Complete renunciation leads to enlightenment. Enlightenment answers all the questions, whose answers we have sought in running after the things of the senses and the world.

With the senses restrained, mind focused on the Supreme Lord of the Universe, and empty of desire, we are the complete renunciate. Anytime we imitate this complete renunciation of the outer by replacing it through some inner act, we can help prepare ourselves for that complete inner renunciation.

Our attempts at meditation are ways to imitate complete inner renunciation. Even though the attempt to meditate is not successful, it will yield results. We may struggle through the entire time we sit for meditation. The senses scream for attention, the mind runs like a herd of wild horses, and we are in painful agony or utter restlessness the whole time. We are completely relieved to be done with our sitting time and leave our asana like a racehorse leaving the starting gate!

Yet strangely enough, the after-effect of our time in meditation is quite wonderful. Either immediately after, or later in the day, we feel purified, at peace, and very centered; the complete opposite, but hoped for, experience in meditation. The mind wonders if the meditation was a waste of time, yet we feel this way afterward. The stringency of the meditation is directly responsible for the uplifted mood, later on.

The difference in how we get to sensory satisfaction and spiritual satisfaction can be compared to how we earn and spend money. Sensory satisfaction is like getting a credit card and running up the bill, paying only the minimum amount due. The fun is all up front, with an increasing debt load, added to by the accumulating interest charges. Whatever is purchased in this way costs many times the original amount.

By working and saving, however, the most difficult part is done first, and the savings compared to the credit method is really significant. When we "spend" our life-energy on the senses first, we accumulate a debt. By investing in the body and the world all of our life-energy, we forget our Divine origins. This forgetfulness results in a huge expenditure on the body and world that: 1) will go away all too soon, and 2) leaves us spiritually bankrupt when we leave this body.

Attending church once a week will not balance this account. Leaving this body with a huge "amount owing" to this world requires we come again to work out the balance. At least if we live a moral life, we will not be so much in the red, but God help us if we fudge the numbers or were outright corrupt. The debt can be staggering.

Renunciation is the diversion of these funds, our life-energy, and transferring them to our spiritual bank account. Even at ten percent of our life-energy, the savings account can grow substantially. Ten percent of our time, ten percent of our energy, and ten percent of our interest is what traditional religion asks for, yet who is even ready to give that?

That would be two and a half hours a day, withdrawing the life-force from the body and senses and giving it to God. Most people would call such a person a fanatic! Yet this ten percent is the tithe that God asks for. This illustration is given to prompt us to think about how we spend our days, our time, and our life-energy. It is something to think about.

What most people do not realize is the tremendous payoff of this investment. The peace, happiness, and even higher productivity of worldly duties, come as a natural result of this investment.

As with most financial plans, the encouragement is to start today! Even if ten percent seems too high, start with five percent, or less, but start today! And be consistent, invest every day. What begins as a discipline and an act of will becomes a time of haven and necessity for our inner happiness and balance.

There is no one else to live our life for us! So, the decision must be, and always has been, ours. Let us determine to be a steady and consistent saver of life-energy for our spiritual bank account and watch our account grow. We will accrue unending peace, joy, and intuitive wisdom. Not a bad payoff in the here and now; not to mention the time when it comes to leave this body and world behind us. One day, with the balance of past debt paid, we will be free to come or go, but compulsory return will be a thing of the past. We will smile at that investment portfolio!

Loyalty

Loyalty is a timeless virtue, but it seems it is also timely. I have been asked in recent times what my view is on signing loyalty oaths. My view is that no realized spiritual master would require such a thing and it does not reflect teachings based on the highest Truth.

Loyalty is something that is earned, and if we want loyalty, then we must give it. But loyalty cannot be something that is mandated. The more one tries to demand loyalty, the more one reveals their deep-seated insecurity.

When we have a high level of respect and/or love for someone, loyalty is given naturally and freely. There are many instances in history of loyalty running so deep that one gives up their life for another. This must be said to be a very highly developed sense of loyalty when done for some noble purpose.

Today we tend to give little thought to loyalty. As long as things are working for us and we have some happiness, then we stay with a friendship, marriage, or work situation. But when things are not going quite the way we want them to, or when some other situation looks easier or better to us, then we leave our commitments and run to what promises to be expedient happiness.

This tendency to disloyalty when difficulties arise makes a deep impression on our soul. A pattern of such behavior will weaken our character and bring us suffering. Giving no loyalty to another, we see the world as unwilling or unable to give us loyalty. Deep down, we trust no one because we project our own inability to give loyalty onto others. Even if others show us loyalty, we will think them to be not very smart, to not have the courage to leave when they should, or always secretly scheming to get away or get revenge on us. It breeds a devious mindset that is always calculating the odds in our favor, or when we need to leave or find a scapegoat.

Loyalty, on the other hand, provides a solid core inside. When we go through difficulties with others, it tends to bring us closer together. As families experience crises and weather storms, they build a bond that they know can withstand practically any season; in business, in friendships, go right down the line and there are no exceptions to this rule.

Now that I have said that, I will say there is an exception, but it violates what loyalty is really built upon; that is when one stays loyal for the wrong reasons. What might those reasons be? Wrong reasons for staying loyal to others are when we are too fearful to separate; for reasons of greed, thinking we will get something by staying; for base reasons like lust or even revenge. But staying for these reasons is not loyalty; it is self-interest. Real loyalty cannot be compared to these pseudo-loyalties. Real loyalty will raise the soul up to a higher plane of consciousness that ennobles all whom it touches.

How can we compare such a lofty idea and ideal of loyalty to a demand that someone sign a piece of paper pledging their loyalty? I am surprised anyone can bring themselves to do it, even when they feel such loyalty to an individual or an organization. It flies in the face of the kind of relationship that creates a sense of trust, respect, and mutual regard that engenders loyalty. I can only believe that any who propagate such practices are not on good terms with loyalty and how it is generated. For myself, I would rather the world abandon me in time of need than for any to feel bound to me because they signed a piece of paper.

When my own Guru went through much physical suffering and many started to stay away, she never spoke ill of one person. Once in a while, she would say, "You know, I have been missing so and so." It was not that she had no feelings; she loved more deeply than anyone I have known. But it was an impersonal love that did not infringe on another's deciding power to come or go. She always held out the highest ideal for all and would do her best to help everyone live up to that ideal. She would teach, suggest, and speak very forcefully about her perception of truth, but she always left it up to the individual do to what they thought best. She gave all who came to her respect, love, and the loyalty of a truly realized teacher.

In return, she expected the same. But when others did not live up to their best and did not reciprocate that loyalty as students/disciples, she let them go gracefully.

I cannot imagine that anyone would stay with something because they signed a piece of paper, and if they did stay for that reason, would they be the kind of person we would want to stay? All of these thoughts have come about as a result of listening to some others who encountered these rules from some different spiritual organizations. It is always timely to contemplate, meditate, and spend some time on the meaning of loyalty. What does it mean to be loyal? How do we know when to commit ourselves to being loyal? Are there times when loyalty is not really loyalty, but a form of cowardice or some other less-than-noble reason for staying with someone or something?

When I came to this path at twenty years of age, I had not given much thought to the idea of loyalty. Mother would mention it in her talks, and when I thought about it, my mind would always go to this sense of knowing when I was on the right track—following that inner direction. Mother would point out that loyalty to the inner guru always came first; this inner sense of knowing what was right was my inner guru. But that inner barometer of truth was not all that existed in me. I was also full of desire nature, fears, and uncertainties, undefined regions of thought and feeling. So, Mother also gave me guidelines designed to put me in touch with a more refined sensitivity to this inner knowing. It is like learning what is healthy for the body. When I am eating a lot of junk food, I will taste a carrot and not think it is very sweet. But when I clean my system of sugary items, that same carrot will taste very sweet. Staying "loyal" to a diet free of the sugary items will prepare the body to recognize the sweet taste of the carrot.

Spiritual disciplines and guidelines are like switching from a diet high in sugar to appreciating natural sweetness. When I was inundated with stimulation through the senses and by my desire nature, my sensitivity to my Spiritual Nature was blunted. By following the simple rules Mother proposed and focusing my mind in the way she guided me, my awareness of that inner guru grew. I did not know the Truth of all that Mother taught from the beginning. By staying loyal to her teachings, I garnered the experiences that showed me that what she taught was, and is, the Truth. Loyalty to her teachings changed my nature and refined my perception of Truth. I found the Truth discovered within and what was taught to me by Mother to be one and the same.

The movement or flow of energy in a group of people goes through ups and downs. All things in the world change: the weather, what is being talked about, enthusiasm, everything. When we join a spiritual group, there may be a lot of fresh energy flowing that sweeps many people up in its grip. When the predictable ebb of energy comes into the picture and the energy is more difficult to feel, either individually or collectively, then those who were there for the "ride" of the energy current will drop off. When we go through an individual or group crisis of down energy, loyalty and commitment are put to the test. These are the times that build that solid base of character, or we enter the quicksand-shifting loyalty of convenience.

The reason that loyalty is so critical to the sadhaka is due to the fact that no real spiritual progress can occur without the kind of commitment that comes with loyalty. I overheard a participant at a retreat talking about his spiritual path. This individual was in charge of some kind of a "spiritual" center. He said, "I can't really meditate. I am into Krishna Das (the singer) right now." Now, what kind of aspirant is that, and how far do you think he will go in his spiritual journey? With that kind of loyalty, he will be on to the next thing that captures his attention, and he has set himself up to lead others on their spiritual path—quite amazing.

Mother described a period she went through: for three years, she questioned her Master's spiritual attainment. She was a Center Leader and was holding meditations in her home. During that time, she mentioned her doubts to no one. She continued on with her spiritual practices and served all who came to her. Through her steadfast approach, she came out of that doubt and realized the incredible influence Master had on her life and what she had inwardly attained. She saw that attainment would not have been possible if not for Master and what he had given her. Her loyalty to her Guru and her steadfastness to her inner Guru of Truth weathered the storm and brought her to a greater degree of realization. It was not a blind faith that took her through the crises, but a sincere search for Truth combined with loyalty to the inner and outer guru.

All sadhakas will have crises of faith. These wilderness times will be some of the most difficult experiences we will have to face. It is loyalty that will see us through those times. Not a blind loyalty, not a faltering loyalty, but a loyalty first to Truth, and therefore to our spiritual path. When each experience we encounter drives us deeper into our search for Truth, then we will find what we seek. If we are "loyal" for the wrong reasons or that loyalty is misplaced, it will be shown to us in our search for Truth. For example, Sri Yukteswar asked young Yogananda to bring him back to the path if he found that he, Sri Yukteswar, was faltering on the path. What humility the great Master had. But also, he was teaching Yogananda about the complete loyalty of friendship, for that is what one friend does for another. When we have such loyalty for one another, no one will be a stranger; we will see our Beloved within all. Loyalty of this kind cannot be demanded, but only freely given. Indeed, it is the most precious gift in the world.

The Universal Religion

My great Guru Mother Hamilton often said, "There is one God, one religion." It has also been said that one person's myth is another person's religion. Myth in this case implies a fable, something not true, and religion means it is true. Thus begins the never-ending argument over religion. These discussions follow one of two veins.

One: "My religion is truth, and your religion is false." Or: "Your religion has some truth, but mine is the truer, and to be truly spiritual or saved you should follow mine." With this religious superiority, the world is divided into camps; sometimes spilling over into war or protracted separation.

We have to ask ourselves, "Is this what God truly wants for his children of the earth?" I propose it is not, and further, I propose there is a way out, without anyone having to give up their religion—their pathway back to God.

That every great religion is humanity's approach to the Divine Nature as the real source of origin is intuitively understood. Each religion and subdivision of those religions vary in philosophy, language, and ritual to either a small degree or in large measure. These differences are compounded by a provincialism that says, "My way is the right way or the only way." And: "When I see the variances in language, philosophy, and customs, I am even more convinced you are wrong, and I am right."

In order to understand there is but one God and one religion, we must be able to identify what is common to all religions. Through identifying universal principles, universal truths, we can then speak of a universal philosophy that varies by language and customs only. It may be said that the color of skin may vary, but all humans bleed red. If God be truly the Creator of all, then equally there will be universal aspects to the heart and soul of humanity.

> **Postulate One:** There is a right way and a wrong way, or a superior way and an inferior way, of understanding the nature of creation and our individual relationship to it.
>
> **Postulate Two:** Religion addresses itself to those in error, or with inferior understanding, with an eye to teaching individuals the right way to approach their life.
>
> **Postulate Three:** By following these teachings, a change will be effected that will lead to the rectification of the previous fallen state into a condition of being saved and/or transformed.

Postulate Four: The spiritual health of individuals and the community depends on the acceptance and implementation of the teachings.

These four postulates, I would submit, are universal to all the major religions. The common point that applies to all religions may be said to be the establishment of the spiritual health of the individual and the community at large.

There is an obvious point to be made here. All individuals hold beliefs, by and large, because they truly think those beliefs represent the highest truth. If they did not believe that they would change their beliefs. The two exceptions to this rule are due to individuals either being too lazy to think things through, or too fearful to change due to social pressure.

First Principle of Universal Perspective

The number one principle of a universal perspective should be the recognition that all individuals have a right to their beliefs. It should be assumed that each individual's belief represents their sincere effort at creating their own spiritual health as well as that of the community. There are, of course, those who are indifferent, or in antipathy, to the direct spiritual health of themselves or the community. Yet those too should be thought of as doing their best at creating some good for themselves and/or others. Barring direct harm they incur on others, which secular law should address, they should be allowed to believe as they see fit.

Finding Points of Agreement

In the pursuit of universal understanding, we may ascertain areas of universal principles that comprise a healthy spiritual life and community.

The three areas of Universal Spiritual Life are:

1. **Worship**

   All religions seek to direct the mind to some transcendent Being or Consciousness. Whether it be called God, Allah, Satchidananda, The Tao, Nirvana, or any number of designations, this worship or meditation upon this transcendent principle is core to any religion. Typically, there are centers of worship: a church, synagogue, temple, mosque, etc. For these places of worship to be respected and remain invariably protected, by one and all should be the watchword of all religions. In return, the keepers of these holy places should protect the sacred purposes for which they are created and not violate that sacred trust by becoming involved as centers for secular foundations, such as revolutions.

2. **Love and Compassion**

   Not only do the great religions speak to the worship of a transcendent principle, but they also relate these principles to humankind: one's brother and sister. All too often, these universal sympathies become constrained by local identification. "Only those of my belief or community or country are deserving of my love and compassion." All great religions and religious leaders call on us to expand our love and compassion to one and all. Are we not called upon to emulate the great ones in whose steps we follow and find the means to love all? Surely universal love and compassion must be the foundation for a universal outlook.

3. **Learning From Our Differences**

   The variety of ways of striving for the higher ideal can and does add richness and interest to all who strive to follow a high road. When an individual is truly secure in his or her own way, that individual can then afford to examine the ways of another. Our attempts to "live the one life" meet with challenges and obstacles on every front. Who is to say he or she has the best answer to every dilemma?

To learn and derive inspiration from those sincere in their desire to follow their spiritual way is wise and efficient. Sorting through externals and perceiving the essential principles, in addition to following one's own way, one may then find applying the ways of another an added means toward accomplishing the difficult task.

We can marvel at the wonderful and diverse ways individuals have evolved to worship the one God of all. Of course, not all ways will appeal to us equally and some we may find repulsive. But we can go back to the number one principle of a Universal perspective: respect for everyone's right to worship as they feel inwardly directed.

In supporting Universal ways of practicing beliefs and allowing for the practices of others in their religion, a very important phenomenon will happen. By uniting the efforts of those interested in the spiritual health of a community, that community's spiritual health will grow. Kindred spirits who differ on some philosophies but have agreement on some core principles will strengthen the community in living those principles.

Jointly aspiring for higher-mindedness, universal sympathy, and purity of lifestyle will advance the health and well-being of all. Acknowledging the areas of agreement will strengthen those areas for all. Leading a religious life, showing tolerance for differences but strength in principles, will inspire others to do the same. A knitting together of those who are pursuing the spiritual health of a community can only mean good for the community.

As our world shrinks with improved travel and communication, the imperative for not only tolerance of others but for the reinforcement of universal spiritual principles, becomes essential to the spiritual health of all. Spiritual health is under terrific attack today.

There is one banner under which that attack may be defeated, and spiritual health established: one God, one religion. This is not to say all religions become one religion. It does mean a recognition of the one religion of humanity: the individual's relationship with his or her Creator.

There are many roads leading to a City of Light upon the hill. Let travelers by diverse roads lend support and inspiration to one another so that all may reach that blessed destination.

You Are a Divine Instrument

We are told the two-fold path to realization comes through dispassion for things of the world while keeping attention fully focused on God. The end result is a perfect union between the self of individuality and the Self of Universal Consciousness. This union brings about a condition in which the stillness of absolute Spirit and the activity of creation is seen as a singular existence of one absolute reality, God. With this vision, the whole of humanity, creation, and formless Spirit are all seen as seamless Divinity.

What is required for this Universal Vision is the two-fold purification of the mind from all limiting attachments. Thus, the two-fold approach of dispassion for things of the world, and a complete focus on God. In the lives of many realized Beings, an itinerate lifestyle was adopted, with the simplest of needs for the body begged from others in order to free the mind from worldly concerns so as to keep the focus on God. This life cannot and should not be adopted by all. Lahiri Mahasaya came as an example of one who lived in the world as a Householder, yet remained "Not of the world," keeping his spiritual freedom in the midst of activity.

The problem encountered by sadhakas aspiring for the Universal Vision is to make their way in the world yet remain out of the snare of attachment. Marriage, home, children, business, and social life tend to draw the mind outward, enmeshing it in attachment to things of the world. How does one then enter into the field of activity and remain free?

The answer to this question is the substance of the Householder's sadhana. The method described as the outer renunciate rejecting the world and its lures will not be effective for the Householder. The Householder moves right into the world's activities. The means of viewing this activity, voluntarily chosen, will differ for the Householder. All aspirations for the world may be seen by the Householder as willed by the Divine.

For Householders, acceptance of Divine Will through the desire nature is not license for an "anything" attitude. Rather, it requires a keen sensitivity to separation between the observer of a desire and the desire itself. Through inward acknowledgment that this desire comes from God, we as the Householders should feel an inner connection to the Divine and a loosening of identification with the ego nature. This inward freedom of Spirit is the keynote from which the Householder may gauge the effectiveness of this practice.

We can then feel more an instrument of Divine Will. In the beginning, start with the big picture of life. Are our goals sought in alignment with good and positive qualities? Whether it be marriage, raising of children, career, or social activities, are they of a high spiritual quality? To say we are leading an inwardly spiritual life but spending time and effort on a useless or destructive lifestyle is hypocrisy. To say we aspire for God-realization but are contemplating marriage to an abuser of drugs or someone engaged in other negative behavior just does not make sense. Bringing life goals into alignment with spiritual values begins the inner/outer congruity of Divine Will.

Next comes adherence to a spiritual method or discipline. We all know that to make progress in a chosen field, we must dedicate time and effort toward that goal. The greater we are consumed by a goal, the more likely we are to make progress. There are those who have prenatal talent that makes the accomplishment of a goal very easy for them in that field. This is both a blessing and a caution. Sometimes, the prize of spirituality does not go to the hare who makes rapid progress with just a little effort, but to the plodding turtle who takes one step after another, never giving up! Make meditation a humble surrender to the vast field of spirit that seeks to make its Sacred Goal known to the devotee.

With the goals of life correctly calibrated for a spiritual life and the daily practice of meditation and prayer in place, then we may reasonably look to the movement of Spirit throughout the day. In those times of meditation when we feel a great sense of peace and attunement—versus those times when it seems like wild horses have taken us for a ride and then ran us over—a natural kind of knowing will be present. Reflecting on certain situations, conversations, or choices in life—feel the rightness or wrongness of it all. It may come as a "gut feeling;" we just *know*. Most often, the thought of a situation will spontaneously come to mind, and we know what is in the highest alignment.

This intuitive knowing comes more often as we listen and respond to it. Living according to this inner direction brings a sense of alignment from ourselves to our Self. A certain feeling of purity emanates from the inside out, along with peace. These manifest qualities affirm that we are on the right track. Others may comment that they feel peaceful when around us, or they can always count on our opinion; it just seems to be always in the right direction.

This is the place for another caution. We can start feeling quite full of ourselves at this point. The sense of peace, purity, and wisdom can trigger the ego into thinking, "I've made it. I've arrived at that stage of perfection." It can be an overt thought or one that is lurking in the shadows, giving a certain smugness or secret arrogance.

The safest route here, as always, is a humble recognition that: "I of myself am nothing; it is my Father who doeth the works." The guru role can be an enormous help here. By surrender to the guru as teacher and guide, the right attitude is brought to the fore. No matter what your degree of spiritual development, the guru is acknowledged as the reason for that progress—easily give all credit to him or her.

This inner surrender helps inoculate us from spiritual pride. This does not create any sense of inadequacy or low self-esteem. Because the humble recognition is based on truth, it is a simple acknowledgment of a fact. Spiritual masters and God have no need or desire for groveling and pandering. True humble recognition that the power and feeling of God have come and remain with us as a result of a deep inner surrender is essential to growth. This attitude, applied to the movement of God through us, will bring happy harmony with Divine Law and Spirit.

By deepening attunement with the Divine Presence within, we will feel its guidance throughout the day. Easy compliance and alert recognition of this guidance strengthen its role in life to the point to where we feel but a witness to the Spirit within. Those times we fail to recognize intuitive direction from the Superconscious mind, or deliberately go against it, produce such painful circumstances that we grow more determined, stating that, "no matter what," we will adhere to God's will; even if that means the death of this body—death is preferred to the painful absence of the Divine Presence. This wholehearted commitment makes us a perfect instrument of Divine Will.

Feel that we are the machine and God is the operator. Far from making us a mind-numb automaton—feel more alive, more conscious, and more at peace. Be a witness to the fascinating drama of life as it unfolds within and without. In perfect surrender, let us feel as if we are a musical instrument played by a master musician. Become boundless in our experience and feel more and more that, "I am nothing; God is everything."

However, this does not lead to extinction; rather, we identify with the nature of God. What God is, so are we—Infinite, eternal, all-powerful, and all wisdom. The drop enters the sea; it ceases to be a drop but knows itself to be one with the sea. The sea also contains the drop, so may express itself as the drop if it wishes or may explore vast realms of itself.

For example, if we are learning a new task, say playing the piano, we may focus our full attention on our right hand in working to master the finger movements of a certain piece of music. In a high state of concentration, we may lose all conscious awareness of the room and the whole rest of our body except the fingers on our right hand. Over and over, we go through the movement of the right hand to be able to play those notes correctly. In that moment of concentration, we could say the whole world has become our right hand. As far as our conscious awareness is concerned, this is true, although the rest of our body continues all of its normal functions as always. When we release the concentrated attention from our right hand, our awareness returns to whole-body consciousness. At that time, we become aware that our right leg went to sleep because of the way we were sitting, it's a little bit warm in the room, etc. All things we were unaware of when focused so intently on our right hand.

Even so has the Divine All-consciousness become focused on our form and thought patterns, etc., to the exclusion of the universal omniscience. The All-conscious Being makes Himself unconscious as inert gases. Then He gradually becomes more and more conscious through minerals, vegetables, animals, and then humans. Like the practicing pianist awakens his or her hand to be an instrument of intelligent life-force until it can deftly play beautiful notes, so does the awakening God practice through His human instrument, making it a capable conduit of more and more refined consciousness. Gradually, the human body is fitted to express the highest consciousness even as God is! No longer the walking dead, the son of man, the human ego, has transcended into the Son of God, the Divine Manifestation—this is the fulfillment of the awakened one, the Buddha, the Christed one.

We are now fit to be the Divine Instrument for the ages. Divinity has at last found full expression through its human instrument. The steps toward this attainment as outlined earlier are available to all.

The question is, "Who is willing to make the effort to become that fully awakened instrument of Divinity?" The calling is here today, as it ever has been. Who will hear? "Awake, Arise!"

Moral Courage

The development of moral courage is the essential basis for a spiritual life, without which all advanced practices are doomed to crumble and fall. The moral tenants have been known to us since time immemorial in various forms such as the Ten Commandments of the Bible and the Yamas and Niyamas of Patanjali.

Laws upon laws are piled upon the people of a nation by humans, but simple observance of basic morality with a courageous, selfless attitude would replace the millions of words of complex and conflicting law. To tell the truth, even when it goes against one's interest, is a basic for the spiritual aspirant. This does not mean we need to blurt out whatever comes to mind in the name of truth, no matter who it hurts, for this goes against another law: non-injury to others. This is most beautifully summed up as the Golden Rule: "Do unto others as you would have them do unto you." In fact, if this one Golden Rule were to be universally observed, it would single-handedly replace all other laws. Just think of a world where other people's interests were important to all! How this world would change.

"But," says the pragmatist, "that is not how the rest of the world is. If I were to take that attitude, I will be crushed by the greedy and careless!"

What do the spiritual masters advise us on this count? Jesus said the greatest thing a man can do is lay down his life for his fellow man. (John 15:13) In what way did Jesus lay down his life? He did it through total surrender to the Divine Will. He bore the slander and defamation from others in silent love. He may have lost the battle of the moment, but he won the war by shaping the world through his example.

But, he was not reticent to speak and act against misdeeds when he felt prompted; he was no coward. Indeed, he reflects the teaching of another world teacher, Krishna. Krishna says we must enter the arena of conflict when called as a duty. (Gita 1:31) To avoid conflict from ignorance that leads to reticence does harm to ourselves and the world at large. Jesus drove the money changers from the temple because they destroyed the holy vibration of a sacred temple. Thus, we must stand up for what is right, even give our life for that purpose if called upon.

We live with the courage of our conviction and surrender to Divine Will. This courageous morality comes to us through practice, just like using muscles in exercise strengthens the muscles through use.

Which of us has not succumbed to the temptation to lie when caught with guilt, shame, or an unwillingness to face the consequences of our actions? Each time we give in to moral weakness, we deflate our moral muscle. Conversely, each time we step onto the field of action and plainly speak the truth with injury to none, then we strengthen that muscle. Each time we treat another with the same care and consideration we would like to have shown to ourselves, we glow a little brighter. The moral muscle is gradually transformed from the muscular noodle of a weakling to the courage of a warrior's strength!

As spiritual aspirants, we must give due consideration to developing and perfecting our moral courage. The first step is to stop all dishonest behavior, make amends where we can, and leave the rest behind. Then we set our lives in order so that any action of ours may be shouted from the rooftops and not cause us shame or regret.

Next, practice every day with every person to treat them as we would like to be treated. As Jesus says, it is easy to love those who love us, what is tough is to love those who hate us. (Luke 6:31–35) This is a great test of our moral strength. We can be wise as a serpent—that is, we can avoid those who mean us harm, or we can hiss if necessary, rattle our tail in warning—but we are harmless as the dove. (Matthew 10:16) We don't return hate for hate, but prayerful love for hate. When we exercise our moral courage in this way, we glow with righteousness. This is the way to grow in God.

After all, how long has the Infinite put up with our insolence, indifference, neglect, and abuse? How would we have known to be different if not by the example of those spiritual souls that have gone before us? It is said that the Buddha had five hundred lifetimes of compassionate service to others before his shining example as the Buddha, the Anointed One! Are we to not follow in those hallowed footsteps? Surely, we are called. Who will follow?

Moral courage does not come naturally; selfish action to protect self-interest and the body is what is natural. The child gains in self-awareness and learns to say: "Mine!" This attachment continues as the natural way to be, into adulthood. It is not the natural way of worldly attachment we are called to live by, but the spiritual way of Divine giving. With developed moral courage, we overcome lower tendencies and become free and joyful spirits obeying a higher principle. May that moral courage so grow in us that it becomes a glowing example for all to follow and we can one day replace inferior human laws with a few simple verities of the Absolute.

Compassion

Compassion is the very watchword of saints and realized masters. Compassion is the extension of empathy for all suffering. In gaining realization of our oneness with the all-pervading Reality, it is realized that there is no difference between ourselves and all that we survey. Realized Beings have experienced existing as blades of grass over which people walk, they feel the vibration of stone and mountain while knowing it is not inert matter but living substance with vibration, consciousness, and spirit! With this expanded sense of identity, how could the Realized Beings not have an identification, understanding, and compassion for all suffering? It would be literally impossible.

There are those who, once gaining their realization, make a vow to continue to come back to this sphere where ignorance reigns in order to help those suffering from that ignorance to gain realization as well. Such is the love and compassion produced in such ones. In that pursuit of awakening humanity, fully realized Beings take on a garb of flesh and ignorance for the sake of humanity. They will see themselves, at least for a time, as separate from the realized state they hold so dear. With a crushing sense of confinement, they voluntarily focus their attention on a tiny mass of flesh and bone and identify with that, leaving behind their omnipresence, their bliss, their absolute oneness with the whole. The narrow confines of this state of ignorance, so newly worn, chafes against their freedom-loving nature. They feel themselves driven to regain the lost status of their Divine Heritage. Similar in nature to those souls who are nearing their "final mile" of realization, these great Beings enact the drama of gaining their realization once again. Oftentimes, they take on a much greater load of karma than the average individual, for they have come to pay the price of ransom for many. Far from having an easier time of it, since their cloak of ignorance has been so newly donned, they suffer greater extremes. Like the adults who take a load from their children's backpacks when they tire on a hike—so does the Realized master assume the burden of those who God has brought to them for help on their way.

More than others, these compassionate masters realize the paradise lost by all humanity. They know the huge loss entailed in suffering through narrow identification of body consciousness. They yearn to awaken us all to our real nature. But they find that although suffering abounds, most want to continue sleeping. Rather than the suffering spurring on the desire to awaken, the sleepyheads only roll over for some more sleep, asking for a happier dream! So, humanity dreams on. What can be done? Free will is the birthright of each soul. Our Mother Hamilton was such a one, a soul who came of her own free will. Not compelled by the law of cause and effect, only the law of compassion brought her to this vale of tears. She, along with her great Guru, Paramhansa Yogananda, came to awaken humanity from their terrible sleep.

In the same century that was graced with great spiritual masters and scientific advancements, it was also a century stricken with unparalleled suffering. It is said that Adolph Hitler killed twenty million people, Lenin twenty million, Joseph Stalin forty million, and Mao Tze Tung topped them all with sixty million. The additional horror to all? Most of these deaths were not of victims of war with another country, but of those who lived within the borders of the very same countries as these vicious leaders. It is an unaccountable mystery, how a Hitler, Lenin, Stalin, and Mao can coexist on the same planet as a Mahatma Gandhi, Paramhansa Yogananda, Mother Hamilton, and Babaji.

I believe that it was not only brave individuals giving their lives for freedom on the battlefield that has seen the brutality of these movements beaten back again and again, but the sacrifice of these great spiritual masters as well. These spiritual masters came at a crucial time in history. With the rapid development of scientific intelligence, in combination with these dark forces unleashed on the earth, the world could have easily seen ruthless dictators with nuclear weapons. And could there be any doubt that if any one of these cruel and ruthless leaders were in sole possession of such weapons, they would have hesitated to use them to advance their own selfish interests and self-aggrandizement? It is a dark thought to think of Hitler in sole possession of nuclear bombs and rockets. Master once stated that it was Jesus and Babaji who planted the idea in Hitler's vain mind to attack Russia. Without that blunder, it is very conceivable that Hitler would have overwhelmed Britain and had the time to develop not only the intercontinental missile, but nuclear weapons as well.[19] What a different world this would be!

True spiritual masters are ever helping the world to come into its rightful inheritance of the Kingdom of Heaven. But equally so, the supreme Creator has endowed each soul with free will. It is soul choice, individually and collectively, what kind of world we create. Really, we have everything needed to make this a paradise on earth. But the human heart must change from selfish self-interest to universal compassion. Think of the resources wasted in wars and conflict, and the intelligence and creativity employed for destructive ends. If this human genius can be focused on health, physical, mental, and spiritual, we could indeed have a heaven on earth. Simple laws of behavior make it so. Jesus summed it all up with the teaching to love God above all else, and to demonstrate that love toward all of humankind. If we emulated even a portion of the compassion that these great masters show us, how we, and this world, would change. We could not lie to another, cheat, steal, commit adultery, or even hurt and destroy our bodies through drugs, alcohol, or other destructive habits.

Compassion is not being a mush-head. It does not mean that feelings rule our actions. Rather, it is the clear knowledge that we cannot separate our own interests from all those around us. There is a saying that you "do not foul your own nest." Well, this world is our nest: not just our little family unit, but the world is our family; not just our local community, but the world is our community. In these days of overstimulation by the media, that may seem too much. But that is because we try to grasp the idea with our mind. Rather, it is something to be grasped by the spirit. We can start by opening

_____

19   That, along with Germany's declaration of war on the United States rank as two of the greatest blunders made by Hitler. Master said they also tried to stop the war, but karmic forces and human free will swept nations into the onslaught.

ourselves to those around us. We can do this silently, inwardly, by simply making forays of conscious compassion to the world around us. Most of us exist with a covering around us, around our hearts. We have toughened ourselves as proof against being overwhelmed by the misery within us and in the world at large. What will protect us in the forays of compassion? It is by first becoming established in Spiritual Consciousness.

Now that does not need to be an overwhelming assignment in itself! It can be quite simple. Let us start by feeling oneness with the heart of God, very simply, right inside our own heart. See the world as God must see this world. Most people wear veneers of knowing what they are about, but inside, they are not at all certain. We can feel ourselves in touch with a capacity for empathy for this human condition while, of course, including ourselves in this compassion as well. Remaining above it all, yet intimately connected with the pain and suffering of all, feel the pulse of humanity. So that we do not drown in the emotions of it all, it is important that we keep ourselves separate from it as well as connected with it. With conscious awareness, we feel the rhythms of all humanity, but even more so we feel Divine Compassion. From that compassion flows a continual stream of love. As the parent watches the child struggling to build something, the child wants no help, the wise parent realizes that the child must struggle on his or her own, and yet the parent can feel for the struggle of the child. There may be moments when a word from the adult here and there clears the way for the child, but timing is important. Likewise, struggling humanity is often not in need of advice, but wise compassion.

I have heard of a principle in physics that states: anything observed will be changed. Not through the intention of the observer, but as a natural course of nature. Human beings certainly fall under that principle as well. Whenever anything is observed, the observed will change. If the observer tries to change that which is observed, the observed oftentimes reacts with oppositional will. We can think of times when we have been on the receiving end of well-intentioned advice. Sometimes, even when we know it is sound advice, we may fight against it just out of general principle, being that the idea did not originate with us! But let someone be with us, compassionately, understandingly, and we will know the right thing to do spontaneously. Through acceptance from another, we learn acceptance of ourselves. Through self-acceptance, we automatically come into deeper touch with what our wisdom would naturally want us to know. From being compassionately observed, we find that we change automatically.

The purer the consciousness that is observing us, the more perfect a reflection we may see in our own soul. The more perfect the consciousness under observation, the more perfect a soul reflection may be seen by the observed. This is the principle underlying darshan. Darshan means literally "the sight of" another person. In India, it is being in the Presence of a realized Being. When a sincere devotee comes into the province of a realized Being, a transmission of compassionate Grace is transmitted to devotees, allowing them to know the true reflection of their Soul. The more refined the devotees, the more they may see for themselves their true Spiritual Nature. This is the Grace of being in the purified company of saints and realized Beings. To one who has no such sensitivities, they see an ordinary person and/or a reflection of themselves. However, the compassionate Grace flows to all alike.

Where East and West Meet

Why take on the ways of Eastern Mysticism when, born here in the West, we have traditions of the Judeo-Christians, Greek philosophers, and modern science philosophy? In my view, it is in the East, and particularly in India, that the true spirit of religion has been preserved. Not necessarily in the masses who attend religious fairs and practice temple worship, although, like all religions, men and women of Realization may be found in the outer reaches, here and there. Realized souls have kept ablaze the real purpose of life—conscious realization of God—and the means of achieving that lofty goal.

There is much evidence this was also part of early Judaism and Christianity. Mother Hamilton found a description of the Kriya Breath in the Old Testament. Jesus proclaimed the Kingdom of Heaven is within, and in the Gospel of St. Thomas, he taught that, "The kingdom of heaven is spread all over the earth." Through Jesus saying, "Keep thine eye single and thy whole body shall be filled with Light," he was drawing the attention inward. But material humans, weighted with body consciousness, brought these inner teachings to a worldly status. True, if enough of humankind were to achieve Heavenly Consciousness, the world as a whole would become Heavenly. But Jesus said there would be some standing here that shall not pass away before the coming of the Kingdom. (Matthew 16:28) He did not preach, nor do I think the prophets proclaimed, a distant event. They were speaking of imminent reality. The Kingdom of Heaven is at hand! That truth *is*; it always has been. But countless millions look to a distant day, now Jews and Christians together, for over two thousand years. Even for God, this represents a bit of time. Does he have no mercy in his timing, so fraught with shattered lives?

I say no! His promise has been fulfilled and continues to be fulfilled. Saints of all times and places have experienced the second coming and continue to do so. These are not dead promises, nor are they speaking of some unfulfilled future. They are living words demanding action and vigilance today. But what action? Certainly, we know the Ten Commandments, or at least we should, and we know the Golden Rule, (whether we practice it is a different question). We may say Grace before eating and when we attend church on Sunday. Beyond that, what do we do?

That is the question answered in the science of Yoga. It teaches that the Kingdom of Heaven is within, a state of Being to be realized, and it teaches the means for realizing it. For although it may be rightly said the Kingdom comes as a gift of Grace, nevertheless it requires the utmost effort to attain it. Are these not contradictory statements of fact? (No, in fact, they are both true.) Humans cannot, through their own effort, create or make the Kingdom of Heaven manifest. The fact is: it is our inheritance; it is built into us from our first inception as an individual soul. No amount of effort can take away from it nor add to it. It is ours already, a fact of Grace by design.

But, we must come of age to be able to accept our inheritance. It is like a young boy who is given the finest sports car in the world as a gift from his father. The boy in fact and in theory has the car, but really it cannot fulfill its real meaning and purpose for the boy until he has grown to maturity, both physically and emotionally. He first gets a tricycle, then a bicycle with training wheels, and so on; he progresses to more sophisticated modes of transportation. It would be a foolish and negligent father who gave the boy access to the most powerful and sophisticated car in the world on his sixteenth birthday. No, the father is going to look for signs of maturity, skill, and balance as the boy continues to work his way up to his inheritance.

So must we, as souls, work our way up in consciousness, proving as Jesus' story of the talents, we use what we have well. Otherwise, we may cause ourselves and others greater harm by having more than we have proven we can handle. When we are ready, we are given more. If we squander what we have been given, then even that which we have been given will be taken away. Harken well to this lesson; the law is exacting. But if we use well what we have been given, we receive more to work with. For Kriyabans, this means to exercise to full effect what we have been given. And, when experiences come and we handle them well by cultivating humility, selfless service, love, and wise decisions, and we fulfill our duties to the world and to God, then we earn greater capacity in God.

The wisdom of the East brings to us a guiding Light. We find the same seeds were cast into Judaism and Christianity, finding occasional flowering, but not the fullness realized in India. Why then, the material mind may ask, is India materially poor, and America materially rich? Like all nations, India has a karmic pattern. I doubt Jews or Christians of early eras would argue Rome's superior military and economic power proved it a superior spiritual power. But through all the dark times it has been subjected to, India survives with its universal outlook, realized Beings, and scriptural truths intact, dating back many thousands of years before our common era.

Yogis, those involved in worldly life and those separating themselves, even as Jesus did, from material possessions and relations, continue to hold aloft a Light for struggling humanity. And of all humanity, one here and there raises their head above the toil of the day to look to a further Light. And the Light, our inheritance, is there, waiting for maturing souls to come into their own. The East of India has kept both the goal and the means to the goal: i.e., methods of meditation, life-force control, pure love and devotion, sacred chanting, etc., in the forefront of their culture and philosophy.

The more I know of the sacred techniques and lore of India, the more I appreciate the wisdom of what I grew up with. Far from distancing me from Christianity, Judaism, Greek philosophy, or scientific philosophy, it has brought me closer to the beauty of what these have to offer. I find in what is called the Old Testament, beautiful truths of the highest nature. And the life and teachings of Jesus, the anointed of God, are filled with all the wisdom and perfection I find in the Eastern masters. In fact, the unfolding consciousness of humankind may draw inspiration from any of these wells, and others besides, and find themselves fed with the same sweet-tasting living waters of truth. To say the water from only one well will quench our thirst, or that other wells are filled by human effort and only our well by God's Grace, would be arrogant and shortsighted.

Would an omniscient God not provide the means of salvation, realization of our oneness with Him, to all people at all times when a sincere desire was present to do so? Who could look at the various religions of the world and say God forsook all but a chosen few? This would hardly prove to be just, or even make sense to a little human perspective, much less to a Divine one. Through God's Grace, we have available wisdom of the East that is also latent in all we have in the West. It is latent but not explicit. It is time for a grand awakening for all—everywhere. The need is great to establish the goal for humankind to fulfill their evolutionary destiny of Realization to their highest Nature, to become fully engaged in self-less service, and to acknowledge the transcendent love of God—and through the love of God, love for all His creation. We may all partake of the method-means of the East while deepening our appreciation and understanding of the ways of the West. One supports the other. No vanity, jealousy, narrow-mindedness, or other obstruction need inhibit our focus on how God has provided for the salvation of all humankind, East, West, North, and South. May it be ever so! God, Christ, Gurus.

What is True Joy

What is the nature of true joy?
If all the nations call me blessed
This is not everlasting joy.
But if all nations should revile me,
Persecute me, sneer at me,
And I stand unaffected,
One with God,
That is true joy!

If friends and lovers
Should say sweet things,
Honor me with praise,
This is not enduring joy.
But if close intimates
Should betray me,
Seek to destroy me

And I am forgiving in my heart
That is true joy!

If I should have all wealth,
Success and fame come my way,
Associates seek my favor and advice,
All the world, as it were,
Sits at my feet
That is <u>not</u> unfading joy.
But if fame and fortune desert me,
And my love remains complete
That is true joy!

If health and pleasure
Heap their bounty upon me,
And I say, "life is good,"
This is not absolute joy.
But if sickness visits me,
Beauty fails me, old age overtakes me,
And residing in my Spirit I say, "Life is good!"
That is true joy!

If I were to lead a good life
And at the end of my days
I enter the Heavenly Abode,
This is not supreme joy.
But if I were to live a life of slavery
And at the end, God should put me in hell,
And I saw some good I might do there,
And I felt gratitude to God for the opportunity,
<u>That</u> is true joy!

The Twenty-Four Aspects of Creation

Introduction

This addendum is my companion to a portrait of "The Cosmic Man." This drawing is inspired by Sri Yukteswar's description in *The Holy Science* of the creation of the cosmos. As the microcosm of man is designed as a reflection of the macrocosm of all creation, nay, even of God Itself, I have applied the various aspects of Sri Yukteswar's delineation of all creation to that of the inner cosmic man. This may give a deepened appreciation for this wonderful body temple—the temple not made with hands. Not only an appreciation for its remarkable design, but its ultimate potential to become a worthy temple of worship, that is a place of realization.

I have numbered twenty-four aspects to Sri Yukteswar's account, to be found in Chapter One of *The Holy Science*.[20] This should not be confused with his twenty-four principles he enunciates in his commentary on the scriptures, both of East and West. This correspondence of numbers came about as a synchronicity after I had drawn the portrait and then decided to add this companion writing with numbers. You will note my twenty- four aspects begin with Sat, that which is formless, beginningless, and endless. Sri Yukteswar's twenty-four principles represent the formation of creation after the effects of the ideas of time, space, and atom.

The creation of this picture and companion writing was done over a couple of days at a feverish pace, as if it could not be completed soon enough. As with all occurrences these days, I feel it was done through me, not coming, or originating, from me. I am aware that Divine Intelligence is perfect, pure, and complete unto itself. Whatever errors are inherent are due to the limitation of the human instrument. I say inherent because human instruments will always express some apparent flaw. The greater the purity of the

---

20   *The Holy Science* by Jnanavatar Swami Sriyuktewsar Giri, Chapter 1, Sutra 2, published by Yogoda Sat-Sanga Society of India, 3rd Edition, 1949.

consciousness of the instrument, the closer will be the approxima-tion to the original purity of Divine Consciousness.

The fact that any truth expressed comes through a human mind, no matter how purified, and the fact that it is received through a human mind, require that it will never represent absolute Truth. The greatest work an expressed truth will generate will be for the inspiration and guidance provided to bring questing souls to their own direct perception of Truth, which resides beyond the mind. This is my wish for you: as you read, think about, absorb, and real-ize the great potential that man is, being a Son of God.

I have added a number of quotes from the Bible, particularly from Genesis, that will add appreciation for those ancient scripts and a sense of wonder at their close approximations to their Hindu cousins. At the time of this writing, my body feeling the strain of inflexible creative flow of the last few days, I bow down in gratitude to Sri Yukteswar and the great spiritual Masters, both East and West.

Those who are granted views from places on high stand on the shoulders of these great spiritual giants. May you be blessed, as they were so obviously blessed, to realize your inherent oneness with Sat Chid Ananda and ever reside in the consciousness of the Son of God.

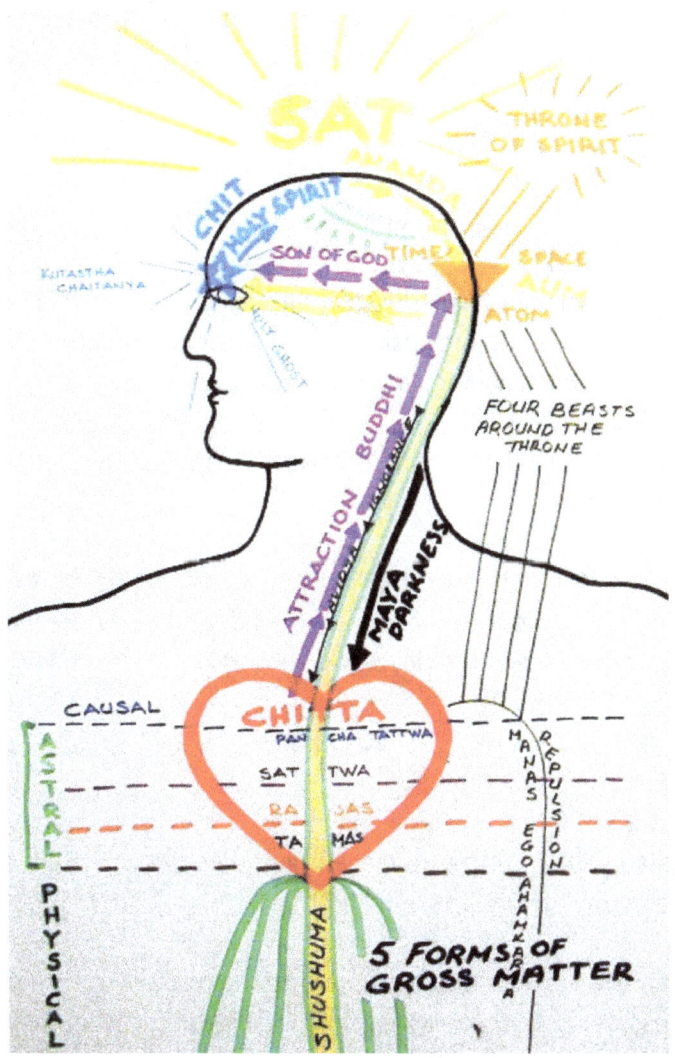

The Cosmic Human.

Twenty-Four Aspects of Creation

Sutra 1

Aspect 1

SAT: Eternal Father: the only Real Substance. Sat is one, without a second. It is without form, beginningless and endless. It is unknowable by the intellect, and resides beyond all creation; yet, it is the very Substance from which all of creation is created.

> Hear O Israel, the Lord our God is one Lord. (Deuteronomy 6:4)

> In the Beginning, God created heaven and earth. And the earth was without form and void, and darkness was upon the face of the deep. (Genesis 1:12)

Sutra 2

Aspect 2

CHIT (also CHID): Omniscient feeling makes the world conscious; it is the source of Divine Love and Light.

> And the Spirit of God moved upon the waters (consciousness). And God said, Let there be Light: and there was Light. (Genesis 1:2–3)

Aspect 3

ANANDA: Eternal Joy: Shakti, Almighty Force, that produces the world.[21]

---

21   *The Holy Science* originally states Ananda (Eternal Joy) *produces* this world; editors later changed this to *produced*.

Let there be a firmament in the midst of the waters, and let it divide the waters from the waters (the idea of separation required for creation)... and God called the firmament Heaven... and God said, Let the waters under heaven be gathered together in one place, and let the dry land appear (the idea of physical creation)... and God called the dry land Earth. (Genesis 1:6–10)

Aspect 4

Prakriti: Chid and Ananda together demonstrate the Nature (Prakriti) of God the Father (Sat).

And God made the firmament (Light of heaven, Chid), and divided the waters (through the Shakti of Ananda) which were under the firmament (of a lower vibration rate) from the waters which were above the firmament (Sat nature of God): and it was so. (Genesis 1:7)

Sutra 3

Aspect 5

Aum: The manifestation of Prakriti is the vibration of Aum, Amen (the Word). It comes as the sound vibration of all creation.

These things saith the Amen, the faithful and true witness, the beginning of the creation of God. (John 1:1–3)

And Aum, the Word, manifests as:

Aspect 6

Desa: the idea of division.

And God divided the Light from the darkness. (Genesis 1:4) And God said Let there be a firmament in the midst of the waters, and let it divide the waters from the waters.

> And God made the firmament, and divided the waters which were under the firmament from the waters which were above the firmament (Genesis 1:6–7) and called the dry land Earth; and the gathering of the waters, seas (Genesis 1:10) and God said Let the earth bring forth grass, the herb yielding seed, and the fruit tree yielding fruit after his kind, whose seed is in itself (multiplicity through division after division of that which is indivisible Substance is made possible by Maya). (Genesis 1:11)

Aspect 7
Kala: idea of change.

> And God said, Let there be Lights in the firmament of heaven to divide the day from the night; and let them be for signs, and for seasons, and for days and years. (Genesis 1:11)

The ensuing effect is:

Aspect 8
Anu: the idea of particles—Innumerable atoms.

> And God said, Let the waters under heaven be gathered together (density of mass) unto one place (material creation) and let the dry land appear. (Genesis1: 9)

The Word (Aum, Amen), time (Kala), Space (Desa), and the atom (Anu) are the four ideas projected by the Eternal Father (Sat) through Mother Nature (Prakriti). The Aum vibration of the Word resonates with the highest vibrational nature of God, Sat. Therefore, it can be said that the Word (Aum) and God are one. The analogies often quoted are: just as fire and its burning power cannot be separated, and, just as the substance of milk and its color of white cannot be separated, so God (as formless Spirit) and His creation (God with form through Aum) are inseparable.

Sutra 4

Aspect 9
Throne of Spirit: Aum, Kala, Desa, and Anu make up the throne of Spirit. The Creator shining upon this Throne creates this universe.

> And immediately I was in the Spirit (raised in high consciousness): and behold (through inner vision), a throne was set in heaven (a revelation of the creative forces became clear in high spiritual vibration). (Revelation 4:2)

Aspect 10
Maya: These four ideas of the throne, which are represented by the idea that atoms beget creation, which in total create Maya, the darkness, as they delude the senses into thinking creation is absolute reality, keeping the individual from comprehending, or realizing, the great Light of God's Being.

> And God said Let there be light (of Chid nature), and there was Light (feeling consciousness). And God saw that it was good (an uplifting vibration): And God divided the Light from the darkness (lower creative vibration). And God called the Light day (enlightenment). And the darkness he called night (uncomprehending of Truth, Light, the Real Substance of creation). (Genesis 1:3–4)

Aspect 11
Avidya is the individual atom that creates ignorance, as it makes man ignorant of his own Self.

> In him (the Word) was life; and the Life was the Light
> of men. And the Light shineth in the darkness; and the
> darkness comprehended it not. (John 1:3–5)

Aspect 12

Four Beasts in the midst and around the throne: When man identifies with body consciousness: i.e., the darkness of Maya and the
ignorance of Avidya, the mind is confused with the seemingly final
realities of time, space, and materiality built of atoms. These illu-
sionary ideas emanate from the Aum power vibration and interfere with the deluded mind's ability to comprehend the primordial
Light of God. Therefore, these four creative principles are pictured
as four beasts around the Throne of Spirit when seen from manas,
sense-deluded mind. In his revelatory vision, St. John the Divine
sees the true nature of this reality as omniscient, simultaneously
seeing before and behind.

> And in the midst of the throne, and round about the
> throne, were four beasts full of eyes before and behind.
> (Revelation 4:6)

Sutra 5

Aspect 13

Kutastha Chaitanya: Omniscient love (Chid) manifests as the Self.
Kutastha Chaitanya (centered in the body at the ajna) is the power
of attraction of love, which is the power of God Itself. It is the savior aspect sown throughout all creation. This Light that draws all
to SAT, God the Father, may be seen at the ajna, the third eye point.

> The Light of the body is the eye: if therefore thine eye
> be single, thy whole body shall be filled with light. But
> if thine eye be evil (Avidya or ignorance consciousness),

thy whole body shall be full of darkness (perceiving only delusive Maya). If therefore the light that is in thee be darkness, how great is that darkness! (The Consciousness is filled with confusion, error, separation, and ignorance of tamas. How very true to call this state a great darkness!). (Matthew 6:22–23)

Aspect 14

The Holy Ghost: The Omniscient love of the Kutastha Chaitanya shines out to all creation (as the Holy Ghost), calling its children home. But the children are full of Avidya, ignorance, and do not care for the Light. They reject the light that is constantly shining upon them.

That was the true Light which lighteth every man that cometh into the world. He (the Light) was in the world, and the world was made by him, and the world knew him not. He came unto his own, and his own received him not. (John 1:9–11)

Aspect 15

Son of God: When man accepts this light, is able to comprehend it through Self- realization, and is attracted by the love of universal Nature, he becomes a Son of God, Purusha.[22]

But as many received him, to them gave he power to become the Sons of God, even to them that believe on his name (are uplifted on the sound current of Aum, Amen): which were born not of blood, nor of the will of flesh, nor of the will of man, but of God (drawn up by the Grace of

---

22   In Sankya Philosophy, Purusha is the capital "S" of Self. In other Indian philosophies, purusha is a lower-case "p," and will translate to mean man, or the animating principle in man. Sri Yukteswar draws from the analytical Sankya meaning.

Divine love and reborn in the light of the Kutastha Chaitanya, Christ Consciousness). (John 1:12–13)

Sutra 6

Aspect 16
Chitta: This atom (Avidya, individualized ignorance), under the influence of Chid, universal love, creates a spiritualized field, like a magnet aura, whereby the atom becomes conscious with the power of feeling. This is called Chitta (the calm state of mind). And like a magnet, Chitta has a positive and negative pole. The positive pole takes on the quality of Chid, the magnetic drawing power of Divine Love. The negative pole is repulsion to the light and continues the outward, or downward, journey of the atom of ignorance and darkness.

Aspect 17
Buddhi: The positive pole of Chitta, when spiritually oriented, becomes Buddhi, or Sattva, discriminative Intelligence. With Buddhi, the individual can determine Truth, the Real, Sat (God the Father) from the unreal (ignorance and darkness) and is drawn up by Divine Love.

Aspect 18
Manas: The negative pole of Chitta has repulsion to the Light and manifests as Manas, drawn to ananda (lower-case "a"), enjoyment of the senses.

Aspect 19
Ego: It is in Manas, the sense-oriented mind, that jiva, the self, is formed with Ahamkara, the ego, the idea of separate existence.

And God made two great lights: the greater Light (the sun of Kutastha Chaitanya, centered in the ajna) to rule the day (Buddhi that brings the light of discernment) and the lesser Light (solar plexus, human intuition, the moon or second sun center) to rule night (to guide manas through intuition while under the influence of darkness, Maya, and ignorance, Avidya). (Genesis 1:16)

Sutras 7–10

Aspect 20

Pancha Tattwa: (Pancha: five, Tattwa: aura, electricity, or principles.) The Chitta, the spiritualized Atom of the heart, produces five different sorts of aura electricities as the Causal Body. These five electricities,[23] being under the influence of the Holy Ghost, drawing them to Sat, produce a magnetic field of Sattva Buddhi, the Intelligence. These five ideas create the body of the Causal Being, the Purusha or Son of God.

And God said, Let the waters (consciousness) bring forth abundantly the moving creature (that which allows for movement, or a body: the primal body of Causal Man), that hath life (electricity ideas or the principles that make up the body), and fowl (higher-flown thought forms) that may fly above the earth (resides beyond the material mind) in the open firmament (the *firmament* is the astral heaven and the *open firmament* goes beyond the astral to the Causal Realm). (Genesis 1:20)

---

23   The number 5 is a recurring theme for man: five senses, five fingers per hand, five toes per foot, and when man stands upright with his feet apart, arms outstretched, and head erect, he is in the form of a five-pointed star. These physical attributes have their root cause in the Pancha Tattwa. The five-pointed star of Christ Consciousness, beheld at the Kutastha Chaitanya, leads man back to pure causal consciousness. By going through the star, man ascends to Sat, God the Father.

Aspect 21–23

The Astral Body: Made of the five electricities (idea principles) drawn from the Causal Realm or body. At this point, the three Gunas come into manifestation. The three Gunas are sattva (positive), rajas (neutral), and tamas (negative).[24]

Aspect 21

Sattva: The positive attributes of the five electricities are Jnanendriyas (the organs of sense for both astral and physical experience, these make up the body of Manas.)

Aspect 22

Rajas: The neutralizing attributes of the five electricities are the organs of action (Karmendriyas). These organs allow for excretion, generation, speech, motion (feet), and manual skill (hands). These electricities make up the energetic body (prana) from the heart.

Aspect 23

Tamas: The negative attributes of the five electricities are the objects of the senses and when united with the organs of sense (rajasic organs of action), they satisfy the desires of the heart (for sensory life). This completes the astral body.

> And God created great whales (under water is the subconscious mind repository of Tamasic qualities, the original word in Genesis also meant sea monsters and dragons)...and every winged fowl (birds are lofty thoughts of sattvic qualities)...And God said, let the

---

24   Sri Yukteswar again uses Sankya designations for the Gunas that may vary from other definitions you have heard. There are six main philosophical systems in India, Sankya being one of them. These philosophies share many words but give differing definitions. (Fortunately, becoming realized does not require mastering all six philosophical systems!) These scriptural interpretations are meant to orient the mind to the true purpose of life: the realization of God as Sat Chid Ananda.

earth bring forth the living creature after his kind (earth is neutralizing rajasic qualities). (Genesis 1:21–24)

Sutras 11, 12

Aspect 24

Five Forms of Gross Matter: The five tamasic electricities of the astral body combined together produce the idea of gross matter, which appear to us in five varieties: The solid (Kshiti), the Liquid (Ap), the fiery (Tejas), the gaseous (Marut), and the ethereal (Akasa or Vyona).

> And God said let us make man in our image (according to the creative principles just enunciated), after our likeness (having his origins in Sat, unmanifested Spirit): and let him have domain over fish of the sea (self-mastery of the subconscious mind), and over fowl of the air (higher intelligence), and over cattle, and over all the earth, and over every creeping thing upon the earth (self-mastery over the body consciousness and the subtle astral and causal bodies. Guided by the twin Lights of Divine Christ Consciousness of the ajna and human intuition of the solar plexus (the second sun), man was designed to live free in harmony with nature and Spirit through the guidance of intuition at the solar plexus and the wisdom Light at the ajna). (Genesis 1:26)

Summary: This completes the 24 Principles that clothe the Son of God (Purusha), in Its various bodies. They are:

1. Chitta: Intelligent Consciousness, power of feeling
2. Buddhi: Discriminative intelligence
3. Manas: Sense Mind
4. Ahamkara: Ego

5–9.   Jnanendriyas: Five instruments of sense
       perception
10–14. Karmendriyas: Five instruments of action
15–19. Tanmatras: Five objects of the senses: smell, taste,
       sight, touch, and sound
20–24. Gross matter: Five ideas of gross matter.

And around about the throne were four and twenty
seats; and upon the seats I saw four and twenty elders.
(Revelation 4:4)

Creation comes about as a projected idea from Sat, brought to
conscious awareness through Chid, and into being through the
Blissful vibratory power of Ananda. God assumes a mask, then
divides into innumerable forms for His masquerade play, His
lila. We are meant always to remember our Divine origin and not
become attached to the ephemeral creation. This attachment creates identification with the forces of duality and causes misery and
suffering.

And the lord God commanded the man, saying, Of every
tree of the garden thou mayest freely eat (all vibratory
creation is good to experience and does not bind the
soul): But of the tree of the knowledge of good and evil
(duality consciousness), thou shalt not eat of it (not identify with duality): for in the day that thou eatest (bring
the idea in for consumption), thou shalt surely die (will
enter into realms of birth and death and through that
identification, create suffering for yourself by forgetting
your Divine origins). (Genesis 2:16–17)

God's essential Nature is Bliss (Ananda), Conscious Awareness
(Chid), and knowledge of the Eternal Self (Sat). By reestablishing

our consciousness in Him (realizing our Sat-nature or His likeness), we establish the correct relationship with creation (His image). We once again are seated on the throne of Supreme Consciousness.

To him that overcometh (raises life-force to Christ Consciousness) will I grant to sit with me in my throne (reside in Christ Consciousness), even as I overcame (gained self-mastery and surrendered all) and am set down with my Father in His throne (in Christ Consciousness one rises to know Sat Consciousness as well). He that hath an ear (one who has receptive consciousness), let him hear what the Spirit saith unto the churches (open that receptivity to the vibratory power that awakens the "churches" of all the chakras). (Revelation 3: 21–22) (From 2001 version.)

Behold, I stand at the door (the ajna) and knock (the sound of Aum, Amen at the medulla): if any man hear my voice (the Aum), and open the door (enter through the ajna into Light of Chit), I will come in to him (the soul will be uplifted into Christ Consciousness) and will sup with him, and he with me (the individual soul will be in communion with Christ Consciousness). To him that overcometh (gains self-mastery and withdraws life-force up the spine to the ajna) will I grant to sit by me in my throne (become established in Christ Consciousness), even as I also overcame (gained complete self-mastery and surrender), and am sat down (no longer struggling i.e., in a natural state) with my Father in His Throne (Christ Consciousness merges with Sat Consciousness in Sahaja Samadhi). He that hath an ear (one who has receptive attunement), let him hear what the Spirit saith unto the churches (experience the Aum vibration awakening the chakras to higher spiritual Consciousness). (Revelation 3:20–22) (From 2018 version.)

This creation was meant for soul enjoyment and experience while remaining one with the Father, Sat-Consciousness. May you be awakened to the real Nature of your Father God and become established in Sat Chid Ananda, forever and ever! Aum-en.

... And God saw everything that he had made, and behold, it was very good. (Genesis 1:31)

Creation Story

I am going to tell you a story of Creation.

In the beginning, God was. Of course, there was not really a beginning because God is beyond time, but we have to use that kind of language in order for it to make sense to us. Anyway, as I say, in the beginning, God was. God was complete, whole, one without a second.

Then the creative juices in God thought up a play, a wonderful drama to express Himself. Why create? Because it is His Nature to create, that's why. He thought to Himself (He could only think to Himself since there was no other), "Wouldn't it be fun to create scenery and characters that are not omnisciently aware at all times? These characters, who are none other than Myself, since there is no other, can carry on operating through limited sense perception, growing and developing along individual lines. Let's just see where My mind takes Me in creating all of this."

So quick as a thought, God (Sat) projected out lovely stage lighting (Chid) so He could see what He was doing. Then He made a joy-filled backdrop screen (Ananda/Prakriti) for contrast. On that backdrop, God got busy and one could hear the sound (Aum) of further construction. Up popped a stage, creating a space (Desa), and then a really unique creation that allowed for a sequence of events called time (Kala). Oh, God was really pleased with this beginning and was having so much fun, and exclaimed, "This is Good!"

The show, God's lila, was really starting to get interesting, and He was most fascinated to see what He would dream up next! Suddenly, a large vibrational sound (Aum) could be heard, stage left. Particles (Anu) streamed onto the stage (Maya). At first, it did not look like much, but then in a sudden burst of thought (Causal), the particles exploded like fireworks in the sky; all exclaimed in thrills of ooohs and aaahs. A big bright explosion of Light, looking like a large colorful balloon (Astral Worlds), formed into gorgeous expanses of galaxies, stars, and planets. Oh, what variety and beauty, this was getting better all the time!

Now different ones emerged out of the whole as individual points of consciousness (jivas or souls), thinking they too would like to create. These Causal Beings were a combination of producers and screenwriters for the play, the idea people. Others wanted to be directors and actors for the play and dove right into the action as Astral Beings. As quick as a thought, they projected themselves into the dream creation of the Astral Worlds, which became teeming with life. They donned costumes of various forms and learned to operate the sense controls, moving pieces of the sets around and interacting with others doing the same. Oh, the joy, fun, and love of it all were wonderful.

God then thought to Himself, "All are having such a great time acting, having control of the sets, and playing their individual roles. What more can I do? Hmmmm? I know, let's slow down the rate of vibration of the particles, making it different from the bright balloon of the Astral Worlds, thus making the particles denser, more like molasses."

"Hmmm, what is molasses?"

"Don't know, have yet to think that up. I will figure that out as I go along." (God talks to Himself like that, probably a product of spending too much time with Himself!)

On stage left again was heard a deep rumbling sound. A stream of different particles other than the Astral World came onto the stage. Well, this new development had the attention of the audience, writers, and actors. What in the world was going to happen now?! The deep rumbling grew louder and with a sudden bang! (That made everyone jump in delight.) A much smaller, denser Material Creation came about. All felt Joy and Love as they gazed on this new arrival; much darker than the balloon, it hung like a dense basket under the colorful balloon.

What marvels might there be next, they wondered? The actors in the Astral balloon were especially intrigued about the Material Creation since they were having so much fun in the Astral. God said to all:

> Ok, here's the deal. If you go into this new creation, the Material World, it has some unusual properties. I made this creation an even more complex maze than you have seen before. If, in your sojourn there, you stay focused on your connection with Me, you can get out anytime you want. But! If you identify with your character while there, you will become lost (Avidya) in the maze (Maya). Now, of course, in reality, you are never really separate from Me, but if you identify with your character in the maze, you will forget Me. This is a much denser world, so it is harder to move and there are not as many control options. However, I think many of you will find it a very interesting challenge to enter this maze and then find your way back out. Like all creation, what you experience is really a projection of your own thoughts.

Some stood back, not sure they wanted anything to do with this darker, less free Material World. Others had their curiosity aroused and looked deeper into this dark maze, fascinated at the challenge of finding their way through it. Some thought, "What if I get lost? But did the Creator not say I could never really be separate from Him, it was all a projection of my own thoughts?"

As the creative "Bang" started to coalesce, there appeared some interesting prospects. "Oh, there is a planet forming now! Watch as it all comes together, isn't it fascinating and beautiful?" Losing any inhibition, gazing at the forming planet, wondering what it would be like to experience oneself as flowing red-hot lava rock, the soul, quick as a thought, merged into that projected creation.

"Oh, isn't this interesting? Flowing from mountain to sea as molten rock, hardening now, feeling the pressure of other rock pushing against me. Ahhh." And so, the play proceeds. When one is done exploring the idea of being mineral, the mineral idea falls away like an outer sheath revealing a new life as vegetation. When the soul is done exploring vegetation, another sheath falls away and reveals the freedom of movement as animal. And when done exploring animal, that sheath layer falls away to reveal human. Working from one maze to another, mineral, vegetable, animal, and then human, the course is run.

Through each successive layer, an unconscious principle prompts the soul to become more conscious of the various levels of Material Creation. Maze after maze presents itself, going deeper into identification with these strange, fascinating, and mysterious creations. An unconscious drive leads the soul on and on, all the while a certain feeling of connection with the Creator is always in the background. At last, the soul knows what it is to be human.

At first, the human incarnation is much like the animal. Instinct and conditioning form most of the behavioral patterns. The animal mind (manas) is rooted in body consciousness and its immediate surroundings. It is rough play, but all the while, the soul feels committed to working its way through the maze. Through successive human births, the brain and capacity for higher thought develop. The higher-functioning mind (Buddhi) is at first focused on solving human dilemmas. Unlike the animal, humans are self-aware. Through that self-awareness, they think more about their world and its creative possibilities. Rules of conduct, organization, and modes of worship begin to take shape.

When animal instinct dominates the human's thinking, the idea of "I," "me" and "mine" are limited in scope. With this higher-functioning mind, those ideas become more developed. The mind recognizes the notion of free will and the consequences of choice. The play for the soul gets even more complex and interesting at this time. Higher thought leads to more experimentation than before. Deeds not even considered to this point, now have an allure. Sensual, delightful, soul-forgetting joys and worldly ambitions look interesting. But somewhere, deeply embedded in the consciousness, is a warning signal. It is telling the soul, "No, don't go there! If you do, you will lose all connection with Me!" The signal keeps sounding, but... "Wouldn't it be nice to try? It couldn't hurt to try." The idea of willfully going against an inner knowledge of what is right increases the idea of "I" and "mine."

When the soul chooses to go against that inner warning, a predictable set of consequences is set into motion. A series of inner states of mind emerge: shame, fear, jealousy, anger, and even murder. And, murder is not killing for food or self-protection, but due only to these new lower states of mind. The idea of a fall can only come from self-awareness that knows better. This means a self-awareness of good and bad and a freedom of will to go against what one knows to be right. This act of will completes the identification with "I" and "mine" and seals off the connection with the Creator. This is the fall of the human. Once some souls discover the apparent power of "I" and "mine," they go about indoctrinating newly emerging humans from the animal kingdom into this new ideal. Life after life reinforces the notion of separation from the Creator and the predominance of might makes "right" until it is an unquestioned belief. Life loses real Love and Joy.

Development of language, the study of mathematics, observation of the stars, systems of laws and other signals of higher intelligence gradually become more pronounced as the information produces more successful and stable societies. Philosophers question the human's place in creation; the whys and wherefores of existence challenge some of the great minds. Superstitions are debunked and reason gains more of a foothold. The development of ethics from the higher reasoning brain (Buddhi) works in competition with the wants and desires of Manas, making for many ethical challenges. The increasing body of human knowledge increases their dominance in the world and heightens the sense of safety and control. However, the development of reason without the guidance and the directional rudder of the pure vibration of the Holy Spirit (Chit) ultimately results in both an unstable human personality and society.

Gaining outward dominance does not produce the hoped-for bliss the earlier human had once thought it would. The development of higher reason is but a stepping-stone to something higher still. The reasoning mind, disappointed by the results of its worldly gains, is then turned inward to discover more fundamental truths of existence and the meaning of life (an important direction in the maze has been turned). An inner attraction draws the consciousness to realms beyond the Material World. This results in an inner illumination that transcends the reasoning mind. It taps directly into the intuitive apprehension of Truth (the Buddhi Mind illumined by the Holy Ghost). With this transcendent perception fresh in the mind, the soul begins its upward ascent in earnest in order to become established in higher Spiritual Consciousness.

In this ascension, the soul's upward pull from the Holy Ghost is intersected by the repulsion (Ahamkar) exerted by attachment to the body (Manas). This polarity represents the greatest potential for the fall of the human, for it is here that the soul can most profoundly turn away from its inner calling. When the desire for inner illumination draws the devotee to God, simultaneously, the temptation for earthly existence is very strongly felt. By turning away from the higher calling to God, humans push away the inner prompting for their own Awakening. This leads individuals further away from the light of their redemption—rather, into the maze and away from freedom.

As humans ascend this spinal stairway of consciousness, at each successive level the horizontal opposition of the worldly attraction seeks to deflect or turn downwards the upward Spiritual drive. The meeting of this oppositional energy and the overcoming of it is the Mystical Crucifixion. The horizontal worldly desires cross the vertical Spiritual energy coming up the spine and forms the cross at each one of these junctures: the heart, the throat, and the medulla.

Through overcoming each of these obstacles and drawing all energies up to the third eye point (the ajna or Kutastha Chaitanya), the world is seen as a dream and the inner Light is seen as the preeminent Reality (exit stage right). Through the overcoming of the lower mind (Manas) and the purification of the higher mind (Buddhi), the power of the Holy Spirit (Chit) magnetically draws the consciousness, and thereby the soul, back to its origins of pure God (Sat). The inner and outer Realities are now seen as one complete whole, as the Creator and creation are known to be one, without separation. This illumination leads humans out of the maze (Maya) and back to their origins of universal Love and Bliss. They are once again established in the Truth of their origin as Self—in absolute freedom as Sat Chid Ananda.

OM TAT SAT

APPENDIX

Babaji-Inspired Clearing/ Charging Exercises

Yogacharya David R. Hickenbottom

Which of you has sat for your practice of meditation and felt restless, distracted, wanting to "do anything other than this," tired (all of a sudden)—in short: resistant? Well, everyone! You may have the will power to "gut it through," or may develop a pattern of avoidance, cut your mediation short, or other coping mechanisms. The problem, in case you were wondering, is not unique with you! Your spiritual path requires eternal vigilance, tenacity, strength, and surrender. And, fortunately for those on the Kriya path, shortcuts!

Do shortcuts amount to cheating? No. It is the use of intelligent will to use universal principles to enhance growth. There was a movie called "Chariots of Fire." In the movie, as the story is told, an athlete from England went to a prestigious university. The student had employed a coach, something "one just does not do." The student argued with school authorities who had the assumption that an athlete was somehow just "born." It was somehow unbecoming to sweat, learn, and grow into someone who excelled. It was ironic that professional educators of the mind were insistent that professional education of the body was inappropriate. With the help of the coach, the student athlete won a gold medal at the Olympics.

So, with yogis, for those who have a definite practice for Self-realization, the application of intelligent coaching helps all to excel. Now, a new process for helping to clear the physical, emotional-energetic, and mental bodies has been put forward. Through inner revelation, a means of clearing the nadis, the subtle nerves of the astral body, and recharging the whole system, is available.

In a 3-day silent retreat, you will learn how to start cleansing the body of disturbances that lead to physical, emotional, and mental unrest and imbalances. These imbalances may also result in illnesses in any of these three bodies. In these safe, simple but powerful techniques, sadhakas will learn, step by step, the methods for clearing disturbances, or starting a clearing process and then powerfully charging the system with the prana of life-force. The retreat begins Friday evening and ends midday on Monday.

Retreat Schedule

April 6–9, 2001

(* * Indicates bell 5 minutes before we start, except for Wake up.)

Friday

    6:00 pm . . . . Evening Meal

    7:30 . . . . Orientation

Saturday

  * * 5:30 am . . . . Wake Up Bell

  * * 6:00 . . . . Kriya Yoga (initiates only)

  * * 6:30 . . . . Meditation (for all)

    7:00 . . . . Group Chanting (for all)

    7:30 . . . . **Breakfast & Morning Chores**

  * * 9:00 . . . . Energization and Light Stretching

    9:15. . . . . Introduction to Exercise 1

    9:30 . . . . Practice Exercise 1

    10:30 . . . . Write Observations

    . . . . **Break**

  * * 11:15. . . . . Read Responses to Observations, Questions & Answers

    12:00 . . . . **Lunch, Afternoon Chores, & Rest**

  * * 2:00 . . . . Introduction to Exercise 2

    2:15. . . . . Practice Exercise 2

```
       3:15. . . . . . . . . . . . . . Write Observations
            . . . . . . . . . . . . . Break
  * * 3:45 . . . . . . . . . . . . . Read Responses to Observations,
                                     Questions & Answers
       4:00 . . . . . . . . . . . . . Introduction to Exercise 3
       4:15. . . . . . . . . . . . . Practice Exercise 3
       5:15. . . . . . . . . . . . . Write Observations
            . . . . . . . . . . . . . Break
  * * 5:45 . . . . . . . . . . . . . Read Responses to Observations,
                                     Questions & Answers
       6:00 . . . . . . . . . . . . . Dinner, Evening Chores,
                                     & Rest
  * * 7:30. . . . . . . . . . . . . . Introduction to Fire Ceremony
       7:50 . . . . . . . . . . . . . Fire Ceremony
       8:15. . . . . . . . . . . . . End of Day's Schedule
```

Sunday

```
  * * 5:30 . . . . . . . . . . . . . Wake Up Bell
  * * 6:00 . . . . . . . . . . . . . Kriya Meditation (initiates only)
  * * 6:30 . . . . . . . . . . . . . Meditation (for all)
       7:00 . . . . . . . . . . . . . Group Chanting
       7:30 . . . . . . . . . . . . . Breakfast & Morning Chores
  * * 9:00 . . . . . . . . . . . . . Energization and Light Stretching
       9:15. . . . . . . . . . . . . Introduction to Exercise 4
       9:30 . . . . . . . . . . . . . Practice Exercise 4
      10:30. . . . . . . . . . . . . Write Observations
            . . . . . . . . . . . . . Break
  * * 11:15. . . . . . . . . . . . . Read Responses to Observations,
                                     Questions & Answers
      12:00 . . . . . . . . . . . . . Lunch, Afternoon Chores, & Rest
  * * 2:00 . . . . . . . . . . . . . Introduction to Exercise 5
       2:15. . . . . . . . . . . . . Practice Exercise 5
       3:15. . . . . . . . . . . . . Write Observations
            . . . . . . . . . . . . . Break
```

* * 3:45 . . . . Read Responses to Observations,
Questions & Answers

4:00 . . . . Introduction to Exercise 6

4:15. . . . . Practice Exercise 6

5:15. . . . . Write Observations

. . . . **Break**

* * 5:45 . . . . Read Responses to Observations,
Questions & Answers

6:00 . . . . **Dinner, Evening Chores, & Rest**

Evening is free: read additional materials, walk, meditate, etc.

Monday

* * 5:30 . . . . Wake Up Bell

* * 6:00 . . . . Kriya Meditation (initiates only)

* * 6:30 . . . . Meditation (all)

7:00 . . . . Group Chanting

7:30 . . . . **Breakfast & Morning Chores**

* * 9:00 . . . . Putting It All Together: Integrating
Clearing/Charging Exercises

9:30 . . . . Practice Integrating Exercises

10:30 . . . . **Break**

* *11:00 . . . . Questions and Answers, open
talking for all who wish

12:00 . . . . **Lunch, Afternoon Chores, Rest, &
Closure**

Babaji-Inspired Clearing/ Charging Exercises

Yogacharya David R. Hickenbottom

Introduction

The Clearing/Charging Breathing Exercises help you to clear away life-energy blocks and enter into deeper states of meditation. You learn, through simple and easy-to-use breathing techniques, how to clear the subtle nadi nerves.

According to yogis, there are seventy-two thousand nadis, subtle astral nerves, in the human body. Each of these nerves is a carrier for a subtle intelligent energy called prana. Prana is responsible for your life in the physical, etheric, and astral bodies. It is the intelligent force of prana that brings health. As well, it enhances the ability to move, to breathe, and to in all ways function.

Prana is interactive; that is, it carries out functions of the body automatically, and it is responsive to our mental and emotional instructions. Prana operates through your physical system to, for example, make adrenal glands respond to danger, ready for fight or flight. When you are in chronic danger without the possibility of fight or flight, then you start to shut down your connection with the body to protect yourself. This mental/emotional reaction restricts prana from areas of the body. Many people are in the position of either being constantly stimulated to a reactive mode of fight or flight or with no outlets of fight or flight, they shut down their ability to respond. Either way, they throw their system out of balance, and waste, or shut off, life-energy.

Imagine, if you will, that the intricate system of pranic nerves (nadis) are like busy freeways, with entrances/exits and surface streets. When the instructions are given by the brain to close down parts of the pranic traffic system (due to some trauma), a "traffic jam" starts in one area and begins to affect other areas. This traffic jam of prana creates disturbances in the physical, emotional, and mental bodies. If these disturbances are temporary, the crisis leaves, new instructions come that open the highway systems again, and balance is restored. Gradually, all the nadis are soon flowing again carrying their vital, life-giving energy to the whole system.

However, if no new instructions are given, the nadis/nerves will continue to be overly stimulated or shut down and a chronic condition ensues. This lack of balance in the pranic system can lead to chronic fatigue, post-traumatic stress syndrome, and other physical, emotional, and mental disturbances or illnesses. No new instructions are given to restore balance because it is judged by the conscious and/or unconscious mind that you are in an unsafe world. This view of an unsafe world leads to chronic rajasic stimulation, leading to restlessness of the body and mind.

When you attempt to enter into deeper states of meditation, you find yourself facing chronically closed or stimulated systems. The process of meditation withdraws prana from the body and focuses it in the higher regions of the spine and brain. This inward meditative state and the withdrawal of life-force require that all nadi passageways be as open as possible. When the nadis are not open and balanced, you experience distress in the body. This imbalance in the pranic system is what you come face to face with when you are trying to meditate. Imbalance results in restlessness, flashbacks to times of trauma, sleepiness, spontaneous feelings of anger, fear, dejection, or any other of numerous symptoms.

Two things are needed to restore balance in the pranic system to help you enter into deeper meditative states. The first thing needed is to clear the life-energy roadblocks; the second is to recharge the depleted system. The Clearing/Charging Exercises can effectively perform both these tasks. These simple but powerful exercises help restore the functioning of your energy pathways and bring your system back to the feeling of calm awareness. The Clearing/ Charging Exercises have been tested and proven to be highly effective tools for bringing the mind, body, and feelings into greater balance. Achieving a calm, relaxed state helps you enter a deeper meditative state, leaving an open highway to higher Consciousness. Help is here, and I trust you find these next couple of days useful and fruitful.

BABAJI-INSPIRED CLEARING/ CHARGING EXERCISES

First Step

Please write down all physical disturbances you would like to resolve or begin a reharmonization process with. This can be anything from restlessness to aches and pains to long-term illnesses. Try to distinguish these from focusing on mental and emotional disturbances in this section, although there are bound to be overlaps. Write as much or as little as you would like. It is for you. But, do give it serious thought. If it makes you anxious at all, just take a deep breath, hold it as long as comfortable, and release. Then do the best you can.

Place in an envelope marked "physical."
Do not seal the envelope at this time.
Now, on a separate piece of paper, write down all the emotional disturbances you would like to release or reharmonize. Go into as little or as much detail as you would like. A good method is to let your hand begin to write and let your emotions "speak." Again, if you get to a stuck place, take a deep breath and hold as long as comfortable, then release.

Place in an envelope marked "emotional."
Do not seal the envelope at this time.
Third, write down mental disturbances that you would like to let go of. Those thought patterns that may keep you stuck or are not useful to you. Again, in as little or as much detail, this is for your eyes only. The more you put into these exercises, the more you are likely to get out of them.

Place in an envelope marked "mental." Do not seal at this time.
You will have tonight and tomorrow to work on these, although I
think it best to do the bulk of this before we begin our exercises
tomorrow. The reason for leaving the envelopes unsealed is to add
anything that may come to you during the exercises tomorrow.

BABAJI-INSPIRED CLEARING/ CHARGING EXERCISES

Day 1: Exercise Introduction

Today's sharing includes three phases of exercises and a ceremony this evening. The three exercises today are designed to clear and cleanse your physical, emotional, and mental bodies of obstructive blockages that limit the true power you were born to have. Through these exercises, you learn techniques not only for today, but methods you can take with you to use for the rest of your life.

All of you have been troubled by disturbing thoughts, feelings, and sensations that are not strictly, or at all, connected to the present. When I was at Cloud Mountain Retreat Center for my time of silence, Babaji inwardly revealed to me these techniques for the removal of disturbances. It is his wish that these techniques be taught to sadhakas (spiritual aspirants), helping them to become more attuned to the Divine.

You will notice that these exercises are simple and safe. Yet, they have the power to remove troubling disturbances that may have blocked your meditation practice for a very long time. Although there is nothing here that is harmful, you may stop the practice at any time you would like. Although, you are encouraged to see it through to the end as I am sure you will find relief through the practice.

The best way to enter the practice is from the "observation deck" of the Ajna, or the 6th chakra point (sometimes called the 3rd eye). From this observation deck, you can observe all experiences as a third person would safely watch the conversation between two other people. Since you may be dealing with sensations, feelings, and thoughts that reside deep in the psyche, there can be times of discomfort, strong emotions, or intense thoughts emerging. These are the moments you may be tempted to "abandon ship" and leave the practice. I would like to encourage you to stay with the breathing if such things should emerge, as I think you will find relief in a fairly short time. On the other hand, you may not feel like much has gone on at all, but may be quite surprised at how fast the time has gone. Let go of expectation. Your experience will be what it will be. Rest assured, whatever the experience, you are in a safe environment and may move to the observation deck of the Ajna at any point in the exercise.

The emphasis during this exercise is: "Whatever may emerge as sensations, feelings, or thoughts, stay the calm observer and breathe into the disturbance." The usual temptation is to try to make a disturbing feeling just go away, or to identify with it. Here the goal will be to simply breathe into it and stay the observer, seeing the distressing feeling or thought itself begin to breathe. If you sense an area of your body that is very painful or distressing, then see an aura or wrap a bubble around that area. See the aura or the bubble breathe, move the aura, or energy field, out further if it does not easily move. For example, your attention is drawn to your knee and you find it very painful. Sense the energy around that painful area radiating out several inches or more. Begin with the outside of the radius and see it, or feel it breathing with you. Gradually, work closer to the center as you experience some relief from the intensity; eventually, you will work to the center.

During these exercises, you will focus on a specific chakra. However, your attention may be drawn from that chakra to any part of your body; this is part of the exercise and is all right. After your initial focus on a chakra, you will not be controlling where your mind goes, but rather, you will be following where your attention leads you. Your starting point is your Home Base. You begin and return there when nothing else is calling your attention. Being called by a part of your body can include any feeling or sensation; it may be a feeling of pain or tightness, anything at all. Keep your focus on that sensation, that part of your body, until you feel a resolution or a softening to that part, or a softening of the sensation, or feel a stronger calling from any other part.

For example:

- Your attention may go back and forth to different parts of your body during the exercise.
- Daydreams can play a role and be connected with the physical area of the body and the chakra with which you started. It is important to remain consciously aware during the daydreams. See or feel a bubble around the images in the daydream and then see or feel that bubble breathe in rhythm with your breath.
- You may feel overwhelmingly tired. Go to the center of the tiredness in your body and allow it to breathe.
- You may feel anxious, go to the center of the anxiety and allow it to breathe.

Your focus may remain in one place for just a moment or an extended period of time (it may extend for several days of practice or more). The time spent is strictly between you and the energy in that part of your body. If the intensity is too high, you may always find relief through a shift of focus to the Ajna (observation deck) where you can observe your body from there. (And remember, once you have identified an issue that needs further attention, it is fine to acknowledge this and, if needed, seek the best practitioner to gain further assistance.)

At the end of each exercise, there will be a sheet for that exercise marked **OBSERVATIONS.** This sheet will be for me to read and to make any comments. Please write what you observe during the exercise, whatever you think is useful. These observations may include what you experienced mentally, physically, and emotionally or any shifts, blockages, and insights that have occurred. When you get the forms back, they are yours to keep. There will be time at the end of each phase for comments, thoughts, and observations from the group.

Now let us start

CLEARING BREATH EXERCISE 1
PHYSICAL CLEANSING

Introduction

You are now going to receive instructions on the first Clearing Exercise. Once you receive the instructions and have had an opportunity to ask clarifying questions, begin practice. Practice for about fifty minutes. At the end of that time, I will sound the bell and then you can write out your observations. You may then leave for a break, while maintaining your silence, drink some tea, go for a walk, or however you would like to use the time. When you come back, pick up your Observation Sheet with my comments. At that time, we will have an open discussion period.

The Practice

First Breath.

Sit comfortably upright and take a breath in. Observe the course of your breath from its entry into the nose all the way to the lungs. Let the exhalation come naturally, neither willfully holding it nor pushing it out. After this first breath, you will then observe the stomach while continuing to breathe. The stomach extends out during the in-breath, and draws in during the out-breath. This should seem natural, but go on observing it for some breaths.

In-Breath, stomach out,
Out-Breath, stomach in.

Breathe this way for a little while until this pattern becomes comfortable.

Breathe Into the Stomach Area

When you have a comfortable pattern, take the breath "into" the stomach area. Mentally draw the breath to the stomach and see/feel the stomach area as if it were breathing, expanding out during the in-breath. See/feel the stomach come back in during the out-breath. The focus on the stomach area will be just above the navel in the center of your body.

Follow Your Awareness

Once established in this pattern of breathing, your awareness may be drawn to any part of your body, or you may find yourself with a certain train of thought. Unlike other meditation practices, you do not curb this sporadic tendency of the mind. Rather, you follow this awareness to any part of your body or to any train of thought. In following the awareness of your body or thought, you will breathe into that part of your body, or into the thought. If you start to daydream, wrap a bubble around the daydream and see/feel the bubble breathe, or see/feel your character in the daydream breathe with you.

For instance, you observe the breath drawn into the stomach area. Your stomach is in a comfortable pattern, stomach moving out with the in-breath, and then drawing in on the out-breath. Perhaps you are then made aware of a feeling of pressure or pain in your shoulder area. As you feel some pain in your shoulders, see/feel that area "breathe" with you, the aura of pain moving in and out with your breath. Now a thought about work comes into your mind; you daydream about some situation. Continue to either see yourself in the daydream, breathing even as you are currently breathing, or put a bubble around the daydream picture and see it breathing with you. Now your attention is drawn to your knee; that is all right. See/feel the aura of pain in your knee; expanding on the in-breath and contracting on the out-breath. And so on, following your awareness wherever it leads, staying conscious of your breathing.

If your body wants to shift, move, or sigh, gently accommodate it. You do not need to stay in a fixed position; in fact, it is preferable to stay flexible and move with it. However, be mindful that this is a group practice, so do not become too noisy or move so much that it disturbs others.

Do Not Try to Make a Tense/Painful Area Change; Just Let it Breathe

Do not try to make a painful area do anything, simply breathe with it or into it. Do not try to get it to relax, or make the pain or daydream go away. By getting an area to breathe with you, allow it to change if it wishes, or at most, see it moving in rhythm with your own breath. Trying to get it to change will only set up a tug-of-war that will be counterproductive for this exercise. Coax it into the breathing pattern, seeing it, perhaps at first just slightly, breathing in rhythm with your breath.

Continue breathing this way until I ring the bell (Approximately 50 minutes).

Clearing Exercise 2
Emotional Cleansing

Introduction

Clearing the emotional body means moving to the 4th chakra, the Heart Center. The Heart Center is, of course, the center for the emotional body and the astral being. When you focus on a chakra center, the resultant associations of physical sensations, feelings, and thoughts will usually be connected with that center. You may observe that as you focus on the 4th chakra, different places in the body will become painful or call your attention. Even though these physical aches or the daydreams coming to you may not be obviously associated with emotions of the Heart Center. If you spent enough time analyzing the chain of associations, you could see that the connecting weave of thoughts and feelings would most likely eventually lead you back to the Heart Center. This Clearing Breath does not require you to make an analysis of thoughts or feelings, it only requires that you breathe into the thoughts and feelings until they find resolution or soften into the breath.

The Practice

Start with the instructions for the practice and you will have time to ask questions after they are given. Begin by sitting in a comfortable, upright position.

1. Mentally follow the breath from where it enters the nose and follow it down to the lungs. On the second breath, direct your stomach to expand on the in-breath and contract on the out-breath. Do not make this an exaggerated movement, but a natural expansion and contraction.
2. Once this is an easy, established pattern, draw your focus to the Heart Center. Your Heart Center is located in the center of

your chest. If you draw your shoulder blades back together until they touch, you will have the right height. At that height, mentally locate the middle of your chest, halfway between the front and the back. See this area expanding on the in-breath, contracting on the out-breath. Expanding on the in-breath, contracting on the out-breath. Continue with this pattern.

If your attention is drawn to some part of your body, or to a daydream, just follow it. Your Home Base is your Heart Center. This is where you return any time there is nothing calling in your body or daydreams. Like the first breathing exercise, breathe into the physical sensation or the daydream. When this is resolved, move to what calls you next or return to the Heart Center.

Any questions?

Ok, continue with this breathing pattern until you hear the bell.

CLEARING EXERCISE 3
MENTAL CLEANSING

Introduction
Now we are going to move to the 5th chakra at the throat, which is
the Mental Dharma Center. The Buddhi, or the higher reasoning
mind, may be illuminated by the Divine Intelligence or clouded
by ignorance. The fundamental reason for this ignorance is due to
the idea of separation from God. When clearing the 5th chakra, your
Home Base this time, you are clearing yourselves of the mental disturbances that reflect this ignorance. However, this ignorance may
be locked into the body, or it may manifest as disruption in the
pranic energy. So, when focusing on the Throat Center, you may be
drawn to physical pains in the body or you may feel blockages of
energy or emotions as well as daydreams. Again, you can use the
Observation Deck of the Ajna if you feel overwhelmed with any feeling or emotion.

The Practice
1. Sit in an upright, comfortable position. Watch the breath
   move from the nose to the lungs and back out again. Allow
   the stomach to expand on the in-breath and contract on the
   out-breath.
2. Once the Clearing Breath is established, draw the focus to
   your 5th chakra. You can locate the 5th chakra by rolling your
   head side to side and feeling where the cracks come from in
   your neck. Then mentally sense the location half between
   the front and back of your neck at that place where your neck
   cracks. See/feel that area expand on the in-breath and contract on the out-breath. In essence, this area is breathing with
   your breath.

As with Exercises 1 and 2, if some area of your body calls to you, or some daydream comes to you, allow your attention to follow what calls and gently encourage that area of your body or the daydream to breathe in the same rhythm as your physical breath. Your Home Base is the Throat Center. Always return there if nothing else is calling to you.

Any questions? Ok, continue with this breathing on the 5th chakra until you hear the bell, about 50 minutes.

CHARGING EXERCISE 4
PHYSICAL CHARGING

Introduction

Now you are going to move into charging the three-body system. What was revealed to me was a remarkably simple method for re-directing the prana life-force energies to any part of the body, or back to their source, the powerhouse chakras.

What was shown to me, sometime after the "blueprint" of the nadi astral nerves and their relationship with the breath, was how the body naturally performs these Clearing/Charging Exercises.

The Clearing/Charging Exercises systematize what the body does naturally and thereby increase its effectiveness many hundred-fold. When you sigh, you are performing a Clearing Breath. When you yawn, you are performing a Charging Breath. Similarly, when you stretch like a cat, you are unconsciously performing Yogananda's "Energization Exercises." It is quite wonderful how nature designed the body to create balance in our system. Through Yoga, you can intelligently apply methodical principles to greatly enhance balance in the three-body system, overcome obstacles, and realize your human nature's greatest potential, God-realization.

The practice of the Charging Breath is very powerful. There are times when one or two of these breaths were all I needed or could do; this is particularly true if you are experiencing surges of kundalini. You may also become quickly "full" with the Charging Breath if your system has traffic jams in its pranic highway. For these reasons, or because you have simply reached a balanced condition, you may quickly feel filled up, or that the Charging Breath is creating pressure, increased heat, or other uncomfortable conditions. You should stop the Charging Breath at this time and switch to the Clearing Breath. These discomforts are not to be treated as something to overcome or to push through. They are signals to you that you have reached a saturation point and should not continue.

I would like to emphasize again, if you get an inner signal to stop the Charging Breath, even after one or two breaths, do not ignore it or try to push through it, but respond to the signal by switching to the Clearing Breath. You cannot overdo the Clearing Breath, especially if you breathe naturally; you can definitely overdo the Charging Breath. The grand summation of the Clearing Breath (after much yogic practice) will result in your coming into a still point of consciousness, breathlessness. Entering breathlessness will be your signal that you do not need to continue to practice the Clearing Breath.

Now, let's move on to the practice
instructions of the Charging Breath.

The Practice
1. Sit upright in a comfortable position.
2. Observe a natural breath coming in from the nose, down to the lungs, and then back out again.
3. For the Charging Breath, the movement of the stomach is going to be reversed from the Clearing Breath. During the in-breath, the stomach will be drawn in; during the out-breath, the stomach will move out. **Breathe in, stomach-in, breathe out, stomach-out.** Work with this pattern for a few breaths until it feels like a comfortable pattern. Do not exaggerate this movement; it should not be painful. There are times when you will want to take very deep breaths and the stomach will be completely drawn in. Other times, it will be a gradual movement contracting in during the in-breath, a gradual relaxation and extension of the stomach during the out-breath. Go according to what feels right in the moment. Breathe in, stomach-in, breathe out, stomach-out.

4. Once you have established a comfortable pattern with the Charging Breath, Locate the 3rd chakra, right above the navel, midway between the front and back of your body. Now take the Charging Breath to the 3rd chakra location and see that area of your body breathing with your Charging Breath. This time, feel the energy contracting into that area of your body on the in-breath, and then relaxing and expanding in golden light on the out-breath. The energy contracts on the in-breath and expands in golden light on the out-breath. See/feel that Light gently expanding out in a radius from that part of your body.

During this practice, your attention may be drawn to other parts of your body or to daydreams. Allow your attention to follow what draws you, charging that part of your body or charging the daydream. Charging a part of your body means seeing that part of your body (or a radius of energy around it) contracting during the in-breath. Then, smoothly radiate out the energy as golden light on the out-breath. For the daydream, see yourself in the daydream using the charging breath, or wrap a bubble around the daydream image and see the whole image doing the Charging Breath. If at any time you feel full or uncomfortable from the Charging Breath, immediately switch back to the Clearing Breath. You can switch back and forth as much as you would like—experiment.

Any questions?

**Now continue until you hear the
bell ring (approximately 50 minutes).**

CHARGING EXERCISE 5
CHARGING THE HEART CENTER

Introduction

The Heart Center is in charge of emotions and the astral body. The Heart Center strengthens your courage—gives you fortitude in emotional distress, and gives you additional power to love God— you may use the Charging Breath at the Heart Center. Also, as with using the Charging Breath at the 3rd chakra—anytime that area of your body feels charged enough, switch to the Clearing Breath. Your attention may be drawn to another part of your body or to a day-dream—use the charging breath for that body part by seeing/feeling that area of your body contract with energy during the in-breath and expand out in golden light during the out-breath—contract in during the in-breath—expand out in golden light during the out-breath. For a daydream—see/feel yourself using the Charging Breath in the daydream—or wrap a bubble around the daydream and see it breathing with the Charging Breath.

The Practice

1. Now, let's sit upright in a comfortable position. Follow the breath from the nose to the lungs and back out again in a natural breath.
2. On the next in-breath, draw the stomach in during the in-breath—let the stomach move out during the out-breath— repeat this until it is an easy pattern.
3. Now, focus on the Heart Center—see/feel the breath and energy coming into the Heart Center during the in-breath— then see/feel the Heart Center expand in golden light during the out-breath—repeat this several times. Charge any area of your body or a daydream that your attention is drawn to.

Any questions? Continue the Practice until you hear the bell.

Charging Exercise 6
Charging the Mental Body

Introduction

This is the last exercise in the Clearing/Charging Exercises. You will be charging your 5th chakra, the Mental Body—giving strength and purpose to your thoughts and increased power to mental dharma: knowing the right thing to do in your life.

The Practice

1. Sit upright in a comfortable position. Follow the breath from your nose to your lungs and back out again in a natural way.
2. On the next breath, draw the stomach in during the in-breath—let it out during the out-breath—in during the in-breath—out during the out-breath.
3. Now, focus your attention on the Throat Center—during the in-breath see/feel the breath and life-force entering into the 5th chakra—then expand out in golden light during the out-breath. Breath/energy in during the in-breath—out on the out-breath. As before, if thoughts or body sensations draw your attention, go with them and charge them. If you feel "full" of energy or sense pressure or pain, switch to the Clearing Breath.

Are there any questions? Continue until you hear the bell.

Clearing/Charging Exercise 7
Integration into Meditation

Introduction

This is the final step for using the Clearing/Charging Exercises; that is, integrating it into your meditation practice. As I have mentioned before, this practice is not strictly a meditation practice, as it does not put your attention on God; rather, it helps prepare you for deeper meditation through clearing and charging your three-body system. Through the practices you have been engaged in over the last couple of days, you have begun to see the possibilities for creating a truly calm state of mind. Yet, even a calm state of mind is not, of itself, the fullest experience to be gained through direct God-perception. This 7th step can fill in the missing link that will take you to these higher states of Consciousness.

All who practice the Kriya path know that piercing the Ajna and entering into Christ Consciousness (Chit-Consciousness) will bring you to that highest state of total God-Union (Sat-Consciousness), which is the object of Yoga and all the great religions of the world. In trying to focus attention on God alone, you all know what happens to the body and mind. The mind wanders in daydreams, the body starts to call attention to itself with anxiety, aches, and pains, or a desire to fall into an unconscious state. All these obstacles can be discouraging, and the penalty is that while fighting those obstacles, God-Consciousness is not attained.

In using the Clearing/Charging Breathing Exercises, keep in mind that the ultimate aim is to move through the Ajna into absolute Being, Consciousness, and Bliss. Instead of trying to ignore distractions, you breathe into them. The Charging Breath can move right into the root cause and bring resolution to it; this brings calm and an easier access to the Ajna. Rather than fighting these distractions, which at times only adds power to the distractions, the breath can clear the distractions. Then the Ajna is accessed, and thereby, deeper states of meditation. So many times, in the battle to ignore distractions, it seems that the battle is lost, if not the war. Many times, even when in the higher states of Consciousness, new distractions can arise that challenge inner peace. This effective method through the Clearing/Charging Breaths can remove obstacles efficiently and allow you to return to a closer oneness with God

Here are the instructions and then I will answer any questions you may have about this 7th exercise.

The Practice

This practice brings integration: the practices of clearing and charging your three-body system are going to integrate with your meditation practice. You have been instructed in a step-by-step process that takes you from one chakra level to the next. It is very useful to learn where the chakra centers are and what they do. These earlier practices may have also highlighted some problematic areas for you, in that some of the chakras were more difficult to work with than others. Keep those challenging areas in mind for future reference and return to those areas as places for more work. Through persistent practice, you may find that those problematic areas shift, change, and eventually resolve themselves. Contact helpful trained wellness professionals in regard to your work on these specific areas if you find them not yielding to your practice over time. This integrated practice assumes that you have some self-mastery in all these areas. This gives you a sense of the complete practice and where you are headed. You may also find that this integrated practice works fine for you now, and you slip into it quite easily.

Let's go over the practice, and then we will see if there are any questions.

1. Sitting upright in a comfortable position, I want you to focus on the Clearing Breath. As you remember, the Clearing Breath is:

Breathe-**in,** stomach **out,**

Breathe-**out,** stomach **in.**

2. Once you have established a comfortable pattern for the Clearing Breath, focus on your 3rd chakra, just above the navel. Sense any blockages in that center or wherever your mind may be drawn. Stay present on the 3rd chakra for some time. If you feel no great calling by the 3rd chakra, or any body parts, you may move on to the Heart Center. Due to the fact that you are learning Exercise 7 as a complete set, I am going to move you through all the stages, whether or not you have completely cleared the chakra on which you have been focused.

3. After about 10 minutes, I am going to ring the gong; this will signal you to move from the 3rd chakra to your 4th chakra at the Heart Center.

4. When you work through the Heart Center and would like to move on the 5th chakra at the Throat Center, the Mental Body, feel free to do so.

5. When the bell rings again, feel free to move on to the 6th chakra, the Ajna, if there is nothing more calling you at the Throat Center, the Mental Body.
   With the continued use of the Clearing Breath, see the Ajna expanding and contracting very gently in rhythm with your own breath. You may accompany this movement with either the Hong Sau chant, or Om Sri Ram if you wish.

6. Note: **Do not use the Charging Breath on the Ajna Center at any time. Keep to this simple practice of doing the Clearing Breath, seeing the Ajna expand with the in-breath and contract with the out-breath.** This is a very slight, gentle movement. If your attention is called insistently by any body part or daydream, then go to that area and use the Clearing Breath on it. If you are feeling any weakness,

for instance, your neck is allowing your head to fall forward, then use the Charging Breath to charge the neck and back area and feel it grow in strength. If you have been using the Charging Breath to clear or strengthen an area, when you come back to the Ajna, switch to the Clearing Breath once again and see/feel the Ajna gently expanding and contracting with the breath.

Stay with the Ajna until you hear the final gong. Then you will write your observations.

A Brief Summary

- Begin with the Clearing Breath at the 3rd chakra.
- Move at your own pace through the chakras if it is faster than the timed bells.
- Whether or not you are finished with the chakra when the bell rings, move to the next chakra when you hear the bell.
- Move from the 3rd chakra to the 4th then 5th and then 6th chakra at your own pace or with the bell, using the Clearing Breath and using the Charging Breath any time you feel the inclination.
- For the Ajna Center, use the Clearing Breath only.
- If something draws your attention insistently while at the Ajna Center, use the Clearing/Charging Breath on the disturbance until it is resolved, then return to the Ajna once again using the Clearing Breath only.

Are there any questions? Let us begin.

Clearing/Charging
Exercises for Couples

Getting Started

Sit either facing one another or side by side; prepare to "clear the air" between you.

Clearing the Air

If there are things that need to be talked through or just said and heard, this is the time to make peace with one another.

Strengthening a Stressed Relationship

If there is major discord right now in the relationship, words may only inflame emotions. You may choose to go directly to the Clearing Exercise to stabilize and strengthen the emotional bodies.

Building the Bond

It is also a time to say things of appreciation and affection that build the bond of connection between a couple. Each word of true appreciation and affection is like a deposit in the bank. It's good to have a rainy-day fund.

Clearing Breath

Now, as you sit facing or next to each other, begin with the Clearing Breath. Be aware of your partner next to you. You are not only clearing the pathways within your own body, although this will be your main focus, but you will also be clearing those pathways between the two of you.

Awareness of Blockages

Be aware of blockages in your own system. As you sit with your partner, you may be aware of how you are blocked in a part of your body. Start at your Heart Center with the Clearing Breath and let your attention go to whatever area is asking for attention. Once that is cleared, go to the next area calling for attention, or go back to the Heart Center.

Time

You may want to have an agreed-upon amount of time that you want to spend on a clearing session. One partner may feel they are cleared before the other partner. Stay with the Clearing Breath until both partners feel cleared.

How Long Will This Take?

This may take many such sessions of clearing, especially in the beginning. Do not feel pressured to be cleared of blockages if your partner has reported they feel cleared. This will only create a blockage in you. Besides, your partner may feel cleared only to drop to a new level and find he or she is now working on a previously unknown blockage.

Deeper Levels

The partner who feels cleared first will continue with their Clearing Breath, exploring all the nuances of the vital flow of connection within, and connecting to their partner. There is no boredom here.

Boredom

If you find yourself bored, sleepy, or irritated that your partner is taking so long, etc., these are blockages and something for you to clear with the Clearing Breath.

Exploring What It's Like to Be Clear

When both of you report being clear, spend some time being aware of how the play of life-energy goes between you. Most people are not so highly attuned to this play of intermingling energy, but now you can explore your awareness of how this flow of life-energy resonates. It is delightful, stimulating, and informative. Each of you may want to keep a journal of your experiences and read passages to each other. This brings intimacy; if this creates discomfort, use the Clearing Breath to resolve it.

Charging

Once you have taken the time to become thoroughly acquainted with the openness of being clear, you may want to move to charging. I am cautious about this because charging is powerful.

Don't Feel Pushed

If there are blockages that continue for one or both partners, the charging exercise may intensify the blockage. This can cause irritation, feeling bad about yourself or the relationship, etc. So, by no means feel pushed to move to the charging stage. Far better to stay with clearing for as long as it takes.

May Need to Do More of Your Own Work

Also, you may have blockages that do not relate to your relationship but have yet to be cleared. Better to do your own work first, taking the clearing in the relationship as far as it will go.

Charging

If you both think you are ready to do charging (you can always experiment and either one of you can bring it to a halt), then once again sit alongside each other or face each other. Switch to the Charging Breath. Be aware of subtle shifts of energy within you and between you.

Let Go of Expectations

Changes can be subtle; they can start small and grow larger; they can be very different for each partner. It can feel like not much has happened, but then, later on, you feel a profound difference. So be aware but let go of expectations as these only tend to create more blockages.

Results

Notice short-term and long-term results. You may notice increased energy in yourself and in your relationship. You may feel your relationship open itself into a wider field of consciousness: i.e., more connected to God. More creativity or energy for joint projects may emerge.

Possibilities

You may feel, with the increased strength of the relationship, the motivation to create something on your own (i.e., getting a degree, starting a business, etc.) for which, in the past, you did not think you had the strength, courage, or energy to do.

Stay In the Moment

Or, it may be just a nice, pleasant exercise. Be aware of what occurs and stay in the moment.

CLEARING AND ENERGIZING YOUR SYSTEM

Stubborn Traffic Jams

If you run into places (physical sensations, emotions, or thoughts) that do not give way easily when moving the breath into that area, do not get into a fight with them. It is easy to be drawn into a tug-of-war with a part of you that does not respond easily. Rather than get into a battle of wills, one which you may well lose, simply observe the stuck area while breathing life-force into it. Allow it to "free up" by moving it in rhythm with the breath. Stay with it for as long as necessary. Know that the overall system wants balance and unseen forces will be working with you.

One stuck place may move to another. Freeing up an area in the body, or partially freeing it up, may lead to another part. For instance, you may start with a pain in the back. After a few breaths, your awareness is drawn to an anxious feeling in the stomach. Allow your attention to go to the area calling most loudly; from there, your attention may get focused in your throat, then your Solar Plexus, then your back pain again, etc. Move from one area to the next. It may not feel like a logical sequence to you, but there is an internal logic to it.

A physical sensation may trigger thoughts and/or emotions. Again, if that calls the loudest, let your mind go to it. Breathe into those thoughts or emotions in the same way as you would a physical sensation. Maintain yourself as the witness and allow the "traffic jam" of thoughts/emotions to clear. Once the log jam is cleared, things tend to move rather rapidly. If nothing then calls your attention, go back to the body area you were instructed to focus on. Some stubborn jams do not clear so easily. Trust in the process.

Make sure you are not attached to getting it to move as that sets up a battle of wills. Be calm, patient, and persistent. Sometimes you are removing jams that have been there a very, very long time. A few minutes, hours, days, or weeks to work with a stuck area is not long compared to how long you have carried it.

CLEARING EXERCISE AND KRIYA

Before or after Maha Mudra, take time for the Clearing Breath exercise. Both in worldly life and dream life, the body absorbs the knocks of stresses and worries produced by the mind. To clear the body of any disturbances or blockages created by these knocks, the Clearing Breath exercise will prove to be highly useful. In addition to the knocks of the day, there may be triggered subconscious associations that get reflected in disturbances of the energy pathways, the nadis. In either case, when sitting down to meditate, these disturbances will create problems in entering an interior state of mind.

In addition to these disturbances, or perhaps as a part of them, tamasic moods and rajasic energy may be running rampant throughout the energy body. Tamasic moods may make you feel sluggish, experience low energy, feel depressed, and note an overall resistance. Rajasic energy may include a rapid flow of thoughts, multiple thoughts or ideas seemingly coming all at once, restless energy ("fired up," "jazzed up," etc.), anger, or a sense of being in fighting mode. Of course, these energies run counter to the sattvic energy of meditation. The Clearing Breath can help to shift these tamasic and rajasic energies. The Clearing Breath works toward getting both tamasic and rajasic energy pathways open and free, thus either beginning a harmonizing process or achieving a dynamic balance. The wrong approach tends to increase resistance. The Clearing Breath helps to harmonize the pranic rhythm of the affected area or issue. Remember, this can take a time of diligent practice.

Clearing Breath Exercise

Before starting your Kriya Proper, take time to start the Clearing Breath and allow your attention to go to any area of the body calling you. Then see that area breathing in rhythm with your breath.

As soon as that area resolves itself, move to the next area. Clear out all areas calling your attention. When the body is cleared of blockages and distracting energies, shift the attention to the Ajna and begin the Clearing Breath there. If some part of the body calls your attention, or some thought stream comes to your attention, apply the Clearing Breath to what has called your attention. Once you are established in the Ajna with the Clearing Breath, then you are ready for Kriya Proper.

The Kriyaban will notice the Kriya practice is a Charging Breath. Kriya charges the spine and brain, creating a magnetic field that draws wayward particles of ignorance the way a magnet will attract iron filings. These particles of ignorance are drawn to the Ajna where they are surrendered to the Light and thereby the Kriyaban gains Union, Yoga, with the Supreme Consciousness of God.

Advanced Clearing/Charging Exercises

Upon awakening, while still in bed:
- Wake up thinking of God
- Activate pleasant contemplative thoughts
- Chant Ram Nam
- Chant Hong Sau, or a mantra of your choice

Stretch like a cat a couple of times and charge the body with Master's energization exercise through the medulla.

Clearing Breath

Start with the top of your body and work all the way down to the bottom of your feet. One of the reasons birds can fly is due to the fact that they have hollow bones. Feel as if the nadis from head to foot are hollow and flowing with prana life-energy. Once you have worked on clearing any backlog of blockages from the subtle body, this daily clearing will work as a day-to-day maintenance practice. By starting your day this way, you can clear any blockages that have resulted from the subconscious mind during your dreams. When you feel light as a bird from head to foot, you are ready to switch to the Charging Breath.

Charging Breath

Feel all the cells of the body vibrating with pure pranic energy. You may hear the AUM sound in the right ear, medulla, or all over, connecting you with the cosmic sea of the AUM vibration. This is a very good way to start your day and to prepare yourself for being at the altar of Kriya meditation.

You are now awake and ready!

Fire Ceremony

An important ingredient for clearing your system is to be aware of what you are intentionally letting go of and placing in the fire. You have listed those areas you would most like to be seen in the rear-view mirror in life.

The act of writing and the symbology associated with intentionally letting things go provide strong messages to the mind. Letting go is usually a process, that is, it extends over time and goes in stages. One does not know if they are at the beginning, middle, or end of letting something go. The best you can do is get really good at letting things go and know that eventually your "basement" of consciousness will be cleaned out.

You have all worked today in releasing physical, emotional, and mental issues that distress you. Tonight, you are going to enact a ceremony that will signal the conscious and subconscious minds to take a deeper step in letting go. The subconscious mind responds powerfully to pictures. That is why symbolism is so powerful.

Tonight, you will use that symbology for a good purpose. You are going to see your problems go into the flames and become as ephemeral as smoke. The more deeply you think of connecting the things you have written to this symbolic act of burning them—the clearer will be the message to the subconscious mind.

Taking the envelope marked "physical" in your right hand—think of all the physical difficulties and lack of harmony you want to let go of. Think of the fire as the flame of God and that you will be releasing all of these things as you prepare to place the envelope into the fire.

Pray to God to make it so and when you feel ready to release it, do so—watch it burn—turn into smoke.

Also, the same with the "emotional" and "mental" envelopes.

The ceremony will end with several loud Oms.

CLEARING/CHARGING EXERCISES FOR EVERYDAY USE

When sitting in meditation, a sudden anxiety hits you. All you want to do is get up and run. Instead of fighting it, or giving into it, you breathe into it. Letting the Clearing Exercise do its work of making the nadis open and run as they are designed to do. Locate the epi-center of the dis-ease and allow the stomach to move out with the in-breath. Mentally see the breath go to the affected area. See the area itself breathe with your breath. On the out-breath, the stom-ach goes in.

Do not try to change the tenseness of the area. Just breathe into it. If it releases and seems all right with a few breaths, fine and well. If it takes longer, then it takes longer, just stay with it. If it shifts to another part of your body, if thoughts or feelings get triggered, then breathe into those new sensations, thoughts, or feelings. Do not worry about the time it takes; you are making the paths straight and it is necessary. You can remove lifetimes of patterns in a rela-tively short time.

There may be physical symptoms you thought were just part of being in a human body. These discomforts may be helped with this exercise. Knee pains, back pains, stomach upset, and headaches can all respond to the Clearing Exercise.

Once the area is cleared, you may want to take the time to charge the area. Simply reverse the stomach movements of the exercise and continue to see the affected area breathe with you, only this time, instead of the area releasing clogged pathways, it is being positively charged with new energy for the newly-opened path-ways. Be sure you've cleared the area first or you may experience an uncomfortable buildup of energy in the area with the charging. If this becomes the case, then reverse breathing to the Clearing/Cleansing Breath.

Whenever you sit for meditation, you can use these exercises when distractions draw you away from your focused attention on the Ajna. Also, you may use it during your day to tend to low energy, relaxing the body before eating, headaches, other pains, etc.

CLEARING/CHARGING EXERCISE FOR OVER/UNDER EATING

For overeating, become aware of your cycle of eating. Become mindful of what happens in your body.

You are sitting in a chair and the thought comes, "Something sweet would taste good right now." Increasing self-awareness, you check in with your stomach. It is neither full nor demanding food. You then notice the demand is coming from your mouth. Salivary glands are secreting juices in preparation for something to eat. It is strange; your body is not hungry, but your mouth and some part of your mind tell you, with increasing urgency, to eat now!

Your normal reaction would be to seek out something sweet, something salty—whatever your mouth and brain tell you to have. Instead of this usual reaction, you are going to utilize the Clearing/Charging Exercise.

Using the Clearing/Cleansing Breath, let the stomach move out on the in-breath, breathe into the salivary gland area. With quiet attention, move the breath in and out of this area. Notice how your body responds. For example, your attention is then drawn to your tightened stomach; you follow it. From there, you have a daydream that relates to food and then a stressful situation. Breathe into the daydream. When the daydream resolves itself, return to the body. Check if you still need to breathe into the stressful situation: if so, do that. Next, you are aware of pain in your back. Respond to it with the Clearing/Cleansing Breath. Continue to clear all the channels that relate to this "need" to eat. Notice the overall response to the body as you do this.

Through this example, you can get an idea of how to apply this technique to your own case. People overeat for many reasons—fear, pain, overwhelming feelings—many reasons. What is common to all of these is that overeating is a symptom, not a cause. In other words, it is a reaction to something else happening in life.

Perhaps you did not get enough to eat when young, or you were shamed about how much you ate. That part of your mind is still very active and now that you are an adult, it is determined to eat as much as it wants, whatever the consequences! You can breathe right into that mental image and help clear those old associations from the subconscious mind.

For undereating, many of the same dynamics occur as with over-eating, only the message of the body is: "Don't you dare put that food into my mouth! I'll make you sick. I will punish you, etc." In this case, you will focus either on the body part or the mental fantasy that relates to not eating. Breathe into it, and if it shifts, follow it. Careful not to get into a tug of war with it! Rather, quietly work with getting those areas to breathe. If they will not completely clear now, can you negotiate with them for the moment? For instance, if your body lets go some but not all the way, consider something you think the body might find acceptable to eat. If it gives a green light of "That's ok," then eat that for now and no more. It may come in steps, but you can win your body's cooperation for normal, healthy eating.

For both under or overeating, when the clearing is done, or at least gone as far as it—or you—can go for the moment, try some Charging Breaths. If these breaths feel right, then continue. If the Charging Breath is agitating to that area, then leave it for the moment. If an area is not cleared, you may work on it with the Clearing Breath at odd moments during the day when you can focus on the breathing.

Victory to the Light within you.

CLEARING/CHARGING EXERCISES FOR KUNDALINI EXPERIENCES

During kundalini experiences, the dynamic energy of kundalini is working on clearing the nadis and strengthening them. You can help it to do its work through the Cleansing/Charging Exercises.

Large and small body movements and twitches are part of the kundalini working through knotted areas. By focusing the Clearing Breath on the core of the affected area, you are helping to clear the problem on which the kundalini is working. Proper energetic alignment can be facilitated and nothing is lost in the experience through the Clearing/Cleansing Breath.

Also, areas of intense heat can be helped with the Clearing Breath and associated symptoms of headache, nausea, and fatigue.

You may very carefully experiment with the Charging Breath. If it tends to intensify an already overly-charged system, then stay focused on the Clearing/Cleansing Breath. However, the charging can help bring needed supplies of prana to a stressed part of the body and may feel relaxing and re-energizing. Short experiments will let you know which effect will occur. Always adjust to the current situation.

A CHARGING BREATH QUESTION

(An un-dated question included in the documentation.)

Question:

For the Charging Breath, on the in-breath, it is stomach in, focusing on the area you are taking the breath to, then the out-breath, and the area expands. Is the breath going in or is it pictured going out as with Kriya? Then in on the out-breath. I know you have said this is like a Kriya breath, so I have been a little confused on this point.

Answer:

I am going to take you through the steps of the Charging Breath and let us see if this clears the confusion.

Step 1: Sit in a comfortable, upright position; later, you may do these breaths in any position.

Step 2: Observe your breath from its entry through the nose, down to the lungs and back out again in natural breathing; do this a few times.

Step 3: Now, when you breathe in, draw your stomach in, when you breathe out, let your stomach move out. These do not need to be exaggerated and should not produce any pain. There may be times when this movement is slight, other times when you will feel you want to draw the stomach as far in as it will go and hold it for extended times; this is all right. You will feel the rightness of the breath by following what your body system wants. Do not enforce an idea you have from the mind, but follow what the body wants in that moment. So: The Charging Breath

Breathe-**in,** stomach **in,**
Breathe-**out,** stomach **out.**

Practice this way of breathing until you feel you have a natural rhythm occurring. This Charging Breath may not feel as natural as the Clearing Breath at first, but it should not be painful in any way. Once you have a comfortable breathing pattern in place, then:

Step 4: Draw the breath into the 3rd chakra. For the purposes of these breathing exercises, your focus of attention for the 3rd chakra will go to an area one inch above your navel, and midway, between the front and back of your body. One way to establish the location in the spine is to sharply draw in the navel area and feel where that connects in the spine. Then move to the midway point, halfway between the spine and the front of your body. You are going to bring the breath to that area.

On the in-breath, you will see the breath/energy going into that area and see the area contract. On the out-breath, you will see the breath/energy expand out from that area, suffused with a golden light.

Breath-in: breathe into that area and see it contract; breath-out: see the area relax, expand, and see/feel that area radiate a golden light.

Breathe-in/stomach in/energy in,
Breathe-out/stomach out/energy out.

In later practice, you may take it to the Heart Center and then to the Throat Center. You will not use the Charging Breath on the Ajna. If you are called to another part of your body while focused on the 3rd, 4th, or 5th chakras, you will go to the area you are called to, see it contract with energy on the in-breath, expand with the energy of golden light on the out-breath.

If you are drawn into a daydream, you can either see your character in the daydream breathing the Charging Breath, or you can wrap a bubble around the daydream and see the whole bubble contracting with energy on the in-breath, expanding in golden light on the out-breath.

Another use for the Charging Breath is to strengthen your body, emotions, or thoughts for a particular event. Say you are going to give a talk in front of a group. In the past when giving a talk, you have felt uneasy, unsure of yourself, nervous, nauseous, or just plain scared! What to do?

Mentally picture yourself standing before the group, about to give a talk. With the Clearing Breath, clear the butterflies that are fluttering in the stomach. Once those are cleared, then switch to the Charging Breath. Charge that area in the stomach where the butterflies had been with Prana, Life-energy. Feel the power and fullness of that area as you charge it. Gradually, feel/see yourself radiating the golden light out from your body to the whole group until the whole room is pulsating with golden light in rhythm with your breath. When golden light fills the room, where is there room for fear? You may practice this method however many times you wish before the event, and then when the event arrives, do it in "real time" as you prepare to speak, and even while you are speaking. You can also focus on the heart for courage in emotional difficulties, and charge positive thoughts at the 5th chakra.

Please let me know if this covers the salient points. Do not try to connect the Charging Breath as described to the Kriya Breath other than the fact you may notice that when doing the Kriya Breath, you have been doing a Charging Breath for the entire spine and brain.

Om Namaste, David

REFERENCES

Asch, Shalom. (2011). *The Nazarene*. Tolmitch E-Books.

Asch, Shalom. (2012). *The Apostle*. Tolmitch E-Books.

Asch, Shalom. (2013). *Moses*. Tolmitch E-Books.

Campbell, Joseph. (1990). *Transformation of Myth Through Time.* New York: Harper Perennial.

Guillaumont, A; Puech, Henri; Quispel, W.; and Masih, Yassah; Translators. (1959). *The Gospel According to Thomas.*

Hickenbottom, David. (2019). *My Spiritual India*. Camano Island, Washington: The Cross and The Lotus Publishing.

Hickenbottom, David. (2021). *Climbing the Sacred Mountain: Poems and Prayers of a Western Yogi.* Camano Island, Washington: The Cross and The Lotus Publishing.

Hickenbottom, David. *Householder Yogi: Journal of a Western Yogi 2001–2002.* In development.

Kemp, Harry. (1925). *The Home Book of Modern Verse*. London: Henry Holt & Co.

Paramhansa Yogananda. (1946). *Autobiography of a Yogi.* New York: The Philosophical Library.

Paramhansa Yogananda. (1994). *Sayings of Paramhansa Yogananda*. Los Angeles, California: Self-Realization Fellowship.

Paramhansa Yogananda. (1995). *God Talks with Arjuna: Bhagavad Gita.* Los Angeles, California: Self-Realization Fellowship.

Purdom, C.B. (1964). *The God-Man*. South Carolina: Sheriar Foundation.

Roman, Rolland. (1953). *The Life of Vivekananda*. San Francisco: Vedanta Press.

Sri Ramakrishna. Translator. Swami Nikhilananada. (1964). *The Gospel of Sri Ramakrishna*. Madras, India: Sri Ramakrishna Math.

Swami Satchidananda. (1990). *The Gospel of Swami Ramdas*. Kasaragod, Kerala: Anandashram Press.

Swami Sri Yukteswar Giri. (1949). *The Holy Science*. India: Yogoda Sat-Sang Society of India. 3rd Edition.

Bible References

King James Bible Online: https://www.kingjamesbibleonline.org

The Cross and The Lotus: www.crossandlotus.com

Editor's Acknowledgments

A beautiful thank you to Yogacharya David who asked me to assist him with publishing his teachings. Sadly, he left his body far too soon, before we could begin that endeavor. After David's passing, Carla, his devoted wife and disciple, invited me to organize and present David's brilliant writings, his modern-day views of a Western Yogi, in text form, for all to benefit. It is a privilege to work with David's legacy—teachings designed to support wise stewardship in today's world.

My thanks to friends and colleagues who assisted with the proofreading: Catherine Ralphs did the first reading of Part One, as did Mira Lutz. Rebecca Harvey read the whole manuscript; her keen eye has added much perfection. Moreover, she has access to many of David's computer files and knows how to find the most obscure details. Much appreciated. Zia Cole, my editor, then took the manuscript and polished all our hard work, refining the micro-details.

Gratitude to Jan Westendorp of Kato Design who used her creative talents to bring us this beautiful book, featuring David's teachings in the best possible manner.

David's image portfolio provided us with all the images, and Mike Victory, with his highly professional photography skills, has ensured that each image looks its best—including the cover image of David at Cloud Mountain. A gracious thank you to all sadhakas who gave permission to have their image included in this book.

My appreciation to Reverend Larry Koler and his wife, Cate Koler, and The Cross and The Lotus Publishing. They answered my questions and shared their knowledge while ensuring that the book was published in a timely fashion.

www.ingramcontent.com/pod-product-compliance
Lightning Source LLC
Chambersburg PA
CBHW070856120626
46546CB00001B/21